D1477239

Trinity College Library Dublin

This is the first comprehensive, scholarly history of Trinity College Library Dublin. It covers the whole 400 years of the Library's development, from its foundation by James Ussher in the seventeenth century to the electronic revolution of the twenty-first century. Particular attention is given to the buildings and to the politics involved in obtaining funding for them, as well as to the acquisition of the great treasures, such as the Book of Kells and the libraries of Ussher, Claudius Gilbert and Hendrik Fagel. An important aspect is the comprehensive coverage of legal deposit from the beginning of the nineteenth century, viewed for the first time from the Irish perspective. The book also draws parallels with the development of other libraries in Dublin and with those of the universities of Oxford and Cambridge, and features throughout the individuals who influenced the Library's development – librarians, politicians, readers, book collectors and book thieves.

PETER FOX has over 30 years' experience at a senior level in academic libraries, including 15 years in Trinity College Library. In 2009 he retired as the Librarian of the University of Cambridge, having held the post since 1994. Before that he was the College Librarian and Archivist at Trinity College Dublin. He was also a Curator of the Bodleian Libraries, Oxford, and a member of a number of committees at the British Library. He has edited several books, including *Cambridge University Library: The Great Collections* (Cambridge, 1998), the commentary volume to *The Book of Kells, MS 58, Trinity College Library Dublin* (1990) and *Treasures of the Library: Trinity College Dublin* (1986).

Trinity College Library Dublin

A History

———

PETER FOX

CAMBRIDGE
UNIVERSITY PRESS

CAMBRIDGE
UNIVERSITY PRESS

University Printing House, Cambridge CB2 8BS, United Kingdom

Cambridge University Press is part of the University of Cambridge.

It furthers the University's mission by disseminating knowledge in the pursuit of education, learning and research at the highest international levels of excellence.

www.cambridge.org
Information on this title: www.cambridge.org/9781107011205

First published 2014
Reprinted 2015

Printed in the United Kingdom by TJ International Ltd. Padstow Cornwall

A catalogue record for this publication is available from the British Library

Library of Congress Cataloguing in Publication data
Fox, Peter, 1949–
Trinity College Library Dublin : a history / Peter Fox.
    pages   cm
Includes bibliographical references and index.
ISBN 978-1-107-01120-5 (hardback)
1. Trinity College (Dublin, Ireland). Library – History.   2. Academic libraries – Ireland – Dublin – History.   I. Title.
Z792.5.T75F68   2014
027.7418′35 – dc23   2013049902

ISBN 978-1-107-01120-5 Hardback

For Isobel, Louise and Jenny

Contents

Illustrations

Colour plates

Figures

Illustrations are reproduced by courtesy of the following: Peter Barrow, European Photo Services (Plate 1); Hubie de Burgh, Oldtown, County Kildare (Plate 2); Irish Architectural Archive (Figure 19 and Plate 7); *Irish Times* (Figures 24 and 25); Board of the National Library of Ireland (Figure 3); Collection Rijksbureau voor Kunsthistorische Documentatie (RKD), The Hague (Figure 9). All other illustrations are reproduced by permission of the Board of Trinity College Dublin and are © The Board of Trinity College Dublin.

Tables

Acknowledgements

Although the intensive research and the writing of this book have taken place since my retirement in 2009, it has been many years in gestation and I have benefitted from the advice of a large number of people, some of whom are sadly no longer with us. My interest in the history of the institution of which I was then the Deputy Librarian was sparked by an invitation to write a guidebook for visitors to the Library and encouraged by the then Keeper of Manuscripts, William O'Sullivan. Billy's successor, Bernard Meehan, has provided support and advice throughout my research, as well as reading every word of the draft for this book and offering comments and suggestions. Veronica Morrow, the former Keeper (Collection Management), has also read and advised on the whole text. To both of them I owe an immense debt of gratitude. Others who have kindly read and commented on sections of the book are Robin Adams, Charles Benson, Ciaran Brady, Elizabethanne Boran, Lydia Ferguson, Mirjam Foot, Louise Fox, Anne Jarvis, Patrick Kelly, Edward McParland, Caoimhe Ní Ghormáin, Trevor Peare, Bill Vaughan and Dennis Wood.

Most of the research has been carried out in the Manuscripts Room at Trinity, where the staff, especially Aisling Lockhart and Jane Maxwell, have gone out of their way to assist with my requests, however unreasonable. I am also grateful for the unfailing helpfulness of librarians and archivists at the National Library of Ireland; the National Archives of Ireland; Marsh's Library; the Representative Church Body of the Church of Ireland; the Royal Irish Academy; the Irish Architectural Archive; the High School, Dublin; the King's Inns, Dublin; University College Dublin; the Public Record Office of Northern Ireland; the British Library; the Central Archive of the British Museum; the National Archives at Kew; the Bodleian Library; the university libraries of Edinburgh, Glasgow, Manchester and Reading; and, in particular, Cambridge University Library, where most of my non-Trinity research has been carried out.

My work has been facilitated by all manner of help from other former colleagues in Trinity College Dublin, especially Paul Corrigan, Anne-Marie Diffley, Anne Fitzgerald, Catherine Giltrap, Jessie Kurtz, Sharon McIntyre,

Michael Murray, Jane Ohlmeyer, Felicity O'Mahony, Sharon Sutton and Gillian Whelan.

Robin Adams, until recently the College Librarian, provided moral support and encouragement and arranged for the cost of the illustrations to be underwritten and a subvention to be provided, which should allow this book to be found not only in academic libraries but also, it is hoped, on the shelves of individuals interested in the history of libraries in general and that of Trinity in particular. I would like to thank the Trinity Long Room Hub for electing me to a Visiting Fellowship in 2011, which enabled much of the research in the College archives to be undertaken, to Selwyn College, Cambridge and the University of Cambridge Foreign Travel Fund for research support, and to Anne and Malcolm Cadoo, Bill Vaughan, Edward McParland, Irene Kingston and Simon Bridge for their generous hospitality during my visits to Ireland.

At Cambridge University Press, Andrew Brown was an enthusiastic champion of the project, and I am grateful to Linda Bree, Tom O'Reilly and Anna Bond for their help throughout the production process.

For permission to quote from documents in their care, I thank the Board of Trinity College Dublin and the Director of the National Archives of Ireland. The Chief Executive Officer of the Publishers' Association has kindly allowed me to quote from his Association's *Members' Circular*.

Finally, I should like to acknowledge the patience and support of my wife Isobel, for whom my 'retirement' has consisted of long absences, either in Dublin or in my study, and who has also cast a critical eye over my writing style. Despite all the help I have received, it is hardly possible that a book of this sort will pass without errors, and for these, of course, I take full responsibility.

Abbreviations

Abbott, *Incunabula*	T. K. Abbott, *Catalogue of fifteenth-century books in the Library of Trinity College, Dublin, and in Marsh's Library, Dublin, with a few from other collections* (Dublin: Hodges Figgis, 1905)
Abbott, *Manuscripts*	T. K. Abbott, *Catalogue of the manuscripts in the Library of Trinity College, Dublin; to which is added a list of the Fagel collection of maps in the same library* (Dublin: Hodges Figgis, 1900)
Abbott and Gwynn	T. K. Abbott and E. J. Gwynn, *Catalogue of the Irish manuscripts in the Library of Trinity College, Dublin* (Dublin: Hodges Figgis, 1921)
Annual Bulletin	*Annual Bulletin of the Friends of the Library of Trinity College, Dublin*
Annual Report	Annual Report, Trinity College Library Dublin (MUN/LIB/32/177–8)
BA	Bachelor of Arts
BL	British Library
Boran, 'Libraries'	Elizabethanne Boran, 'Libraries and learning: the early history of Trinity College Dublin from 1592 to 1641' (unpublished Ph.D. thesis, University of Dublin, 1995)
BNB	British National Bibliography
Cambridge history	*The Cambridge history of libraries in Britain and Ireland*, 3 vols. (Cambridge University Press, 2006)
Colker	Marvin L. Colker, *Trinity College Library Dublin: descriptive catalogue of the mediaeval and renaissance Latin manuscripts* (Aldershot: Scolar, 1991)
Commons Jn Ireland	*The journals of the House of Commons of the Kingdom of Ireland*, 19 vols. (Dublin: George Grierson, 1795–1800)
Craster	Sir Edmund Craster, *History of the Bodleian Library, 1845–1945* (Oxford: Bodleian Library, 1952)
CUA ULIB	Cambridge University Archives, Archives of Cambridge University Library
Decantations	Agnes Bernelle, ed., *Decantations: a tribute to Maurice Craig* (Dublin: Lilliput Press, 1992)
DU Calendar	*The Dublin University Calendar, 1833–*

DU Commission	*Report of Her Majesty's Commissioners appointed to inquire into the state, discipline, studies and revenues of the University of Dublin, and of Trinity College, together with Appendices containing Evidence, Suggestions and Correspondence*, [1637], 1852–3, XLV, 1
EPB	Early Printed Books Department
Essays	Vincent Kinane and Anne Walsh, eds., *Essays on the history of Trinity College Library Dublin* (Dublin: Four Courts Press, 2000)
Harris	P. R. Harris, *A history of the British Museum Library 1753–1973* (London: British Library, 1998)
HC	House of Commons
HEA	Higher Education Authority
HL	House of Lords
HMC	Historical Manuscripts Commission
HMSO	Her (His) Majesty's Stationery Office
Holland	C. H. Holland, ed., *Trinity College Dublin and the idea of a university* (Dublin: Trinity College Dublin Press, 1991)
Irish book	Raymond Gillespie and Andrew Hadfield, eds., *The Irish book in English 1550–1800* (Oxford University Press, 2006) *The Oxford history of the Irish book*, vol. III
JRSAI	*Journal of the Royal Society of Antiquaries of Ireland*
Kells facsimile	Peter Fox, ed., *The Book of Kells: MS 58, Trinity College Library, Dublin* (Luzern: Faksimile Verlag, 1990)
Lords Jn Ireland	*Journals of the House of Lords [of Ireland]*, 8 vols. (Dublin: William Sleater, 1779–1800)
MA	Master of Arts
McDonnell and Healy	Joseph McDonnell and Patrick Healy, *Gold-tooled bookbindings commissioned by Trinity College Dublin in the eighteenth century* (Leixlip: Irish Georgian Society, 1987)
McDowell and Webb	R. B. McDowell and D. A. Webb, *Trinity College Dublin, 1592–1952: an academic history* (Cambridge University Press, 1982)
McKitterick	David McKitterick, *Cambridge University Library: a history; the eighteenth and nineteenth centuries* (Cambridge University Press, 1986)
Mahaffy, *Epoch*	John Pentland Mahaffy, *An epoch in Irish history: Trinity College, Dublin, its foundation and early fortunes, 1591–1660* (London: Fisher Unwin, 1903)
MP	Member of Parliament

MS	Manuscript (MS numbers quoted are from Trinity College Library unless otherwise indicated)
MUN	Muniment (Trinity College Dublin archives)
NAI	National Archives of Ireland
NLI	National Library of Ireland
Old Library	W. E. Vaughan, ed., *The Old Library, Trinity College Dublin: 1712–2012* (Dublin: Four Courts Press, 2013)
Partridge	R. C. Barrington Partridge, *The history of the legal deposit of books throughout the British Empire* (London: Library Association, 1938)
Proc. RIA	*Proceedings of the Royal Irish Academy*
PRONI	Public Record Office of Northern Ireland
RIA	Royal Irish Academy
RUL	Reading University Library
SCONUL	Standing Conference of National and University Libraries [of the United Kingdom and Ireland]
Smyly	J. G. Smyly, 'The Old Library: extracts from the Particular Book', *Hermathena*, 49 (1935), 166–83
Tanner letters	Charles McNeill, ed., *The Tanner letters … extracted from the collection in the Bodleian Library, Oxford* (Dublin: Irish Manuscripts Commission, 1943)
TCD	Trinity College Dublin
TD	Teachta Dála (member of Dáil Éireann)
TNA	The National Archives [of the United Kingdom]
Trans. RIA	*Transactions of the Royal Irish Academy*
Treasures	Peter Fox, ed., *Treasures of the Library: Trinity College Dublin* (Dublin: Royal Irish Academy, 1986)

Introduction

Trinity College Library is the oldest and by far the largest library in Ireland and one of the most important university libraries in Europe. It is unique in the variety of roles it performs. Its special collections, built up over 400 years, combined with its right to claim copies of books and journals published in both Ireland and the United Kingdom, under legal-deposit legislation, have made it a quasi-national library and a research resource of international importance. As home to the Book of Kells, which is housed in the magnificent setting of the Old Library, it is one of the most popular tourist attractions in Ireland and, unusually for an academic library, provides a significant income for its parent institution.

In many ways, the Library is the College's greatest asset. Certainly, when the name of Trinity College is mentioned outside its walls, more often than not it is the Library that springs to mind. The speed with which it was established, in the first few decades after the foundation of the College in 1592, was remarkable, and the early Fellows were clear that its purpose was to support Trinity's principal function of promoting 'civility, learning and Protestant piety' among the youth of Ireland.[1] Until the nineteenth century, its role was essentially a custodial one and in this respect it differed little from other university libraries, where 'collections were acquired, catalogued, gloated over and admired'.[2] Yet much of its history is characterised by periods of relative neglect, interspersed with bursts of activity initiated by individual energetic and efficient Librarians. The Fellows as a whole showed little interest in the running of the Library and its development, which, for much of the seventeenth and eighteenth centuries, owed more to the influence of external forces than to internal planning. Indeed, until the second half of the nineteenth century, the majority of the manuscript treasures and great collections arrived as the result of donations or bequests, with little active intervention on the part of the College: Ussher's library came as a gift from the Irish House of Commons, sanctioned by Charles II; Claudius Gilbert's library was a bequest; and the Fagel collection was

---

[1] McDowell and Webb, p. 5.
[2] Peter Freshwater, 'Books and universities', in *Cambridge history*, vol. II, pp. 345–70 (p. 358).

bought for the College by the Erasmus Smith Trust. Even the Library's legal-deposit status was an incidental result of a political decision made for other reasons, and the College remained indifferent at first to what was the most important gift in the Library's history.

There are, of course, exceptions to this passive approach, and the impact – for good or ill – of those Librarians who held office for more than a handful of years is one of the principal features of this story. In the late eighteenth century, Thomas Leland's involvement with Irish studies, his encouragement of scholars and his ability to persuade the College to part with its money for the purchase of manuscripts created a suitable environment for the gift of the Sebright collection, which placed the Library in the first rank among holdings of Irish manuscripts. In the nineteenth century, Jacky Barrett and James Henthorn Todd capitalised on the College's periods of relative affluence to develop the collection by extensive purchasing and by employing sufficient staff to process not just what was being bought but also the growing flood of materials arriving under the terms of the Copyright Acts. The Library's copyright or legal-deposit status has had an overwhelming influence, not only on the collection itself, but on all aspects of the way the institution has been run and used since the early nineteenth century. The need to find space to house the ever-growing collection has been a perennial problem for successive Librarians.

Until the mid nineteenth century, use of the Library was restricted to graduates, which meant that the number of readers using its books and manuscripts was relatively low. Changes to the curriculum and the admission of undergraduates led to a growth in use, particularly after the First World War. Unfortunately, this coincided with an unprecedented increase in the amount of material being received by legal deposit, a growing impoverishment of the College following Irish independence, and the incumbency of a Librarian, Josiah Gilbart Smyly, whose involvement with the running of the Library was minimal. As a result, resources became very thinly spread and the Library suffered a period of serious decline. It was not until the 1950s that efforts to restore the standing of both the College and its Library began to bear fruit. Despite the relative poverty of the Irish universities in comparison to those in other parts of the developed world, Trinity College is now a major player on the world scene and its Library not only plays a fundamental role in the support of teaching and research in the College but is an internationally important resource for scholarship, heavily used by students and scholars from all over the world.

The highlights in the story of the Library were retold in various publications during the nineteenth century, but relatively little primary research has been undertaken until recently on its history, its collections, its users and its staff. The collections themselves have now been covered extensively in two books: *Treasures of the Library* and *The Old Library*.[3] The publication of a book of *Essays* in 2000, and more recent research, have unlocked a considerable amount of new information, but the editors of the *Essays* noted that there was at that time an insufficient critical mass of research to provide the background for a full academic history.[4] The College muniments (archives) document the organisation, buildings and acquisitions reasonably well – at least from the eighteenth century onwards – but there are still gaps in our knowledge of the Library's history. In particular, its impact on teaching and research in the College and on the wider world of scholarship, and its use by individual readers are both areas which deserve further study.

The purpose of the present book is not to duplicate the work on the collections that have already been published, but to provide a chronological narrative showing how the Library has developed, the context into which its collections fit, the buildings in which they were housed and used, something of its organisation and, as far as current research permits, a glimpse at the use that has been made of it by readers. No library operates in isolation and, although this is not intended as a comparative history, the fortunes of other libraries have been included where they are relevant to the story of Trinity College Library. As an institution which had an English queen as its foundress and Cambridge men as its first five Provosts, Trinity College has traditionally related more closely to the ancient English universities than to the Scottish ones – and of course it was the only university in Ireland until the middle of the nineteenth century. This relationship applies equally to the Library, particularly after its inclusion among the British legal-deposit libraries in 1801, a status lost by the Scottish universities in 1836. Most of the comparative statistics that have been included, therefore, are for the other two university legal-deposit libraries, the Bodleian Library in Oxford, and Cambridge University Library, as comparison between Trinity and other Irish or British university libraries is less straightforward, none being comparable in size to those three and all having to acquire most of their books and journals by purchase.

A note on terminology

The terms Trinity College Dublin and the University of Dublin are a frequent source of confusion. The Elizabethan College charter contained the curious

---

[3] *Treasures; Old Library.*   [4] *Essays.*

phrase '*mater universitatis*'. Quite what was meant by the designation of Trinity College as the 'mother of a university' is unclear, and the phrase has been interpreted in a number of ways. Was the University of Dublin founded on the model of Oxford and Cambridge, with Trinity as its first college and the assumption that others would follow, as nearly happened in the 1650s? Or was it a precursor of colonial foundations such as Harvard and the College of William and Mary, with a single authority acting as both college and university? 'To say that Trinity was founded as a college and became a university is a convenient way of explaining to the bewildered the oddity of an institution which manages to be both simultaneously.'[5] The distinction between the University of Dublin and Trinity College has changed over the years, but in essence it is the College which provides the teaching and research facilities, including the Library, and the University which confers degrees, though for most day-to-day purposes the two institutions are synonymous.

The University has a Chancellor and several Pro-Chancellors (the office of Vice-Chancellor was abolished in 1964), but all of those roles are primarily of a formal or ceremonial nature. The head of the College is the Provost, a post equivalent to Vice-Chancellor or President elsewhere, and the College is run by the Board, which until 1911 consisted of the Provost and the seven Senior Fellows. After that date its membership was gradually extended to include representatives of the Junior Fellows, professors and, later, students and other members of staff. Until the nineteenth century, most of the 'annual officers' were elected from among the Senior Fellows on 20 November each year. The principal officers included the Vice-Provost, Bursar (responsible for the financial management of the College), Registrar (who maintained the records of both the College and the University) and Senior Lecturer (responsible for undergraduate studies). Although these offices still exist, much of their work has now been taken over by professional administrators, but for most of the period covered by this book the officers were academics who worked with little or no administrative support. The Librarian was also one of these officers, but his election on an annual basis ceased in the eighteenth century. It took until 1965 for Trinity to appoint its first full-time Librarian, long after other comparable institutions, but this was in the context of a university which, even in 1939, had only five full-time administrative staff and the same number of secretaries.[6]

---

[5] Aidan Clarke, 'Responsibility: the administrative framework', in Holland, pp. 89–105 (p. 89). See also McDowell and Webb, pp. 1–5.
[6] McDowell and Webb, p. 443.

Copyright and legal deposit

Throughout the book I have used the term 'legal deposit' rather than 'copyright' to refer to the process by which publishers are obliged to deposit copies of their books with specified libraries. Until 1842, publishers wishing to protect the copyright in their books were required to register them at Stationers' Hall in London, which then rendered them eligible for deposit in the libraries. The 1842 Copyright Act removed the link between copyright protection and deposit, but legal-deposit legislation continued to be included in successive Copyright Acts until 1911 and the term 'copyright library' persisted until the late twentieth century.

Conventions

In quoting from manuscript material I have not changed spellings, but abbreviations and ampersands have usually been filled out, and archaisms such as y^e and y^t, punctuation and capitalisation have been modernised. Throughout this book references to MUN and MS numbers without any further indication of location are invariably to documents in Trinity College Library. In all other cases the holding library or archive is indicated.

In September 1752, Britain and Ireland adopted the Gregorian calendar, which prescribed that the year should start on 1 January, rather than 25 March. I have followed that convention for all dates (i.e. the day following 31 December 1603 is rendered here as 1 January 1604, not 1 January 1603, as would appear in the sources) and the day and month are given as they appear in the original documents.

Currency amounts quoted are those recorded in the documents themselves, and, unless specified, they refer to Irish pounds at times when those were different from sterling. Throughout the eighteenth century thirteen Irish pounds equalled twelve pounds sterling, and in 1826 the Irish currency was assimilated to the British. This arrangement lasted until 1979, when Ireland joined the European Monetary System, breaking its link with sterling, and in 2002 the Irish pound was replaced by the euro.

1 | Early days: 1592–1640

At various times during the fourteenth and fifteenth centuries attempts had been made to found a university in Dublin, but as Ireland entered the 1590s it was still without such an institution. By that time, England's two universities were already around 400 years old and Scotland had three that had been founded before 1500. With the relative peace following the religious upheavals of the earlier part of the sixteenth century, there was a flowering of new universities and colleges across Europe: Jesus College, Oxford was established in 1571, Leiden in 1575, Edinburgh in 1582, Emmanuel College, Cambridge in 1584 and Graz in 1585.

In Ireland, it was recognised from the 1560s that, if the Reformation was to become embedded, its inhabitants needed to be educated and its clergy to be trained in the Protestant faith. After a number of proposed schemes had come to naught, the mayor and corporation of Dublin were persuaded in 1590 to set aside the land and the largely ruined buildings on the site of the former Augustinian priory of All Hallows, about a kilometre to the east of the city wall. Application was made to the Queen, Elizabeth I, and on 3 March 1592 the College of the Holy and Undivided Trinity near Dublin was granted a charter.

Unlike several of the colleges of Oxford and Cambridge, Trinity's foundation was not accompanied by a handsome endowment. The Queen, notorious for her frugality, encouraged the establishment of the new university but failed to provide any financial support. The initial funding to set up the College had to be collected by means of a public appeal, addressed to gentlemen in every county of Ireland. The appeal raised over £2,000, but throughout the first decade of its existence the College was beset by financial difficulties. It was granted estates in the 1590s, but the uprising of the Earl of Tyrone meant that the rent from those estates could not be collected until after Mountjoy's victory at the Battle of Kinsale in 1601.[1]

Some building did take place in the early years. By the end of the Elizabethan era, the College consisted of a quadrangle of three-storey buildings,

---

[1] Mahaffy, *Epoch*, pp. 60–111; Colm Lennon, '"The bowels of the city's bounty": the municipality of Dublin and the foundation of Trinity College', *Long Room*, 37 (1992), 10–16.

with Chapel, Hall and Kitchen on the north side, incorporating part of the former monastery, the Library on the south side, and students' chambers forming most of the remainder. A later drawing shows this layout. (See Figure 3.) When the first students arrived in 1594, only the west and north sides had been completed, but work was proceeding on the remaining buildings, including the Library, for which Roger Parker, described as the 'steward', was paying bills for woodwork, hinges, nails and glass in 1595 and 1596.[2]

Challoner and Ussher

During the first few years of the College's existence, its Library collection consisted of a mere handful of books. The Particular Book, the earliest extant record of College affairs, contains a list of '*libri in publica Collegii Bibliotheca*', dated 24 February 1601.[3] (See Figure 1.) It records around forty printed works, including editions of classical writers such as Aristotle, Plato and Cicero, atlases by Mercator and Ptolemy, and a number of theological titles. Seven of the books were a gift from Richard Latewar, a former Fellow of St John's College, Oxford, who was killed in County Tyrone in 1601 whilst serving with Mountjoy's forces and who left books and manuscripts to his Oxford college, as well as to Trinity.[4] Most of the printed books, and probably at least one of the manuscripts listed as being in the Library in 1601, are still present, but the majority of the entries for manuscripts have been crossed through, probably indicating that they were subsequently found to be missing. Three were gifts from Christopher Ussher, Ulster King of Arms.

The early members of the College had access to many more books than those represented in this small collection. Luke Challoner, one of the three founding Fellows, had amassed a substantial library of over eight hundred books by the 1590s, including works on philosophy, theology, history, astronomy, mathematics and geography, with maps by some of the important sixteenth-century cartographers. It is clear that Challoner was collecting not just for his own use, but also for that of students and other Fellows, to

---

[2] MS 2640 (transcription, MS 2641).

[3] The Particular Book is now MUN/V/1/1. See also: TCD, *The Particular Book of Trinity College, Dublin: a facsimile from the original*, with an Introduction and appendices by J. P. Mahaffy (London: Unwin, 1904). References to the Library were collected by J. G. Smyly in 'The Old Library: extracts from the Particular Book', *Hermathena*, 49 (1935), 166–83, and for convenience these, rather than references to the original manuscript, are cited below (as Smyly).

[4] Mahaffy, *Epoch*, pp. 141–2; K. J. Höltgen, 'Richard Latewar, Elizabethan poet and divine', *Anglia*, 89 (1971), 417–38.

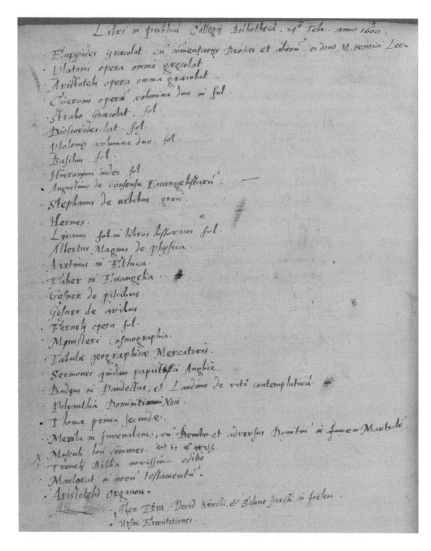

Figure 1 The first list of books in the Library, 24 February 1600/01 (MUN/V/1/1, fol. 216v.)

whom he lent books from his collection.[5] One of his notebooks contains three catalogues of his library, dated 1595, 1596 and 1608, and lists of books lent, dated 1601 and 1610, with the names of the borrowers, including several of the Fellows, with the titles crossed out to indicate their return.[6]

[5] Elizabethanne Boran, 'Luke Challoner's library, 1595–1608', *Long Room*, 37 (1992), 17–26; Boran, 'Libraries', p. 5.
[6] MS 357, fols. 1–15.

The year 1601 marks the beginning of the College Library proper. As well as being the date of the first list of books, it was also the year when a Library Keeper was appointed and when the first recorded purchases took place. Between then and 1613, several members of the College undertook book-buying visits to England. Funding for the books bought on those expeditions came from a donation that had been promised to the College in 1593 but which was not received until 1601. A legend prevailed for over 200 years that a sum of £1,800 for the purchase of books had been donated by the officers of the army after Mountjoy's victory at Kinsale. That legend, almost certainly started in 1656 by Nicholas Bernard, the keeper of Archbishop Ussher's library and his first biographer, was conclusively disproved by J. P. Mahaffy in 1903.[7] The amount donated was smaller than Bernard claimed and, though its source was indeed a gift from officers of the army, it dated from 1593, not 1601, and it was made to assist with the founding of the new College and not specifically for the Library. Bernard manipulated the story for political purposes, as will be seen in the next chapter. It appears that the soldiers were owed payment for their service in Ireland and that they decided to donate this money to the College.

The process of extracting the money from the Queen and Lord Burghley, however, turned out to be far from simple. In February 1593 the Lord Deputy, Sir William Fitzwilliam, sent to Burghley and the Privy Council a number of bills 'given by certain captains towards the building of the college', asking for reimbursement.[8] The following month Challoner and others also wrote to ask for the money, amounting to £623 0s. 8d., owed to the 'captains serving in Ireland', requesting that it be transferred to the College as the soldiers had requested.[9] A further letter from the Lord Deputy followed a year later, repeating the request, but it took until 1601 for the first payment to be released.[10] Even then, the money seems to have arrived in small sums over a period of years, mostly through the hands of Sir James Carroll, an official of the government in Ireland, who was closely involved with the College finances.

The first of the book-buying expeditions was undertaken by Challoner in June 1601. He bought around 350 items from a number of London book-sellers, including Gregory Seton of Aldersgate, from whom he purchased

[7]　Nicholas Bernard, *The life and death of the most reverend and learned father of our church, Dr James Usher* (London: Tyler, 1656), p. 42; J. P. Mahaffy, 'The Library of Trinity College, Dublin: the growth of a legend', *Hermathena*, 12 (1903), 68–78.

[8]　H. C. Hamilton, ed., *Calendar of state papers Ireland, Elizabeth, 1592–1596* (London: HMSO, 1890), pp. 77–8.

[9]　*Ibid.*, p. 81.　　[10]　*Ibid.*, p. 248.

145 titles at a total cost of £58.[11] On his second visit to England, in 1603, Challoner was accompanied by the 22-year-old James Ussher, who had taken his MA at Trinity 2 years earlier and was later to become his son-in-law. (See Figure 2.) Ussher knew Challoner's library and used books from it, but this journey was his first introduction to the wider world of serious book-collecting and scholarship, when he began to assemble the nucleus of what was to become one of the most renowned private libraries of the age. On this visit, Challoner again bought extensively for the College. The Chester port-book for 1603 records the shipment by him of two barrels and one dryfat [chest] containing books valued at £100. In one year, possibly 1603, the College spent £568 9s. 0d. on the purchase of books and a further £20 on library desks.[12]

Ussher's journey to England was the first of what was to become a series of visits every 3 years until 1612, during each of which he spent about 3 months, not only buying books for the College and for his own growing library, but also undertaking research in Oxford and Cambridge. On those trips he met other scholars and collectors such as William Camden, Sir Thomas Bodley and Sir Robert Cotton, and after the visit of 1606 Camden asked Ussher to provide a description of Dublin for the next edition of his *Britannia*. Ussher did so, saying little about the College other than that it had been 'furnished of late with a notable library', a phrase added verbatim by Camden to the 1607 edition of his book.[13]

Challoner made one more visit, accompanying Ussher in 1609 and buying not just books but also globes and other items, to the value of £107 6s. 0d.[14] The two men were mainly responsible for building up the Library, but they were not the only people entrusted to spend the College's money on books. In 1608, the Provost, Henry Alvey, travelled with a similar purpose, and in 1611 Anthony Martin, a Fellow, received payment for books that he had bought in England. Alvey's visit, and that of Challoner in 1609, are both well documented, and the booksellers from whom they made purchases are recorded: Adrian Marius, John Norton and John Bill in London, John Legate in Cambridge and Joseph Barnes in Oxford, several of whom were also

---

[11] Seton's bill, MS 2160a/10, is transcribed in William O'Sullivan, 'The Library before Kinsale', *Annual Bulletin*, (1952), 10–14. MS 2160a/1–17 consists of book lists from 1601–10, some in the hands of Ussher and Challoner and usually including the prices paid.

[12] D. M. Woodward, *The trade of Elizabethan Chester* (Hull: University, 1970), p. 21; MUN/LIB/10/4a.

[13] C. R. Elrington, ed., *The whole works of the most rev. James Ussher*, 17 vols. (Dublin: Hodges & Smith, 1847–64), vol. XV, p. 11; William Camden, *Britannia* (London: George Bishop, 1607), p. 751.

[14] MUN/LIB/10/4.

supplying Sir Thomas Bodley. Expenditure included calfskins for wrapping the books, a 'dryfat' in which they were transported, carriage by cart from London to Chester, storage in a warehouse there, where they were checked by customs officers, and then the cost of shipping to Dublin. The total price paid by Alvey in 1608 was £57 6s. 6d. and to this was added £7 4s. 4d. for packing and carriage.[15] In 1612–13, a further £60 was spent on books for the Library.[16] From entries in the Particular Book it has been estimated that £244 was spent on the purchase and carriage of books between the summer of 1608 and early 1613, the year of Challoner's death and the end of the initial development of the Library.[17]

The first Library collection

Although the officers' donation to the new College had not been given specifically for the Library, the Fellows decided to use it for that purpose. This must have been partly at the instigation of the great book-collector, Challoner, but it also demonstrated the importance they attached to developing the Library, even when Trinity was facing serious financial difficulties. This was a period when academic libraries were experiencing a revival after the turbulence and religious strife in the mid sixteenth century. Cambridge University Library, which had been almost abandoned in the middle of the century, was being restored to usefulness from the 1570s; in 1598, Sir Thomas Bodley offered to re-found Oxford's university library, which had effectively disappeared earlier in the century; and the new university in Edinburgh acquired a library that had been given to the city 2 years earlier.[18]

The collections in existing academic libraries had traditionally been built up on the basis of donations, such as those of Matthew Parker to Corpus Christi College, Cambridge, Andrew Perne to Peterhouse, Cambridge and Clement Little, whose books formed the basis of Edinburgh University Library. Trinity College Dublin was not favoured with major benefactions like these until after James Ussher's death, and so almost all of its initial collection had to be bought. This had the advantage of meaning that the Library was not subject to the private academic or collecting interest of an individual and that the developing collection could reflect the purpose of the Library as envisaged by the early members of the College. As in all universities of the time, that meant principally the training

---

[15] MS 2160a/14–15; Smyly, pp. 172–3, 176.   [16] MUN/P/1/66.   [17] Smyly, p. 176.
[18] Kristian Jensen, 'Universities and colleges', in *Cambridge history*, vol. I, pp. 345–62.

of the clergy – in Trinity's case, specifically the Protestant clergy. In due course, as the collection grew and as the College became more established, the Library also became a resource for the research that helped to shape the theology of the Church of Ireland, and it provided Irish Protestant polemicists with the ammunition to refute the arguments of their Catholic compatriots.[19]

The undergraduate curriculum of the time was based loosely on the medieval *trivium* and *quadrivium*. The former covered grammar, logic and rhetoric and the latter arithmetic, geometry, music and astronomy, and undergraduates received a thorough grounding in Latin, Greek and Hebrew. Most students left Trinity after gaining their BA; those intending to proceed to ordination were then required to read political science, mathematics and physical science in order to obtain an MA, before they were allowed to study divinity.[20] The layout of the early Library reflected this pattern, with the books arranged in two main categories, theology and humanities. The lower (or outer) library contained the humanities books, which included those regarded as suitable for students reading for the BA and MA. The upper (inner) library, to which students were not admitted, was divided off by a partition and held the theology books. This arrangement by subject, rather than alphabetically, was similar to that adopted by Bodley.[21] It seems that, as in Oxford, printed books and manuscripts were shelved together, though Ussher's receipt for the loan of Roger Bacon's *Opus maior* (MS 381) from 'the presse of the manuscripts' suggests that some manuscripts, at least, were housed separately even at this early date.[22]

The humanities section was divided into ten class-divisions, and theology into fourteen. The first two divisions of the humanities section consisted of dictionaries, Latin, Greek and Hebrew grammars, and books on logic and rhetoric, in fact all the elements of the *trivium*. The collection was strong in the teaching of Petrus Ramus, evidence of the influence of Cambridge, where the first Provosts had been educated and where Ramist thought had become predominant. The influence of Ramist philosophy was not confined just to the subjects of the *trivium*, but in Trinity it had become an 'all embracing methodology'.[23] Mathematics and astronomy were well represented, with

[19] Alan Ford, *James Ussher: theology, history, and politics in early-modern Ireland and England* (Oxford University Press, 2007), pp. 63, 174.
[20] McDowell and Webb, pp. 5–9.
[21] *The first printed catalogue of the Bodleian Library, 1605: a facsimile* (Oxford: Clarendon Press, 1986), pp. viii–ix.
[22] MUN/LIB/10/8.
[23] Boran, 'Libraries', p. 248. Boran's dissertation includes a detailed analysis of the contents of the early Library, on which much of this section is based. See also K. Theodore Hoppen,

some 300 titles, of which the majority were by recent writers such as Tycho Brahe, Copernicus and Gesner. The music section was dominated by psalms, reflecting the Calvinist view of their divine inspiration, but there were also madrigal texts, including works by Byrd and Tallis. History, not yet regarded as a curriculum subject in its own right, was represented by a range of chronologies and national histories. The founders of the College had intended medicine and law to be taught, and both were included in the early Library, although neither subject actually became part of the curriculum until the later seventeenth century. The medical books were principally those of the ancient writers, notably Galen and Hippocrates, but they included more recent authors such as Paracelsus and Vesalius. Botany and medicine were closely linked at the time, and the Library contained works by most of the important contemporary botanists. The legal section largely ignored English common law and concentrated on canon and civil law. The Roman law section was preceded by books on ancient history and politics by writers such as Tacitus, Sallust and Livy, and the English history books included major works by Camden and Francis Bacon.

The theology section accounted for more than half the Library, and it is clear that Challoner and Ussher intended it to be as comprehensive as possible. There were many Bibles, in English and the biblical languages, as well as polyglot editions. The commentaries included those by the Church Fathers and by more recent writers, chiefly Calvinist commentators. The polemical works reflected a similar pattern, with many by Puritan writers. The provision of books by members of the reformed church is unsurprising, but Challoner and Ussher also ensured that users of the Library had access to a collection of books by Catholic authors, to provide them with material upon which to base both their defence of the Protestant cause and criticism of their opponents. Ussher was conscious of the risks of including such controversial material, and this is presumably the principal reason why the theology section was kept separate and not accessible to students. In 1612, and again the following year, when sending books over from London, he asked Challoner to ensure that 'the English popish books be kept in a place by themselves, and not placed among the rest of the library, for they may prove dangerous'.[24]

By 1613, the Library contained around 4,500 books. Its scale and breadth far surpassed what was required purely for the teaching of the curriculum,

The common scientist in the seventeenth century: a study of the Dublin Philosophical Society, 1683–1708 (London: Routledge and Kegan Paul, 1970), pp. 59–61.

24 Ussher, *Works*, note 13 above, vol. XVI, pp. 318–19, and vol. XV, p. 74.

and it is clear that Challoner and Ussher sought to develop a collection that was not only comprehensive but also reflected the most recent scholarship. The priority accorded to its development by the first group of Fellows meant that, within less than 20 years of Trinity's foundation, its library had surpassed in size those of much older colleges at Cambridge, such as Sidney Sussex, Trinity and Emmanuel, all of which contained fewer than two thousand books, and Cambridge University Library itself, which held no more than a thousand.[25] In Oxford, on the other hand, Sir Thomas Bodley's efforts to rebuild the University's library were on a grander scale even than those in Dublin, and by the time of Bodley's death in 1613 the library had grown to about seven thousand volumes.[26]

In Trinity, the arrangements for readers were generous. By allowing students to use the lower (humanities) library, the College followed more closely the practice of the university libraries in Oxford and Cambridge, which admitted graduates, rather than that of their colleges, which normally allowed access only to the Fellows. Books could also be borrowed by, it seems, most categories of reader. A list of loans with the names of the borrowers has survived from around 1617.[27] When he was Archbishop of Armagh, Ussher borrowed not just the manuscript of Bacon's *Opus maius* but also a printed edition of Dionysius.[28] Men who were not members of the College were also permitted to use the collection; indeed, in 1602, Henry Fitzsimon, a Jesuit missionary who sought to engage Protestants in debate, was allowed access to books from the Library for one such disputation.[29]

Readers normally worked in the lower library, which in the early years of the century was equipped with three tables and six benches for the purpose. In January 1611, ten benches were provided and a partition was built between the lower library and the upper section. It is unclear whether this was new or the repair of an existing partition, but its presence clearly offended one reader, who was fined later that month for 'offring violence' to the partition door.[30] The Library also contained a list of benefactors, twelve large maps and many smaller ones, four 'dutche tables, a sceliton with taffety hangings' and a table with two globes. In the gallery were another map and a revolving 'standing desk' for reading large folios.[31]

---

[25] Boran, 'Libraries', pp. 9–11; J. C. T. Oates, *Cambridge University Library: a history; from the beginnings to the Copyright Act of Queen Anne* (Cambridge University Press, 1986), p. 152.

[26] Ian Philip, *The Bodleian Library in the seventeenth and eighteenth centuries* (Oxford: Clarendon Press, 1983), p. 14.

[27] MUN/LIB/10/5.   [28] MUN/LIB/10/8.   [29] Ford, note 19 above, p. 13.

[30] Smyly, p. 170.   [31] *Ibid.*, p. 171.

The shelfmarks of both books and manuscripts were written in black ink on their fore-edges, which faced outwards. They consisted of four elements: a letter T (for theology) or H (for humanities), and three numbers, the first representing the class-division, and other two denoting the shelf and the book's position on that shelf.[32] A typical shelfmark might, therefore, be T.3.5.11. Many of the early shelfmarks have been lost as a result of later rebinding and trimming, as they were not normally inscribed inside the book as well as on the fore-edge. Some books contain a manuscript note, 'Collegii Sanctae et Individuae Trinitatis juxta Dublin', but a more common, if brutal, method of indicating ownership took the form of stab-marks made by an awl or chisel driven into the title page and extending up to 1.5 cm into the text-block. The practice appears to have been employed by the first Library Keeper, Ambrose Ussher, who may have considered it to be a quicker method of indicating that the book belonged to the College than writing the lengthy *ex libris* at a time when books were arriving in the Library in considerable numbers.[33] The Particular Book records payment in 1611 to the Library Keeper for mending a chain, but as there are no marks of chains on the books themselves, it is assumed that the chain was stretched across the front of each shelf to prevent the books being removed.[34]

Though Trinity now possessed a very respectable Library, notebooks kept by both Challoner and Ussher contain the names of people who had borrowed books from each of their private collections, an indication that they continued to be used to augment that belonging to the College. Indeed, the lack of overlap between the three collections provides evidence that, in their book-buying, the two men regarded them as complementary. Ussher's library covered similar subjects to Challoner's and was particularly strong in history and Protestant controversy, 'the prevalent tone of both collections [being] that of a Calvinist controversialist'.[35] Ussher's notebooks contain lists both of the books he loaned to other people and those which he borrowed, including a number from Challoner.[36] This network of borrowing by members of the College community, to augment the

---

[32] MS 2; Norma MacManaway and Charles Benson, '"A sceliton with taffety hangings": the early College Library', in D. Scott, ed., *Treasures of the mind: a Trinity College Dublin Quatercentenary exhibition* (London: Sotheby's, 1992), pp. 143–50.

[33] Anthony Cains, 'The Long Room survey of sixteenth- and seventeenth-century books of the first collections', in *Essays*, pp. 53–71.

[34] Smyly, p. 172.

[35] Elizabethanne Boran, 'The libraries of Luke Challoner and James Ussher, 1595–1608', in Helga Robinson-Hammerstein, ed., *European universities in the age of Reformation and Counter-Reformation* (Dublin: Four Courts, 1998), pp. 75–115 (p. 104).

[36] For example, MS 793, fol. 169.

official collection, continued for at least the first decade of the seventeenth century.

Challoner died in 1613, leaving his books to his daughter Phoebe, and on his deathbed is said to have asked her to marry Ussher. She did so and the library assembled by her father became part of Ussher's own and thus, eventually, part of the College Library. A later Provost, J. P. Mahaffy, remarked: 'whether that great lover of books [Ussher] regarded the lady as an appendage to the books, or the books to the lady, we do not know'.[37]

Managing the Library

As the Library grew, it had to be managed and catalogued. In 1601, Ambrose Ussher, James' younger brother, who had graduated that year, appears in the records as the first Library Keeper. The small collection recorded in the simple list produced in 1601 was growing rapidly and a more sophisticated catalogue was required. Three complete or partial catalogues survive from the decade following the start of the book-buying expeditions.[38] The first, now among the Library's collection of papers of the seventeenth-century divine John Drury, appears to be in Challoner's hand. It is incomplete, covering only theology, with a few titles in law and politics, and has been dated to 1601 by Elizabethanne Boran, who believes that it could be a record of the first round of purchasing.[39] The next two catalogues, now MS 2 and MS 358, are alphabetical lists, which Boran has dated to 1604–5. MS 2 is missing its title page, but a mid-seventeenth-century copy of it (MS 1) includes a transcription of what was probably the now-missing first folio, recording that it was prepared by the Librarian, Ambrose Ussher, in 1604. The latest entry in the hand of the main compiler of MS 2, presumably Ussher, is for a book published in 1604, which suggests that it was initially completed that year, but as it contains later entries in different hands it appears also to have been used as an accessions catalogue, recording the subsequent acquisition of books. MS 358 is a copy of the original entries in MS 2 and may well have been made so that those engaged in buying books for the Library could take it with them to avoid the purchase of duplicates.

When Ambrose Ussher gained his MA in 1605, he resigned as the Library Keeper. His immediate successors were also men of BA status, who held

[37] Mahaffy, 'The Library', note 7 above, p. 78.
[38] For a discussion of these catalogues, see Boran, 'Libraries', pp. 5–7.
[39] This catalogue is MS 295, fols. 78r.–86v.

office for between 1 and 4 years, earning an annual salary of £2 5s. 0d. The duties of the Library Keeper were to be present in the Library when it was open, to supply books to those readers who did not have the right of access to the shelves and to add entries to the catalogue (or 'register'). Ussher received 2s. 6d. for paper and binding of the 'library regester [*sic*]' and payments to his successors refer to 'keeping the library and the regester', though Randall Holland was paid an additional six shillings in 1611 for 'making an index of Library books'.[40] Maintaining the fabric of the building also came within the Library Keeper's responsibilities; the Particular Book records payment to Ussher for 'a new lock to the library dore' and to Holland for mending a chain.[41] At this period, students entered the College in their early teens, and so most of the first Library Keepers, as recent BAs, were probably still under twenty, a fact sometimes reflected in their behaviour. In 1612, Holland was fined 2 months' worth of Commons (meals) for being locked out of the College late at night and for entering by breaking a window in the Chapel – though this did not prevent him from retaining his post as Library Keeper for another 2 years, until he had taken his MA.[42]

William Temple, who became Provost in 1609, was a man of prodigious administrative ability. Through careful financial management, he was able to fund an increase in the number of scholars to seventy and the Fellows to sixteen, of whom he designated seven as Senior Fellows and the remainder as Junior Fellows.[43] Salaries were increased in 1617, with that of the Library Keeper rising to £3 a year, that of the Bursar to £10, a Junior Fellow to £27, a Senior Fellow to £56 and the Provost to £100.[44] Temple's reforms included a codification of the statutes, undertaken in about 1615, but evidence of these now exists only in an incomplete form. It seems likely that they included changes to the regulations for the Library Keeper. In May 1618 John Garrald (or Fitzgerald), already an MA, was appointed to the office and was later required to sign a bond for £20 stating that he would 'looke diligently and carefully to the library of the said College, wherof he is appoynted the keeper'.[45] Garrald remained in office until at least 1625, by which time he had become a Fellow and, like most of those who were to follow him as College Librarians until the twentieth century, he held the post simultaneously with other offices, which in his case were those of Junior Fellow, Junior Dean and philosophy lecturer.[46]

---

[40] Smyly, pp. 168, 177.   [41] *Ibid.*, pp. 169–70.

[42] *Ibid.*, p. 167; MUN/P/7/1, quarter beginning 26 June 1614.

[43] Mahaffy, *Epoch*, pp. 160–9.   [44] MUN/P/7/1.   [45] MUN/LIB/10/6.

[46] MUN/P/7/1, quarter beginning March 1618 to MUN/P/7/12, quarter ending March 1625; MUN/P/1/152.

Temple died in January 1627 and was succeeded as Provost by William Bedell. On 19 August 1627, 3 days after Bedell was sworn in, the newly instituted Board Register recorded the decision that 'the registers place and the custody of the Library is devolved to one of the senior ffellowes in perpetuum; his stipend is six pounds per annum'.[47] That arrangement fell into abeyance almost immediately, however, as within a year of his election Bedell began to revise Temple's statutes. The new statutes, dated 24 September 1628, required the Librarian (*Bibliothecarius*) to be chosen not from among the Senior Fellows but from either the Junior Fellows or the scholars who had taken their BA or, if none were willing, from among the MAs.[48] The Bursar's accounts record payments to an unnamed Library Keeper at the old rate of £3 a year from 1625 to 1628. After that, the new statutes notwithstanding, Thaddeus Lysaght simultaneously held the offices of Senior Fellow, Bursar, Library Keeper and Registrar. In 1631, he resigned and was followed by a succession of Junior Fellows, paid £3 a year.[49]

The 1628 statute relating to the Library was included in that covering College property, where it was stated that, 'of all the College goods, the books are most valuable'.[50] For that reason, the person chosen as Librarian was to be resident in the College, 'careful . . . , given to study, and a lover of books'. He was to be elected on 20 November each year, along with the other College officers. His principal duties were to attend the Library daily from 9 a.m. until 11 a.m. and from 3 p.m. until 5 p.m. He was also to compile an annual 'register' of the books, 'that it may appear what was lost the preceding year, and how'. Admission to the inner library continued to be restricted to the Provost, Fellows and Bachelors of Divinity, who were also permitted to borrow up to three books at a time, after depositing an appropriate security. Any borrower failing to return a book was obliged to replace it within a month or be fined twice its value. The outer library, to which books were fetched for readers by the Librarian, was open to 'any others who have a mind to make use of the conveniency and benefit of the Library'. This category included readers from outside the College as well as its own undergraduates, and the statutes specified that books such as commentaries, 'which are in frequent use with students', could not be borrowed. If any book was discovered to be lost, a search of students'

---

[47] MUN/V/5/1, 19 August 1627.

[48] MS 760, transcribed in Mahaffy, *Epoch*, pp. 327–75. An English translation of the Library section of the Laudian statutes of 1637, which are almost identical to Bedell's, is printed in Robert Bolton, *A translation of the charter and statutes of Trinity-College, Dublin. Together with the Library-statutes* (Dublin: Nelson, 1749), pp. 87–91.

[49] MUN/P/7/14–MUN/P/7/64.   [50] Bolton, note 48 above.

rooms was to be instigated and, if the book were not found, the Bursar was empowered to replace it and charge the cost to the Librarian's salary. Anyone found to have removed a book 'contrary to the rule' was barred from the Library for a month for a first offence, a year for a second and permanently for a third.[51] This was not the only punishment meted out. For the theft of books, a scholar, Edmond Rawley, was obliged to make 'a publick confession of his fault in the Hall upon his knees'.[52]

In 1637, the College statutes were revised again, this time by the Chancellor of the University, William Laud, Archbishop of Canterbury. Laud introduced major changes, both constitutional and educational, but as far as the Library was concerned, the Bedell statutes remained almost unaltered, except that the opening hours were changed to 8–10 a.m. and 2–4 p.m.[53] In the same year the Board enacted a regulation that anyone who had borrowed a book and not returned it should be fined five shillings a week until the book was brought back.[54]

By the early 1630s the number of students who were enrolled in the College exceeded the institution's ability to provide them with lodgings and, whilst some lived at home, others were accommodated in premises outside the walls, of which the most important was Kildare Hall, in Back Lane, close to Christchurch Cathedral. This possessed a collection of books for students' use and may also have been used for teaching. Lists of the books in the library there in 1633 contain around seventy titles.[55] By 1638, Trinity no longer used Kildare Hall, but in that year the College appealed to Wentworth, the Lord Deputy, seeking to initiate proceedings against a number of men who had borrowed and failed to return books from either the Hall or the College Library, or who owed debts to the College. The list included several who had been Fellows or MAs and had moved on to ecclesiastical posts, and others who may have been external readers, as their names do not appear in the register of College graduates. The list of those summoned to appear as witnesses included a Mr Barry, described as the 'keeper of the library' at Kildare Hall.[56]

After the burst of activity in the first decade of the seventeenth century, there were comparatively few purchases during the rest of the 1600s, though the annual accounts for several years between 1617 and 1623 record a

---

[51] *Ibid.*   [52] MUN/V/5/1, 4 July 1629.

[53] *Charta, sive Literae Patentes, Caroli I* (13 Charles I), in *Chartae et statuta Collegii Sacrosanctae et Individuae Trinitatis Reginae Elizabethae juxta Dublin* (Dublin: Gill, 1844), pp. 80–4; Bolton, note 48 above.

[54] MUN/V/5/1, 7 June 1637.   [55] MS 2160/2 and 2a; Mahaffy, *Epoch*, pp. 213–18.

[56] MUN/LIB/10/7, reprinted in Mahaffy, *Epoch*, pp. 249–50.

modest level of expenditure on books.[57] There were equally few donations until after the restoration of the monarchy in 1660, but the Library did receive the papers of Ambrose Ussher, bequeathed at his death in 1629 (MSS 285–91). These comprise commentaries, sermons and a number of his unpublished manuscripts on a range of subjects, including an Arabic dictionary and grammar, a partial translation of the Bible, and a political tract on the question of Scotland's union with England.

In selecting books for the College, Challoner and Ussher had been motivated by the desire to put together a library that would be comprehensive and scholarly, and not a mere ornament, but even by the first half of the seventeenth century it had become a part of the College which the Fellows proudly showed to visitors. Sir William Brereton, later to become a parliamentary general in the English Civil War, travelled through Ireland in 1637 and visited Dublin. He was taken to the Library and saw various manuscripts, including Bacon's *Opus maius*. The Fellows, he reported, 'glory much in their library', but, as an Oxford man no doubt familiar with the Bodleian, Brereton was surprisingly unimpressed, describing it as 'not large, well-contrived, nor well furnished with books'.[58] He was told that a new Library was to be built, though in fact it was to be almost another century before this dream was realised. Brereton also dined with James Ussher at his house in College Green, and was taken into his library, where he was shown the archbishop's collection of Waldensian manuscripts.

---

[57] E.g. MUN/P/1/109, MUN/P/1/118, MUN/P/1/119 and MUN/P/1/151.
[58] Sir William Brereton, *Travels in Holland, the United Provinces, England, Scotland and Ireland, 1634–1635*, ed. by Edward Hawkins (Manchester: Chetham Society, 1844), p. 143.

2 | Ussher, Kells and Durrow: 1641–1665

The first four decades of the seventeenth century were a time of relative peace and increasing prosperity for the fledgling College, but in 1641 all was to change, in the wake of the political upheavals under way across the water. Wentworth, the former Lord Deputy and later Earl of Strafford, was executed in May 1641. Four years later the same fate befell William Laud, Archbishop of Canterbury and Chancellor of the University of Dublin. In 1640, James Ussher, who was the Vice-Chancellor, as well as Archbishop of Armagh, made a routine visit to England, from which he never returned. Rebellion broke out in Ireland in October 1641, and the Provost, Richard Washington, along with several of the Fellows, followed the Vice-Chancellor to England. The College, which had already been forbidden by Parliament to elect any more Fellows, remained without a Provost until 1645. Throughout the anarchy of the 1640s it staggered on, receiving very few students and being forced to sell plate to survive, because many of its estates had fallen into the hands of the insurgents and income from rents had almost dried up. It received a little help from the government in the form of small grants, but these were hard won. One petition to the Lords Justices described the College as being in danger of having to be dissolved through poverty, and pleaded that, even if the scholars could not be kept together, 'for the preservation of learning... at least the fabric of the house and public library may be preserved'.[1]

From 1637 to 1641, the Library was in the care of John Bishop (or Bushop), who had been elected first a Fellow in June 1637 and then the Library Keeper a month later.[2] In November 1641 he was replaced by Richard Welsh (or Walsh), who – presumably because there were so few Fellows then available – was neither a Fellow, nor even an MA. He continued to serve until at least 1644, but seems to have been ineffectual as the custodian of the Library, as the statutes were ignored and considerable numbers of books were lost.[3] The records contain a draft petition, dated April 1643, referring to the fact that 'divers bookes of the Coledge Library are inbezeled and thence

---

[1] MUN/P/1/346.   [2] MUN/V/5/1, 7 June 1637; MUN/P/7/39–MUN/P/7/47.
[3] MUN/V/5/2, 20 November 1641; MUN/P/1/342.

taken away and detained since and before the beginning of the Rebellion'.[4]
The petition noted that Ussher, as Vice-Chancellor, had appointed Edward
Parry to be Pro-Vice-Chancellor with a particular responsibility to ensure
that the statutes relating to the Library 'bee put in execution', and sought
authority for Parry to nominate Fellows or graduates of the College resident
in Dublin to search for books belonging to the Library anywhere in the
College or city 'where they shall suspect any such bookes to bee'.[5]

By 1650, Trinity had reached a low point in its history, with Dublin
ravaged by a plague that carried off half the population and the College
almost closed. However, in that year Cromwell's government in Ireland
seized the possessions of the see of Dublin and used the income to increase
Trinity's endowments. They also appointed trustees with the authority to
remove the Fellows and run the College according to the demands of the
regime.[6] As part of this cleansing process, the strongly puritan Samuel
Winter was appointed as Provost. Winter, whose annual salary of £100 as
Provost was supplemented by a further £200 as a state preacher, became
a generous benefactor to the College, assisting poor students as well as
donating 'a large summ of money disbursed out of his own purse' to provide
books for the Library.[7]

Henry Jones

One of the few men to survive in office throughout this period was Henry
Jones, who had succeeded his uncle, James Ussher, as Vice-Chancellor in
1646 and held the post until the Restoration. Jones was one of the Commissioners appointed after the rebellion of 1641 to investigate the claims of the
dispossessed, an undertaking that led to the compilation of the 1641 Depositions, which were donated to Trinity by John Stearne a century later. In
1651, Jones spent £400 on refurbishing the Library with 'a faire staire case,
windows, classes, seates, and other ornaments'.[8] It was long assumed that
the two staircases now at the west end of the Long Room were those that had
been donated by Jones and that they had been moved from the old Library,
but this has now been disproved.[9] Jones' contribution was commemorated
on a brass plaque which was placed above the door to the original building

---

[4] MS 2160/14.   [5] *Ibid.*

[6] T. C. Barnard, *Cromwellian Ireland: English government and reform in Ireland 1649–60* (London: Oxford University Press, 1975), pp. 198–211; Mahaffy, *Epoch*, pp. 293–5.

[7] J.W., *The life and death of the eminently learned, pious, and painful minister of the Gospel, Dr Samuel Winter* (London: Parkhurst, 1671), p. 36.

[8] MS 571, fol. 3v.   [9] See below, p. 64.

and is now in the Old Library.[10] Generous though this benefaction was, it was later dwarfed by his gifts of what were to become the College's two greatest treasures, the Book of Kells and the Book of Durrow.

Several misconceptions about both of these manuscripts survived into the nineteenth century. Both were associated with – or, indeed, were thought to have been written by – Colum Cille (St Columba), but the Book of Durrow is now normally dated to the late seventh century, a hundred years after the death of the saint, and the Book of Kells was produced at least another century later. It was also thought that they formed part of Archbishop Ussher's library but, though they arrived in Trinity within a few years of the Primate's books and manuscripts, the evidence points to Ussher having studied both without possessing either.[11]

The Book of Kells (MS 58) is the most lavishly decorated of the surviving Gospel manuscripts produced by Irish monks between the seventh and ninth centuries.[12] The main text is that of the Gospels in Latin, preceded by canon tables (concordances of Gospel passages) and *breves causae* (summaries of the narratives). Each Gospel is introduced by a full-page symbol of the evangelist and there are other pages with portraits of Christ and scenes from his life. As well as these great illustrated pages, the wealth of decorated initials and interlinear drawings is unparalleled. Almost every page contains 'writhing, chasing, struggling, frolicking creatures, now hiding, now scampering between the lines, filling the gaps at the ends of paragraphs'.[13] The manuscript is thought to have been written around the year 800, either in the Columban monastery of Iona, off the west coast of Scotland, or in Kells, County Meath, to which the monks moved after the sack of Iona by Vikings in 806, or – perhaps more likely – it was begun in Iona and brought to Kells for completion. The manuscript remained in Kells throughout the Middle Ages and, according to the Annals of Ulster, it was stolen from the church there in 1007 because of the heavily ornamented *cumdach* (shrine) in which it was kept. It was found 3 months later, buried in the ground and without the *cumdach*. It remained in Kells, where, in the twelfth century, property transactions were recorded in previously blank spaces. The town

[10] F. Elrington Ball, 'Extracts from the journal of Thomas Dineley or Dingley, Esquire, giving some account of his visit to Ireland in the reign of Charles II', *JRSAI*, 43 (1913), 275–309.

[11] Aubrey Gwynn, 'Some notes on the history of the Book of Kells', *Irish Historical Studies*, 9 (1954), 131–61; Bernard Meehan, 'The history of the manuscript', in *Kells facsimile*, pp. 317–29.

[12] For recent scholarship, see *Kells facsimile*, which contains a comprehensive bibliography; F. O'Mahony, ed., *The Book of Kells: proceedings of a conference at Trinity College Dublin, 6–9 September 1992* (Aldershot: Scolar, 1994); Carol Farr, *The Book of Kells: its function and audience* (London: British Library, 1997); and Bernard Meehan, *The Book of Kells* (London: Thames and Hudson, 2012).

[13] George Otto Simms, 'Early Christian manuscripts', in *Treasures*, pp. 38–56 (p. 44).

suffered during the unrest of the mid seventeenth century. The surveyors carrying out preliminary work for the Down Survey reported in 1655 that horses were stabled in what remained of the church and that the manuscript believed to have been written by Colum Cille had been sent by the governor of Kells to the Commissioners of the Commonwealth about a year and a half previously.[14] This dates its transfer to Dublin fairly precisely to 1653, though where it remained after that, until it was donated to Trinity, is not known.

The Book of Durrow (MS 57) is thought to be the earliest surviving fully decorated insular Gospel-book. Though closely related to the Book of Kells, it is less sumptuous. It contains eleven pages of decoration, including symbols of the evangelists and 'carpet' pages of abstract design: spirals, roundels and biting animals. Unlike the Book of Kells, most of its pages of text have little ornamentation, but the calligraphy is of a high order. It was probably written in the monastery founded by Colum Cille in Durrow, County Offaly, where it was placed in a *cumdach* adorned with a silver cross, around the year 900. After the dissolution of the monastery at Durrow in the mid sixteenth century, it is not known where the manuscript was kept, although it still seems to have been in Durrow around 1630.[15]

Both manuscripts were collated by James Ussher, probably in the 1620s or 1630s, and at some point they passed into the custody of Henry Jones and thence to Trinity. The date of Jones' donation is not known, but it seems most likely to have been soon after 1661, when he became Bishop of Meath, in which diocese both Kells and Durrow lie. In 1681, he told William Palliser, then Professor of Divinity at Trinity, that he had assisted Ussher with the work of collating the two manuscripts and confirmed that he, Jones, had been the donor of them to the College.[16] He described them as 'S. Columkill's and the Cupboard MS'. The first is undoubtedly the Book of Kells, which was long known as 'St Colum Cille's manuscript' and the second is almost certainly the Book of Durrow, which, because of its silver *cumdach*, would have been kept in a cupboard separately from the other manuscripts. Samuel Foley's 1688 catalogue of the College manuscripts lists both, noting the shrine of Durrow and allocating a shelfmark to Kells, but not to Durrow.[17] The *cumdach* was stolen during the Jacobite occupation of the College in 1689–90 and the Book of Durrow was then bound, given

---

[14] Charles McNeill, 'Copies of Down Survey maps in private keeping', *Analecta Hibernica*, 8 (1938), 419–27.

[15] A. A. Luce, G. O. Simms, P. Meyer and L. Bieler, eds., *Evangeliorum quattuor Codex Durmachensis*, 2 vols. (Olten: Urs Graf, 1960); Bernard Meehan, *The Book of Durrow: a medieval masterpiece at Trinity College Dublin* (Dublin: Town House, 1996).

[16] Palliser to Henry Dodwell, 19 April 1681, quoted in *Tanner letters*, p. 440.

[17] William O'Sullivan, 'The donor of the Book of Kells', *Irish Historical Studies*, 11 (1958–9), 5–7.

a shelfmark and placed with the rest of the manuscripts. Narcissus Marsh wrote in 1699 that he remembered seeing the shrine with its 'monumental silver cross' when he was Provost (1679–83), but that the manuscript had later been bound in a 'plain brown rough leathern cover'.[18]

Ussher's library

In 1600, at the age of 19, James Ussher had been elected a Fellow of the College, and he served as the Professor of Divinity from 1607 until his appointment as Bishop of Meath in 1621. Four years later he was translated to Armagh as the Primate of All Ireland. His regular visits to England, which had begun in the company of Challoner, continued after the latter's death, and by the 1620s Ussher was moving in the highest circles, political as well as scholarly, in both countries. His journey in 1640 turned out to be his last, and he never returned to the land of his birth. The rebellion the following year deprived him of his home, his income and – almost – his library. His books and manuscripts were in the Primate's residence near Drogheda, in the care of his chaplain, Nicholas Bernard, when the town was attacked. Despite the damage done by the rebels, Bernard reported that 'it pleased God' to save Ussher's library from the 'barbarous multitude'.[19] After the siege was lifted in 1642, the books were shipped to Chester for safety and later to London.

Ussher was by that time becoming increasingly identified with the royalist cause. He refused to recognise the Westminster Assembly, set up by the Long Parliament to restructure the Church of England, and, as a result, his library was confiscated by Parliament and ordered to be sold. Some of the manuscripts were stolen, but the bulk of the collection was bought by his friend John Selden, who had saved other libraries destined to be dispersed, and Selden returned it to its owner.[20] With the King and Parliament now at war, Ussher moved first to Oxford and then to Cardiff, taking with him

---

[18] Marsh to Arthur Charlett, 30 November 1699, quoted in Henry Ellis, ed., *Original letters of eminent literary men of the sixteenth, seventeenth and eighteenth centuries* (London: Camden Society, 1843), pp. 295–8 (p. 298).

[19] Nicholas Bernard, *The life and death of the most reverend and learned father of our church, Dr James Usher* (London: Tyler, 1656), p. 94; Hugh Jackson Lawlor, 'Primate Ussher's library before 1641', *Proc. RIA*, series 3, 6 (1900–2), 216–64.

[20] *Journals of the House of Commons*, vol. III, pp. 394, 612 (9 February, 30 August 1644); *ibid.*, vol. IV, p. 429 (6 February 1646); C. W. Russell and John P. Prendergast, eds., *Calendar of state papers Ireland, James I, 1603–1625*, 5 vols. (London: Longman, 1872–80), vol. I, pp. xcv–c; C. R. Elrington, ed., *The whole works of the most rev. James Ussher*, 17 vols. (Dublin: Hodges & Smith, 1847–64), vol. I, pp. 227–32.

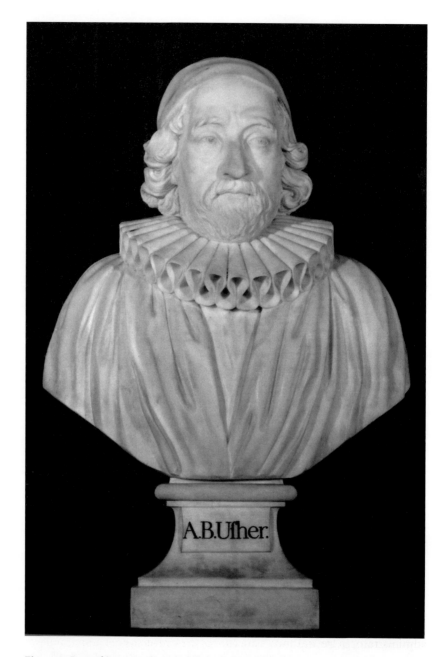

Figure 2 Bust of James Ussher, Archbishop of Armagh, in the Long Room (College Art Collections, TCD)

several chests of his books. When Cardiff became unsafe, he set off for St Donat's Castle in Glamorgan, but during the journey his party was waylaid and many of his books and papers were stolen. The local clergy and gentry appealed for their return, and within 2 or 3 months almost all had been restored to him, though two manuscripts on the history of the Waldenses were never recovered, a loss that 'did much grieve him'.[21] In 1646, Ussher returned to London, where he was appointed to a preaching position at Lincoln's Inn and where space was provided to house his library. He lived at various locations around London for the next 10 years, but on 20 March 1656 suffered a violent pain in his hip, which he thought to be a recurrence of the sciatica 'which about 35 years agoe, he had by sitting up late in the Colledge Library of Dublyn'.[22] He died of an internal haemorrhage the following day. Despite Ussher's royalist sympathies, Cromwell provided £200 for a state funeral, which was conducted by Nicholas Bernard.[23]

Ussher's intention had been to leave his personal library to Trinity, knowing the extent to which it complemented the holdings of the College Library. In this way his plan for the Library, as an amalgamation of his and Challoner's collections, together with the books he had bought for the College half a century earlier, would have been realised. The events of recent years, however, meant that it had become his sole remaining worldly possession, and so he bequeathed it to his only daughter, Elizabeth, the wife of Sir Timothy Tyrrell, who had defended Cardiff for the royalist side during Ussher's stay there. The Tyrrells were impoverished and, as the library's pecuniariary value mattered more to them than its scholarly importance, they put it up for sale. According to Ussher's seventeenth-century biographer Richard Parr, offers were made for it by Cardinal Mazarin and the King of Denmark, but Cromwell intervened to prevent its being sold abroad.[24]

At its meeting on 12 June 1656, the Council of State nominated three prominent clergymen to consult the catalogue of the library and 'report what manuscripts or other books should be bought by the state'.[25] In the meantime the sale was forbidden. In December, the Council appointed five of its members to negotiate with Tyrrell and advise on appropriate action. Several institutions were interested in acquiring the collection. Sion College in London offered £2,500 for it and it was reported at the Council meeting in February 1657 that Thomas Barlow, Bodley's Librarian, hoped that it would be 'conferred on the public', by which he no doubt meant the Bodleian Library.[26] Cromwell's son Henry, who had been appointed chief administrator in Ireland and Chancellor of the University of Dublin, and was

[21] Bernard, *Ussher*, note 19 above, p. 101.   [22] *Ibid.*, p. 108.
[23] *Mercurius Politicus*, No. 303 (27 March–3 April 1656), 6076.
[24] Richard Parr, *The life of the most reverend father in God, James Usher* (London: Ranew, 1686), p. 102.
[25] M. A. E. Green, ed., *Calendar of state papers, domestic series, Commonwealth, 1649–60*, 13 vols. (London: Longman, 1875–86), vol. IX, p. 370.
[26] *Ibid.*, vol. X, pp. 199, 271; T. C. Barnard, 'The purchase of Archbishop Ussher's library in 1657', *Long Room*, 4 (Autumn/Winter 1971), 9–14.

later to become the Lord Deputy, was planning to establish a second college in the University. Ussher's collection would provide it with an excellent and ready-made library. However, he had to find the £2,500 that had already been offered for the books, and the government in Ireland was in no position to produce that amount of money. Whilst these negotiations were under way, Nicholas Bernard published the sermon that he had preached at Ussher's funeral. It included a biography of the archbishop in which he gave an account of the founding of Trinity College Library on the basis of donations from the army after the Battle of Kinsale. Though now disproved, that story was believed at the time. Bernard's clear political message was that, if soldiers could buy books to establish a library for a new college (Trinity) in 1602, then the current generation of soldiers ought to be able to do the same for Cromwell's planned new college in 1656. The propaganda worked, and in March 1657 the army agreed to provide the money to buy Ussher's library.[27]

By the end of the month, Sir Anthony Morgan, one of Henry Cromwell's subordinates, was already negotiating with Tyrrell. The contract was signed and Tyrrell was paid £500, with the remaining £2,000 due 3 months hence. He was allowed £50 towards the cost of packing and for making a new catalogue, which was to be compared with the old one, 'that wee may see what is wanting which he is to make good'.[28] The catalogues were checked, very few items were found to be missing and so, as Tyrrell had added books and a chest of manuscripts that were not listed, Morgan considered that the terms of the agreement had been fulfilled.[29] The books were taken to Chester and arrangements were made for them to be shipped to Dublin as soon as 'the Kinsale Frigate . . . or some other man of warre' was available to provide an escort.[30]

Cromwell had designated Cork House as the site of the library for his new college, but when the books arrived in Dublin it was not ready to receive them, and so they were stored in the adjacent Castle.[31] Caesar Williamson, a Fellow of Trinity, was appointed to superintend the library and catalogue the books, and from an invoice dated 1658 it appears that he also supervised the binding of some of them.[32] He was promised an annual salary of £20, but had

---

[27] *Mercurius Politicus*, No. 353 (12–16 March 1657), 7672.

[28] Morgan to Cromwell, 7 April 1657, BL MS Lansdowne 822, fol. 9. See also Peter Gaunt, ed., *The correspondence of Henry Cromwell, 1655–1659, from the British Library Lansdowne manuscripts* (Cambridge University Press, 2007).

[29] Morgan to Cromwell, 21 April 1657, BL MS Lansdowne 822, fols. 53–4.

[30] Thomas Herbert, Clerk to the Irish Council, to Charles Whalley, Chester, 8 July 1657, quoted in William Urwick, *The early history of Trinity College Dublin, 1591–1660* (London: Fisher Unwin, 1892), p. 92.

[31] Urwick, *Early history*, note 30 above, pp. 63–9.   [32] MUN/LIB/10/9.

to petition the Irish House of Commons several years later before he received payment, and it took the College until 1664 to pay Horatio Beverley, brother of the by-then-deceased binder.[33] During 1658 and 1659 plans were drawn up to convert part of Cork House to hold Ussher's collections as a 'publique library', and Williamson and some of the trustees of Trinity College were summoned to advise on how the library 'may be disposed . . . for public use'.[34] However, the death of Oliver Cromwell, his son's return to England and the restoration of the monarchy in 1660 meant that none of those plans was implemented and the library remained in Dublin Castle. On 31 May 1661 the Irish House of Commons ordered that it be transferred from the Castle to Trinity, 'there to be preserved for publick use', a gift that has been celebrated in the College ever since as that of 'the Most Serene King Charles the Second'.[35]

During its stay in the Castle the collection suffered losses, but the Cromwellian authorities successfully recovered most of the missing items.[36] The library that was transferred to Trinity numbered about ten thousand volumes. Despite its sundry vicissitudes and earlier losses, it was still one of the largest and finest private libraries of its time, exceeding in size that of Ussher's friend Selden, whose collection of about eight thousand volumes is often cited as one of the largest of the mid seventeenth century.[37]

Among nearly seven hundred manuscripts, which have formed the core of the Library's collection of medieval manuscripts ever since, Ussher's library is particularly rich in items from English religious houses, especially the former monasteries of northern England, such as Fountains and Rievaulx. More than twenty medieval manuscripts have been identified as coming from the collection of Henry Savile, of Banke in Yorkshire, which was broken up and sold after his death in 1617. The sale of manuscripts belonging to the mathematician and astrologer John Dee yielded several more medieval manuscripts, including the thirteenth-century Anglo-Norman *Vie de Seint Auban* (MS 177) by the celebrated historian Matthew Paris.[38]

Ussher was well placed to acquire these and other manuscripts from the English monasteries: he was collecting within a century of their dissolution, he was in England for lengthy periods and he knew the main collectors of

---

[33] *Commons Jn Ireland*, vol. I, p. 404 (15 June 1661); MUN/LIB/10/9–10.

[34] Quoted in Urwick, *Early history*, note 30 above, p. 93.

[35] *Commons Jn Ireland*, vol. I, p. 400; the wording on the gold frieze in the Long Room.

[36] Barnard, 'Purchase', note 26 above, p. 13.

[37] David Pearson, 'The English private library in the seventeenth century', *Library*, 13 (2012), 379–99.

[38] Robert Atkinson, ed., *Vie de Seint Auban: a poem in Norman French ascribed to Matthew Paris* (London: Murray, 1876).

the day.[39] Manuscripts were frequently loaned among these scholars and collectors, some of them remaining with those to whom they had been lent. Ussher both gained and lost from this traffic, and it has been argued that the manuscript collection owned by Ussher during his lifetime should not be regarded as static but as 'an essentially fluid entity', to which he was constantly adding and subtracting.[40] One of the finest items in the collection, the twelfth-century New Testament and Psalter from the abbey of Winchcombe in Gloucestershire (MS 53), had previously been in the Royal Library, a collection that lost a number of items during the early seventeenth century, including several to Ussher, though Bodley's plans for the wholesale removal of the library to Oxford were thwarted.[41] Through his friendship with Sir Robert Cotton, Ussher had access to the greatest collection of manuscripts in England. He borrowed extensively from it, and Cotton was also generous in giving manuscripts, several of which are now in the College Library bearing Cotton's marks of ownership.[42] Some of the manuscripts that left Ussher's library before his death passed to other collectors and frequently thence to institutions such as the British Museum and the Bodleian Library. Others were later acquired by Thomas Barlow, Bodley's Librarian, and by Ussher's grandson James Tyrrell. Both of those collections were eventually presented to the Bodleian.[43]

Ussher possessed few Irish-language manuscripts, and this aspect of the collection was further impoverished by the loss of the Book of Lecan and the Book of Ballymote from the College Library between 1689 and 1720. Among Trinity's Irish manuscripts the provenance of the *Liber hymnorum* (MS 1441), an eleventh-century collection of hymns in both Latin and Irish, was a matter of doubt until the late twentieth century, when the Library's first Keeper of Manuscripts, William O'Sullivan, produced convincing evidence that it had belonged to Ussher.[44] Less secure was T. K. Abbott's attribution

---

[39] William O'Sullivan, 'Ussher as a collector of manuscripts', *Hermathena*, 88 (1956), 34–58; Bernard Meehan, 'The manuscript collection of James Ussher', in *Treasures*, pp. 97–110.

[40] Elizabethanne Boran, 'Ussher and the collection of manuscripts in early modern Europe', in Jason Harris and Keith Sidwell, eds., *Making Ireland Roman: Irish neo-Latin writers and the republic of letters* (Cork University Press, 2009), pp. 176–94.

[41] James P. Carley, 'The Royal Library as a source for Sir Robert Cotton's collection: a preliminary list of acquisitions', in C. J. Wright, ed., *Sir Robert Cotton as collector: essays on an early Stuart courtier and his legacy* (London: British Library, 1997), pp. 208–29.

[42] Colin G. C. Tite, '"Lost or stolen or strayed": a survey of manuscripts formerly in the Cotton library', *British Library Journal*, 18 (1992), 107–47.

[43] Barnard, 'Purchase', note 26 above.

[44] William O'Sullivan, 'Notes on the Trinity *Liber hymnorum*', in John L. Sharpe, ed., *Roger Powell: the compleat binder* (Turnhout: Brepols, 1996), pp. 130–3; J. H. Bernard and R. Atkinson, eds., *The Irish Liber hymnorum* (London: Henry Bradshaw Society, 1898).

to Ussher of two early Irish Gospel manuscripts, to which he gave the names *Usserianus primus* (MS 55) and *Usserianus secundus* (MS 56, also known as the Garland of Howth).[45] During the early 1620s William Bedell, later to become Provost, had lent Ussher the eleventh-century Psalter and martyrology written in about 1079 in an Irish script and with decoration by the Welsh scribe Ricemarch or Rhygyfarch. Now known as the Ricemarch Psalter (MS 50), the manuscript was returned to Bedell, who died in 1642 and bequeathed it to Ussher.[46] At least three, and possibly more, of Ussher's manuscripts came from the collection of George Carew, Lord President of Munster. After Carew's death in 1629, Ussher tried to acquire his manuscripts of Irish interest but was rebuffed by Carew's son, to whom they had passed, though the College later acquired the Irish maps.[47]

For his biblical research, Ussher employed agents in Aleppo and Constantinople to seek out oriental copies of Bible texts and to have transcriptions made when originals could not be obtained. One such is a Syriac text of parts of the New Testament (MS 1509) transcribed for Ussher in the 1620s.[48] He also commissioned transcriptions of texts in continental libraries such as the Vatican and the Escorial. His library contained ten volumes of documents relating to the Waldensian sect of the Alpine region of France. This movement began in the twelfth century as a reaction against the outward splendour of the Church and, after the Reformation, adopted a Calvinist form of Protestantism. The manuscripts are mostly religious tracts, written in Provençal and dating mainly from the sixteenth century (MSS 258–67).[49]

Among the contemporary papers acquired with the collection were those of Ussher himself (MSS 773–794), Luke Challoner (MSS 354–8), Richard Hooker (MSS 118–121 and 774), and John Bainbridge, Professor of Astronomy at Oxford and a close friend, who left his papers to Ussher in 1643 (MSS 382–6).[50] There is only one music manuscript that can be attributed

---

[45] O'Sullivan, 'Ussher', note 39 above.

[46] Hugh Jackson Lawlor, ed., *The psalter and martyrology of Ricemarch* (London: Bradshaw Society, 1914).

[47] William O'Sullivan, 'George Carew's Irish maps', *Long Room*, 26/27 (1983), 15–25.

[48] John Gwynn, 'On a Syriac MS belonging to the collection of Archbishop Ussher', *Trans. RIA*, 27 (1886), 269–316; Iskandar Bcheiry, *Catalogue of Syriac manuscripts in Trinity College Dublin* (Kaslik: Parole de l'Orient, 2005), pp. 3–5.

[49] James Henthorn Todd, *The books of the Vaudois: the Waldensian manuscripts preserved in the Library of Trinity College, Dublin* (London: Macmillan, 1865); Lisa Shields, 'Medieval manuscripts in French and Provençal', *Hermathena*, 121 (1976), 90–100.

[50] P. G. Stanwood, 'The Richard Hooker manuscripts', *Long Room*, 11 (Spring/Summer 1975), 7–10.

with certainty to the collection: the so-called 'Dublin virginal manuscript' (MS 410), a collection of keyboard pieces dating from around 1570.[51]

The printed books included those which Ussher himself had collected, as well as those that he had inherited from Challoner. As in the case of the College Library that both men helped to establish, the collection was dominated by theological works. It included grammars in the three biblical languages, Hebrew, Greek and Latin, many editions of the Bible and a large collection of translations of the Psalms. Biblical commentaries by Protestant writers such as Luther and Calvin were balanced by the works of the Church Fathers and Roman Catholic writers, seen as essential ammunition in the polemical warfare of the time. Historical works were also well represented, including Roman histories by Livy and those of more local areas such as Ireland, Scotland and England. Geography and astronomy were particular interests of Challoner's, and the collection contained many of the most important works on the subject, including texts by Ptolemy and Copernicus. Law, medicine and economics, on the other hand, were less well represented.[52]

The acquisition of Ussher's library placed Trinity in the first league in terms of collections, not only in size but also in the richness of its holdings. In the sermon at Ussher's funeral, the Swiss theologian Friedrich Spanheim was reported to have described it as 'the library of the learned world'.[53] Narcissus Marsh, however, was less impressed. Writing to Edward Bernard at Oxford shortly after his appointment as Provost of Trinity, he said, 'though I must whisper him in the ear, that I would not have it divulg'd, that Primate Usher's library (both MSS & printed books) comes very short of its and its owners fame; it might have been thought a good library for another man, but not for that learned Prelate'.[54]

It presented the College with huge problems of scale, as it tripled the size of the Library. Ussher's manuscripts, which were in a separate sequence from the printed books, were placed in a room at the north-east corner of the Library. Once the principle of separating printed books and manuscripts had been established, later Library Keepers placed all newly acquired manuscripts in this, the first Manuscripts Room, and the manuscripts already in the College were gradually moved there. There is no evidence

---

[51] J. M. Ward, ed., *The Dublin virginal manuscript*, 2nd edn (Wellesley, Mass.: Wellesley College, 1964); John Ward, 'The lute books of Trinity College Dublin', *Lute Society Journal*, 9 (1967), 17–40.

[52] Elizabethanne Boran, 'The libraries of Luke Challoner and James Ussher, 1595–1608', in Helga Robinson-Hammerstein, ed., *European universities in the age of Reformation and Counter-Reformation* (Dublin: Four Courts Press, 1998), pp. 75–115; Elizabethanne Boran, 'Libraries and collectors, 1550–1700', in *Irish book*, pp. 91–110.

[53] Bernard, *Ussher*, note 19 above, p. 7.   [54] 16 October 1680, Bodleian MS Smith 45, fol. 19.

as to whether the Library had to be extended to accommodate the acquisition of Ussher's books, but it seems unlikely that the improvements made in 1651 at the expense of Henry Jones would have provided a large enough space, unless of course Jones had already anticipated the arrival of the collection. At any rate, the Library now occupied the whole length of one of the quadrangles, on the floor above the student rooms, and Ussher's books were housed at the west end, in a separate section, behind a lattice screen.[55]

When Ussher's collection arrived in Trinity it was accompanied by two catalogues, one listing the manuscripts and the other the printed books. Both have been attributed to Sir James Ware, though it is possible that the catalogue of the printed books is that which Caesar Williamson compiled whilst the collection was in Dublin Castle.[56] It is a shelf-list (now MS 4), and the College clearly decided that an alphabetical catalogue was also needed. This was compiled around 1666 and contains a note stating that it was 'written by S[r] Tindall & S[r] Staughton', two recent BAs.[57]

Ware's catalogue of Ussher's manuscripts has not survived, but its existence at the time is indicated by a list compiled in about 1670 (MS 7/2), the entries in which are brief and contain a number of references to fuller descriptions in Ware's lost catalogue, usually in the form 'v. S[r]. James Ware'.[58] Copies of the catalogue of 1670 exist also in the British Library and Trinity College, Cambridge, and it is possible that it and the 1666 list of printed books were produced to fulfil the requirement of the Commons, when the collection was transferred to Trinity, that catalogues should be prepared and 'entered in the Journal Book of the House'.[59]

The catalogue of manuscripts (MS 7/2) was also used to record the receipt of later accessions, such as the gifts from Thomas Halley in 1673 (MS 90) and Henry Prescott in 1681 (MS 49). The only other donations of note in the middle of the century were the half-dozen medieval manuscripts from English monasteries given by the College's first Professor of Mathematics, Miles Symner, between the 1630s and 1650s.[60] In comparison to the spectacular gifts of the 1660s, all of these, and the other few acquisitions of the period, pale into relative insignificance.

---

[55] John Dunton, *The Dublin scuffle* (London: printed for the author, 1699), p. 412.
[56] *Commons Jn Ireland*, vol. I, p. 404.
[57] The catalogue is now MS 5, and MS 6 is a fair copy of it.
[58] E.g., MS 7/2, fol. 29v.; William O'Sullivan, 'Introduction to the collections', in Colker, pp. 21–33.
[59] *Commons Jn Ireland*, vol. I, p. 400; O'Sullivan, 'Introduction', note 58 above.
[60] Colker, entry for MS 208; MUN/LIB/1/53, fol. 2r.; T. C. Barnard, 'Miles Symner and the new learning in seventeenth-century Ireland', *JRSAI*, 102 (1972), 129–42.

Sir Jerome Alexander's library

Jerome Alexander was born in Norfolk and, after graduating from Cambridge, was called to the English bar. His career was for the most part a scandalous one, involving no less than four periods of imprisonment on charges including the forging of legal documents, intimidation of witnesses and misappropriation of funds. Forbidden to practise in England, he moved to Ireland, where he continued his legal career whilst, at the same time, proceeding to acquire forfeited lands in various parts of the country. He was knighted by Charles II and appointed as second Justice of Common Pleas in Ireland, in which office he was renowned for his harsh judgments and for the unscrupulous manner with which he managed to secure property to which he had no claim. He died in 1670, leaving the bulk of his considerable fortune to his youngest surviving daughter, on condition that she did not marry an Irishman or a Catholic, in which case her inheritance would transfer to Trinity.[1] She duly married an English baronet, but Trinity benefitted considerably from other provisions in Alexander's will. He left the College his library of over six hundred books and manuscripts, apart from those on medical subjects, which went to his daughter.[2] Over half the collection consisted of legal and statutory material, but it also covered politics and religion, geography and history, including 125 volumes of pamphlets published during the English Civil War.

In making his gift to the College, Alexander took pains to ensure that it adequately commemorated him as benefactor. He laid down strict instructions about how the transfer was to be handled and how the collection was to be administered. He specified that the books were not to be moved to

---

[1] Charles Rogers, 'Notes in the history of Sir Jerome Alexander', *Transactions of the Royal Historical Society*, n.s., 1 (1872), 220–40 includes the text of the will (cf. also MUN/LIB/10/17).

[2] Virginia Teehan, 'The Alexander collection in the library of Trinity College, Dublin, with special reference to the law books' (unpublished M.Phil. thesis, University of Dublin, 1991); Elizabethanne Boran, 'Libraries and collectors, 1550–1700', in *Irish book*, pp. 91–110. MUN/LIB/10/18 is a catalogue of the collection, dated 1675; MUN/LIB/1/15 is a later catalogue, containing shelfmarks.

Trinity until they had been catalogued, a task for which two people were to be appointed, one by his daughter and the other by the Provost. He left £500 to erect a new building for the College and a further £100 to house his library and provide accommodation for a Library Keeper, whose salary was to be met from part of the rent received from lands in County Westmeath, which he also gave to Trinity. The Library Keeper was to be appointed by the Provost and Fellows at a special meeting to be held on Christmas Day whenever a new incumbent was required. The security of the books was a particular concern to him. They were not to be lent or otherwise removed from the library, 'being very many of them small and easily pocketted up and yet very scarce, and rarely to be gotten for love or money'.[3] On appointment, the keeper was to be given a 'perfect catalogue' of the library to sign, and on demitting office was required to pay the College £5 for every book 'that he shall loose, or suffer to bee imbezilled' during his term of office. The first record of the appointment of a Library Keeper was that of George Mercer, a Senior Fellow, on Christmas Day 1674, as required by the will, but later elections to that office took place at various times in the year whenever there was a vacancy.[4] The College accounts record payments to the 'Librarian of Sir Jerome Alexander's Library' until the late 1760s, though by then the post appears to have become a sinecure.[5]

The library itself disappears from the record between the late seventeenth century and the nineteenth. It and its building seem to have suffered serious damage during the occupation of the College in 1689–90. Those manuscripts that survived were transferred to Burgh's new building in 1732 and merged with the rest of the Library's collection of manuscripts. According to evidence given to the Dublin University Commission in 1852, Alexander's printed books, together with books given by Claudius Gilbert and a bequest from Provost Murray, were merged in 1800 to create a new Lending Library.[6]

The Countess of Bath's library

Henry Bourchier, later Earl of Bath, entered Trinity as an undergraduate in 1597 and became a close friend of James Ussher. He was elected a Fellow and was described as a 'lover of learning'.[7] After a political career, he died

---

[3] MUN/LIB/10/17.   [4] MUN/V/5/2, 25 December 1674.   [5] MUN/P/1/751.

[6] William O'Sullivan, 'Introduction to the collections', in Colker, pp. 21–33; DU Commission, 'Appendix A: Evidence', p. 192.

[7] Thomas Fuller, *The church history of Britain*, 3rd edn, 3 vols. (London: Tegg, 1842), vol. III, p. 440.

in 1654. It was believed in Trinity that he had left a bequest to the College, and in 1665 William Shaw, the College's agent in London, was sent to investigate. Though Shaw could find no specific legacy, Bourchier's widow told him that it had indeed been her husband's wish to support the College and, he reported, 'therefore she is resolved to bestow sumthing ... that may keepe up his memory'.[8] However, she appears to have taken no action to carry out this wish as, in 1670, Thomas Madden, a Trinity graduate now at the Inner Temple in London, reported to the Provost, Thomas Seele, on a conversation that he had had with the Countess' brother, Sir Francis Fane. Fane had been under the impression that Bourchier had bequeathed his library to the College and was disturbed to hear that the books were not in Dublin.

Fane investigated further and was told by his sister that she had not made the gift, as the books had been sold by her second husband. She was, however, now ready to contribute £200 to the College 'towards the perpetuating of her Lords memory'.[9] Madden visited her and it was agreed that the College would provide a list of books needed for the Library and that she would select titles from this list to the value of £200.[10] This allowed the College to guide the selection, and later borrowing records suggest that she was steered in the direction of science and medicine in order to provide a balance to the heavy preponderance of theology in the existing Library.[11] This guidance was possible only up to a point, however, as the Countess had firm views on what she wanted to buy. Madden reported to the Provost that, from the College's list, she had rejected all the books in English apart from Ussher's *Annals of the world*, and all the smaller books, 'resolving to send none but such as are in (Folio)'.[12] She was particularly attracted by illustrated multi-volume works such as Sanderus' *Flandria illustrata*, and rejected Heylyn's *Cosmographie* in favour of what Madden described as 'Cytty's of the World in 8 vol: a gaudy Book with whose beauty her Ladyship was soe well pleas'd, that she wish'd all the rest like them'.[13] The Countess clearly considered that the books should not only constitute what she regarded as a fitting memorial to her husband but also one to herself, as she arranged for each volume to be embellished with her coat of arms and a specially engraved book-plate, recording her donation in the year 1671.[14] She made a gift of books to the same value and with the same embellishments to Emmanuel

---

[8] MUN/P/22/92(20). See also MUN/P/1/470.
[9] MUN/LIB/10/13b.   [10] *Ibid.*; MS 2160/8/1.
[11] Elizabethanne Boran, 'Book-borrowing in Trinity College in the early eighteenth century', in *Old Library*, pp. 79–87.
[12] MUN/LIB/10/13.   [13] *Ibid.*   [14] MUN/LIB/10/16.

College, Cambridge, which had been founded by one of her ancestors, Sir Walter Mildmay. In Trinity, the books were kept as a separate collection, at the east end of the Library, facing the Manuscripts Room. It was specifically remarked upon by John Dunton, visiting in 1698, who described it as 'filled with many handsome folios and other books, in Dutch binding, guilt [*sic*], with the Earls arms imprest upon them'.[15] An alphabetical index (MS 8), dated 1720, lists about 1,300 volumes in the 'Bath Library', but this cannot be regarded as an accurate record of the donation, as later acquisitions, including those from 'forfeiting papists' in 1690, were added during the intervening years.[16]

Provosts Marsh and Huntington

The restoration of the monarchy in 1660 brought a brief period of stability to the College. The annual election of officers resumed and the Library was restored to the care of a Library Keeper. The first of those, John Jones, was probably elected early in 1661 whilst still a BA and not yet a Fellow, but after that the Keeper was normally chosen from among the Junior Fellows. Each man rarely held office for more than a year or two, and then responsibility for the Library was passed to the next most recently elected Junior Fellow. As a result, between 1661 and 1689, there were fourteen Library Keepers. In 1677, the officers' salaries were increased, that of Library Keeper rising to £8 (plus £10 Fellow's salary).[17] It remained at that level until 1722, when it rose again, to £15.[18]

Additional tasks frequently attracted a supplementary payment. In 1662, Jones received £4 'in consideration of his pains about the olde books'. This was part of £12 received that year from tithes owed to the College, the remainder of which was ordered to be spent on the Library 'as it shall be thought fit'.[19] In 1675, Richard Acton was elected as the Library Keeper and at the same time was paid £10 'in consideration of the pains he tooke in writing a catalogue of the Spanish books', a task that he must have carried out before his appointment.[20] The books in question were probably works of Spanish origin that had been confiscated from Roman Catholic clergy

---

[15] John Dunton, *The Dublin scuffle* (London: printed for the author, 1699), pp. 411–12. See also John Dunton, *The Dublin scuffle*, with an Introduction and notes by Andrew Carpenter (Dublin: Four Courts Press, 2000).

[16] MUN/V/5/2, 16 September 1690.   [17] MUN/P/7/64–MUN/P/7/65.

[18] MUN/V/5/2, 12 October 1722.   [19] *Ibid.*, 12 May 1662.

[20] *Ibid.*, 20 November 1675; O'Sullivan, 'Introduction', note 6 above.

and given to the College. It appears that some of them were later sold, as two of the Fellows were dispatched in 1686 to William Norman's shop to demand payment for 'a quantity of supernumerary Spanish books deliver'd into his hands'.[21]

Later in the century, the young Claudius Gilbert was elected as a Junior Fellow and Library Keeper.[22] He held the post for 3 years, and his involvement must have been considerably greater than that of some of his predecessors, as he received additional payments of £6 15s. 5d. for his 'diligence' in 1694, and £4 5s. 0d. 'for his service in the Library' on his replacement by a new Library Keeper in 1696.[23]

As a junior College officer, the Library Keeper played little role in developing the collection. Those acquisitions that did arrive were either donations, such as those from Alexander and the Countess of Bath, or occasional purchases, and all such transactions were generally handled by the Provost.

Even though he was primarily a scholar, with little taste for the administration of the College, Narcissus Marsh, elected Provost in 1679, took a keen interest in the running of the Library. He criticised the process of electing a different Library Keeper almost every year, which, he said, amounted to having 'no Standing Library Keeper', and he regarded the salary as inadequate.[24] Before his appointment, some of the Library Keepers seem to have shown little commitment to their duties, with the result that the Library had begun to fall into neglect. Marsh discovered that books were missing, and so he enforced the statute governing the Library Keeper's responsibilities. He issued instructions that a list should be hung at the end of every bookcase showing the titles and shelfmarks of the books that were housed there. He checked those lists with each new incumbent: 'when another Library Keeper was chosen, I carry'd both the old and new Library Keeper up, and run all over the Library, as before (which was not above two hours work,) and what books were wanting I made the old Library Keeper restore or pay for to buy others of the same kind'.[25]

From the 1680s the borrowing of books from the Library was more carefully controlled, by means of a series of loan books which recorded the names of borrowers and the titles they borrowed.[26] The earliest entry in the

---

[21] MUN/V/5/2, 20 November 1686.   [22] *Ibid.*, 20 November 1693.

[23] *Ibid.*, 20 November 1694 and 20 November 1696.

[24] Bodleian MS Smith 52, fols. 121–5. See also Raymond Gillespie, ed., *Scholar bishop: the recollections and diary of Narcissus Marsh, 1638–1696* (Cork University Press, 2003).

[25] *Ibid.*

[26] MSS 2087–90. For a detailed analysis of these loan books, see Boran, 'Book-borrowing', note 11 above.

books dates from February 1685, and the series continued until 1731, just before the opening of the new Library, though the volume for 1701–11 is now missing. Whether this was a late implementation of Marsh's reforms or the initiative of his successor, Robert Huntington, is not clear. The records are arranged by year, with a page allocated to the Provost and to each Fellow. The entries consist of the titles of books borrowed, the date and the amount of caution money deposited. When the book was returned, the title was crossed through. Though the pattern is not entirely consistent, the appointment of a new Library Keeper usually coincided with the start of a new list and a new series of pages for borrowers. Books still on loan were transferred from the old list to the new one. Borrowers were usually assiduous about returning their books, and almost all the entries are crossed through, though, in November 1685, the Board had to instruct George Mercer, a Senior Fellow described as the College's 'Agent', to demand the return of books borrowed by two former Fellows, now both parish clergy, 'and to pursue them at law if they satisfied not the Colledge'.[27]

The lists provide an insight into the use being made of the Library around the turn of the century. Some Fellows used it heavily (or at least borrowed from it); others have completely blank pages against their names. Claudius Gilbert was the most consistent borrower, taking up to fifty books a year, and several Fellows had between twenty and thirty titles. Fellows could also take books out on behalf of their students. Unsurprisingly, given the College's principal role as a seminary for Church of Ireland clergy, the most commonly borrowed subject was theology. This was followed by history, literature and science, reflecting the demands of the curriculum at the time.[28] Manuscripts could also be borrowed, even the most precious. Between December 1686 and May 1687, Richard Acton had over a dozen items, including 'a manuscript commonly called St Columba's Gospels' (presumably either the Book of Durrow or the Book of Kells) and 'another old ms of the New Testament in Latin', against a caution of £3 10s. 0d. each. Both were returned.[29]

Marsh was one of a group of scholars and collectors of books and manuscripts who collaborated intensively in the last two decades of the seventeenth century. The links between Dublin and Oxford were particularly close. The Irish group included Marsh, Huntington and one of the city's leading physicians, Charles Willoughby (all of whom had held Fellowships at Oxford), Dudley Loftus (who had been educated at both Trinity

---

[27] MUN/V/5/2, 20 November 1685.   [28] Boran, 'Book-borrowing', note 11 above.
[29] MS 2087.

and Oxford), St George Ashe and William Molyneux. Among their colleagues in Oxford were Henry Dodwell, who had been a Fellow of Trinity, Edward Bernard, the Savilian Professor of Astronomy, and Thomas Smith, the unofficial librarian of the Cotton Library. Their interests ranged from oriental and antiquarian studies, the latter now becoming fashionable in the universities and among the clergy, to the new sciences, reflected in Ireland by the foundation of the Dublin Philosophical Society by Molyneux. The first recorded meeting of the Society was held in Huntington's rooms in the College. Of the fourteen founder members, eleven were either Fellows or graduates of Trinity, and the Society retained a close relationship with the College.[30]

Whilst still at Trinity, Henry Dodwell had corresponded with Edward Bernard in Oxford about manuscripts in Ussher's library, and Marsh produced for Bernard a list of Trinity's Greek manuscripts.[31] Dodwell later became the Camden Professor of History at Oxford, but remained a steady donor of books, mostly his own publications, to his old College. He maintained a regular correspondence with his contemporaries at Trinity, particularly St George Ashe, who thanked him more than once for his 'many kindnesses' to the College, particularly his gifts of books.[32] After his appointment as Provost, Ashe asked Dodwell to supply information about books recently published in Oxford and London, so that he could buy them both for himself and the College Library, and he sought advice on which booksellers to use 'to have them speedily'.[33] In 1681, Marsh, as Provost, sent Dodwell 'hearty thanks' for the gifts of his books, and in 1705 a later Provost, Peter Browne, repeated the thanks.[34]

Dublin at the time was a rich source of biblical manuscripts in languages such as Syriac and Aramaic, collected with the view that they would help to elucidate the scriptures. Those from Ussher's library were already on the shelves in the College. Marsh owned over eight hundred such manuscripts and Huntington over six hundred, most of which had been acquired whilst he was chaplain to the Levant Company in Aleppo. Dudley Loftus, an indefatigable translator from Syriac, Armenian, Persian and other languages, arranged for his Latin translation of Dionysius Syrus to be taken to Oxford for publication. He also persuaded the College to send Ussher's copy of the Syriac text of the manuscript when the University Press was ready to publish

[30]   K. Theodore Hoppen, *The common scientist in the seventeenth century: a study of the Dublin Philosophical Society, 1683–1708* (London: Routledge and Kegan Paul, 1970).
[31]   Bodleian MS Smith 45, fols. 9, 11, 19–20.
[32]   Bodleian MS Eng. Lett. C. 29, fol. 1. See also *ibid.*, fols. 2, 19, 20.
[33]   *Ibid.*, fol. 22.   [34]   Bodleian MS Eng. Lett. C. 28, fols. 11, 69.

it, on condition 'that it be returned not injured'.[35] Marsh approved the loan of the College manuscript and Loftus later acknowledged its safe return to Dublin.[36]

As Oxford-educated Englishmen who had reached high positions in Ireland, both Marsh and Huntington had divided loyalties as far as the future of their collections was concerned. Huntington's oriental manuscripts eventually went by means of sale and bequest to Merton College, Oxford, the Bodleian, Trinity and to Marsh's Library. Those in Trinity number about a dozen, almost all in Arabic, and as they are inscribed with the date 1682, before Huntington became Provost, they may have been sent by him to Provost Marsh.[37] Marsh tried to obtain Huntington's western manuscripts for his own library but discovered that they had already been sold to the Bodleian.[38] His own oriental manuscripts were, likewise, bequeathed to the Bodleian, but his books eventually became one of the founding collections of the new Marsh's Library.

It is for the establishment of that library, the first public library in Ireland, situated next to St Patrick's Cathedral in Dublin, that Marsh is best remembered. He resigned as Provost in 1683 to pursue a career in the Church, which he found infinitely more amenable than the burdensome administrative duties in Trinity. In 1694, he became Archbishop of Dublin and in 1703 was translated to the Primacy in Armagh. The idea of building a library occurred to him whilst he was Provost, but it was only after his appointment as archbishop that he had access to the land and the money to carry out his plan.[39] In a letter to his friend Thomas Smith in Oxford in 1700, he said that he was planning to build a library:

for publick use which will be of great use here where is no publick library, that of the College being open only to the Provost and Fellows and where the booksellers shops are furnisht with nothing but new trifles, so that neither the divines of the citty, nor those that come to it about business, do know whither to go to spend an hour or two upon any occasion at study.[40]

---

35   *Tanner letters*, p. 437.
36   *Ibid.*, pp. 441, 446. See also G. T. Stokes, 'Dudley Loftus: a Dublin antiquary of the seventeenth century', *JRSAI*, 5th series, 1 (1890), 17–30; M. Mansoor, 'Oriental studies in Ireland from times of St Patrick to the rise of Islam', *Hermathena*, 62 (1943), 40–60.
37   MSS 1510, 1518–28, 1678; O'Sullivan, 'Introduction', note 6 above, pp. 21–33.
38   Bodleian MS Smith 45, fol. 23a.
39   For Marsh's Library see Muriel McCarthy, *Marsh's Library: all graduates and gentlemen*, revised edn (Dublin: Four Courts Press, 2003); and Muriel McCarthy and Ann Simmons, eds., *The making of Marsh's Library: learning, politics and religion in Ireland, 1650–1750* (Dublin: Four Courts Press, 2004).
40   Bodleian MS Smith 52, fol. 85.

In a passage from a later letter to Smith that has been much quoted since, he repeated the statement that only the Provost and Fellows were permitted to study in the College Library, and that anyone else wishing to read had to be accompanied at all times.[41] In fact the statutes were not as restrictive as he stated, though his reference to the needs of the 'divines' suggests that his concern was probably about Ussher's collection and the inner library, which contained the theological books, access to both of which was certainly more limited.

As part of his reorganisation of the College Library, it seems likely that it was Marsh who instigated the preparation of a catalogue of the manuscripts. The work was entrusted to Samuel Foley, another of the founder members of the Dublin Philosophical Society. In 1682, Foley reported that he had completed about half the collection, but acknowledged that progress was slow, partly because of 'the great confusion of all the MSS and the untoward character of some'.[42] He began work by inserting new entries into the old shelf-list and making corrections to those already there. He then indicated against each entry the letter under which it was to appear in the new alphabetical catalogue.[43] He resigned his Fellowship in 1684, by which time the catalogue was probably completed.

Three years later, the Board ordered that a catalogue should be transcribed, to include the books 'in both the great libraries, the Countess of Bath's Library, and the manuscripts in Primate Ussher's MSS Library'.[44] The manuscripts catalogue, a fair copy of Foley's earlier list, concludes with a note, dated 1688, stating that it lists about 720 manuscripts, including about 250 on vellum.[45] The decision to compile a list of the Library's contents was no doubt precipitated by fears for their safety as tension in the country grew following the accession of James II in 1685. For Trinity, as a Protestant institution, the perceived threat became more real in early 1687 with news that the Catholic Richard Talbot, Earl of Tyrconnell, had returned to Ireland as Lord Deputy. The Board's anxiety turned out to be well-founded, given the turmoil into which the College was shortly to be thrown.

Tyrconnell began to replace Protestants in positions of civil and military power with Catholics, with the result that, when James II fled from England after the landing of William of Orange in November 1688, Tyrconnell's forces controlled most of Ireland. Protestants were fleeing to safety across the water. Trinity's income from rents had dried up and the College was

[41] *Ibid.*, fols. 121–5.   [42] *Tanner letters*, p. 462.
[43] O'Sullivan, 'Introduction', note 6 above, pp. 21–33. The versions of the catalogue are MS 7/1–3.
[44] MUN/V/5/2, 17 January 1687.   [45] MS 7/1, fol. 83v.

'reduced to a low condition by the infelicity of the times'.[46] Plans were made to sell or pawn the plate, meals in Hall for Fellows and scholars were reduced to one a day and it was decided that the manuscripts should be sent to England. The Fellows also started to leave. A Board minute recorded that 'the dangers of staying in the College seem'd so great, that it was judg'd reasonable that all those that thought fit to withdraw themselves from the College for their better security, might have free liberty to do so'.[47] By the beginning of March 1689 only four Fellows remained, including the Vice-Provost, Richard Acton, and within just over a year two of the four had died. Provost Huntington was already in England, having crossed the previous September to attend the installation of the Duke of Ormonde as Chancellor of the University of Dublin and having then judged it prudent not to return.

In March 1689, King James landed at Kinsale in an attempt to use Ireland as a springboard to regain his throne. Within a fortnight his forces were in the capital. In September, the College was seized by the King's troops and converted into a barracks for the soldiers and a prison for Protestants. The remaining members of the College were turned out and ordered to take nothing with them but their books. At the instigation of Tyrconnell, James appointed Michael Moore, a Dublin-born priest, as head of the College, and Teigue McCarthy, a priest and chaplain to the King, was given charge of the Library. Fortunately, both were scholarly men and appreciated the importance of the College's books and manuscripts. In October, the Chapel was seized, the Library broken open and many of the College buildings were damaged, but the contents of the Library were largely preserved 'from the violence of the souldiers' by the action of Moore and McCarthy.[48] Some years later, a grateful Board ordered the payment of £5 to McCarthy's nephew, in consideration of his uncle's efforts in 'preserving the books of the Colledge Library'.[49]

As an act of defiance, the Vice-Provost and the other three remaining Fellows met as the Board on 20 November 1689 and re-elected the College officers from the previous year.[50] They also composed a petition addressed to the King, from the 'Vice-Provost, Fellows and Scholars', complaining about the occupation of the College, allegedly on James' orders, about the fact that

[46] MUN/V/5/2, 24 January 1689.
[47] *Ibid.*, 19 February 1689. This and subsequent entries are transcribed in John William Stubbs, *The history of the University of Dublin, from its foundation to the end of the eighteenth century* (Dublin: Hodges Figgis, 1889), pp. 127–34.
[48] MUN/V/5/2, 21 October 1689; Liam Chambers, *Michael Moore, c.1639–1726: Provost of Trinity, Rector of Paris* (Dublin: Four Courts, 2005), pp. 44–50.
[49] MUN/V/5/2, 28 February 1711; MUN/V/57/1, 2 March 1711.
[50] MUN/V/5/2, 20 November 1689.

they had been ejected and that private property belonging to members of the College had been stolen. In April 1690 the King ordered a visitation of the College by the Lord Chancellor, Sir Alexander Fitton. The Fellows were instructed to give up their keys to the Library, and to the trunks and presses containing the College records. They initially refused, but after receiving an order to hand over the keys or 'answer the same at their peril', they complied on the advice of the Vice-Chancellor, Anthony Dopping.[51]

The plan to move the manuscripts to England had not been carried out and, though Moore and McCarthy have been justly credited with saving the Library, it did nonetheless suffer some losses. These included the silver *cumdach* of the Book of Durrow and the fifteenth-century manuscript known as the Book of Lecan. The latter subsequently turned up in Paris, in the possession of a collector who claimed to have purchased it from Sir John Fitzgerald, the officer commanding the Jacobite troops occupying the College, and it is now in the Royal Irish Academy.[52] Sir Jerome Alexander's library, which was housed separately from the main Library, suffered more serious losses.[53]

After the Boyne

After William's victory at the Battle of the Boyne, the Provost and Fellows began to return. Before leaving Ireland, the new King had ordered the College to seize the books that had been confiscated from Catholics who had supported the Jacobite cause, but, as this order did not reach the Fellows for about 6 months, many of the books were by then beyond their reach.[54] A contemporary list in the Library of 'forfeited books at Galway' contains about three hundred titles, of which about three-quarters are in Latin but with a substantial number in Spanish and a few in French and Italian.[55]

The occupation of the College by the troops had led to some damage to the buildings, but recovery was swift. At the end of 1690, Provost Huntington wrote to the Archbishop of Canterbury, William Sancroft, describing the ruin and desolation in the country at large, but of Trinity he said: 'we don't despair ... our Library is in a good condition, and I hope to see it in a better'.[56] The annual election of College officers resumed, but the state of

[51] *Ibid.*, 11 April 1690.
[52] Marquis MacSwiney of Mashanaglass, 'Notes on the history of the Book of Lecan', *Proc. RIA*, C38 (1928), 31–50.
[53] Rogers, 'Alexander', note 1 above, p. 115.   [54] MUN/V/5/2, 16 September 1690.
[55] MS 2160a/21.   [56] *Tanner letters*, p. 507.

the College funds precluded the election of new Fellows or scholars until 1692, and there is no mention of a Library Keeper until the same year, when William Carr, a new Junior Fellow, was appointed.

St George Ashe succeeded Huntington as Provost in 1692, but resigned after only 3 years to become, in succession, Bishop of Cloyne, Clogher and Derry. Though undistinguished as a theologian, he played a major role in Irish intellectual life and was keen to promote the latest thinking in philosophy, science and mathematics. Marsh, William Molyneux and Charles Willoughby met in Ashe's lodgings to revive the Dublin Philosophical Society in 1693 and the College's centenary celebrations the following year emphasised both the continuity of the traditional religious learning and a commitment to the new interest in science.[57] Ashe was a Fellow of the Royal Society, contributed to its *Philosophical Transactions* and knew its President, Sir Isaac Newton, who presented him with a copy of Joseph Raphson's *Historia fluxionum* (London, 1715). This was bequeathed to the Library on Ashe's death in 1718 along with his collection of mathematical books, which included a first edition of Newton's *Principia mathematica* of 1687. Ashe was among those who borrowed from the library assembled by Willoughby, which included nearly eight hundred volumes, mostly on medical and scientific subjects. The College Library contains a catalogue of that collection (MS 10), which lists, in addition to the titles themselves, the names of those to whom Willoughby lent books. In 1691, he gave £200 for the purchase of books for the College, and until the opening of the new building in 1732 these were kept as a distinct collection.[58]

The growing interest in antiquarian studies in the later seventeenth century created the need for a guide to manuscripts in public and private collections. In 1698, the University of Oxford met this demand with the publication of the *Catalogi librorum manuscriptorum Angliae et Hiberniae*. Known ever since as Bernard's *Catalogi* of 1697, after its editor in chief, Edward Bernard, and the date printed on the title page, it represented the culmination of cataloguing work that had been under way in Oxford for several decades. Roughly a third of the book was devoted to the manuscripts

---

[57] Helga Robinson-Hammerstein, '"With great solemnity": celebrating the first centenary of the foundation of Trinity College, Dublin, 9 January 1694', *Long Room*, 37 (1992), 27–38.

[58] T. Percy C. Kirkpatrick, 'Charles Willoughby, M.D., Fellow of the King and Queen's College of Physicians', *Proc. RIA*, C36 (1923), 239–48; Elizabethanne Boran, 'The sceptical collector: alchemy and chemistry in early modern Irish libraries', in Danielle Westerhof, ed., *The alchemy of medicine and print: the Edward Worth Library, Dublin* (Dublin: Four Courts Press, 2010), pp. 75–88.

in the Bodleian; it covered the collections in Oxford in a comprehensive manner, those in Cambridge very much more sketchily, and included most of the significant private collections of manuscripts in England. Five Irish collections were listed, including Trinity's and four in private hands: those of Dudley Loftus, Narcissus Marsh, John Madden, a Dublin bibliophile whose collection was later to come to Trinity, and the manuscripts collected by Sir James Ware, then in the hands of Henry Hyde, Earl of Clarendon. The list of the College's manuscripts is a transcription of Foley's catalogue, omitting his cross-references.[59] Foley's work was not acknowledged by Bernard, but George Browne, the Provost at the time of publication, was thanked, even though it seems to have been his predecessor, St George Ashe, who supplied the material. In 1694, Ashe had written to Dodwell in Oxford, thanking him for his account of 'the printed catalogue of MSS to which we have contributed what little addition we were able'.[60]

A new Library needed

By the time of the College's first centenary the Library was still in its original location, described as 'but an ordinary pile of building, and can't be distinguish'd on the out-side'.[61] Internally, its layout reflected the major collections that had been acquired and kept as separate entities. They were referred to as the Old Library (still with its division into theology and humanities), the Ussher Library, the Countess of Bath's Library and the Willoughby Library, and each had its own sequence of shelfmarks.

Despite its unprepossessing physical appearance, the Library attracted the occasional visitor. Around 1670, the French cartographer Albert Jouvin de Rochefort met the Provost, Thomas Seele, who showed him the Library, '*où il y avoit des livres tres-rares*' [*sic*], and Camden's *Britannia* was brought out for him to admire.[62] More detailed descriptions of the late-seventeenth-century College were provided by the English antiquary Thomas Dineley and the London bookseller John Dunton. Dineley's reports of his travels in Ireland in 1681 contain many drawings, including a plan of the College dating from just before the start of Provost Marsh's building programme. It

[59] Edward Bernard, *Catalogi librorum manuscriptorum Angliae et Hiberniae*, 2 vols. (Oxford: Sheldonian, 1697), vol. II, part 2, pp. 16–48; O'Sullivan, 'Introduction', note 6 above, pp. 26–7.
[60] Bodleian MS Eng. Lett. C. 29, fol. 23.   [61] Dunton, note 15 above, p. 412.
[62] A. Jouvin, *Le Voyageur d'Europe*, 3 vols. (Paris: Thierry, 1672), vol. III, p. 475.

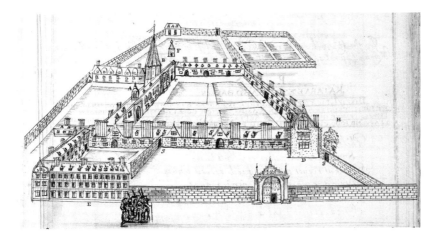

Figure 3 Plan of the College in 1681, by Thomas Dineley. The Library was in the building on the right, marked C. Sir Jerome Alexander's Buildings and library are marked E, and the old Dining Hall and Chapel are A and B (NLI MS 392, p. 71)

shows the old Dining Hall, the Chapel, the Library, and the new buildings erected from the bequest by Sir Jerome Alexander.[63] (See Figure 3.)

A later, more detailed, description was given by John Dunton, who visited Ireland in 1698. The account of his visit was published as *The Dublin scuffle* and, though it is an idiosyncratic document loaded with pages of moralising and plagiarised passages, it includes accurate and detailed descriptions of buildings, including the Library. His account, which corroborates the Dineley drawing, states that the Library was located above the students' rooms and extended for the full length of the quadrangle. At its east end, on the right-hand side, was a room containing the Countess of Bath's library, and on the left was the Manuscripts Room, 'in which I saw a great many manuscripts, medals, and other curiosities'.[64] The curiosities included 'the thigh-bone of a giant' and 'the skin of one Ridley, a notorious Tory, which had been long ago executed', a reminder that the contents of seventeenth-century libraries included more than just books and manuscripts.[65] At the west end, behind a lattice screen, was Ussher's library and a full-length portrait of Luke Challoner. Dunton said nothing about the physical state of the Library but he did note that there were plans to build a new one.

---

[63] NLI MS 392, p. 71; F. Elrington Ball, 'Extracts from the journal of Thomas Dineley or Dingley, Esquire, giving some account of his visit to Ireland in the reign of Charles II', *JRSAI*, 43 (1913), 275–309.

[64] Dunton, note 15 above, p. 412.   [65] *Ibid.*, p. 411.

By the end of the 1670s the number of undergraduates had risen to about three hundred, the old buildings were no longer adequate to meet their needs and Provost Marsh had initiated a building programme that was to last well into the next century.[66] The new residences that had been started with the money from Alexander's bequest were extended and Marsh planned to replace the Chapel and Dining Hall with larger structures. He began with the Chapel, which was consecrated in 1684, shortly after Huntington's appointment as Provost. The inclusion of a new Library in the building programme was already in Huntington's mind by this date. He wrote to Thomas Otway, Bishop of Ossory, asking for a donation towards the building programme. Otway replied saying that charity began at home and that the repairs to his cathedral, St Canice's in Kilkenny, were a more urgent priority for him, but he promised to bequeath his books to the College. In thanking him Huntington noted that, by the time the College received his books, 'we may have raised a structure fit for the reception of such a noble legacy'.[67] Otway later joined with Michael Boyle, the Archbishop of Armagh, and the Limerick physician Jeremiah Hall in donating £100 to buy books for the Library.[68]

Dunton, writing in 1698, said 'I hear they design the building of a new library: and, I am told, the Hoose of Commons in Ireland have voted £3000 towards carrying it on'.[69] The Library had to take its place in the queue, however, and when work started again after the occupation of 1689–90 the College's priority was the Front Square and the residential buildings now known as the Rubrics, which were begun in about 1699 using the £3,000 from the government. By the end of the century it seems to have been common knowledge that a new Library was in the offing. The satirist Edward Ward expressed scepticism, however: 'the Irish Parliament is contriving ways and means for a library for'em, which some think will be built much about the time, as the students who are design'd to make use of it, shall arrive to the knowledge requisite for such studies, and that is never'.[70]

Marsh's plan to enlarge the Dining Hall was delayed until early in the new century and, when work did eventually start, the Library was pressed

[66] McDowell and Webb, p. 23.

[67] Bodleian MS Rawl. B 497, fol. 10. Otway bequeathed £200 to Trinity, but left his books to found a library at St Canice's Cathedral for the use of the clergy.

[68] James Ware, *The whole works of Sir James Ware concerning Ireland, revised and improved* [by Walter Harris], 2 vols. in 3 (Dublin: printed for the author, 1739–46), vol. I, pp. 130, 431.

[69] Dunton, note 15 above, p. 412.

[70] [Edward Ward] *A trip to Ireland: being a description of the country, people and manners* [London?] 1699, p. 11.

into service as a temporary refectory for the students. This marked another low point in the Library's history, and word of its parlous state reached Oxford, from where Thomas Smith wrote to congratulate his friend Marsh on buying Edward Stillingfleet's books for his new library. Smith said that, when this news was received in Oxford, 'a learned man there with whom I correspond' had written to say that he hoped greater care would be taken of them there than at Trinity, where the Library was 'neglected' and 'useless'.[71] The 'learned man' was undoubtedly Thomas Hearne, Assistant Keeper at the Bodleian, who recorded in his notebook that Trinity's Library was 'quite neglected and in no order, so that 'tis perfectly useless, the Provost and Fellows of that College having no regard for books or learning'.[72] Marsh, now Primate and under no obligation to be unnecessarily complimentary about the College, responded to Smith that the Library had indeed been 'utterly uselesse' during the building of the Dining Hall. As the books were not chained, they had been removed for safety 'to some other place, and having no one roome for them, they were constrein'd to lay them in heaps in some void rooms', but they were now back in place and the Library was 'as usefull as ever'.[73]

There clearly were problems, however. In July 1707, the Library Keeper, Robert Howard, reported to his brother that Thomas Herbert, the Earl of Pembroke, had donated £500 to the Library, 'which you know is a very seasonable gift to a place that lies in so wretched a condition'.[74] Howard's wording suggests that this was a recent gift, and Pembroke had been appointed Lord Lieutenant of Ireland in April 1707, but the list of benefactors in the *Dublin University Calendar* for 1858 records the date of Pembroke's donation as 1698. Pembroke had no connection with the College at that time and the earlier date seems less likely, unless he had made the donation in response to a request from Provost Ashe, as both had been Fellows of the Royal Society since the 1680s.

Though it was in a poor state, the Library was not completely neglected. There was expenditure on both purchases and binding in the early years of the new century. Benjamin Pratt, Regius Professor of Laws and a future Provost, was buying books for the Library, some of which, Jonathan Swift reported to John Stearne, 'would set you a longing', and in 1708 the Library Keeper, Richard Helsham, was paid an additional allowance for preparing

[71] Bodleian MS Smith 64, fols. 221–2.
[72] C. E. Doble, D. W. Rannie and H. E. Salter, eds., *Remarks and collections of Thomas Hearne*, 11 vols. (Oxford: Clarendon Press, 1885–1921), vol. I, p. 62.
[73] Bodleian MS Smith 52, fols. 121–5.   [74] NLI MS 38,597/24 (2), 15 July 1707.

a catalogue.[75] The collection was also being used. The borrowing records, which had lapsed in 1688, resumed in 1693, with Gilbert again the heaviest user, borrowing an average of five books a month in some years.[76] The same notebooks were used to record details of items that could not be found when a new Library Keeper assumed office. On 20 November 1702, over 300 volumes were noted as being missing from Ussher's Library and about 75 from Willoughby's, and the following year Robert Howard, the new Library Keeper, recorded over 300 missing from the Old Library. These figures must, however, be treated with caution, as in some cases they consist of runs of shelfmarks, suggesting that the books had been moved elsewhere, possibly during the rebuilding of the Dining Hall. In March 1702, probably for the same reason, the manuscripts were also checked, and a note was added to the front of Foley's catalogue listing thirty-eight missing items, including the Book of Lecan. All but eleven of these were crossed through by John Lyon in 1741–2, to indicate that they had been found.[77]

[75] Harold Williams, ed., *The correspondence of Jonathan Swift*, 5 vols. (Oxford: Clarendon Press, 1963–5), vol. I, p. 114; MUN/V/57/1, 10 December 1708, 10 February 1710.
[76] MS 2088.   [77] MS 7/1, fol. 1r.

4 | A new building: 1709–1737

By 1709, the College recognised the need to act decisively if it was to acquire the new library that was so urgently needed. Progress turned out to be far from smooth, however, and eventual success required considerable political agility on the part of those behind the scheme. Trinity had supported the Williamite settlement, but some of its members were still far from wedded to the new regime and continued to display distinct Jacobite and Tory sympathies. The involvement of students in the daubing of King William's statue on College Green was not uncommon, and in 1708 a Scottish student named Edward Forbes, who was due to receive his MA degree the following day, refused to drink a toast to the 'glorious, pious and immortal memory' of King William and compared him unfavourably to a recently hanged highwayman. This was too much for the College authorities and on this occasion they took firmer action than hitherto by expelling Forbes and depriving him of his degree.

Though the Forbes case was a trivial issue in itself, the way the College had handled it was cited the following year as an indication of its loyalty when the Irish House of Commons petitioned Queen Anne for a grant of £5,000 for the new Library. The Commons' motion, of 1 June 1709, commended Trinity for its adherence 'to the late happy Revolution, her present Majesty's Government, and the succession in the Protestant line', in censuring Edward Forbes for speaking ill of the late King. The Library was needed, said the Commons, 'for the encouragement of good literature and sound Revolution Principles'.[1] The strongly Protestant and Whig tone of the motion as submitted reflected the sentiments of the majority in the Commons, but changes made to the original version displeased those Trinity graduates who had been its proposers. Joseph Addison, Secretary to the Lord Lieutenant, noted that the original motion had been so well written that those against it had not thought it proper to oppose it outright but had amended it in such a way as to cause 'great uneasiness to severall Members'.[2] Sir Richard Cox, a former Lord Chancellor of Ireland and a staunch Tory,

---

[1] *Commons Jn Ireland*, vol. II, p. 596.
[2] Walter Graham, ed., *The letters of Joseph Addison* (Oxford: Clarendon Press, 1941), pp. 145–7.

wrote scathingly to Edward Southwell, MP for the University and Secretary of State for Ireland, then residing in London: 'If you come to Ireland, take care to bring with you Sound Revolution Principles, for you may see by the vote of £5000 to the Colledge, of what consequence they may be to you.'[3]

These 'Revolution Principles' were even less palatable to the Lords and the issue became a source of one of the frequent disputes between the two houses. By the time of the 1711 session of Parliament, the Queen had approved the grant. In its expression of thanks, however, the Lords rejected the case set out in the Commons' motion and asserted that the grant had not been made 'to promote those Principles, upon which it was first applied for, but to encourage university education'.[4] William King, the Church of Ireland Archbishop of Dublin, who was to play a major role in the future of the new Library, was one of only three members of the Lords to object to the insertion of this clause. He wrote to Jonathan Swift that he kept them in debate about it for at least an hour, and, as a result, fell out of favour with his fellow peers.[5]

The insertion of these words incensed the Commons, who protested that they suggested a lack of loyalty and that by adding them the Lords had infringed their rights, misrepresented the reason for the grant and 'unjustly insinuated (to the dishonour of this House) that the principles, for encouragement of which the aforesaid application was made, were such as her Majesty disapproved'. The Commons prepared an address of thanks to the Queen for the grant towards the Library, complaining about this misrepresentation of their position by the Lords and assuring her of their loyalty. To this the Lords responded by referring to the Commons' motion and saying that, although they had not intended to misrepresent the members of the lower house, the latter had not vindicated themselves by their wording of the address.[6]

For the College, however, the important point was not only that the grant of £5,000 had been approved but that half of it had already been paid.[7] By the beginning of the following year stone cutting had started and on 12 May 1712 the Provost and Fellows attended the laying of the foundation stone.

[3] Letter, 4 June 1709, BL MS Add. 38156, fol. 79.
[4] *Lords Jn Ireland*, vol. II, p. 366 (17 July 1711).
[5] David Woolley, ed., *The correspondence of Jonathan Swift, D.D.*, 4 vols. (Frankfurt am Main: Lang, 1999), vol. I, p. 373.
[6] *Commons Jn Ireland*, vol. II, pp. 711, 714; *Lords Jn Ireland*, vol. II, p. 414.
[7] *Commons Jn Ireland*, vol. III, p. cccix; Dublin, Marsh's Library, MS Z2.1.10, p. 10.

They also ordered that £50 be paid to 'the person who sollicited the payment of the five thousand in England'.[8]

Building starts

The architect chosen for the work was Lieutenant-Colonel Thomas Burgh. (See Plate 2.) Educated at Trinity, Burgh served in the army of William III in Ireland and then as a military engineer in Flanders in the 1690s. He returned home and in 1700 was appointed as Surveyor General of His Majesty's Fortifications in Ireland, in which role he oversaw the building of military installations all over the country, including the Royal (now Collins) Barracks in Dublin. Burgh was responsible for continuing the rebuilding of Dublin Castle, started by his predecessor, William Robinson, and for a number of important non-military buildings in the city, including the (pre-Gandon) Custom House, Dr Steevens' Hospital, St Werburgh's Church and the Linen Hall. At Trinity he built the Anatomy House as well as his masterpiece, the great Library. His standing as an architect and his position as a member of Dublin society — indeed, of the short-lived but significant Dublin Philosophical Society — made him an obvious choice to carry out Trinity's great enterprise. Among the members of the Society were Benjamin Pratt, the Provost when Burgh was appointed, the Lord Lieutenant (the Earl of Pembroke), Archbishop King, George Berkeley and Samuel Molyneux, all of whom were to play a role in the unfolding story of the new Library.[9]

The scaffolding poles arrived in the summer of 1712 and for the next 2 years work proceeded apace. The College accounts record regular payments for stone cutting and timber and to masons, bricklayers and carpenters. The craftsmen employed on the Library also worked on other College buildings and, in some cases, families like that of Moses and Henry Darley worked as stonemasons for the College for generations. Some, such as the joiner John Sisson and the carpenter Isaac Wills, worked on the building themselves and also acted as contractors, employing other men as well. Nathaniel Hall, the Head Porter, was heavily involved, carrying out all manner of duties from procuring a pump to drain the foundations to

[8] MUN/V/5/2, 12 and 16 May 1712.
[9] K. Theodore Hoppen, *The common scientist in the seventeenth century: a study of the Dublin Philosophical Society, 1683–1708* (London: Routledge and Kegan Paul, 1970).

organising the carriage of 38 tons of Whitehaven stone from Dublin port to the College. In November 1713, he was paid for the delivery of beams for the Library floor, so by then the shell of the building must have been well advanced.[10] But the grant was almost exhausted and the work was coming to a halt. More money was urgently needed, and a meeting took place on 4 December 1713 with the College's two MPs, John Elwood and Marmaduke Coghill, to consider a petition to Parliament.[11] Objections from both representatives meant that the petition went no further, and, with the accession of George I the following year, the College's ambiguous attitude to the Hanoverian succession placed it in an even more precarious relationship with the establishment.

Into the breach stepped William King, who as Archbishop of Dublin was also Visitor to the University. For King, Trinity played a pivotal role in defending and supporting the established Church and the Protestant succession, both of which he saw as being crucial to the future of Irish Protestants. The College had to be managed in such a way as to ensure that this role was maintained. The completion of the Library and removal of the remaining Tories were essential features of King's agenda, and it became clear to him that the former could not happen without the latter. The dismissal of the Chancellor of the University, the Jacobite Duke of Ormonde, in 1714, and his subsequent impeachment for high treason, provided King with the opportunity he needed. With support from Samuel Molyneux, Secretary to George Augustus, Prince of Wales and the future George II, he successfully encouraged the University to elect the Prince as its new Chancellor in 1716. This he regarded as a significant step towards securing more funds for the Library. He told William Wake, the Archbishop of Canterbury, that the election 'has had a great effect already and has made no small alteration in the humour of the youth in the College likewise in the gentlemen of the Kingdom with whom the College was on ill terms'.[12] He hoped that, with a little encouragement, Parliament would provide the money that was needed.

King met the Provost and one of the Senior Fellows, Robert Howard, to consider approaching the Commons again for a further grant. He discussed the matter with MPs but it became clear that his optimism had been

---

[10] Edward McParland, *Public architecture in Ireland 1680–1760* (New Haven: Yale University Press, 2001), pp. 143–58; Anne Crookshank, 'The Long Room', in *Treasures*, pp. 16–28; Anne Crookshank, *The Long Room* (Dublin: Gifford and Craven, 1976). For the buildings accounts, see MUN/P/2/23–MUN/P/2/59.

[11] MS 2215; E. H. Alton, 'Some fragments of College history – I', *Hermathena*, 57 (1941), 25–38.

[12] MS 2533, p. 149.

premature, as he found them unwilling to support the proposal on two grounds. First, they claimed that they did not wish to apply to London for any more grants in that session; and second, they were still smarting from the attack by the Lords in 1711 and remained suspicious of Trinity's political leanings. King complained to Molyneux that the resistance of the Commons was based upon 'the ill return they had for their last vote, for which the House of Lords in their address to the Queen in effect declared them rebels, and the Universitie did the like, and they pretend that the College haveing bin an infected place they ought to perform a quarantine before they be received as other subjects'.[13] In other words, there would be no more money until the College had been purged of Tories, chief among whom was the Provost, Benjamin Pratt.

Howard shared King's views on the importance of completing the Library and on the nature of the difficulties standing in the way of achieving it. Both men concluded that without the support of the Chancellor there was little hope of obtaining another grant. In October 1716, Howard urged King to continue his efforts on behalf of Library, 'which wee have the greatest want of, and which wee have some sort of right to demand of those in power — since it was promised us upon our choosing the Prince our Chancellour'.[14] In December, Howard reported that some of the Fellows were not willing to cause an 'open rupture' with the Provost, but he felt that a letter to Pratt from Molyneux, as Secretary to the Chancellor, might encourage him to stand down.[15] King maintained the pressure on the College, writing to Howard from London, 'I am afraid till you have a new provost the matter of the library will go heavily' and then, as Visitor, he forced the issue by threatening a formal visitation, which clearly unnerved Pratt, who had spent long periods in London as an absentee Provost.[16] Pratt's price for resignation was a bishopric, but King was having none of it. Pratt was offered, and accepted, the deanery of Down, and resigned his Provostship in June 1717, to be replaced by the Vice-Provost, Richard Baldwin, an avowed Whig. Now the campaign to obtain more funds for the Library could proceed.

King lost no time canvassing the views of MPs and the new Lord Lieutenant, the Duke of Bolton, all of whom he felt were now positively inclined towards the College. He thought that if the Prince of Wales could be persuaded to write to the Lord Lieutenant 'it wou'd be absolutely effectuall and do the work', and he put this proposal to both Molyneux and Archbishop Wake.[17] Wake declined King's request to intercede with the Prince on the

---

[13] *Ibid.*, p. 250.   [14] MSS 1995–2008/1794.   [15] MSS 1995–2008/1796.
[16] MS 2534, p. 52.   [17] MS 2534, p. 277.

grounds that the latter's relationship with his father, George I, was at a low ebb and any intervention at this stage was unlikely to advance the College's cause.[18] Molyneux also warned that this approach would not work.[19] King even came up with a scheme for funding the enterprise 'without any charge to the nation' by diverting to the College revenue that had formerly been used to support rebuilding work at Dublin Castle.[20]

Matters were now moving rapidly to a conclusion. Wake enlisted the support of Addison, now Secretary of State, who advised the Lord Lieutenant that the time was right for a petition to be presented to the Commons in Dublin. Addison reported that the King 'is willing, by this mark of his royal favour, to encourage those honest and loyal principles, which (as he hears with great satisfaction) begin to revive' among the members of the College.[21] The Fellows of the College seized the opportunity to reaffirm those principles. In their petition they reminded the House of the Forbes case, they cited as evidence of their loyalty the election of the Prince of Wales as Chancellor, and they reiterated their steady adherence to the late happy Revolution and the Protestant succession. Having received the first grant, they said, they had spent it carefully, but it was not sufficient to complete the building, 'so as to answer the ends for which it was intended, and be of use as well as ornament to the University and Kingdom'.[22] The petition was read on 21 September 1717 and the Commons asked the Lord Lieutenant to request from the King a sum of up to £5,000.[23] This time there was no dissent from the Lords and a delighted archbishop, whose alternative funding scheme had proved to be unnecessary, was able to tell Wake that: ''tis all that was desired, 'twas thought fitt by every body that it shou'd be his Majesties gift and depend on his pleasure'.[24] Addison informed Bolton that the King intended to approve the request and the first payment, of half the amount, was made in December.[25] The Board asked Coghill, as one of the University's MPs, to present their thanks to the Commons and to offer the degree of Doctor of Laws to any members who wished to take it. At a ceremony the following March the Speaker and thirty-six MPs received their degree *Speciali Gratia*.[26] In the meantime, building work could resume.

During 1718 large sums were paid to Moses Darley for masons, to Francis Quin for bricklayers, and to Nathaniel Hall for the labourers, of which, by

[18] MS 2534, pp. 290, 297; MSS 1995–2008/1828.   [19] NLI MS 38,598/2.
[20] MS 2534, p. 299.   [21] *Letters of Joseph Addison*, note 2 above, p. 376.   [22] MUN/P/2/46/1.
[23] *Commons Jn Ireland*, vol. III, p. 134.   [24] MS 2534, p. 303.
[25] *Letters of Joseph Addison*, note 2 above, pp. 381–2; *Commons Jn Ireland*, vol. III, p. cccix.
[26] MUN/V/5/2, 24 September 1717 and 10 March 1718.

midsummer, there were twenty: ten general labourers, most of them working with the masons, six working with the carpenters, and four 'sawers cutting up timber', including by this stage 2,475 feet (754 metres) of oak for the gallery.[27]

The final payment from the second grant of £5,000 was made by the middle of 1720 but it was still insufficient to complete the work and the College was again forced to apply to the Commons for help. In their petition they once again reaffirmed their 'inviolable attachment to . . . the present Establishment' and assured the House 'that they will always continue utterly to discountenance and exterminate, as far as in them lies, all principles of a contrary tendency'. The previous grants for finishing the Library, they said, 'though expended with the utmost care and frugality', had been insufficient.[28] In October 1721, without any demurring, the Commons asked the King for a further grant of up to £5,000. The first instalment of this was forthcoming the following February and the full grant had been paid by April 1724.[29] By now expenditure, at £15,787, had already exceeded the three grants, and over the next 10 years a further £4,500 was spent on the building, so the College must have started augmenting the grants with its own money.[30]

The structure was now largely complete. Jonathan Cape, the plumber, provided sheets of lead for the roof, worked on it for 2 years and was paid off in full in early 1723. Darley, too, was paid 'for the full discharge' of his masonry work but was brought back over the following 2 years to lay the flagstones in the entrance hall and the 'piazza' under the Long Room. The main craftsmen involved at this stage were Sisson, the joiner, who received payments of £200 on account each quarter between 1723 and 1725, George Spike, the plasterer and painter, and the glaziers. The work was accompanied by the usual irritations associated with a building site. In August 1720, Nathaniel Hall was paid for calling out Mr Oates and his men with 'the ingen and buckets', along with twelve boys to bring water, to extinguish a fire in the Library, and in April 1724 five scholars were caught breaking its windows.[31]

By this stage, however, the College seems to have lost interest in completing the Library, perhaps because it was focussed on the construction of new residential accommodation. Annual expenditure on the building, which had been running at around £1,000 a year, dropped in 1728 to £145 and ranged between that and about £250 annually until 1733, the last year

---

[27] MUN/P/2/37.   [28] MUN/P/2/46/2.   [29] *Commons Jn Ireland*, vol. III, pp. 261 and cccix.
[30] MUN/V/75/4, pp. 8–19.   [31] MUN/P/4/25/18; MUN/V/5/2, 18 April 1724.

for which there was any significant amount spent on the building. It went mainly to Sisson to complete the balustrades for the gallery and for his work on the Manuscripts Room.[32]

Chaos and loss

The quarter century between the College's first approach to Parliament and the completion of Burgh's building had been a time of increasing chaos in the Library, with the old building becoming almost unusable. It was physically dilapidated, the books and manuscripts were either nailed up in boxes or in disorder and subject to theft and Marsh's reforms were being largely ignored.

At the election of College officers in November 1709 it was the turn of the young George Berkeley to become Librarian. He describes the state of the Library and his lack of enthusiasm for the post in a letter to Samuel Molyneux:

I am lately enterd into my citadell in a disconsolate mood, after having passd the better part of a sharp and bitter day in the damps and mustly solitudes of the Library without either fire or anything else to protect me from the injuries of the snow that was constantly driving at the windows and forceing its entrance into that wretched mansion, to the keeping of which I was this day sennight elect'd under an inauspiciary planet.[33]

He was particularly irked by the fact that lack of space meant that the books acquired as a result of the Earl of Pembroke's donation had been put into boxes, an act that 'deprivd me of the only entertainment I could propose to my self in that place'.[34] By the time he had become a Senior Fellow, conditions had deteriorated further. In 1722, in response to an enquiry from his friend Lord Perceval, he wrote that the Library 'is at present so old and ruinous, and the books so out of order, that there is little attendance given'.[35] The English antiquarian, John Loveday, who visited in 1732 and again the following year, dismissed the old Library as 'a vile garret and everything there in the greatest confusion'.[36]

---

[32] MUN/V/57/2.

[33] A. A. Luce and T. E. Jessop, eds., *The works of George Berkeley, Bishop of Cloyne*, 9 vols. (London: Nelson, 1948–57), vol. VIII, p. 24.

[34] *Ibid.*   [35] *Ibid.*, p. 126.

[36] Sarah Markham, *John Loveday of Caversham, 1711–1789: the life and tours of an eighteenth-century onlooker* (Salisbury: Russell, 1984), p. 162.

This confusion and lack of proper supervision placed the collection at risk, and in 1715 the Library suffered a series of thefts carried out by 'sculls', odd-job men or errand-boys employed by the College.[37] The culprits broke into the building and over a period of several weeks systematically stole about forty books to the value of £100. According to the brief for the prosecution, the disordered state of the Library helped to conceal their activities: 'most of the books were in boxes and not putt upon shelves which was the reason they could not be so easily missed'. The brief also provides a witness statement describing the removal of the books: 'deponent . . . saw Cooper [one of the defendants] coming out of the turret over the door which is over the library staircase with 2 books 1 a large Lattin book the other a small book of celebrating the Mass in French . . . Cooper gave deponent the big book to carry out of the gate and Cooper carried the other in his pocket'. Some of the books were sold, but for others the perpetrators could find no market. The theft was discovered by an MA living in College, who, on returning to his rooms one evening, 'did light on four books that were taken out of the library and were laid there ready to be carryed of, such are the same 4 books that Myles Byrne sent Harman back for and were so heavy that he could not carry them away, and that was the occasion of the great discovery'. The case was initially investigated by Nathaniel Hall, the indefatigable Head Porter, who was paid 7s. 7d. to hire a constable and two assistants to search for the books. The Fellows who were brought in to value them and prove that they were from the Library were two former Librarians the Bursar (and bibliophile) Claudius Gilbert and Thomas Bindon. Bindon was subsequently paid £3 14s. 7½d., presumably as reimbursement for the cost of recovering some of the books. Matthew Gunn, one of the booksellers who had bought several of the stolen books, initially refused to return them, but was eventually prevailed upon, on payment of £2 15s. 10½d. The serving Librarian, the 19-year-old Robert Clayton, appears not to have been involved in the proceedings.

Given the state of the Library and the fact that many of the books were in boxes, the annual stocktaking and the requirement initiated by Provost Marsh that the Librarian should replace any missing books at his own expense must have been a haphazard process at best. Even so, it was becoming increasingly difficult to persuade even recently elected Fellows to take

---

[37] MUN/LIB/10/32–MUN/LIB/10/33; MUN/V/57/1, pp. 538–54; M. C. Griffith, 'From the College muniments, 1: depredations in the Library, 1715', *Long Room*, 4 (Autumn/Winter 1971), 15–18.

on the responsibilities of the Librarian. In November 1715, John Madden, the Fellow elected to succeed Clayton, declined the post and had to be replaced by John Kearney, who had already served in 1712–13. In 1717, the 20-year-old James Stopford became Librarian a mere few months after his election to Fellowship. He was followed by Thomas Skelton, who had taken his MA the previous year but was not, and never became, a Fellow. Skelton resigned after less than 2 months and the Board, perhaps in desperation, then ignored the statutes and appointed William Lewis, a graduate yet to take his MA. He received £4 'for attending as Librarian', half the statutory salary.[38]

The caution books listing what was borrowed by the Fellows were maintained, at least in some years, so some control was being exercised, but on the evidence of these records the stock-checks were far from annual, as had been decreed by Marsh. On 19 November 1723, his last day in office, James King noted thirteen books that had been lent to Fellows that year and not yet returned, and the same exercise was carried out 3 years later by Robert Berkeley at the end of his 2 years as Librarian, recording twenty-eight titles still on loan to eleven Fellows. Keeping track of who had what was made more difficult by the practice of some Fellows of keeping books out of the Library for many years. In 1720, George Berkeley had four books on loan, one of which he had had since 1707, and John Elwood, the Regius Professor of Laws, had twenty-two books out, some of them since 1702 and had loaned some on to his pupils.[39]

Acquisitions

Despite the state of the old building and the general air of chaos, the Library was not completely neglected during this time. In 1718, the 'great globes' were repaired and fitted with new frames. A few books were bought: in 1717 the College began to subscribe to Montfaucon's *L'antiquité expliquée*, the following year to Pope's translation of Homer, and in 1721 to Addison's *Works*.[40] Joseph Caddy served as Librarian for most of 1720 and had as his principal duty the production of a catalogue of printed books. For this he received an additional allowance of £10 in July and a further £23 the following April.[41] The catalogue is probably the undated *Catalogus librorum in Bibliotheca Collegii Sanctae et Individuae Trinitatis Reginae Elizabethae juxta*

---

[38] MUN/V/5/2; MUN/V/57/1, p. 674.   [39] MSS 2089–90.
[40] MUN/V/57/1, pp. 602, 634, 722.   [41] *Ibid.*, pp. 698, 722; MUN/LIB/10/37.

Dublin printed by John Hyde of Dame Street. It is arranged alphabetically by author but does not include shelfmarks. Although, on the face of it, the catalogue lists around twelve thousand volumes, the total number of items is greater, as some entries include many titles under headings such as 'Pamphlets of divers sorts'. The catalogue was no doubt compiled as part of the preparations for the transfer of the Library into the new building, and this may explain the lack of shelfmarks, given that the books were to be shelved differently in their new locations.

More significantly, the prospect of a new building began to attract serious donations. The first to arrive were the mathematical books bequeathed by St George Ashe in 1718. In 1726, Robert Gibbon, a Trinity graduate who had been a clergyman in England, left £100 to purchase books for the new Library, and an order was placed with the firm of Dublin booksellers John Smith and William Bruce. They duly supplied about ninety titles at a cost of £100 1s. 0d. Most were classical texts with Paris, Leiden and Amsterdam imprints and many were in fine sixteenth- and seventeenth-century editions.[42]

On New Year's Day 1727, William Palliser, the Church of Ireland Archbishop of Cashel (see Figure 4), died leaving a will in which he set out in detail what was to become of his substantial library.[43] The College was to receive any books that it did not already have, and these were to be 'sorted and set out' by his son and Claudius Gilbert, the Vice-Provost. The books were to be kept together as the 'Bibliotheca Palliseriana' and housed in the Long Room next to the library 'now called the Bibliotheca Ussheriana'. If the College should fail to carry out this instruction, the bequest would be nullified. According to Ware, Palliser also left £200 as a fund to buy books to add to the collection.[44] He had held the Chair of Divinity from 1678 to 1692 and, though the subjects represented by most of the four thousand books selected by Gilbert were theology, canon law and classical literature, the collection also contained the occasional surprise. It included, for example, a number of fine atlases, including a hand-coloured copy of the 1630 edition of Mercator. In the late nineteenth century William Reeves discovered, bound among the five maps of Ireland in this atlas, a map dated 1661 of the barony of Inishowen, produced by Wenceslaus Hollar for the owner of that barony, Arthur Chichester, Earl of Donegal. This is one of only three

---

[42] MUN/LIB/10/54 (list of books supplied); *DU Calendar*, 1858, p. 248.

[43] The will is transcribed in MUN/V/5/2, 4 May 1727.

[44] James Ware, *The whole works of Sir James Ware concerning Ireland, revised and improved* [by Walter Harris], 2 vols. in 3 (Dublin: printed for the author, 1739–46), vol. I, p. 487.

Figure 4 William Palliser, Archbishop of Cashel (College Art Collections, TCD)

known copies, the others being in the British Library and the Royal Library at Windsor.[45]

Completion

Finally, in 1732, Thomas Burgh's masterpiece was finished. Though he did not live to see its completion, Burgh was closely involved with the

---

[45] J. H. Andrews, 'An early map of Inishowen', *Long Room*, 7 (Spring 1973), 19–25. The Inishowen map has now been removed from the Mercator *Atlas*.

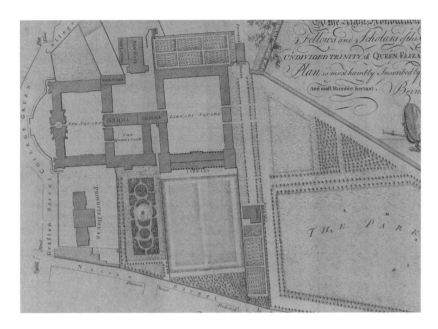

Figure 5 Plan of the College in 1761, by Bernard Scalé (MUN/MC/7)

building until shortly before his death in 1730, and his signature appears on the craftsmen's bills up to November 1729. An English visitor to the College in 1732 remarked that 'a large square and a spacious Library are new built'.[46]

The Library formed the southern side of this new square (Library Square), while the other three sides consisted of residential buildings. (See Figures 5 and 6.) Only those on the east side (the Rubrics) remain today. They and the western range, added in the 1720s, directly abutted the two pavilions of the Library. These pavilions, which were three storeys high, were connected by two open arcades, separated by a wall that ran along the centre spine of the building. In the centre of the wall was a door that provided access to the Fellows' Garden. (See Plate 3.) Students were confined to the less sunny north side of the piazza, and the Library must have towered over the residential accommodation around it. (See Figure 12.) Above the arcades was the Long Room, designed to house the collections and to provide space for readers. The entrance was via a grand staircase in the West Pavilion designed by Richard Castle, a leading architect of country houses and of Leinster House, the Rotunda Hospital and Trinity's Printing House. The

---

[46] *A description of the city of Dublin, by a citizen of London* (London: printed for the author [Edward Lloyd], 1732), p. 15.

staircase seems not to have been completed when the building opened, as the Board resolved in 1750 'to finish the Library staircase according to a plan by Mr Castle'. The following year, payments were made to carpenters and painters for work on the staircase and to the plasterer for stucco work.[47]

In creating the Long Room, Burgh had designed 'the grandest room in Ireland'.[48] It is 64 metres long and 12 metres wide, and the flat plaster ceiling with a lozenge decoration was originally about 15 metres high. The room contains forty alcoves, twenty on each side, formed by bookcases that had a desk fixed to the lower shelf, facing a bench that ran parallel to the shelves. The bookcases terminate in oak Corinthian pilasters carrying a rich entablature. The cases are identified by means of letters, which run A to W on the north side and AA to WW on the south side, and a traditional fixed-location numbering system (for example, AA.3.15) was used to indicate the location of each book by case, shelf and position on shelf. Above the bookcases is a gallery that extends around the whole room, surrounded by a handsome balustrade. When the Library opened, this gallery was devoid of any bookcases or other furniture. The layout of the Long Room can be seen in Malton's illustration of 1793. (See Plate 4.) At the west end are two fine staircases, once thought to have been donated by Henry Jones in the 1650s and, it was assumed, to have been transferred from the old Library into the Long Room. However, this suggestion has now been disproved, both on stylistic grounds and on the basis of invoices paid in 1732 to Isaac Wills for gallery staircases.[49] A room for manuscripts and other particularly valuable items occupied the whole of the first floor of the East Pavilion, with the only access through double doors at the end of the Long Room. The Manuscripts Room was wainscotted and fitted with oak cupboards for the better preservation of its contents. According to John Loveday, the room above was intended as a museum of curiosities.[50] On the first floor of the West Pavilion was the Librarian's Room but the remainder of the pavilions was allocated to academic, not library, purposes. The ground-floor room at the east end contained the Philosophy School, and the Law School occupied the equivalent room at the west end, with an astronomical observatory on the top floor, reached by a secondary staircase.

---

[47] MUN/V/5/3, 16 June 1750; MUN/V/57/3, March 1751–September 1752; E. H. Alton, 'Some notes on the Library and the cost of its building', *Annual Bulletin* (1948), 10–12.

[48] Edward McParland, 'Trinity College Dublin – I', *Country Life*, 159 (1976), 1166–9, (p. 1169).

[49] Crookshank, *Long Room* (1976), note 10 above, p. 5.

[50] John Loveday, *Diary of a tour in 1732 through parts of England, Wales, Ireland and Scotland* (Edinburgh: Roxburghe Club, 1890), pp. 54–5.

It has been argued that Thomas Burgh's great library was modelled on that of Sir Christopher Wren at Trinity College, Cambridge, which was completed in 1695. There are undoubted similarities, particularly of scale and splendour, and it would be unthinkable for Burgh not to have been inspired by Wren's vision, but some of his design features can be found closer to the banks of the Liffey than the Cam. Placing the library at first-floor level was a well-established method of avoiding damp, adopted already in Dublin by William Robinson at Marsh's Library. The open arcade underneath the Library was a feature that Burgh's design shares with Wren's library at Cambridge and with two nearly contemporary Oxford college libraries, Queen's, which pre-dates Burgh's building, and Christ Church, which was begun a little later, in 1717, and was intended to rival in splendour the libraries in Cambridge and Dublin.[51] Neither Wren's building nor the library at Queen's College has a gallery, and in buildings that do, such as the Bodleian's Arts End, the feature was usually designed as a means of reaching a second level of bookcases, rather than as an open promenade as in the case of Burgh's Long Room.

Most contemporary libraries, such as those at Queen's College, Oxford and Trinity College, Cambridge, run north–south, an orientation that accorded with the advice of commentators on library design such as Naudé, but Burgh's runs east–west, an undesirable alignment, as it allows damaging sunlight to fall directly onto the books through the south-facing windows.[52] This problem is compounded by the fact that the windows are nearly the full height of the bookcases, unlike Wren's, which start above the level of the shelves. Wren's arrangement also allowed him to space the bookcases at wider intervals and use the wall space below the windows for shelving, thus creating alcoves with a table and chairs for scholars to work. Burgh followed the more traditional approach of placing a seat parallel to the bookcases in each alcove, and using the lower shelf as a desk, in the same way as at Marsh's.

The building has been described as 'the culmination of Burgh's classicism'.[53] The arcades surmounted by bays of rectangular windows are reminiscent of his other work, most notably the Royal Barracks. The lower part of the building is austere compared to the 'flamboyant elaboration of the exterior entablature' and the splendour of the joinery in the Long

[51] Jean Cook and John Mason, eds., *The building accounts of Christ Church Library, 1716–1779* (Oxford: Roxburghe Club, 1988).

[52] Gabriel Naudé, *Instructions concerning erecting of a library . . . now interpreted by Jo. Evelyn* (London: G. Bedle, T. Collins and J. Crook, 1661).

[53] McParland, note 10 above, p. 154.

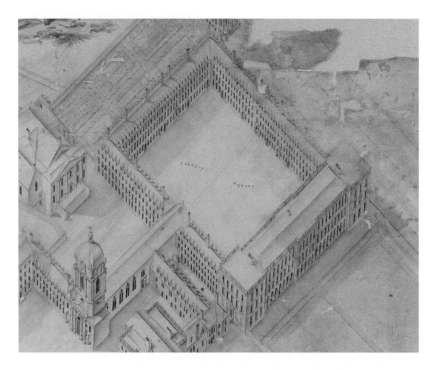

Figure 6 Isometric view of the College in 1780, by Samuel Byron, with the Library in the bottom right and residences forming the other three sides of Library Square (MUN/MC/9)

Room.[54] It seems possible that, as plans developed, designs that were initially simple became more elaborate. This might explain the fact that Burgh originally estimated that the cost of the building, excluding the bookcases, would be £7,100, whereas in the end it came to over £20,000. As he rarely exceeded his estimates and the costs of materials and labour did not rise during the progress of building, this increase is less likely to be a spectacular miscalculation than the result of changes to the design during construction. Unfortunately, no plans exist and so any answer must be merely speculation.

The capacity of the Long Room as laid out in 1732 was about 45,000 volumes, roughly more then twice the size of the collection that the College had assembled during the 140 years since its foundation. In the light of this, the intended role of the gallery is far from clear. It was certainly not needed as additional storage space and served no obvious purpose, as shelving was not installed in it for another 100 years. Was the upper storey an afterthought,

[54] *Ibid.*, p. 152.

a response to an increased budget, or part of an increasingly grandiose design intended to show that Trinity could build a library that equalled or surpassed those at Oxford and Cambridge?[55]

Rebinding and recataloguing the printed books

Once the new Library building had been completed, work could start on the collections. Responsibility for this devolved upon Edward Hudson, who served as Librarian almost continually from 1729 to 1740.[56] Hudson's duties covered not just the transfer of the books and manuscripts from the old Library to the new one but also the incorporation of the recently acquired collections and the organisation of a major binding programme. In April 1732, the College porters moved the manuscripts into their new place of honour, the room in the East Pavilion that had been panelled and fitted with oak cupboards.[57] Loveday, on his second visit in August 1733, noted that the Manuscripts Room contained 'two ancient Greek stones' inserted in the wainscotting. Presumably these were the 'stoon figures in the manuscript library' for which John Daniel had made cramps in 1730.[58] Hudson's preoccupation, however, was not with the manuscripts but with the printed books, and so the reorganisation of the former had to wait until John Lyon was given specific responsibility for them in 1741. In the meantime they remained, according to Loveday, 'in great disorder'.

The magnificent setting of the new Library demanded that the books should also look appropriately splendid, and so large numbers were sent off to be bound, rebound or refurbished. The agent for this work was Joseph Leathley, a bookseller and binder based in Dame Street, who also supplied paper, pens and account books to the College and service books for the Chapel. For the next 25 years Leathley was to undertake most of the binding for the Library, with the exception of the programme for the manuscripts during the 1740s, which was entrusted to John Exshaw.[59] Many of the printed books were sent to Leathley before they were transferred to their new location. The Library accounts contain a list, dated 9 May 1732, of several hundred books 'given out of the Old Library to be bound'.[60]

---

[55] *Ibid.*, pp. 155–8.   [56] MUN/V/5/2, 1729–40 *passim*.

[57] MUN/LIB/10/43.   [58] Markham, note 36 above, p. 162; MUN/P/2/59/2.

[59] For Leathley and Exshaw see M. Pollard, *A dictionary of members of the Dublin book trade, 1550–1800* (London: Bibliographical Society, 2000); McDonnell and Healy, pp. 41–55; M. Pollard, 'The "College Binder" – Thomas Whitehouse?', *Long Room*, 38 (1993), 17.

[60] MUN/LIB/10/43a.

Sometimes more than half the books on a shelf were dispatched, and the list also includes about thirty titles still in sheets. By the end of the year Leathley had bound about 950 volumes and been paid £80 17s. 7d. He charged trade terms for this binding in bulk and billed the College on the basis of format alone, at prices ranging from 7d. for a duodecimo to 5s. 6d. for an imperial folio, with octavos at 9d. and quartos at 1s. 4d. Between 1733 and 1736 he bound a further 5,000 volumes. His bills also include charges for either lettering and numbering (5,300 volumes) or just numbering (10,600 volumes), so over the course of 5 years he must have applied the new shelfmarks to a high proportion of the Library's collection. For this work he was paid between about £30 and £40 a quarter.[61] By 1736, the main programme had been completed, but Hudson continued to supply Leathley with occasional work, though only to the value of around five or six pounds a year.

When the books were moved into their new locations, the shelves on the south side were allocated to the two major donations, starting at the east end with that of James Ussher, which was placed in the first five bays (AA to EE). The Palliser books were located next to it, as specified in the donor's will. On the north side, the books were arranged in broad subject divisions, as they had been in the old Library, and the Bath and Willoughby books, which had previously been kept as distinct collections, were assimilated within the main sequence.

From the outset, the Board recognised that Hudson's commitment would far exceed that required of the Librarian under the statutes, and he received several payments in addition to his salary. For 'his extraordinary trouble in moving and binding books in the Library' he was paid £30 in 1732, a further £60 the following year, and £112 in March 1735 for 'the trouble he has taken and is hereafter to take in settling the Library'.[62] In July 1735 his salary was increased from £15 a year to £60, in accordance with the new statutes.[63] Thirteen years later, the Board paid him a further £228 for 'his extraordinary trouble in ranging the books and making catalogues both general and particular'.[64] It is unclear whether this was a planned payment that had been greatly delayed or, if not, why the Board should have made this decision so long after his resignation, as there is no evidence that he had any involvement with the Library after 1740.

---

[61] MUN/LIB/10/45 and 48–76; MUN/V/57/2; M. Pollard, 'Plain calf for plain people: Dublin bookbinders' price lists of the eighteenth century', in *Decantations*, pp. 177–86.

[62] MUN/V/5/2, 20 November 1732 and 1733, 25 March 1735.   [63] *Ibid.*, 8 July 1735.

[64] MUN/V/5/3, 29 June 1748; MUN/V/57/3, June quarter 1748.

New statutes

The old ways of managing were no longer adequate for a library on the scale of that which the College now possessed. To effect any change, however, would require an alteration to the statutes, and that involved the government. James King, one of the Senior Fellows, travelled to London with letters asking the Lord Lieutenant to have the changes put in hand, and in May 1733 he and George Berkeley, now Dean of Derry, called on Berkeley's old friend Lord Perceval to seek his advice. Perceval had become a significant figure in the English political world, close to both the King and the Prime Minister. His view on the matter, as recorded in his diary, was unequivocal: 'I gave Dr King my opinion that it was a dangerous thing for them to meddle in, because if once they come to altering or procuring new statutes, the Crown, which always takes advantage of such matters, will probably increase its power over them, and add something they may not like.'[65] The three men agreed that King would relay Perceval's views back to the College before approaching the Lord Lieutenant. In Dublin, however, the view remained that, regardless of Perceval's concerns, the old statutes were so restrictive that they had to be changed. Marmaduke Coghill, still MP for the University, wrote to Edward Southwell, who had succeeded his father as Secretary of State for Ireland, asking him to convey the Board's views to King, whom he regarded as an innocent in these matters: 'I fear his not being used to publick business may make him too easily submit to great mens opinions.' The Library, he went on, urgently needed new statutes and had suffered in the past from the inadequacy of the present ones. He ended his entreaties with a comment designed to stiffen King's resolve: 'I know of some great benefactions intended for the Library, which I fear they will not get, if they [new statutes] shoud be rejected.'[66] This was clearly a reference, at least in part, to the great collection that was being assembled by Claudius Gilbert, the Vice-Provost.

King seems to have been poorly briefed before he left for London as, in a further letter to Southwell only three weeks later, the increasingly exasperated Coghill said that he hoped the Board would give King the authority to act, 'tho at the same time I cant but suspect them to be idle and lazy, since no one step has bin made'. He set out at length the objections to the present statutes and how the new ones would redress these failings. The

[65] HMC, *Manuscripts of the Earl of Egmont: diary of Viscount Percival*, vol. I, [Cd. 8264], 1916, XI, 323 (p. 378).
[66] Coghill to Southwell, 4 December 1733, BL MS Add. 21123, fol. 11; D. W. Hayton, ed., *Letters of Marmaduke Coghill: 1722–1738* (Dublin: Irish Manuscripts Commission, 2005).

salary of the Librarian, at £10 a year, was inadequate and could not be raised unless the income of the College grew, in which case the statutes required the increased revenue to be divided among the Provost, Fellows and scholars, of which there were about eighty in all, with the result that 'the Library keepers share will be but a trifle'. The process of electing a new Librarian each year had been 'vastly inconvenient', and the College now wanted to place this process on the same footing as that for Fellows. They also wished to remove the restriction of choosing a Librarian from among the Fellows or MAs resident in the College and 'have liberty to choose elsewhere, if they find a man better qualified for this employment; than one of their own body'. Recent losses from the Library meant that security had to be increased, and to this end they proposed to remove the right of Fellows to borrow books by preventing borrowing altogether. They also considered that it was unreasonable for the Provost to be allowed a key, 'for when the Librarian is answerable for the books under his care, how can it be expected from him to answer for those books when another has as much power to go into the Library as himself'. Finally, in a rather different vein, they considered that access to the Library was too restricted and proposed that 'others may be admitted on takeing the oath proposed, which makes the Library usefull to all sorts of people'.[67]

The interference that Perceval had feared did not materialise and new statutes were approved by Letters Patent of George II on 30 July 1734.[68] In most respects they were similar to what Coghill had noted as being desirable, though a few changes had been introduced. In future, the Librarian was no longer to be elected annually but 'whenever the place shall be vacant', but the proposal to allow election from a wider field of candidates had been dropped and only Fellows or MAs of the College were eligible for the office. The salary of the Librarian was increased to a minimum of £60 a year, a sum that could be raised further at the discretion of the Board, independently of the salaries of other College officers 'because on the care and diligence of the Librarian, the safe custody of this literary treasure principally depends'. The Librarian was to be in sole charge of the keys to the Library and was required to be present from eight to ten in the morning and two to four in the afternoon, except on certain specified days. Nobody was to be admitted to the Library except in the presence of the Librarian. 'None of

---

[67] BL MS Add. 21 123, fols. 80–1. By 1733, the Librarian's salary had already been increased to £15.

[68] *Literae patentes, sive 'Statutum de Bibliotheca bene ordinanda'*, 8 George II, reprinted in *Chartae et statuta Collegii Sacrosanctae et Individuae Trinitatis Reginae Elizabethae juxta Dublin* (Dublin: Gill, 1844), pp. 327–37. The College petition is MUN/P/1/688.

the students in the College shall be admitted into the Library to the use of the books' until they had taken their BA degree. Fellows or resident MAs were allowed to introduce 'strangers' but were required to remain with them at all times. A scale of fines for causing damage to books was set out, with the ultimate sanction being permanent exclusion. No book was to be removed from the Library, by the Librarian or anyone else. Rules for the use of the Manuscripts Room were even more restrictive. The Librarian was required to remain with any users of the room and was not permitted even to open the chests in which 'the coins, medals and things of greater value' were stored, except with the permission of the Provost or Vice-Provost. The statutes also recognised the special situation currently facing the College and specified that, as soon as the books had been transferred to the new Library 'and settled in the places appointed for them', a catalogue with shelfmarks was to be prepared both for the printed books (including the listing of pamphlets within a bound volume) and for the manuscripts. The Library was to be inspected by the Board on the third Monday in October each year and if any books were found to be missing 'the Bursar shall out of the salary of the Librarian immediately, or as soon as may be, make good and return to the Library another book of the same edition and condition'.[69]

According to Coghill, the statutes were based on those of the Bodleian, and many of their provisions do indeed resemble those in force in Oxford.[70] They had nonetheless been devised by a bibliophile conscious of the losses that had taken place over the previous decades, and some of the conditions proved to be irritatingly restrictive to future generations. John Hely-Hutchinson, Provost from 1774 to 1794, commented in the draft of his unpublished history of the College 'that more attention appears to have been given to the preservation, than to the use of the books; and in respect of the manuscripts the cautions are so extremely strict as to render them almost totally useless'.[71] Hely-Hutchinson maintained that it was Gilbert who had framed the statutes and that the difficulties caused by restricting access to graduates only were eventually acknowledged even by their author who, in addition to the enormous collection bequeathed to the College on his death in 1743, left money to establish a lending library for the students.

[69] Robert Bolton, *A translation of the charter and statutes of Trinity-College, Dublin* (Dublin: Nelson, 1749), pp. 119–35.

[70] *Oxford University statutes*, translated by G. R. M. Ward, 2 vols. (London: Pickering, 1845–51), vol. I, pp. 240–62.

[71] MS 1774a, fol. 50.

The preparation of a new catalogue was seen as a matter of urgency, and work on the printed books began late in 1734 with the appointment of Basil Jervis and Robert Lester as clerks, each earning 15s. a week. Jervis worked for just 6 months but Lester's appointment continued until 1742.[72] The catalogue consisted of about six volumes, of which three (A–C, M–Q and R–Z) still exist.[73] The entries indicate the shelfmarks in the new Library and also specifically identify those books in the collections from Ussher (usually by 'B. Usser' or 'B.U.') and Palliser ('B.Pall' or 'B.P.'). Books from the Gilbert bequest are not included, as this catalogue was completed before their arrival. The Library archives also contain just the volume for A of '*Catalogus generalis impressorum librorum bibliothecae novae . . . cura & opera Eduardi Hudson*' dated 1737.[74] This seems to have started as a fair copy of the earlier catalogue, but the Gilbert books have all been added later, in a different hand. There are also many subsequent amendments and additions, including those reflecting the change in the form of shelfmarks in the nineteenth century from LETTER/figure/figure (for example, A.3.15), to denote the case, the shelf and the position of the book on the shelf, to LETTER/letter/figure (for example, A.c.15).

[72] MUN/V/57/2; MUN/LIB/10/136.   [73] MUN/LIB/1/6.   [74] MUN/LIB/1/5.

The academic standing of Trinity in the second quarter of the eighteenth century has been dismissed by the standard modern history of the College. 'It must be confessed that few of the Fellows of the time showed evidence of even a blighted promise or of intellectual creativity,' say its authors, who claim to have been unable to trace a single word, not even a sermon or a textbook, published between 1722 and 1753 by anyone in possession of a Fellowship.[1] However, even if the written output from those in academic positions in the College was minimal, there was a level of intellectual curiosity and excitement among many who had passed through its doors. In part, this was manifested in a growing passion for book-collecting among members of the clergy, lawyers and doctors, many of whom were Trinity graduates. This group of like-minded individuals patronised the Dublin and London booksellers, with some also buying at continental sales, and in due course theirs was a passion from which Trinity and other institutional libraries in the country were to benefit. The donations to the College from Ashe and Palliser have already been noted, and they were to be followed by Claudius Gilbert's library and the manuscripts and pamphlets acquired by John Stearne. Most of Stearne's printed books and the extensive collection built up by Narcissus Marsh were bequeathed to the library founded by Marsh in Dublin. William King, Marsh's successor as Archbishop of Dublin, owned a library of about seven thousand books which he intended should become a public resource, perhaps in his former diocese of Derry, a place that he considered was more in need of books than the capital. At his death in 1729, however, he had left no specific instructions concerning the library, and so it passed with the rest of his estate to his nephew Robert Dougatt, Keeper of Marsh's Library, and subsequently to Dougatt's nephew Robert Spence, who sold about six thousand of the books to Theophilus Bolton, Archbishop of Cashel, some time in the 1730s. Bolton added them to his own substantial collection to create a new diocesan library which, though it has enjoyed mixed fortunes over the succeeding centuries, continues to survive in Cashel as the Bolton Library. Some of King's Hebrew books and the bulk

[1] McDowell and Webb, pp. 38–9.

of his manuscripts, particularly the voluminous correspondence, are now in Trinity, but acquisition of the manuscripts by the College was piecemeal and for the most part did not take place until the twentieth century.[2]

Bibliophily was not confined to the clergy of the established Church. Among the medical men of the time, Edward Worth stands out not just as a distinguished physician but also as a book collector of note. His library of 4,400 sumptuously bound volumes was bequeathed to the newly founded Dr Steevens' Hospital, of which Worth had been a governor. He evidently intended his collection to be available more widely than just to the physicians, chaplains and surgeons at Dr Steevens', as he specified that three copies of the catalogue should be made, one to be chained in the library at Dr Steevens', one to be kept in Trinity College Library and the other at Marsh's.[3] Edward Worth's father John, Dean of St Patrick's, also assembled a substantial library, which was due to pass to one of his sons as long as they took holy orders. If they did not, the books would be inherited by his nephew, confusingly also called Edward. Since neither of John's sons went into the Church, Edward duly acquired the books, of which about a thousand were bequeathed to Trinity in 1742 and some joined those of cousin Edward at Dr Steevens' Hospital.

John Stearne

In July 1742 William Clement, Edward Hudson's successor as Trinity College Librarian, was dispatched by the Board to Clogher in County Tyrone 'to examine what books in the Bishop's library are not in the College Library, and take care to send them up to Dublin'.[4] The bishop in question was John Stearne, son of the John Stearne who had founded the Royal College of Physicians of Ireland and after whom Trinity's Medical Library is now named. (See Plate 5.) It was probably as a student at Trinity in the 1670s that the younger Stearne had been introduced to the study and collecting

[2] Toby Barnard, 'Libraries and collectors, 1700–1800', in *Irish book*, pp. 111–34; Toby Barnard, 'Learning, the learned and literacy in Ireland, *c.*1660–1760', in Toby Barnard, Dáibhí Ó Cróinín and Katharine Simms, eds., *'A miracle of learning': studies in manuscripts and Irish learning. Essays in honour of William O'Sullivan* (Aldershot: Ashgate, 1998), pp. 209–35; Toby Barnard, 'John Lyon and Irish antiquarianism in the time of Swift', in Hermann J. Real, ed., *Reading Swift: papers from the Fifth Münster Symposium on Jonathan Swift* (München: Fink, 2008), pp. 245–54; Robert S. Matteson, *A large private park: the collection of Archbishop William King (1650–1729)* (Cambridge: LP Publications, 2003), pp. xxii–xxv.
[3] The Trinity copy, which contains an extract from Worth's will, is MS 12.
[4] MUN/V/5/3, 21 July 1742.

of books and manuscripts through the influence of bibliophiles like Marsh, King, Palliser and John Madden.[5] His career took him into the Church of Ireland rather than along his father's route into the medical profession, and after serving as Dean of St Patrick's he was elevated to the see of Dromore and then of Clogher, there succeeding St George Ashe. He became Vice-Chancellor of the University of Dublin and donated £1,000 to establish a university press and build the Printing House. In May 1741, aged 81 and unmarried, he clearly felt that it was time to arrange his affairs and write a will, and in this he made generous provision for a number of charities. Over the course of the next 4 years almost all of his substantial library of manuscripts and printed books was given either to Trinity or to Marsh's Library. Broadly speaking, the manuscripts and ephemeral publications went to Trinity and most of the other printed books to Marsh's.

The subject matter of the six to seven thousand volumes in Stearne's library reflected his concern at the precarious state of the Church of Ireland at the time and his perception of the need to collect and make available material that would help to underpin the Protestant cause. This preoccupation was evident in his first two donations, which were made to Trinity in the summer of 1741. In that year, the centenary of the rebellion, he presented the papers that have become known as the 1641 Depositions (MSS 809–41) which he had earlier described as 'a pretty large collection of original examinations' that he thought 'worth the preserving'.[6] He also donated a large collection of pamphlets, many of which relate to the same events and to the unrest of the 1680s. In 1742 came the invitation to the College to select from the books in Clogher those it did not already have and, after Clement had made his choice, Thomas Reilly, 'the carrman', went off with three carriage loads of empty boxes, returning with six boxes of books for the Library.[7] After Trinity had taken its pick it was the turn of Marsh's Library, but that institution had to wait until Stearne's death in 1745. In his will he left to Marsh's those books not already there 'as a small token of the great regard I have for the bountifull creator and endower of that library'.[8] Marsh's selected about three thousand books and the remainder were sold for the benefit of the curates in Stearne's diocese of Clogher.

---

[5] Toby Barnard, 'Bishop Stearne's collection of books and manuscripts', in Muriel McCarthy and Ann Simmons, eds., *Marsh's Library: a mirror on the world* (Dublin: Four Courts Press, 2009), pp. 185–202.

[6] Stearne to Henry Dodwell, 13 September 1709, Bodleian MS Eng. Lett. C. 28, fol. 82.

[7] MUN/LIB/10/153a, 24 August 1742.

[8] Will of Dr John Stearne, PRONI DIO/4/9/5/1/1; MUN/P/1/720.

The 1641 Depositions are without doubt one of the most important collections in the College Library.[9] They comprise about nineteen thousand pages, containing the testimonies of around eight thousand witnesses, mainly Protestants, recording the experiences of those affected by the rebellion of 1641, their losses, the associated military activity and the crimes allegedly committed by the insurgents. The statements were made to a commission consisting of eight Church of Ireland clergymen, headed by Henry Jones (later to become the donor of the Book of Kells and the Book of Durrow), which was established to register the claims of the dispossessed and issue them with certificates of loss. The Depositions are a unique source of information, not just for the events surrounding the rebellion but also for the broader social, economic, religious and political history of these islands in the seventeenth century. They have been exploited by propagandists, politicians and historians for over four centuries and have been published selectively since as early as 1642, with Jones' own *A remonstrance of divers remarkeable passages concerning the Church and Kingdome of Ireland*. It was not until the 1930s that an attempt was made to publish them in full, when, at the instigation of Robin Dudley Edwards, the Irish Manuscripts Commission sought funding for the project from the Department of Finance. Though the government was supportive, its officials were decidedly nervous at the potential effect of 'the more gruesome' of the Depositions, and whilst recognising that selective publication was undesirable they felt that there was 'something to be said . . . for the exercise of the blue pencil'.[10] In the event, the Second World War intervened and the project did not proceed. Full publication had to wait until 2010, when a three-year collaborative project between Trinity and the universities of Aberdeen and Cambridge was completed, with the entire collection being made available online and publication in printed form by the Irish Manuscripts Commission to follow.[11]

The history of the documents themselves is a convoluted one.[12] The 1641 Commissioners deposited them in the office of the Irish Privy Council, where they became the responsibility of Matthew Barry, its clerk. Barry seems to have regarded it as his prerogative to remove papers from the

---

[9] Aidan Clarke, 'The 1641 Depositions', in *Treasures*, pp. 111–22.

[10] Letter J. B. Whelehan (Stationery Office) to J. MacNeill (Irish Manuscripts Commission), 16 October 1935, NAI IMC 97/42/166; see also Michael Kennedy and Deirdre McMahon, *Reconstructing Ireland's past: a history of the Irish Manuscripts Commission* (Dublin: Irish Manuscripts Commission, 2009), pp. 70–3.

[11] http://www.1641.tcd.ie.

[12] William O'Sullivan, 'John Madden's manuscripts', in *Essays*, pp. 104–15.

office and treat them as his private property and at some stage, possibly in the 1680s, he took the Depositions. This turned out to be a felicitous decision as the office and all its contents were destroyed by fire in 1711. Barry subsequently sold the papers to John Madden, a medical practitioner with wide antiquarian interests and a member of the Dublin Philosophical Society. As the brother-in-law of the Society's founder William Molyneux, Madden was close to the centre of the intellectual life of the city. He was particularly interested in genealogy and ecclesiastical history, and he made extensive notes from the manuscripts of Sir James Ware, which were still in Dublin at the time. The Depositions formed the most significant part of his collection, but his genealogical compilations have become an important source of information on English settlers in Ireland. Madden's papers also included documents on the history of Irish religious houses and some official records, which were probably among the items that he bought from Barry. Among these were documents from the Court of Wards and Liveries, which had operated between 1622 and 1641, and the papers of Sir William Davys, Chief Justice of the King's Bench, including proceedings of the Court of Castle Chamber. There were also medieval manuscripts: the fifteenth-century cartulary of the monastery of All Hallows, which occupied the site given to Trinity College (MS 525), a fifteenth-century Hebrew Psalter (MS 17) and a fourteenth-century Book of Hours from Bective Abbey, County Meath (MS 94), as well as the sixteenth-century *Historia et genealogia Familiae de Burgo*, the genealogical history of the Burke family of County Mayo (MS 1440). A remarkable item later discovered between the leaves of a sixteenth-century printed book was a collection of pressed and dried herbarium specimens with a list of contents in Madden's hand, the oldest such collection known in Ireland.[13] During his lifetime Madden assembled one of the largest manuscript collections in the country, significant enough for the catalogue to be published in Bernard's *Catalogi* of 1697, at which time the collection contained twenty-two folio, thirteen quarto, and three octavo volumes.[14]

Madden died in 1703 and his widow sold the collection to Stearne, who had been her husband's near-contemporary at Trinity and wanted to ensure that the manuscripts were not dispersed. Although they formed the major part of Stearne's collection, their new owner added to them, despite his claim of being unable to find any 'old and valuable MSS' in Ireland and

---

[13] MS 709a; E. Charles Nelson, 'A late 17th century Irish herbarium in the Library of Trinity College Dublin', *Irish Naturalists' Journal*, 20 (1981), 334–5.

[14] Edward Bernard, *Catalogi librorum manuscriptorum Angliae et Hiberniae*, 2 vols. (Oxford: Sheldonian, 1697), vol. II, part 2, pp. 57–60.

being 'frightened by the charge and difficulty from seeking them abroad'.[15] Stearne's additions included three or four either wholly or partly in Irish and a collection of visitation returns for Irish dioceses in the 1590s (MS 566).[16] It is difficult to establish precisely which manuscripts were Madden's and which were additions by Stearne, as Madden's own 'Catalogue of my M.S. 1700' has later entries in Stearne's hand, but it is also clear that the list is incomplete even for items that Madden owned.[17] Almost the whole collection, whether a Madden original or a Stearne addition, is now in Trinity, though a handful of manuscripts went with the printed books to Marsh's.

The second of Stearne's gifts to his alma mater in 1741 was that of 4,300 pamphlets. Many of them were spawned by the political and religious unrest of the mid to late seventeenth century, but they also included publications of the 1720s and 1730s. Most are of a polemical nature but there are also several volumes of plays and other items. Among these is the only known copy of the anonymous morality play *The worlde and the chylde* published in 1522 by Wynkyn de Worde.[18] The pamphlets were bound in 387 volumes and placed in class P on the north side of the Long Room, and a catalogue was produced by John Lyon, who had been employed to list the Library's manuscripts.[19]

Claudius Gilbert

An even greater collection than Stearne's was that assembled by Claudius Gilbert, a former Librarian and later Senior Fellow and Professor of Divinity at Trinity.[20] (See Figure 7.) He was a passionate and discerning book-collector whose purchases were guided by his desire ultimately to use his books to fill gaps in the Library's collections, a fact that was noted when Archbishop King and Robert Howard were plotting the removal of Pratt from the Provostship in 1717. Gilbert was seen as an obvious candidate to succeed Pratt, as he 'has credit and authority in the College, [his] heart is here, [he] has no thoughts of marriage, byes books every day to enrich

---

[15] Stearne to Dodwell, note 6 above.

[16] Abbot and Gwynn, p. ix; H. J. Lawlor, 'Two collections of visitation reports in the Library of Trinity College', *Hermathena*, 13 (1905), 319–31.

[17] MS 653, fols. 69–78v.; O'Sullivan, note 12 above.

[18] Ian Lancashire, 'The provenance of *The worlde and the chylde*', *Papers of the Bibliographical Society of America*, 67 (1973), 377–88.

[19] MS 2932 (catalogue).

[20] Robert Armstrong, 'Claudius Gilbert and his books', in *Old Library*, pp. 112–21.

Figure 7 Bust of Claudius Gilbert in the Long Room (Gillian Whelan, Digital Resources and Imaging Services, TCD)

our Library, would be very steady and regular and of unquestionable loyalty both to the church and present government'.[21] In the end, however, the Whig Richard Baldwin was deemed to be the safer choice; Gilbert succeeded him as Vice-Provost and in that office he effectively ran the College on a day-to-day basis until his retirement in 1735. By then it was known that he intended to give the College his library, regarded as one of the finest in Ireland, though it was not actually transferred until after his death in 1743. It was by far the largest collection acquired by the Library up to that date, consisting of over thirteen thousand volumes of printed books, as well as manuscripts.

Gilbert's collecting interests were wide-ranging. There is naturally a heavy concentration on divinity, but law is well represented, as are medicine, mathematics, geography, history, travel, reference works and literature, as well as numismatics, a reflection of his enthusiasm for coin collecting. He also purchased large numbers of contemporary Irish political and economic pamphlets and anti-Popery tracts published in London in the late seventeenth century. His buying was not restricted to sales in Ireland and England and the collection is especially strong in continental publications, with more than 10 per cent in French – over 1,400 volumes, of which 500 deal with French history – evidence of the growing scholarly importance of that language. Collected editions, compilations and periodicals feature extensively. They include 170 volumes of *Le journal des sçavans* (Paris, 1665–1753) and a run of the *Oxford* [later *London*] *Gazette* from 1665 to 1721.[22] Though Gilbert was not principally interested in buying early editions or fine bindings, the collection contains three of Trinity's eight Grolier bindings and Abbott identified thirty-one fifteenth-century books, including two of the Library's five Virgil incunabula.[23]

Among the manuscripts are those bought by Gilbert at the sale of Samuel Molyneux's library on 20 January 1730. They include minutes and papers of the Dublin Philosophical Society, acquired by Molyneux on the death of his father William, founder of the Society, though the formal minutes and register books, sold on the same occasion, are now in the British Library.

---

[21] Howard to King, 28 February 1717, MSS 1995–2008/1804.

[22] Charles Benson, 'Some private libraries in eighteenth-century Ireland', in Danielle Westerhof, ed., *The alchemy of medicine and print: the Edward Worth Library, Dublin* (Dublin: Four Courts Press, 2010), pp. 48–56; Francis M. Higman, 'Holdings and acquisitions in French, 1750–1850', *Hermathena*, 121 (1976), 100–8.

[23] Abbott, *Incunabula*; Helen Conrad-O'Briain, 'Trinity incunable TT.c.11: a home Virgil from the first age of printing', *Long Room*, 52/53 (2007–8), 49–57; Gabriel Austin, *The library of Jean Grolier: a preliminary catalogue* (New York: Grolier Club, 1971); Veronica Morrow, 'An unrecorded Grolier binding', *Long Room*, 39 (1994), 30–2.

There are also drafts and papers for a planned natural history of Ireland begun by William Molyneux in 1682 and the manuscript used as printer's copy for his *The case of Ireland's being bound by Acts of Parliament in England, stated*, which challenged the right of the English Parliament to legislate for Ireland. These few manuscripts (MSS 883–90), together with a handful of printed items bought by Gilbert at the same sale, are the only works from William Molyneux's extensive library to come to Trinity, despite the fact that his will indicated that he intended all of his books and manuscripts to pass to his alma mater.[24]

Gilbert's prolific book-collecting included an extensive range of auction catalogues, many marked to indicate items in which he was interested and some with the prices achieved. He also compiled a catalogue of his collection, indicating the amounts he had paid. The highest were £67 5s. 0d. for the seventeen volumes of Thomas Rymer's *Foedera* (London, 1704–17) and £39 10s. 0d. for twenty-seven volumes of *Maxima bibliotheca veterum patrum* (Lyons, 1677), whereas the Groliers each cost well under a pound.[25]

With the collections from Ussher and Palliser standing next to each other on the south side of the Long Room, it must have seemed obvious that the appropriate place for Gilbert's books was next to them on the remaining empty shelves on that side of the building. They were cleaned and moved into the Library in February 1744 and in April one of the Fellows, Henry Mercier, was appointed as the Assistant Librarian with the duty of arranging and cataloguing them, a task that took him until 1749 and for which he was paid a total of £200.[26] Joseph Leathley bound about 240 of the volumes, applied numbers to 12,914 and lettered 1,930 at a total cost of £112 9s. 0d.[27]

Gilbert's munificence towards the College extended well beyond the donation of his books. He gave 1,881 coins, mostly of Roman silver, a collection that remained little known until the publication of Malet's catalogue in

[24] John Wilcox, *A catalogue of the library of the Honble Samuel Molyneux* [London, 1730]; Patrick Kelly, 'The one that got away, or almost: the Molyneux family library and Trinity College Dublin', in *Old Library*, pp. 94–101; Patrick Kelly, 'The printer's copy of the MS of William Molyneux, "The case of Ireland's being bound by Acts of Parliament in England, stated", 1698', *Long Room*, 18/19 (Spring/Autumn 1979), 6–13; K. Theodore Hoppen, 'The papers of the Dublin Philosophical Society 1683–1708: introductory material and index', *Analecta Hibernica*, 30 (1982) 151–248; William O'Sullivan, 'William Molyneux's geographical collections for Kerry', *Journal of the Kerry Archaeological and Historical Society*, 4 (1971), 28–47.

[25] MS 11; Máire Kennedy, *French books in eighteenth-century Ireland* (Oxford: Voltaire Foundation, 2001), p. 105.

[26] MUN/LIB/10/162; MUN/V/5/3, 28 April 1744, 12 July 1749; MUN/V/57/3, June quarter 1749.

[27] MUN/LIB/10/169.

1839.[28] As the man likely to have been responsible for drafting the statutes for the Library, he will have been aware of their highly restrictive nature, and so he left £550 to provide a small lending library for BAs, including an endowment for the salary of its librarian.[29] The most important bequest apart from his library, however, was the £500 that he gave 'to purchase busts of men eminent for learning to adorn the Library'.[30] This formed the start of the collection of busts that is now such an important feature of the Long Room.

By the early eighteenth century the display of portrait busts in libraries was becoming increasingly common, particularly in France. It was a practice that had been espoused by Gabriel Naudé, of whose book Gilbert possessed two copies in the translation by John Evelyn. In the 1730s, busts were commissioned for two private libraries in England, that of Queen Caroline's Hermitage at Richmond and Pope's library at Twickenham. The adornment of the Codrington Library at All Souls College, Oxford with twenty-four busts of former Fellows was almost contemporary with the commissioning of those for Dublin. Unlike those in Oxford, however, the selection of subjects for Trinity was not intended to reflect the glory of the College's own history but followed more closely Naudé's advice 'to have good copies drawn from such as are most famous in the profession of letters; that thereby a man may at once make judgement of the wit of the authours by their books, and by their bodies, figure, and physiognomy'.[31] The only Gilbert bust to commemorate one of the sons of the house was that of James Ussher. (See Figure 2.)

It was widely believed that the Dublin busts were based on those at Trinity College, Cambridge.[32] However, this cannot have been the case, as a receipt exists from William Keating, joiner, for payment of 2s. 8½d. for putting up busts in the Long Room in September 1746, whilst those in Cambridge were not ordered until the 1750s.[33] Of the many that now adorn the Long Room, fourteen were commissioned as a result of Gilbert's bequest. Six represent classical figures: Aristotle, Cicero, Demosthenes, Homer, Plato and Socrates; six are of modern writers and scholars: Bacon, Boyle, Locke, Milton, Newton and Shakespeare; and two are of benefactors to the

---

[28] J. A. Malet, *A catalogue of Roman silver coins in the Library of Trinity College Dublin* (Dublin: Graisberry, 1839).

[29] MUN/V/5/5, p. 358.   [30] *DU Calendar*, 1858, p. 248.

[31] Gabriel Naudé, *Instructions concerning erecting of a library . . . now interpreted by Jo. Evelyn* (London: G. Bedle, T. Collins and J. Crook, 1661), p. 85.

[32] As, for example, Anne Crookshank, 'The Long Room', in *Treasures*, pp. 16–28.

[33] MUN/P/4/50/25; Malcolm Baker, 'The portrait sculpture', in David McKitterick, ed., *The making of the Wren Library* (Cambridge University Press, 1995), pp. 110–37.

Library: Archbishop Ussher and Thomas Herbert, eighth Earl of Pembroke. In the absence of documentary evidence, it has proved difficult to establish with certainty who was responsible for producing them. Some, and indeed probably all, were commissioned from Peter Scheemakers, a Flemish sculptor born in Antwerp around 1690, who spent all his working life in London. Scheemakers' reputation had reached its height following the unveiling of his memorial to Shakespeare in Poets' Corner, Westminster Abbey, in 1741. His work was also known in Dublin, as his marble effigy of Marmaduke Coghill was installed in 1743 in All Hallows, Drumcondra, a new church in the north of the city erected at the expense of Coghill's sister. One of the Long Room busts (Shakespeare) is signed 'Peter Scheemakers' and seven others (Cicero, Demosthenes, Homer, Locke, Milton, Pembroke and Ussher) are variously marked 'P.S.', 'P.S. fe.' or 'P.S. ft'. On that basis, some commentators have attributed all the busts to Scheemakers, despite the fact that the eighteenth-century writer Horace Walpole stated that half of them were done by François Roubiliac, a French sculptor also working in London who, Walpole said, 'had little business till Sir Edward Walpole recommended him to execute half the busts at Trinity College Dublin'.[34] This was once believed to have been an error for Trinity College, Cambridge, where Roubiliac was certainly responsible for most of the busts. However, recent scholarship has suggested that all those from the Gilbert bequest were indeed commissioned from Scheemakers, but that as he had become overwhelmed with work following the success of the Shakespeare memorial he was forced to sub-contract some of those in Trinity to Roubiliac.[35] The six unsigned busts, therefore, could well be the product of the latter.[36]

The one bust in the Long Room that is indisputably the work of Roubiliac is that of Jonathan Swift. Reporting its arrival in March 1749, Faulkner's *Dublin Journal* stated that it was commissioned by a class of senior sophister students who formed themselves into a 'senate' and 'applied the money usually laid out in an entertainment, to the purchase of this busto, which they have given to be placed in the College Library, among the heads of

[34] Horace Walpole, *Anecdotes of painting in England: with some account of the principal artists; and incidental notes on other arts; collected by the late Mr George Vertue*, 4 vols. (Strawberry-Hill: Thomas Kirgate, 1762–71), vol. IV, p. 99.

[35] Malcolm Baker, 'The making of portrait busts in the mid-eighteenth century: Roubiliac, Scheemakers and Trinity College Dublin', *Burlington Magazine*, 137 (1995), 821–31; Ingrid Roscoe, 'Peter Scheemakers', *Walpole Society*, 61 (1999), 163–304 (pp. 170, 270); Anne Crookshank and David Webb, *Paintings and sculptures in Trinity College Dublin* (Dublin: Trinity College Dublin Press, 1990), pp. 149–52.

[36] The six are: Aristotle, Plato, Socrates, Bacon, Boyle and Newton.

other men eminent for genius and learning; an instance of publick spirit in young persons worthy of praise and imitation'.[37] The bust is inscribed 'Ex dono quartae classis an: 1745 procurante Digbaeo French'. Swift died in 1745 and French graduated in 1747. Faulkner went on to propose that a bust of Berkeley should be added to that of Swift but, remarkably, the philosopher and former Trinity Librarian has never been represented among the Long Room busts, though several portraits of him hang in the College. A bust of Gilbert himself (see Figure 7) was commissioned from Simon Vierpyl, a Florentine sculptor working in Dublin, at a cost of £34 2s. 6d. and possibly bought from funds that remained from the bequest. According to a contemporary report it was placed 'at the head of' his collection in 1758.[38]

Rebinding and recataloguing the manuscripts

After the transfer of the Library's manuscripts from the old building in 1732 they were left largely untouched for almost a decade. They had been augmented by the transfer to the new Manuscripts Room of those from Sir Jerome Alexander's library. The arrival of the Stearne collection provided the catalyst for action, and it was now the turn of the manuscripts to be refurbished, recatalogued and made fit to be displayed in their place of honour just off the Long Room. The work was placed in the hands of John Lyon, a Trinity graduate and an antiquary who had recently been appointed as a canon of St Patrick's Cathedral. There is no record of his appointment to the Library, but by August 1741 he was giving instructions to the binder.[39] In December 1742 the Board decided that a new catalogue of manuscripts was required and ordered 'that the Library Keeper shall deliver the manuscripts to Mr Lyons, who is chosen as Assistant till the catalogue shall be finished'.[40]

Lyon's involvement with the Library's manuscripts was something of a mixed blessing. His cavalier approach to the material with which he was entrusted led to the destruction of much historical evidence, but he also ensured the preservation of documents that might otherwise not have survived. He rearranged the collections, including those of Ussher and Stearne, forcing them into a subject arrangement of his own making, a

---

[37] George Faulkner, *Dublin Journal*, 21–5 March 1749.
[38] *Gentleman's Magazine*, 28 (1758), 91.
[39] MUN/LIB/10/161.   [40] MUN/V/5/3, 1 December 1742.

procedure that he also adopted with the archives of Dublin's two Church of Ireland cathedrals, Christ Church and St Patrick's. He ignored the fact that scholars were now familiar with the arrangement in Bernard's published catalogue of 1697 and, by dint of reordering the collection without providing a concordance between Bernard's numbering and his own, he created a state of confusion that would last for 150 years until the publication in 1900 of Abbott's catalogue, with its new numbering sequence and concordance with those of both Lyon and Bernard.[41] Worse still, volumes that Ussher and Madden had put together were actually dismantled and reassembled in new combinations if they did not fit Lyon's arrangement. The 1641 Depositions were early victims of his attention. When they were in Madden's possession they had been in two volumes, one mainly covering Munster, Ulster and Connaught, and the other Leinster, with additional miscellaneous documents. Lyon rearranged them by county and had them bound in thirty-one folio volumes.

He placed the College's entire collection in seven presses, lettered A to G. The older acquisitions, including Ussher's manuscripts, were arranged by subject in classes A to E, with the biblical and theological material in A to C, philosophy, medicine and poetry in D, and genealogy and history in E. The Stearne/Madden manuscripts occupied press F and part of G, with the rest of G accommodating the Alexander manuscripts. Lyon's catalogue begins with an index of donors, starting with Charles II for the Ussher collection and continuing with Alexander, Stearne and others. Each entry in the catalogue itself consists of a description of the manuscript, its location and, where this is not apparent, the donor. The catalogue was continued by others who later added entries for manuscripts in classes (H to M) that were created as required. Those entries include Deane Swift's donations in 1753 and 1754 of his cousin Jonathan's sermon on brotherly love and an account of his life, both now part of MS 1050. The blank pages at the front of the catalogue were used to record the loan of manuscripts, usually with a signed note of receipt by the borrower and a statement of the date of their return. Between the first of these entries in 1781 and the last in 1822, some thirty loans are noted, mainly to Fellows, but including several to Charles Vallancey and Theophilus O'Flanagan.[42]

The binding programme, which involved about half the collection, was carried out by John Exshaw, a well-known Dublin bookseller, printer and

---

[41] Bernard, note 14 above, pp. 16–48; Abbott, *Manuscripts*, pp. xi–xv.
[42] William O'Sullivan, 'Introduction to the collections', in Colker, pp. 21–33. The catalogue is MUN/LIB/1/53.

binder. Exshaw used three styles of binding on the manuscripts. The major-ity were bound in brown calf; a few were placed in pasteboards covered with marbled paper and provided with vellum spines; and the rest were done in vellum over pasteboards. In general, vellum bindings were used only for paper manuscripts, but calf bindings covered documents on both paper and vellum. Exshaw was familiar with binding books written or printed on paper but seems to have made no distinction between its properties and those of vellum, other than to use heavy glue on the spine of the latter, with the result that the pages suffered from cockling and became difficult to open. In time, the hinges of the calfskin bindings broke down and many were rebacked in the nineteenth and twentieth centuries, but the vellum bindings on paper manuscripts have largely remained intact and are still in use.[43]

Exshaw produced detailed bills in which he listed not just the work carried out but the titles of the manuscripts that had been treated. From these it can be seen that Lyon started with the 1641 Depositions, which were completed by November 1741. The rest of the collection was first rearranged and then sent for binding in the order that the bound volumes were to stand on the shelves in Lyon's seven presses. Exshaw's bills included '46 days wholly spent in pasting cleaning and sewing the manuscripts according to Mr Lion's directions' in August and September 1741.[44] This was presumably the work needed to prepare the Depositions for binding. Work on the other collections began in January 1742 and continued throughout that year. The most expensive manuscripts to bind were the large service books (for example, MSS 77–9 and 109) at 8s. each, whereas the Book of Kells cost only 3s. 6d. and the Book of Durrow, a smaller volume, 2s. On 25 October 1742, Lyon certified an invoice from Exshaw for £48 16s. 5d. to cover the work carried out that year. It comprised £34 18s. 10d. for the binding of 328 volumes, £1 10s. 1d. for lettering 131 volumes, and £12 7s. 6d. for 99 days' work in the Library at 2s. 6d. a day, which, judging from a later invoice, was for repairs and lettering, probably of manuscripts that were not to be rebound. A month later, Lyon noted that all the work had been completed, apart from the Alexander and Stearne manuscripts, and that 'they are delivered and done well according to the prices agreed for'. Forty-four Stearne volumes were bound in the following few months and Exshaw

[43] William O'Sullivan, 'The eighteenth century rebinding of the manuscripts', *Long Room*, 1 (Spring 1970), 19–28; William O'Sullivan, 'Binding memories of Trinity Library', in *Decantations*, pp. 168–76.

[44] MUN/LIB/10/161.

charged for 89 more days' work in the Library 'mending, marking and writing the titles of the manuscripts'.[45]

One of the positive aspects of Lyon's intervention was his binding for the first time of the loose papers belonging to some of the early Fellows of the College, James and Ambrose Ussher, Challoner, and the second Provost, Walter Travers, as well as those of the sixteenth-century theologian Richard Hooker, though in the case of the latter, Lyon's rearrangement of the manuscripts for the sake of uniformity obscured the authorship of some of them for more than two centuries.[46] He accessioned some manuscripts that had been donated in the recent past, including MS 1684, one of the Library's only two Cyrillic manuscripts, given in 1706 by Alexander Jephson, a Trinity graduate serving as a clergyman in London.[47] Lyon was a collector himself, and presented five manuscripts to the College and others to Marsh's Library.[48] His catalogue also provides the first evidence of the existence in the Library of some manuscripts whose provenance is unknown, such as the fifteenth-century *Piers Plowman* text, MS 212.[49]

Lyon identified over a dozen losses since the entry had been made in Foley's catalogue in 1702, including at least three manuscripts that had come to the Library with Ussher's collection: a twelfth-century Greek Gospel manuscript, a thirteenth-century Latin Bible and the Book of Ballymote.[50] The Greek Gospel book was listed in Bernard's catalogue of 1697 and appears to have been lent in around 1702 to Sir Richard Bulkeley, a former Fellow who was collating it for John Mill's 1707 edition of the Greek New Testament. He had not returned it by the time of his death in 1710 and it passed through various hands, eventually coming into the possession of the Marquesses of Bute. In 1907, T. K. Abbott, the then Librarian, tried to recover it, but without success. It subsequently appeared in a sale at Sotheby's in June 1983 at which Trinity was outbid, and it is now in the Schøyen Collection. The missing Latin Bible is in St Columb's College, Derry, having been donated by Sir

[45] *Ibid.* These bills are transcribed in O'Sullivan, 'Eighteenth century rebinding', note 43 above.

[46] O'Sullivan, 'Introduction', note 42 above; P. G. Stanwood, 'The Richard Hooker manuscripts', *Long Room*, 11 (Spring/Summer 1975), 7–10.

[47] C. B. Roberts, 'The Slavonic Calvinist reading primer in Trinity College Library', *Long Room*, 28/29 (1984), 7–14.

[48] Raymond Gillespie, 'Manuscript collectors in the age of Marsh', in *Marsh's Library*, note 5 above, pp. 234–50.

[49] John Scattergood, *Manuscripts and ghosts: essays on the transmission of medieval and early Renaissance literature* (Dublin: Four Courts Press, 2006), p. 156; E. St John Brooks, 'The *Piers Plowman* manuscripts in Trinity College Dublin', *The Library*, 5th ser., 6 (1951), 141–53.

[50] MS 7/1, fol. 1r.

Edward Reid in 1901. Where it spent the intervening years is not known.[51] Anthony Raymond, a former Fellow, borrowed the Book of Ballymote in 1720, when he embarked upon a project to revise Geoffrey Keating's history of Ireland. He died in 1726 and it is unclear what became of the manuscript until the Chevalier O'Gorman presented it to the Royal Irish Academy in 1785.[52] Judging from the descriptions of some of the 'books' stolen by the sculls in 1715 (for example, 'a small book of celebrating the Mass in French'), some of those were probably also manuscripts.[53]

Given the chaotic state of the Library over the previous decades, it is hardly surprising not only that losses were suffered but also that manuscripts noted as missing in 1702 were subsequently found. Lyon annotated the list in Foley's catalogue, by crossing through those no longer missing and added a note of 'Manuscripts wanting in 1742'.[54] Among those found at this time were two leaves from the Book of Kells that had been recorded as missing in the sixteenth century, long before it passed into Trinity's possession.[55]

After Edward Hudson's resignation as Librarian in 1740, Lyon took over responsibility for supervising the binding of the printed books as well as the manuscripts and his name appears on bills from Joseph Leathley in 1743–4. The work for which Lyon had originally been employed was concluded by the end of 1747, when he received a payment of £40 'in full of manuscript and pamphlet catalogues'.[56] He was brought back a few years later to catalogue some charters in the Manuscripts Room, for which he was paid a further £40.[57]

Settling the books and manuscripts into the new building, binding and cataloguing them, and assimilating the new collections, dominated the Library's activities during the 1730s and 1740s and little was spent on the purchase of books. In 1736, William Williams was paid £6 18s. 0d. for his *Oxonia depicta*, Hudson bought some volumes of Hippocrates and Galen in 1737, and several titles were bought in 1748.[58] In 1735, John Hall, who

---

[51] Bernard Meehan, 'Lost and found: a stray of the thirteenth century from Trinity College Library', in *Essays*, pp. 116–19.

[52] Robert Atkinson, ed., *The Book of Ballymote . . . published from the original manuscript in the library of the Royal Irish Academy* (Dublin: Royal Irish Academy, 1887).

[53] MUN/LIB/10/32.   [54] MS 7/1, fol. 1r.

[55] Bernard Meehan, *The Book of Kells: an illustrated introduction to the manuscript in Trinity College Dublin* (London: Thames and Hudson, 1994), p. 92.

[56] MUN/V/57/3, December quarter 1747.   [57] MUN/V/5/3, 10 May 1755.

[58] MUN/V/57/2, September quarter 1736, March quarter 1737; MUN/V/57/3, September quarter 1748.

had been Baldwin's predecessor as Vice-Provost, left £100 to buy books for the Library.[59]

During this period Jonathan Swift made concerted attempts to obtain for the Library the manuscripts collected by Sir James Ware. They had been bought by Henry Hyde, Earl of Clarendon, in 1686 when he was Lord Lieutenant of Ireland and they subsequently passed into the hands of the Duke of Chandos. Swift wrote to Chandos in 1734 asking him to donate the papers, saying 'they can be of no use in England'.[60] Having received no reply, Swift asked Mary Pendarves, the later Mrs Delany, to persuade her uncle, Lord Lansdowne, to intercede, but to no avail. In 1738 he tried again, this time with the Earl of Orrery, but this attempt was no more successful. The papers remained with Chandos until his death and were sold in 1747.[61] Most are now in the Bodleian's Rawlinson Collection and at the British Library. Although Ware was an illustrious early student of the College, the Library possesses very few of his manuscripts. What it does hold includes: a notebook (MS 664) which had belonged to John Madden and came with the Stearne manuscripts; a copy of Keating's history of Ireland (MS 1403) bought by the Library at the Sotheby's sale of Archbishop Tenison's library in 1861; a fifteenth-century text of the English chronicle known as the Brut (MS 5895) bought in 1972; and a notebook (MS 6404) bought in 1974.[62]

---

[59] *DU Calendar*, 1858, p. 248.

[60] Harold Williams, ed., *The correspondence of Jonathan Swift*, 5 vols. (Oxford: Clarendon Press, 1963–5), vol. IV, p. 250.

[61] *Ibid.*, vol. IV, p. 259; vol. V, p. 90.

[62] William O'Sullivan, 'A finding list of Sir James Ware's manuscripts', *Proc. RIA*, C97 (1997), 69–99; Geoffrey Keating, *The history of Ireland*, ed. by David Comyn and Patrick S. Dinneen, 4 vols. (London: Irish Texts Society, 1902–14), vol. II, pp. xxvii–xxix; 'Accessions: manuscripts accessions during the year 1972', *Long Room*, 8 (Autumn/Winter 1973), 43.

6 | The Library in 1750

In 1750, Trinity possessed one of the largest and finest academic library buildings in Europe. The sense of awe that the eighteenth-century visitor would have experienced on entering the Long Room is evoked by James Malton in the description that accompanied his print (see Plate 4): 'we are instantly struck with unspeakable reverence and respect for the place; as if feeling the air impregnated with an emanation of religion and learning... 'tis scarcely possible for the most boisterous and unthinking to enter, but with silent humiliation and whispering enquiry'.[1]

The room contained between 35,000 and 40,000 volumes, most of them in the Ussher, Palliser and Gilbert collections housed on the south side. Books on the north side were more sparse and many of the shelves were still empty. The busts on display in 1750 were the fourteen bought from the Gilbert bequest and the Roubiliac of Swift. Because of the fear of fire there was no heat or artificial light in the Long Room itself, though there were fire-places in the pavilion rooms which, apart from the Librarian's Room, were still used for academic purposes. The fireplaces were obviously used, as the accounts record regular payments for coal.

Externally the building had not changed since it was completed, but the quality of some of the stone was proving to be less than satisfactory. The brickwork which formed the walls was faced on the upper floors with sandstone from Scrabo, in County Down, and in places this had begun to flake. The traveller and antiquary Richard Pococke, visiting in 1752, speculated that this could have been caused by salt water affecting the stone during its journey to Dublin.[2] Repairs to this stonework were not carried out for several more decades.

Since its foundation, the Library's collection had grown principally through donations and bequests, and in 1750 this was still the case, with little attention being given to developing it in any sort of systematic way. In this respect, Trinity was little different from its two sister universities in

---

[1] James Malton, *A picturesque and descriptive view of the city of Dublin* [London, 1799].
[2] MS 887 ('Dr. Pocockes Irish Tour 1752'); John McVeigh, ed., *Richard Pococke's Irish tours* (Blackrock: Irish Academic Press, 1995), p. 36.

England, and in all three institutions the first half of the eighteenth century had been a period of generous benefactions. Those in Dublin have been noted. In Oxford, the Bodleian received the manuscripts and printed books of Thomas Tanner, All Souls the bequest of Christopher Codrington and Christ Church the libraries of Archbishop Wake and Charles Boyle, fourth Earl of Orrery. Cambridge University Library was given the spectacular collection of books and manuscripts that had been assembled by John Moore, Bishop of Ely, a collection roughly twice the size of the University Library itself at the time of acquisition.[3]

Oxford and Cambridge, unlike Trinity, had funds whose income was specifically earmarked for the purchase of books, but they were no larger than the sums provided by Trinity's College Board as the need arose. Between 1750 and 1780 the Bodleian's main fund for books produced an income of about £10 a year and that at Cambridge around £30, though both libraries received occasional monetary bequests and could call on other sources of funds when necessary. The two university libraries were spending considerably less on acquisitions than their more affluent colleges and less than Edinburgh University Library, where various fees and deposits ensured an income of around £250 a year for the purchase of books. The application of the Copyright Act to the English and Scottish universities theoretically placed them at an advantage over Trinity by providing them with new British publications, but it was so ineffectually administered that the libraries received only about thirty or forty titles a year by this means.[4]

The 1734 statutes had abolished the requirement for an annual election of Trinity's Librarian, but the tradition of including him in the appointment of College officers at the Board meeting on 20 November continued. The office of Librarian was one of several that were considered to form part of the Fellows' perks, to be reallocated each November. It was normal for Fellows to hold more than one office at a time and for those to be shuffled regularly. In the 50 years between the resignation of Edward Hudson in 1740 and the election of John Barrett in 1791, no less than twenty men filled the office of Librarian, some more than once, most for just a year or even less, and only three (Thomas Leland, John Lawson and Henry Dabzac) for a period of more than four consecutive years.

[3] Charles Benson, 'Libraries in university towns', in *Cambridge history*, vol. II, pp. 102–21.
[4] Ian Philip, *The Bodleian Library in the seventeenth and eighteenth centuries* (Oxford: Clarendon Press, 1983), pp. 103–4; McKitterick, pp. 349–50; C. P. Finlayson and S. M. Simpson, 'The history of the Library 1710–1837', in Jean R. Guild and Alexander Law, eds., *Edinburgh University Library 1580–1980: a collection of historical essays* (Edinburgh: University Library, 1982), pp. 55–66.

At the beginning of the century, the salary of the Librarian had been £8 a year, in addition to the £10 he was paid as a Junior Fellow. In 1722, the rates were each increased to £15 as part of a general rise in the salaries of College officers.[5] An element of caution is needed, however, when attempting to assess the precise salary of any member of the College staff, as throughout the eighteenth and part of the nineteenth centuries each received, in addition to their 'official' salary, an aggregate of income from a range of different sources, including tutorial, lecture and examination fees and payments for preaching.[6] In the case of the Librarian, further additional payments were also made for specific work such as cataloguing. After 1734, the salary of the Librarian had increased from £15 to £60, and in 1752 the Board exercised the discretion it had been given under the statutes to increase it again, this time to £100, at which sum it remained until the introduction of new regulations in 1817.[7] This meant that in the second half of the eighteenth century the Librarianship was one of the more lucrative College offices, at least as far as the 'official' salary was concerned. In 1766, for example, the salary of the Bursar was £50, while the Registrar earned £63, a professor £100, the Vice-Provost £200 and the Provost £800.[8]

Until the early eighteenth century, the staff had consisted solely of the Librarian and a porter, with a cleaning woman or maid added from the 1740s. Temporary help was provided by graduates or Junior Fellows when required, such as to compile catalogues of printed books and manuscripts following the move into the new building. However, there was no permanent assistant. The term was used for the first time in 1742, when John Lyon was chosen as 'Assistant' for his work on the manuscripts, and it must by then have been obvious that the Librarian could no longer manage the demands of the large new building single-handedly.[9] From 20 November 1743, the Board Register regularly records the appointment of the 'Assistant to the Librarian' at the annual election of College officers, but the first indication of his salary appears in the entry for 1746, when it was noted as £30 a year, at which figure it remained until 1817.[10] The Assistant Librarian was always a Junior Fellow, and from 1743 the Librarian was almost invariably elected from among the Senior Fellows, possibly in order to maintain his seniority over the Assistant, but no doubt also because the Senior Fellows ensured that they derived the income from the more lucrative College offices. The Assistant was required to be present during the Library's opening hours of

---

[5] MUN/V/5/2, 12 October 1722.   [6] McDowell and Webb, p. 511.
[7] MUN/V/57/2, March quarter 1735; MUN/V/5/3, 20 November 1752.
[8] MUN/V/57/4, March quarter 1766.   [9] MUN/V/5/3, 1 December 1742.
[10] MUN/V/57/3, December quarter 1746.

8–10 a.m. and 2–4 p.m. At the November Board meeting one of the Junior Fellows was also appointed as the Keeper of Sir Jerome Alexander's library, at a salary of £7 10s. 0d. This was not part of the College Library and by the mid eighteenth century its role – even its existence – is obscure.

Use of the main Library was restricted to those who had taken their BA degree and sworn the Library oath. That required them to handle the books with care, not to remove them from the Library and to report anyone offending against the regulations.[11] The entitlement of Fellows to introduce 'strangers' was exercised occasionally, as in the case of Leland for scholars wishing to use the Irish manuscripts, but the number of men who could use the Library by right was not large. There were about twenty Fellows, of whom seven were the Senior Fellows, who formed the Board and ran the College, and the rest were the Junior Fellows, who did most of the teaching. Many of the hundred or so students who graduated each year stayed on as resident BAs to prepare for ordination or the bar, and a few sat the examination for a Fellowship. Having taken their BA, they were allowed access to the Library, whilst undergraduates were not. However, given the narrow range of the curriculum, which was based essentially on prescribed textbooks, this probably mattered little to most undergraduates. The restriction was not unique to Trinity. Most students at Oxford and Cambridge were also deprived of access to a library; those studying for their BA were excluded from both Cambridge University Library and the Bodleian, although one or two colleges, such as Trinity in Cambridge, had libraries for their own undergraduates.[12]

A register was maintained from 1737 listing those admitted to the Library, but it simply indicates their names and the date of their first admission.[13] In the absence of any docket system, there are no records showing how much use was actually made of the books in the Library, though a German visitor, noting the apparent ease with which 'strangers' were granted access, commented with approval that the Library was open every day 'and, what is more, it is used!'.[14]

The statutes of 1734 had abolished the right of any users, even Fellows, to borrow books. This brought Trinity into line with Oxford, but distanced it from Cambridge, where members of the Senate and Bachelors of Law and Physic had borrowing rights. Perhaps because of closer municipal involvement in the running of the Scottish universities, a different attitude towards

---

[11] See Appendix 3.   [12] McKitterick, pp. 608–9.   [13] MUN/LIB/6/1.
[14] K. G. Küttner, *Briefe über Irland an seinen Freund, den Herausgeber* (Leipzig: J. P. Haugs Wittwe, 1785), p. 163.

the library and its use prevailed there. In Edinburgh, undergraduates were not only admitted to the University Library, but were also allowed to borrow from it. In Dublin there is no evidence that the Board departed from the statutes as far as lending books is concerned, though the injunction that no one 'shall . . . carry any book out of the Library' seems to have been interpreted literally as referring only to printed books, as they did occasionally allow manuscripts to be borrowed.[15]

Responsibility for supervising the Library and its Librarian resided directly with the Board of the College and not with an intermediate authority such as the Curators of the Bodleian, a body which had existed from the earliest days of Oxford's library, or the Library Syndicate, which was established in Cambridge in 1751. The Trinity statutes required the Board to inspect the Library each October, but there is no record of whether this injunction was carried out during the eighteenth century. It was only from 1799 that the Board minutes started to note the 'Library Visitation', though no further information was provided until the 1830s.

---

[15]   Robert Bolton, *A translation of the charter and statutes of Trinity-College, Dublin. Together with the Library-statutes* (Dublin: Nelson, 1749), p. 125.

Despite the revision of the statutes, it remained the norm throughout the eighteenth century for the Librarian to be elected along with the other College officers on 20 November each year. Some, like Thomas Leland, held office for several consecutive years, but annual changes of office-holder were still common. In the 1760s the lack of clarity between the old ways and the new led to a dispute about who actually *was* the Librarian. Theaker Wilder, Regius Professor of Greek, was elected in November 1762 and again the following November. In March 1764 he was given leave of absence for 3 years and relinquished his Chair, but continued to be paid as Librarian until November 1765. At that point, no doubt preferring to have a Librarian who was actually present in the College, the Board elected one of the Junior Fellows, Thomas Wilson. Wilson was in turn replaced by William Andrews a year later.[1] In March 1767 Wilder's leave of absence was extended for a further 3 years but, undaunted by the fact that he would have been an absentee Librarian for 6 years, he protested to the Board that the election of Wilson and Andrews had been in contravention of the statutes, which stated that an election should not take place each year, but only when the post was vacant. He argued that he had not resigned and was therefore still in post, and would not resign unless found guilty of breaches specified in the statutes. The Board ignored his objection, but he insisted that a note to its effect was inserted into the register.[2] Given the lack of commitment to the post by many of the office-holders, it is hardly surprising that there is little evidence of much activity in the Library during this period except when an energetic and enthusiastic Librarian such as Hudson or Leland held office.

Irish manuscripts

The second half of the eighteenth century was marked, particularly in Dublin, by a growing interest in Irish language, literature and history. Irish

[1] MUN/V/5/3, 1762–7 *passim*; MUN/V/57/4, 1762–5.   [2] MUN/V/5/3, 3 June 1767.

manuscripts were collected and transcribed and societies to promote the study of Irish culture were founded, of which the Royal Irish Academy, established in 1785, was to become the most celebrated. The members of Trinity College and, increasingly, its Library, played a significant role in these developments. The Provost and sixteen Fellows were numbered among the founder members of the Academy, along with politicians, Church of Ireland bishops and clergy, and antiquaries such as Charles Vallancey and Charles O'Conor. The library of the Academy is now considered to have the finest collection of early Irish manuscripts in the world, but for the first half-century of its existence it possessed only a handful, and its Irish collection did not rival that of Trinity until the late nineteenth century. In the 1750s, however, even the College's collection was small, consisting principally of the few Irish manuscripts in the Ussher library and those from the gift of John Stearne, but within 30 years it was pre-eminent in the field, thanks principally to the work of Thomas Leland.

A Fellow from 1746, Leland served as the Assistant Librarian for a year from November 1751. He was Librarian for a short spell in 1761 and then again for most of the period from 1768 to 1781, a post he held simultaneously with the Chair of Oratory. During his initial period of office as Librarian he was responsible for Trinity's first recorded purchase of 'an Irish manuscript' for the not inconsiderable sum of £5 13s. 9d, and in 1766, even though he was not Librarian at the time, he persuaded the College to spend over £140 on Irish manuscripts.[3] These came from three sources.

The first was the sale on 3 February of the library of John Fergus, a Dublin doctor who had assembled a fine collection, not just of medical books but also of Latin and Greek texts and books on Irish history. But it was his Irish manuscripts, of which the sale catalogue listed thirty-seven, that attracted Leland's interest.[4] They included manuscripts that are now some of the most important in the Library: the Annals of Ulster (MS 1282), one of the main primary sources for medieval Irish history covering the period from St Patrick to the early sixteenth century; the Annals of Loch Cé (MS 1293), another sixteenth-century manuscript, in which the narrative begins with the Battle of Clontarf in 1014; and the Annals of the Four Masters (MS 1301), a chronicle of medieval Ireland compiled in the seventeenth century, primarily from earlier annals. The first two together cost £18 and the last

---

[3] MUN/V/57/4, June quarter 1761, March and June quarters 1766.

[4] *Catalogue of the libraries of John Fergus, M.D. and Son, both deceased* (Dublin: For L. Flin, 1766); Diarmaid Ó Catháin, 'John Fergus MD: eighteenth-century doctor, book collector and Irish scholar', *JRSAI*, 118 (1988), 139–62; Abbott and Gwynn, pp. xi–xiv.

£7 19s. 0d.[5] The other manuscript items that Leland bought at this sale were mainly grammars or dictionaries.

The second of the collections from which Leland made purchases in 1766 was that of Francis Stoughton Sullivan, Trinity's first Regius Professor of Feudal and English Law, who had died that year. Sullivan's great interest in early Irish sources extended to an enthusiasm for producing critical editions, and he donated manuscripts to the College throughout his lifetime, purchasing what he could and employing scribes to copy others. The Library now contains at least fifteen documents transcribed for Sullivan by Aodh Ó Dálaigh (Hugh O'Daly) and several more written by the scribe Muiris Ó Gormáin. According to his friend Charles O'Conor, Sullivan intended to leave the rest of his manuscripts to the College Library, but he died suddenly at the age of 50 without, apparently, leaving a will.[6] His library was sold at auction 2 months after his death. The sale catalogue lists only his printed books, but Trinity paid the auctioneer, Michael Duggan, £110 17s. 0½d. in June that year, almost certainly for a private sale of the Irish manuscripts.[7]

The third of Leland's sources was Muiris Ó Gormáin. One of the Irish medical manuscripts in the Fergus sale which was marked down to 'Mr Gorman' was subsequently bought by Leland for the College and is now probably MS 1333. In 1766–7, Ó Gormáin was employed to catalogue the newly acquired manuscripts from the Fergus and Sullivan sales, and the following year he sold a further six Irish manuscripts to the Library for £6 16s. 6d.[8] In 1776, the Library bought another two Irish manuscripts, probably MSS 1281 and 1292 (containing the Annals of Tigernach), from the Catholic Bishop of Cloyne and Ross, John O'Brien.[9]

Leland's own research, which culminated in the publication of his *History of Ireland from the invasion of Henry II* (Dublin, 1773),[10] has not been highly regarded by later historians but he played an important role in promoting the study of Irish history and culture through his development of the College's collection of Irish manuscripts and his friendship and support for others

---

[5] RIA MS 24.E.7 contains a list of the 'Irish books' in the Fergus sale, with the names of their buyers and the prices fetched. See also William M. Hennessey and B. MacCarthy, eds., *Annals of Ulster*, 4 vols. (Dublin: HMSO, 1887–1901).

[6] C. O'Conor, *Dissertations on the history of Ireland* (Dublin: Faulkner, 1766), p. xiv.

[7] *A catalogue of books consisting of miscellanies, canon, civil, and common law to be sold by auction by Michael Duggan. Being the library of Francis Stoughton Sullivan, LLD, lately deceased* (Dublin, 1766); MUN/V/57/4, June quarter 1766.

[8] MUN/V/57/4, March quarter 1768.

[9] MUN/V/57/5, June quarter 1776; William O'Sullivan, 'The Irish manuscripts in Case H in Trinity College Dublin catalogued by Matthew Young in 1781', *Celtica*, 11 (1976), 229–50.

[10] Thomas Leland, *The history of Ireland from the invasion of Henry II*, 3 vols. (Dublin: Moncrieffe, 1773).

engaged in Irish studies. This circle included his Trinity colleague Francis Sullivan, the Catholic polemicists Charles O'Conor and John Curry and the antiquaries Charles Vallancey and Thomas 'The Chevalier' O'Gorman, with encouragement and assistance coming from his Trinity contemporary and close friend Edmund Burke. At Leland's request, the Board allowed O'Conor, Vallancey and O'Gorman to use the College Library and its manuscripts, and even to borrow them.[11]

Leland, Vallancey and O'Conor served on a standing committee set up in 1772 by the Dublin Society to try to locate Irish manuscripts and have them copied. The first meetings of the committee were held in the College Library, with Sir Lucius O'Brien, a leading member of the Irish House of Commons, as Chairman. The committee's minutes book contains a list of manuscripts in the possession of its members, as well as those 'lately added' to Trinity's collection, the whole of which Vallancey proposed to examine and catalogue, on the grounds that many 'bear false titles'.[12]

The first external member of Leland's circle to be admitted to the Library was Charles O'Conor from Belanagare, County Roscommon. A pamphleteer, Catholic activist and historian, O'Conor published the revised edition of his *Dissertations on the antient history of Ireland* in 1766 and this established him as the foremost authority on Irish antiquities.[13] His name appears in the readers' admission book the following year.[14] O'Conor recognised and appreciated the special treatment that he was receiving, writing on more than one occasion to George Faulkner that through Leland's friendship, 'I was made free of the College Library' and had access to the College manuscripts 'notwithstanding the strictness of the university statutes'.[15] Even when he was not in office, Leland made special arrangements for the then Librarian, Richard Murray, to be present outside the normal opening hours to facilitate O'Conor:

If it should suit your convenience to go into the Library next week, Doctor Murray has desired me to assure you that on Tuesday, Thursday and Saturday, from eleven to one, everything shall be made agreeable to you . . . For he supposes, and so do

---

[11] MUN/LIB/6/1.

[12] RIA MS 24.E.7; Toby Barnard, 'The Dublin Society and other improving societies, 1731–85', in James Kelly and Martyn J. Powell, eds., *Clubs and societies in eighteenth-century Ireland* (Dublin: Four Courts, 2010), pp. 53–88.

[13] Walter D. Love, 'Charles O'Conor of Belanagare and Thomas Leland's "philosophical" history of Ireland', *Irish Historical Studies*, 13 (1962), 1–25; Diarmaid Ó Catháin, 'Charles O'Conor of Belanagare: antiquary and Irish scholar', *JRSAI*, 119 (1989), 136–63.

[14] MUN/LIB/6/1, p. 41.   [15] BL MS Egerton 201, fols. 47 and 45.

I, that from eight to ten would be too early, especially when I am not in the way to make breakfast for you.[16]

O'Conor was fulsome in his praise of Leland for acquiring the Fergus manuscripts, noting in his *Dissertations* that they had been added to the Library and commenting: 'nor must the particular attention of Dr. Leland, to this point, be concealed; as it was to his care we owe it, that these old original chronicles have not again fallen into private hands'.[17]

By the 1760s it was well known that Leland was working on his history of Ireland. O'Conor was helping him with the documents in Irish and others were seeking material for him. It was in this context that Edmund Burke, who had noticed some Irish manuscripts on a visit to his friend Sir John Sebright, at his home in Hertfordshire, persuaded their owner to lend him two volumes, so that he could send them to Leland. In December 1769, Leland reported to O'Conor that he had just received from London the two volumes from Sebright's collection, though he mistakenly thought that they were from the manuscripts belonging to the Duke of Chandos that Swift had tried in vain to acquire for the Library 30 years earlier.[18] Leland asked O'Conor to decipher them for him, and the following March he told Burke that they were 'before O'Connor, and in a little time I shall be able to send you a particular account of their contents, which, it seems, are new and curious'.[19] However, despite his considerable linguistic skill, O'Conor was unable to make very much of them and they were passed to Major Charles Vallancey, who identified their content as 'extracts of the ancient Irish laws'.[20]

Charles Vallancey, born in Flanders of French Huguenot parents, had moved to Ireland from England in 1762 as a military engineer and, though he worked on the Irish coastal defences, was much more interested in the country's ancient past. His claims that Irish civilisation and the Irish language had oriental origins were viewed with derision in the nineteenth century, but his pioneering work in Irish studies has been regarded more sympathetically in recent years.[21] He made considerable use of the two

---

[16] Leland to O'Conor, 8 March 1771, RIA MS B.1.2.   [17] O'Conor, note 6 above, p. xiii.

[18] Leland to O'Conor, 9 December 1769, RIA MS B.1.2.

[19] Charles William, Earl Fitzwilliam, and Richard Bourke, eds., *Correspondence of the Right Honourable Edmund Burke between the year 1744 and the period of his decease, in 1797*, 4 vols. (London: Rivington, 1844), vol. I, p. 223.

[20] Leland, *History*, note 10 above, vol. I, p. xxvii. The manuscripts, one of which was later divided into two volumes, are now MSS 1316–18.

[21] Monica Nevin, 'General Charles Vallancey, 1725–1812', *JRSAI*, 123 (1993) 19–58; Walter D. Love, 'Edmund Burke, Charles Vallancey and the Sebright manuscripts', *Hermathena*, 105 (1961), 21–35.

Sebright manuscripts in the early volumes of his *Collectanea de rebus Hibernicis* (Dublin, 1770–1804) and held on to them until about 1777, when he delivered them to Burke, to be returned to their owner. Knowing that there were more Irish manuscripts in Sebright's possession, Vallancey tried to gain access to these, too, so that he could publish more, thinking that they all contained similar legal material to those that he had already seen. However, in this he was initially thwarted because Burke had neglected to send back the first two manuscripts and Sebright refused to part with more until he had received them.[22] Burke finally returned the manuscripts and, rather than *lend* more of them, Sebright decided to *donate* his collection to Trinity. This news was conveyed to the Chevalier O'Gorman by William Burton Conyngham on his return from seeing Sebright. Conyngham, a member of the Dublin Society who had recently inherited a fortune from his uncle, was to become a munificent patron of antiquarian research in Ireland and another founder member of the Royal Irish Academy. O'Gorman relayed the news that Sebright was planning to send his Irish manuscripts 'as a present to the Colledge of Dublin for the use of the nation' and hoped that others with similar collections would do likewise.[23] He suggested to Sir Lucius O'Brien that the Dublin Society should take on this somewhat unrealistic proposal, relaying Conyngham's hopes that various English libraries would 'follow so laudable an example' by transferring their Irish manuscripts, so that they could be made accessible 'to the literati in general' through the publications of the Society.[24]

As users of the College Library, O'Conor and Vallancey were both aware of the constraints that would be placed on access to the manuscripts once they had been received in Trinity, and O'Conor expressed the wish that Conyngham would retain them for a while 'before they are laid up or rather interred in the Manuscript Library of our College'.[25] Vallancey took the matter further and wrote directly to Sebright, receiving the reply that he could study the manuscripts for as long as he 'thought proper, before they were to all eternity immured'.[26]

Rather than being sent directly to the College, therefore, the manuscripts were first conveyed to Vallancey, who recorded in number 12 of his *Collectanea*, published in June 1783, that they were now in his hands. In number 10, published the previous year and dedicated to Sebright, he noted

[22] Vallancey to O'Conor, 23 February 1781, RIA MS B.1.2.
[23] O'Gorman to O'Conor, 19 July 1781, RIA MS B.1.2
[24] O'Gorman to O'Brien, 12 July 1781, RIA MS 24.D.18.
[25] O'Conor to O'Gorman, 25 July 1781, BL MS Add. 21121.
[26] Sebright to Vallancey, 16 December 1782, MS 1316/1, fol. iii.

their intended donation, but commented that 'much time may yet elapse before they are deposited in the library of our University'.[27] Indeed, he kept them for 3 years before passing them on to the College and it was not until 31 October 1786 that the Library minute book could record: 'Rec^d from the Vice Provost and lodged in the MS. room a box of MSS. said to be a present to this College from Sir John Sebright'.[28]

It was the acquisition of the Sebright manuscripts that established Trinity's Irish holdings as a collection of major importance. They had been collected half a century earlier by Edward Lhuyd, a Welsh antiquary who shared the interest of contemporaries like Ware in the history of the Celtic languages and literatures. Between 1696 and 1701 he toured parts of Wales, Scotland, Ireland and Brittany, staying in Dublin to examine the few Irish manuscripts then in the College Library and those in the possession of Archbishop Marsh, and he published the results of his work in *Archaeologia Britannica* (Oxford, 1707). He was Keeper of the Ashmolean Museum, and died in his room there, owing considerable debts to the University of Oxford. His books and manuscripts were seized, but neither his college, Jesus, nor the Bodleian Library would buy them, and in 1716 the manuscripts relating to Celtic antiquities were sold for £80 to Sir Thomas Saunders Sebright, from whom they passed to his son, John, and eventually to Trinity.[29]

Most of the manuscripts are composite volumes, consisting of several, often unrelated, texts that Lhuyd had had bound together. In some cases he even had paper and vellum manuscripts and documents of different sizes bound into the same volume. His interests were primarily archaeological and philological, and the texts in his collection encompass literary and linguistic sources, including many grammars and dictionaries. Those that he prized most highly, however, were the manuscripts containing legal texts. Many of these 'brehon law' documents date from the fifteenth and sixteenth centuries, but the texts they contain are witnesses to the Irish legal tradition of the seventh to ninth centuries, including the great collection of tracts known as the *Seanchas Már* (MS 1316). Such was the importance of Lhuyd's legal manuscripts that they formed the bulk of those transcribed and published from 1865 onwards by the Brehon Law Commissioners.[30]

---

27 *Collectanea de rebus Hibernicis*, no. 10 (1782), p. v, and no. 12 (1783), p. liv.
28 MUN/LIB/2/1.
29 E. G. Quin, 'Edward Lhuyd in Ireland', *Annual Bulletin* (1951), 7–10; Anne and William O'Sullivan, 'Edward Lhuyd's collection of Irish manuscripts', *Transactions of the Honourable Society of Cymmrodorion* (1962), 57–76.
30 *Ancient laws of Ireland*, published under the direction of the Commissioners for Publishing the Ancient Laws and Institutions of Ireland, 6 vols. (Dublin: A. Thom, 1865–1901).

Lhuyd recognised their significance but failed to appreciate that the literary materials in his collection were of comparable importance. MS 1318, a composite manuscript dating mostly from the fourteenth century and known as the Yellow Book of Lecan after the title of a small part of it, was assembled by Lhuyd from individual documents collected during his travels. He had these bound together on his return to Oxford. Though it 'owns no unity save that of the binder', it contains the text of many of the ancient Irish tales, in some cases in the only known copy.[31] In particular, it is a major source of stories from the Ulster cycle, such as the *Táin Bó Cúailnge*. The Tinnakill *Duanaire* (MS 1340), an early seventeenth-century manuscript, contains eighty-three poems, many of them unique, and is one of the most important sources for bardic religious verse.[32] Of equal importance as a literary source, but even more so for its historical information, is the twelfth-century Book of Leinster or *Leabhar na Núachongbála* (MS 1339).[33] This great manuscript of over four hundred pages contains texts of early tales, learned verse, lists of rulers of Ireland and its provinces, historical and pseudo-historical narratives and a mass of genealogies. It has been described as 'a monument to the twelfth-century Irish view of the country's past, and a library of sources for many different aspects of that past'.[34] The Sebright collection also included three of the notebooks from Lhuyd's Irish and Scottish tour and drafts for his *Archaeologia*.

John Lyon's comprehensive rearrangement of the College manuscripts in 1742 had filled cases A to G in the Manuscripts Room. New acquisitions were placed in the next available case, H, and in 1781 these were catalogued by Matthew Young, a Fellow who had entered Trinity in 1766, the year of the great accession of Irish manuscripts. Though his later career took him into the sciences as Professor of Natural and Experimental Philosophy, Young maintained his interest in Irish studies, becoming another of the founder members of the Royal Irish Academy and contributing to the first volume of its *Transactions*. In 1799, he resigned his Chair, on appointment to the see of Clonfert, but died the following year. No doubt in order to assist his widow, the Board decided to buy his papers for £600, but when they arrived the Vice-Provost, Gerald Fitzgerald, objected to the purchase on the grounds that they were 'less perfect than he at first supposed them to

[31] Robert Atkinson, ed., *The Yellow Book of Lecan* (Dublin: Royal Irish Academy, 1896), p. 1; William O'Sullivan, 'Ciothruadh's Yellow Book of Lecan', *Éigse*, 18 (1981), 177–81.

[32] Anne O'Sullivan, 'The Tinnakill Duanaire', *Celtica*, 11 (1976) 214–28.

[33] R. I. Best, O. Bergin and M. A. O'Brien, eds., *The Book of Leinster: formerly Lebar na Núachongbála* , 6 vols. (Dublin: Institute for Advanced Studies, 1954–83).

[34] Gearóid Mac Niocaill, 'The Irish-language manuscripts', in *Treasures*, pp. 57–66 (p. 60).

be'.[35] They remained in the Provost's library until 1845, when they were transferred to the Manuscripts Room.[36] The Young papers now comprise five volumes (MS 950) and four large boxes (MS 949), and it seems most likely that they arrived in two tranches, the first shortly after his death and the second in 1856, when the Library's annual report recorded the donation of papers of 'the late Bishop Young' by Robert Jager, his son-in-law.[37] These were placed in boxes, because they could not be bound, as they contained both memorandum books and loose papers. The boxes contain mainly his scientific writings, but also his catalogue of the Irish manuscripts, which came to light only in the 1970s.[38]

Young listed forty manuscripts in case H, and in 1786 the Sebright volumes were added to them. These arrived in the Library without a list of contents, and so one of Young's pupils, Theophilus O'Flanagan, was set to work to make one. He produced a rough list of forty-six manuscripts, of which about forty can still be identified as having belonged to Lhuyd, but inconsistencies between O'Flanagan's list and entries in later catalogues make it difficult to be sure about the others.[39]

A native Irish speaker, O'Flanagan entered Trinity in 1784 and over the following years developed a considerable reputation as an Irish scholar. He transcribed manuscripts for others, including the Chevalier O'Gorman, and shortly before the arrival of the Sebright manuscripts he was allowed by the Board to borrow the Annals of Tigernach for the purpose of translation and publication.[40] At the behest of Vallancey, he also received a grant of £100 from the Royal Irish Academy to translate the brehon laws among the Sebright papers, a project which came to nought.[41]

Vallancey remained closely involved with both the Royal Irish Academy and the College Library until his death in 1812. He continued to complain about the restrictions on access to Trinity's manuscripts, writing in 1812 that they 'remain untouched, except the small part, given in my Collectanea. Imprisoned forever, as they are, in the manuscript closet of Trinity College, it is more than probable they will never be perused'.[42] This was ungenerous,

---

[35] MUN/V/5/5, 20 December 1800, 9 May 1801; MUN/LIB/11/7/3.
[36] MUN/V/5/8, 15 November 1845. [37] MUN/LIB/17/13.
[38] The catalogue (MS 949/4, No. I, transcribed in O'Sullivan, 'Irish manuscripts', note 9 above) also includes a list of the Sebright manuscripts.
[39] The list is now MS 1945/13a. See also O'Sullivan, 'Edward Lhuyd's collection', note 29 above.
[40] MUN/V/5/5, 13 May 1786.
[41] R. B. McDowell, 'The main narrative', in T. Ó Raifeartaigh, ed., *The Royal Irish Academy: a bicentennial history, 1785–1985* (Dublin: Royal Irish Academy, 1985), pp. 1–92.
[42] Charles Vallancey, *An account of the ancient stone amphitheatre lately discovered in the County of Kerry* (Dublin: Graisberry and Campbell, 1812), p. 59.

given that he had first been admitted to use the Library in 1772, and within a year the Board had allowed him to borrow the Book of Aicill, a volume of the brehon laws (MS 1433).[43] In 1774, with Leland's support, he had requested more manuscripts and the Board again agreed, on the grounds that his work would be 'of general utility, and a credit to the kingdom'.[44] Further manuscripts were loaned to him during the 1770s and 1780s.[45] Whilst in Paris in 1787 he persuaded the Irish College there to give up its copy of the Book of Lecan, taken from Trinity during the Jacobite occupation of 1689–90, but on his return to Ireland he presented it to the Academy, not to its former owner. Trinity did, however, derive some benefit from Vallancey's generosity. In 1784, he donated to the College a large oil painting depicting the Battle of Kinsale, which, according to George Faulkner, he had bought in London.[46] The picture was originally hung in the College Museum but was moved to the Library in the nineteenth century, no doubt because of its association with the story that the English soldiers had donated money for the Library after the battle in 1601. Vallancey's financial situation was at times precarious, and in 1792 he put some of his collection of books and manuscripts up for sale through the bookseller Bernard Dornin. The College paid £26 12s. 2½d. for forty-two volumes of printed books and six Irish manuscripts.[47]

The strange case of Henry Flood's will was nearly the cause of a further, potentially substantial, addition to the Library's collection of Irish manuscripts. Flood, a former attorney-general, died in 1791 leaving most of his estate, valued at £4,000 a year, to Trinity to establish a Chair of Irish and to purchase Irish books and manuscripts. The bequest became a cause célèbre in the public press, and it was reported that schoolmasters were busily collecting Irish manuscripts in the expectation that they would make a handsome profit when Trinity came to buy them. Unfortunately for them and the College, the will was successfully contested by Flood's cousin John, who argued that, as Henry had been born out of wedlock, he, John, was the legitimate heir to the estate.[48] Trinity received nothing, but the story did not end there, as the Board somewhat bizarrely returned to the matter in 1922 and proposed to argue that the College was entitled to the income from the

---

[43] MUN/LIB/6/1, p. 197; MUN/LIB/8/13, p. [i].   [44] MUN/V/5/3, 6 December 1774.

[45] MUN/LIB/1/53, fol. iv; MUN/V/5/5, 27 March 1784; J. H. Andrews, 'Charles Vallancey and the map of Ireland', *Geographical Journal*, 132 (1966), 48–61.

[46] George Faulkner, *Dublin Journal*, 12–14 February 1784.

[47] MUN/LIB/2/1, May–June 1792; MUN/V/57/7, June quarter 1792. The six manuscripts are now MSS 1324–9.

[48] MUN/P/1/1056 and 1383; James Kelly, 'The last will and testament of Henry Flood: context and text', *Studia Hibernica*, 31 (2000–1), 37–52.

bequest. It received legal advice that its case – not surprisingly – was a weak one and the matter was dropped.[49]

Other acquisitions

Irish manuscripts dominated the Library's acquisitions during the second half of the eighteenth century. Very few other manuscripts and only a handful of printed books were bought in most years and the continuing emptiness of the shelves in the Long Room started to be noticed by visitors. Thomas Campbell, in his *Survey of the south of Ireland* of 1777, commented that the number of books had hardly increased since the acquisition of Gilbert's library and 'the modern publications in this library are very few'.[50]

The pattern of purchasing from year to year was quite haphazard and depended on the energy and enthusiasm of either the Librarian or one of the Fellows. In his 2 years as Librarian (1759–60) John Stokes spent no more than £13 4s. 7d. and in several years the accounts record no expenditure at all. On the other hand, in a single year, 1762, during the tenure of William Andrews, about £160 was spent, of which almost all was reimbursed to Leland for books he had bought for the Library. Leland's periods of office as Librarian were, needless to say, the time of greatest expenditure. The accounts show spending on books of £308 8s. 3½d. between June and September 1778. One of the Fellows, Joseph Stock was paid £26 6s. 10d. and the remainder was spent with two Dublin booksellers, William Gilbert and William Hallhead.[51] In June that year, no doubt in an attempt to temper Leland's enthusiasm for buying and in anticipation of the arrival of these large bills, the Board ruled that it must first approve the list of proposed titles before any money was spent on books.[52]

Under Leland's successors, Thomas Wilson and Henry Dabzac, expenditure dropped again to its previous low level. Persuading some Librarians actually to spend money on books seems to have been an issue. In 1774, the English libertarian, Thomas Hollis, a donor to several European and American university libraries, bequeathed £100 to Trinity for the purchase of books 'upon politicks, natural and civil history and mathematicks'.[53] A decade later the money had still not been spent and the Board had to order

[49] MUN/V/5/22, 14 and 21 January 1922.
[50] Thomas Campbell, *A philosophical survey of the south of Ireland* (London: Strahan and Cadell, 1777), p. 11.
[51] MUN/V/57/4–MUN/V/57/5.   [52] MUN/V/5/3, 24 June 1778.   [53] *Ibid.*, 4 August 1774.

the Librarian to apply the legacy to the purposes specified in the will, again without success, and the instruction had to be repeated 4 years later.[54]

In 1788, the Board decided that the entire Library Fund should be used for the purchase of books and that all other expenditure (such as repairs, cleaning and the salaries of the porter and maid) should be charged to general College expenses.[55] This was merely an administrative change that had no effect on the level of purchasing and simply served to demonstrate more starkly the complete lack of expenditure on acquisitions in some quarterly accounts.

The second half of the century saw no donations on the scale of those in the first half. The most significant was the collection assembled by the politician Theophilus Butler, MP for Belturbet and later Baron Butler of Newtownbutler, County Fermanagh. The main strengths of the 1,200 titles in the collection are, as might be expected of a politician and a gentleman, politics, history and travel, but it also contains poetry and music, as well as an important collection of over 180 editions of contemporary plays, and newspapers such as the *Flying Post*. Butler regarded himself as a serious bibliophile and eschewed cheaper Irish printings in favour of the more lavish English editions, with the result that his collection contains few Dublin imprints. Many of the books are marked with his signature or armorial bookplate.[56] Butler died in 1723 and his collection was bequeathed to his brother James. It is not known when it came to the College but in early 1772 the Assistant Librarian, John Forsayeth, was paid £30 for 'arranging and making a catalogue of Mr Butler's books in the Library'.[57] The collection is housed on the north side of the Long Room and was the last collection to be identified by gold letters in the frieze below the gallery.

Also in 1772, the Earl of Rochford, Secretary of State, reported that it was the King's intention to present copies of the *Journals* of the English Houses of Parliament to the College, and deliveries began to arrive shortly afterwards.[58] In 1781, the Irish House of Lords followed suit, ordering that a set of its *Journals*, 'handsomely bound', should be presented to the College,

---

[54] *Ibid.*, 20 November 1783; MUN/LIB/2/1, 15 October 1787.

[55] MUN/V/5/5, 12 February 1788.

[56] Sylvia Earley, 'Theophilus Butler, Cavan MP and book-collector', *History Ireland*, 13(5) (September/October 2005), 7–8; Charles Benson, '"Probationary starts and unprovok'd rants": the drama collection at Trinity College Dublin', *Antiquarian Book Monthly Review*, 14 (1987) 216–18; Charles Benson, 'Some private libraries in eighteenth-century Ireland', in Danielle Westerhof, ed., *The alchemy of medicine and print: the Edward Worth Library, Dublin* (Dublin: Four Courts Press, 2010), pp. 48–56.

[57] MUN/V/57/5, March quarter 1772.

[58] MUN/V/5/3, 22 February 1772 and 14 February 1775.

and William Sleater was paid eighteen shillings a volume for binding the first three volumes in calf, with gilt edges.[59] The Irish House of Commons, as one of its final acts, did likewise in 1800, voting the necessary money for printing nine sets on fine paper for special recipients, including Trinity, Oxford and Cambridge, and binding them in red morocco in such a manner as to 'do credit to the Irish workman'.[60] Thirty-one volumes were received from the King's Printer, George Grierson, in 1802.[61]

Several oriental manuscripts were given in the 1780s and 1790s by various donors, including Edmund Burke and William Digges La Touche, an official of the East India Company, who presented some fine examples of Persian calligraphy.[62] In 1784, Johann Josef Heydeck, who had fled Jewish persecution in Germany and was teaching oriental languages in the College, was appointed to catalogue those Hebrew and rabbinical books not already in the catalogue.[63]

An anonymous writer clearly felt that the College was not receiving an adequate number of donations, and in 1759 an appeal, signed 'Academicus', appeared in Faulkner's *Dublin Journal*, noting that Oxford and Cambridge were entitled to receive books by law under the terms of the Copyright Act. The same arrangement was not proposed for Trinity, but it was suggested that a clause should be inserted into the will of every person who has 'even a moderate collection of books' that they bequeath to the College those books not already in the Library. No response to this appeal has been found and the author has not been identified, but he did acknowledge the generosity of the *Journal*'s publisher, George Faulkner, who presented the Library with many of the books he had printed, including novels, though these were at the time not regarded as suitable material for an academic library.[64]

In December 1778, John Kearney, who had just been elected as the Assistant Librarian, was instructed to select and catalogue books from among those bequeathed by the physician Edward Smyth, a task for which he subsequently received payment of £40 in addition to his salary.[65] This donation

[59] *Lords Jn Ireland*, vol. V, pp. 256 and 463.

[60] MUN/LIB/10/222b; Dermot Englefield, 'Printing the Journal of the Irish House of Commons 1753–1802', in H. S. Cobb, ed., *Parliamentary history, libraries and records: essays presented to Maurice Bond* (London: House of Lords Record Office, 1981), pp. 33–43.

[61] MUN/LIB/2/1, 17 November 1802; MUN/LIB/13/4.

[62] Listed in MUN/LIB/1/53, pp. 257–8.

[63] MUN/V/5/5, 19 June 1784; MUN/V/57/6, June quarter 1784; Susana María Ramírez Martín, 'Juan José Heydeck: un alemán en la corte de Carlos IV', *Asclepio*, 58 (2006), 165–202.

[64] George Faulkner, *Dublin Journal*, 3–6 November 1759; C. Benson, 'A friend of the Library, 1759', *Long Room*, 9 (Spring/Summer 1974), 40; Vincent Kinane, *History of the Dublin University Press, 1734–1976* (Dublin: Gill & Macmillan, 1994), pp. 53–4.

[65] MUN/V/5/3, 17 December 1778 and 30 June 1781.

strengthened the Library's poor holdings of medical books, but the Provost, John Hely-Hutchinson, whilst noting that the collection was a valuable one, wrote regretfully, 'I wish he had left us some of his good works, in which he abounded'.[66]

An unusual donation to the College at this time was that of the harp associated in legend with the eleventh-century High King, Brian Boru, which has been on display in the Long Room since the nineteenth century. The harp dates from at least 300 years after Boru's death, but it is nonetheless the oldest extant harp in Ireland. Its earlier history is the subject of several conflicting stories, one of which was related by Vallancey in his *Collectanea*, where he also recorded its donation by William Burton Conyngham in 1782 to the recently established College Museum.[67] The official records were silent on the subject until the *Dublin University Calendar* of 1834 included it in the list of items on display in the museum, along with other Irish antiquities such as the charter-horn of the Kavanagh family and the silver *cumdach* for the Book of Mulling. In 1853, the harp was 'restored' by the Director of the museum who, having observed the 'mutilated state' in which it had been received, 'restored the parts of the harp to their proper position' and supplied 'from analogy' some lost portions of the foot and the lower end of the bow.[68]

The building

It is sometimes difficult to establish when work was carried out on the Library, as the same craftsmen worked on different College buildings, often at the same time, and their accounts frequently do not identify the specific building to which they refer. During the latter part of the century there were at least two instances of major expenditure on the exterior of the Library but neither of those included replacement of the flaking stonework that had been noticed in the 1750s. In 1777, Thomas Campbell could still write of 'the very bad stone, [which] is unfortunately mouldering away'.[69] The roof was repaired in the 1760s, and in 1791 George Darley was paid £72 4s. 0d. for sixty-eight Portland stone balusters, to replace those that had decayed.[70] These do not appear to have been installed at the time, as the Board decided

---

[66] Letter to Charles Agar, 24 November 1778, PRONI T/3719/C/12/21.

[67] *Collectanea de rebus Hibernicis*, no. XIII (1784) 32–7; Joan Rimmer, *The Irish harp* (Cork: Mercier, 1969), pp. 33, 77–8.

[68] MUN/LIB/13/39a.   [69] Campbell, note 50 above, p. 10.

[70] MUN/P/2/145/18–MUN/P/2/145/23; MUN/P/2/163/11.

in 1796 that the whole balustrade should be taken down, and for this Darley received a further £28 19s. 6d.[71]

Repairs were also carried out to the interior. In 1777, the old ceiling was replaced with a new one 'in compartments and not coloured'.[72] The gold lettering on the frieze below the gallery includes the 'BIBLIOTHECA BUT-LERIANA' and appears in Malton's watercolour of the Long Room (see Plate 4), which suggests that it probably dates from between the cataloguing of the Butler collection in 1772 and the early 1790s, the date of the watercolour. It is possible therefore that it was added at the same time as the new ceiling was installed and painted. The lettering extends right along the south side of the Long Room and marks the location of the three collections housed there: first Ussher's library: 'BIBLIOTHECA USSERIANA EX DONO SERENISSIMI REGIS CAROLI SECUNDI'; then Palliser ('BIBLIOTHECA PALLISERI-ANA'); and then Gilbert's collection: 'CLAUD: GILBERT HUJUS COLL: VICEPRÆPOS: ET SACRÆ THEOLOGIÆ PROFESSOR REGIUS BIB-LIOTHECAM HISCE LIBRIS AUXIT. QUATUORDECIM IMAGINIBUS MARMOREIS ORNAVIT, ET PRETIOSA INSUPER SUPELLECTILI LIT-ERARIA INSTRUXIT. ANNO MDCCXLIII.'[73] On the north side the only collection to be identified in this way is Butler's (BIBLIOTH[A]: BUTLERIANA).

More busts were added as the century progressed. In 1761, Simon Vierpyl was paid £34 2s. 6d. for a posthumous bust of Richard Baldwin, who had died 3 years earlier, having been Provost throughout most of the time the Library was being built. This was clearly the going rate, as Vierpyl had received this sum for his bust of Gilbert, and the Irish sculptor Patrick Cunningham was paid the same amount in 1759 for a likeness of John Lawson, the former Librarian and Professor of Oratory. In 1789, Sir John Parnell presented a bust of the poet Thomas Parnell by another Irish sculptor, Edward Smyth.[74] Two eighteenth-century busts for which there is no record of receipt (though both were included in Malton's description of 1793) are those by Edward Smyth of William Clement, the former Librarian and Vice-Provost, and John van Nost's bust of Swift's close friend Patrick Delany. Cleaning the busts seems to have been something of a preoccupation. In 1754, George and Hugh Darley supervised a mason who spent three and a half days on the work at a cost of 7s. In 1766, and again in 1774, Vierpyl himself was

---

[71] MUN/V/57/7, December quarter 1796.   [72] MUN/V/5/3, 22 July 1777.

[73] 'Ussher's library donated by the Most Serene King Charles the Second'; 'Claudius Gilbert, Vice-Provost of this College and Regius Professor of Divinity, enhanced the library with these books, adorned it with fourteen marble busts and in addition equipped it with valuable literary furnishings. 1743.'

[74] MUN/LIB/2/1, 23 June 1789.

Figure 8 John Barrett, Librarian 1791–1806, 1809–13, 1814–21 (College Art Collections, TCD)

brought in to do them, the first time at the rate of 19s., and on the second occasion at £3 6s. 1d.[75]

John Barrett

John Barrett, universally known as Jacky (see Figure 8), was appointed as the Assistant Librarian in 1784, and he then served as Librarian from 1791

---

[75] MUN/P/2/140, 21 July 1754; MUN/V/57/4, June quarter 1766; MUN/V/57/5, September quarter 1774.

to 1806, and again from 1809, with one year's gap, until his death in 1821. His influence on the Library covered much of a momentous 40 years which included the acquisition of the Sebright manuscripts, the establishment of Trinity as a legal-deposit library, the beginning of the regular purchasing of books, the arrival of the Fagel collection and the visit of King George IV. His tenure also marked the end of the process of electing the Librarian as part of the redistribution of College offices on 20 November each year. From then onwards, those nominated for the office were men who – for the most part at least – saw themselves as having responsibility not just for being present in the Library during the appointed hours but for playing a role in its development. However, since the election of Librarian had to be from among the seven Senior Fellows, the field was of necessity somewhat limited.

The stories of Barrett's eccentricity abound, recording his miserliness, his scruffy dress and his ignorance of the world outside the walls of the College. Many of them are no doubt exaggerated, but even in his lifetime he was regarded as 'an eccentric of the first order . . . [whose] daily peregrinations took place within the quadrilateral defined by the Library, the Chapel, the Dining Hall and his rooms'.[76] He took his responsibilities seriously, however, and was meticulous in his record-keeping. His unmistakeable small, clear hand can be seen everywhere in the archives, noting the arrival of donations and periodical parts, recording the occasional loan of manuscripts and their return, approving invoices from booksellers, sometimes questioning items included in them, and confirming that books received had been entered in the catalogues. Shortly after his appointment as Assistant Librarian he began the 'Library minutes book', a detailed record of activity that was maintained from 1785 until 1949.[77] He also imposed some order on the College muniments and was paid 20 guineas for transcribing several of them.[78]

His work among the manuscripts led to the important discovery of a very early, possibly fifth-century, palimpsest text of St Matthew's Gospel, now known as Codex Z.[79] The discovery was announced to the Royal Irish Academy in November 1786 and the following March the Board allowed Barrett to borrow the manuscript 'marked on the back XYZ and not mentioned in the catalogue' for the purpose of transcribing those parts that he could make out.[80] He published an edition of it in 1801, and a further edition by Abbott appeared in 1880.[81]

[76] McDowell and Webb, p. 82.   [77] MUN/LIB/2/1–MUN/LIB/2/7.
[78] MUN/V/5/5, 30 November 1792.   [79] MS 32.
[80] MUN/LIB/1/53, fol. iv; MUN/LIB/5/5, 7 March 1787.
[81] John Barrett, 'Account of a Greek manuscript of Saint Matthew's Gospel in the Library of Trinity College, Dublin', *Trans. RIA*, 1 (1787) 121–38; John Barrett, ed., *Evangelium secundum*

The failure of Barrett's predecessors to buy newly published books was finally recognised by the Board in 1791, when it agreed to advance £500 for the purpose. In the same year it also allocated £400 to purchase books from the collection of the recently deceased Henry Ussher, the first Professor of Astronomy. These were distributed between the Library and the Observatory that Ussher had established at Dunsink. John Brinkley, Ussher's successor, helped to make the selection and was also commissioned to buy books in London from a list supplied by Barrett.[82] These were opportunities to improve the holdings of recent mathematical and scientific books, and Barrett compiled a list of such works, indicating whether or not they were in the Library. He noted for example that Israel Lyons' *A treatise of fluxions* (London, 1758) and Roger Long's *Astronomy* (Cambridge, 1742–64) were not held and that there were no works at all by the contemporary mathematician William Emerson.[83] He took the opportunity to fill these lacunae, and the nineteenth-century Printed Catalogue lists the books by Lyons and Long, as well as seventeen by Emerson, all in editions of the 1760s and 1770s, standing together on the Long Room shelves.

The Board accepted that this was simply the start of the process of keeping the collection up to date and that a long-term commitment was required. The Librarian and his Assistant were instructed to prepare a list of books needed for the Library, so that the 'best editions of such of the said books, as the Board shall approve of, shall be purchased from time to time', and Barrett ordered a consignment of English sale catalogues.[84] Purchases became more regular, and there are accounts from various Dublin booksellers such as John Archer, Richard Mercier, William McKenzie and James Vallance. The main supplier was McKenzie, who in 1783 had married the widow of the previous College bookseller, William Hallhead, and taken over Hallhead's appointment as bookseller and stationer to the University. McKenzie's relations with the College deteriorated after the appointment of Barrett, who was careful with the College's money as well as his own, and who checked McKenzie's work assiduously and complained when he supplied defective sets and unwanted items and made mistakes in the numbering of series. By 1795, Barrett's patience ran out and the Board dismissed McKenzie from 'the College business of Printer-Bookseller and Stationer'.[85] He was replaced by Richard Mercier.

Matthaeum ex codice rescripto in bibliotheca Collegii Ssae. Trinitatis juta Dublin (Dublin University Press, 1801); T. K. Abbott, *The Codex rescriptus Dublinensis of St Matthew's Gospel (Z)* (Dublin: Hodges, Foster and Figgis, 1880).
[82] MUN/V/5/5, 8 January, 27 July, 29 August 1791.   [83] MUN/LIB/10/187a.
[84] MUN/V/5/5, 25 February 1792; MUN/V/57/7, June quarter 1792.
[85] MUN/V/5/5, 10 October 1795; McDonnell and Healy, pp. 57–75.

Recent publications, including scientific and medical works, formed the majority of the purchases, but antiquarian books were still being bought. In 1786, for example, McKenzie supplied a Latin Bible of 1480 printed by Koberger of Nuremberg.[86] Disposals of private libraries were also a rich source of material, and among those at which the College made purchases were Mercier's sales of Lord Mornington's library in 1795, that of Richard Murray, the late Provost, in 1800, and Vallance's disposal of Archbishop Newcome's library, also in 1800.[87] Most of the modern purchases were in English and, even though chairs had been established in modern languages, the Library's foreign-language books were to be found principally in the Gilbert bequest until the arrival of the Fagel collection in 1802. Antoine d'Esca, appointed in 1776 to teach French and German, bought a few books, including a subscription to Voltaire's *Œuvres* for £11 7s. 6d.[88] His colleague, Antonio Vieyra, the Professor of Italian and Spanish, left about 150 books to the Library on his death in 1797.[89]

In 1800, the politician John Wilson Croker presented the Library with a copy of Sallust, *Opera* (Lyon, 1523) once thought to have belonged to Mary Queen of Scots. It became a celebrated item for display in the Long Room from the later nineteenth century onwards, after having been shown to Queen Victoria on her visit in 1849.[90]

An 'oriental manuscript' was bought from James Vallance in 1796 at a cost of £4 11s. 0d., perhaps inspired by the earlier donations of similar items, and Vallance also supplied a collection of Icelandic documents in 1800.[91] These formed part of a collection of books and manuscripts that had been assembled by the late James Johnstone, when Chaplain and Secretary to the British Embassy in Copenhagen. Their interest to the College no doubt lay in the fact that, according to the sale catalogue, they had been selected 'with a reference to the history of the invasions, and connection between the northern nations and Great Britain and Ireland in early times'. The Library paid 40 guineas and bought only the manuscripts, which were principally seventeenth- and eighteenth-century transcriptions of sagas and chronicles.[92]

---

[86]   MUN/LIB/2/1, 8 July 1786.   [87]   *Ibid.*, 6 August 1795, 10 July and 29 April 1800.

[88]   MUN/V/57/6, December quarter 1781; Máire Kennedy, *French books in eighteenth-century Ireland* (Oxford: Voltaire Foundation, 2001), pp. 33–5; Máire Kennedy, 'Antoine d'Esca: first Professor of French and German at Trinity College Dublin', *Long Room*, 38 (1993), 18–19.

[89]   MUN/LIB/10/209 and MUN/LIB/10/214a.

[90]   MUN/LIB/2/1, 26 July 1800. James Henthorn Todd (*Notes and queries*, 4 (1851), 316–17, 385–6) thought that the book contained Mary's autograph, but the manuscript entries are now not considered to be in her hand.

[91]   MUN/V/57/7, June quarter 1796 and March quarter 1800; MUN/LIB/2/1, 27 February 1800.

[92]   MS 2865 (catalogue); Olai Skulerud, *Catalogue of Norse manuscripts in Edinburgh, Dublin and Manchester* (Kristiania: Moestues Boktrykkeri, 1918). The manuscripts are now MSS 989–1037.

In 1788, the cabinets in the Manuscripts Room, where the collection of coins was stored, were broken into, and a number of silver coins and all the gold ones were stolen. The Board placed advertisements in the newspapers offering £100 for information leading to the discovery of the culprits, who were alleged to have been in possession of keys, but the coins were not recovered.[93]

That case appears not to have been solved, but a theft of books in 1793 was, thanks to the vigilance of the Library porter and prompt action by Barrett. The Library minutes book contains a detailed account of the theft by Timothy Casey, a BA living in the College 'without any visible means of subsistence'.[94] The porter had noticed that books were missing from a section of the Library regularly used by Casey, who ordered small books to be fetched whilst pretending to read large ones. A search of the Library ordered by Barrett yielded nothing, but he later discovered Casey reading alone in one of the alcoves in the Long Room. After the suspect had left the Library, the porter realised that books were missing from that alcove. Casey was apprehended and, on being threatened with prison, confessed to having stolen a number of books, which he had sold to one Dowd, a book-stall keeper on the quays. The porters were sent to Dowd's stand and found about a dozen books from the Library, which Dowd returned on payment of 8s. 8d. Casey was expelled the following day from both the College and the Library.

---

[93] MUN/V/5/5, MUN/LIB/2/1, 19 January 1788; MUN/V/57/6, March quarter 1788; MUN/LIB/2/5, fol. 2.

[94] MUN/LIB/2/1, October 1793; H. W. Parke, 'Mr Timothy Casey's robberies', *Annual Bulletin* (1949), 7–9.

8 | Fagel: 1798–1809

The granting of legal-deposit status in 1801 and the arrival of the Fagel collection the following year transformed the Library both in size and status. The impact of the legal-deposit legislation would be a gradual one; the impact of acquiring the Fagel library, on the other hand, was immediate. The size of the College Library was increased by about 40 per cent at a stroke, and a collection that was essentially secular in nature and continental in origin was added to a library that had grown over the previous two centuries principally on the basis of books acquired by or for Protestant clergy.

The process of buying the Fagel collection began formally on 31 May 1798, when the governors of the Erasmus Smith Schools, meeting in the Committee Room of the Irish House of Lords, decided 'that the surplus money now in hand belonging to the Charity may be well applied in purchasing the library of the Greffier Faghel of The Hague, for the use of Trinity College'.[1]

The thirty-two governors included several members of the nobility, Church of Ireland bishops and archbishops, the Lord Chancellor, the Speaker of the Commons and the Provost of Trinity. They were responsible for administering a Trust established in 1657 by Erasmus Smith, a Leicestershire merchant who had acquired large tracts of land around Ireland in return for his services during Cromwell's campaigns there and in Scotland. By the eighteenth century, the Trust had established five grammar schools, supported over two hundred so-called 'English schools' throughout Ireland and provided scholarships at Trinity. As a major landowner it benefitted from the growing prosperity in Ireland and the resulting increases in rents, and at many of their meetings the governors addressed the issue of how to dispose of the surplus for which they were responsible. Trinity was particularly favoured, with money being granted towards the cost of new chambers for students, grants for several Chairs and for the building of the Public Theatre, also known as the Examination Hall.[2] In this

---

[1] Dublin, High School, Erasmus Smith Trust Archives, BG/1008 (Registry Book of the Governors), 31 May 1798.

[2] W. J. R. Wallace, *Faithful to our trust: a history of the Erasmus Smith Trust and the High School, Dublin* (Blackrock: Columba Press, 2004).

context, the decision to buy the Fagel collection is perhaps not quite so extraordinary, but the resolution of the governors at their meeting in May 1798 nonetheless remains something of a mystery. Among the ten present were the Provost (Richard Murray), the Speaker (John Foster), and Arthur Browne, a Fellow of Trinity and MP for the University. What persuaded them to commit £10,000 towards buying a collection of books belonging to a Dutch statesman and giving it to Ireland's university, which had no link with the collection – nor, indeed, any apparent interest in it? Moreover, the decision was taken in the midst of an armed rebellion, when the city of Dublin was practically under siege, and when the collection was still in Holland and not even on the market.

The driving force was John Foster, a graduate of Trinity, whose role in promoting the purchase is specifically noted in the minutes of the College Board after the collection had been acquired.[3] Foster maintained contacts in several European countries, and his position as Speaker of the Irish House of Commons and a member of the British Privy Council would have given him access to negotiations that were under way in London to secure the position of the collection's owner, Hendrik Fagel.[4] (See Figure 9.)

Fagel was a member of an affluent and cultivated family, several generations of whom had served successively as Greffier der Staaten-Generaal, or Secretary to the States General of the Netherlands, between the second half of the seventeenth century and the end of the eighteenth.[5] The office of Greffier, literally 'Clerk' or 'Secretary', was one of the great diplomatic offices of state; the role included the functions of the modern foreign minister. Each generation of the Fagel family had collected extensively, accumulating what a contemporary described as 'one of the most complete and considerable libraries, and collection of drawings and prints, to be met with in any part of Europe, formed in the course of above a century by a succession of men distinguished for their taste and their knowledge'.[6] This was all in the family home in The Hague when the French forces invaded the Netherlands in 1794. Fagel was sent to London to explain to the allies that the Dutch could no longer continue fighting, and by January 1795 the Republic had capitulated and many of the nobility had fled to England. The new government

3   MUN/V/5/5, 13 March 1802.
4   A. P. W. Malcomson, *John Foster (1740–1828): the politics of improvement and prosperity* (Dublin: Four Courts Press, 2011), pp. 380–1.
5   G. Waterhouse, 'The family of Fagel', *Hermathena*, 46 (1931), 80–5.
6   Charles Bentinck, 21 June 1795, quoted in HMC, *Report on the manuscripts of J. B. Fortescue, Esq., preserved at Dropmore, vol. III*, [C. 9470], 1899, L, part I, 1 (p. 80).

Figure 9 Greffier Hendrik Fagel (Collection Rijksbureau voor Kunsthistorische Documentatie (RKD), The Hague)

that had been installed in The Hague dismissed the absent Fagel as Greffier and temporarily sequestered his property. He was granted a pension by the British government, but this did not solve his financial problems and he was forced to put in train the sale of his library and the rest of the family collections. As Foster was in regular contact with both Lord Grenville, the Foreign Secretary, and Thomas Pelham, the Chief Secretary for Ireland, it seems likely that one of them could have suggested that the purchase of the library would help an ally. The state papers remained in the Netherlands and were sold at auction in The Hague in February 1803, but the rest of the collections were moved to England.[7]

They started to arrive in London in the summer of 1800 and caused Fagel the sort of problems familiar to librarians and book collectors throughout the ages: 'I am in a state of great embarrassment with regard to the books, etc. I would need to take a house with two or three large rooms for them,' he wrote to his brother Jacob.[8] The growing expenses were also causing him concern, and he complained to Jacob that he was having to pay for the rent of the house, the cost of the catalogues, storage (at more than a guinea a week), fire insurance and the fact that he had had to install a servant to live in the house.[9]

He lost little time in putting the works of art on the market and they were sold in 1801. In February that year he had also unpacked more than 160 cases of his books. Initially he decided that the Dutch books should be returned, as he believed that they would fetch a better price in Holland than in London. In the end, however, he decided to abandon this plan, to the great benefit of Trinity College Library.

Fagel employed Samuel Paterson to prepare the catalogue of books for the sale, and planned to sell them through James Christie's auction house. Though a man of unrivalled bibliographic skills, Paterson was renowned for being easily distracted from the task in hand by a book that caught his attention, with the result that on many occasions his sale catalogues were available only a few hours before bidding was due to begin. Paterson's characteristic lack of progress frustrated Fagel, who wrote in November 1801 that 'Paterson is driving me to despair with his slowness, and the amount of money this will cost me is enormous.'[10] He issued an ultimatum, that the catalogue must be completed and printed by the beginning of December or Paterson would not get paid. This seems to have had the desired effect, as advertisements started to appear in the newspapers from 14 December stating that catalogues for the first part of the sale would be available from 1 February 1802.

---

[7] *Catalogus van een uitmuntende verzameling van gedrukte en geschreven resolutien en verdere staatspapieren . . . toebehoorende aan den Hendrik Fagel* [The Hague, 1803].

[8] 3 October 1800, quoted in L. Brummel, *Miscellanea libraria: opstellen over boek- en bibliotheekwezen ter gelegenheid van zijn 60e verjaardag* ('s-Gravenhage: Nijhoff, 1957), pp. 220–1.

[9] 2 December 1800, *ibid.*, p. 221.   [10] Letter to Jacob Fagel, 9 November 1801, *ibid.*, p. 223.

In his Preface to the sale catalogue Paterson waxed lyrical about the importance of the collection, which was, he said, 'one genuine library; which has been accumulating in the family of Fagel ... upwards of one hundred and twenty years ... As an historical, geographical, genealogical and statistical library, it may justly rank among the most distinguished'.[11] Paterson's organisation of the catalogue followed the method that he had pioneered, with the list being arranged by subject rather than by book format. At the beginning of part I, he listed the sections into which he had divided the collection, starting with *Literae humaniores*, followed by theology, classics, philology, literature in various languages, arts, sciences and history.

The sale was divided into two parts. The first was set to begin on 1 March 1802 and scheduled to continue for 30 days. The catalogue for the first part of the sale lists 5,246 lots, to be sold at the rate of between about 160 and 200 a day, with the lot numbers indicated against each day's sale. It is not clear when the catalogue for the second part appeared. It lists the remaining 4,598 lots, bringing the total to 9,844. No dates are marked against the lots, and the number of copies of the catalogue that were distributed was very much less than for the first part, judging by its comparative scarcity in libraries today and the fact that, when the Fagel books were shipped to Trinity, the consignment included 629 remaining copies of the catalogue for part II of the sale, but only 301 of part I. The reasons for this are obvious, given the way that events unfolded in the early months of 1802.

On 5 February, a matter of days after the publication of the sale catalogue, Fagel received an offer to buy the whole collection. He asked for 2 days to think about it and consulted the London bookseller James Edwards, an expert on continental private libraries, who advised him to agree to sell the collection as one lot and to set the price at £5,000. Paterson felt that this was far too little, and in the end Fagel decided to ask for £8,000.

The offer to buy had been initiated by Foster, acting in accordance with the resolution of the Erasmus Smith governors from 4 years earlier, even though the matter had not been formally discussed by them since then, and it is clear that some of the governors had been having second thoughts in the meantime. The bishops, in particular, were far from unanimous in their support for the proposal, perhaps because they felt that the collection's

---

[11] *Bibliotheca Fageliana: a catalogue of the valuable and extensive library of the Greffier Fagel ... digested by Sam. Paterson. Part I: which will be sold by auction, by Mr. Christie* (London [1802]).

secular content would adversely affect the balance of the College Library. The Primate, William Stuart, believed that the government had wanted the library to be used for 'improving the education of the people'.[12] However, pressure was applied by Pelham, now Home Secretary, who wrote to Charles Agar and Charles Brodrick, the archbishops of Dublin and Cashel, asking them to reconsider their position and saying that he had asked Fagel to postpone the auction for a fortnight.[13] He also asked the Lord Lieutenant to try and persuade the governors 'to revive their determination about the Fagel Library'.[14]

The governors met on 6 March. The supporters of the proposal prevailed and it was agreed to spend up to £10,000 British on the purchase. A ten-man committee was established to see that the resolution was carried out, its members including Foster, John Kearney, Murray's successor as Provost of Trinity, the unenthusiastic Agar and Brodrick and the equally unenthusiastic Primate, Stuart.[15] Stuart (who was not present at the meeting) and Brodrick (who was) remained less than convinced about the wisdom of using the Trust's surplus funds in this way. Stuart wrote to Brodrick on the day after the meeting, reiterating his view that 'the education of the people is a matter of so much more importance than an additional library for Trinity College'.[16]

But the decision was now made and things began to move quickly. On 16 March advertisements appeared in the press to the effect that the public sale, which ought to have started two weeks previously, would not now take place and that 'Mr Christie is further happy to make it known, that this collection will henceforth be preserved entire, and that it will form a part of the very valuable Library of Trinity College, Dublin.'[17]

Thomas Elrington, one of the Senior Fellows and a future Provost, was dispatched from Trinity to London to organise the packing and shipping of the collection. He started work on 16 March and kept a detailed diary recording each day's work, the number of cases packed and the contents of each.[18] He paid 'Mr Joye' 20 guineas for valuing the library. This was presumably the bookseller John Joye, employed to provide an insurance valuation, as Elrington noted the amount for each case as it was prepared for shipping. By the end of the first week he had filled fifty packing cases,

---

[12] Stuart to Brodrick, 21 February 1802, NLI MS 8869 (1).

[13] PRONI T/3719/C/36/7; BL MS Add. 33109, fol. 122r.; A. P. W. Malcomson, *Archbishop Charles Agar: churchmanship and politics in Ireland, 1760–1810* (Dublin: Four Courts Press, 2002).

[14] BL MS Add. 33109, fol. 129r.   [15] Smith Trust, note 1 above, 6 March 1802.

[16] NLI MS 8869 (1), 7 March 1802.   [17] E.g. *The Times* and *Morning Chronicle*, 16 March 1802.

[18] The diary is MUN/LIB/12/1.

most of them newly purchased but some bought second-hand from Fagel. He had also had a visit from Foster, who was obviously maintaining a close interest in the process.

Once he had cleared some space by the removal of the first fifty cases, Elrington began to calculate the implications for housing the collection when it arrived in Trinity. He came to the conclusion that it would require 5,200 feet of shelving. On 14 April he paid Fagel £7,500. It is not clear when the other £500 was paid, whether as a deposit or at a later stage. The recording, packing and dispatch continued for five weeks in all, with the final batch of cases (taking the total to 115) being sent off to join the others on 21 April, ready for shipment to Dublin. The following day Elrington paid his various bills and with this his work in London was completed.

The committee established by the Erasmus Smith governors reimbursed the full £8,000 paid to Fagel, met Elrington's expenses for insurance, packing cases, labourers, etc. whilst in London and paid him an honorarium of 200 guineas. The College Board also paid him 100 guineas and met his travelling expenses.[19] These payments to Elrington, totalling over £300, were substantial, considering that the College Librarian's annual salary was only £100. The Board also prepared an elaborate address to the governors, thanking them for the donation which permitted the purchase of 'a library which is scarcely equalled by any private collection in Europe'.[20]

The books arrived in Dublin between 11 and 14 May 1802 and the College was faced with the not inconsiderable problem of where to find about a mile of shelving to house around twenty thousand volumes and how to find the manpower to process them with a Library staff consisting of the Librarian, the Assistant Librarian and a porter.[21] In many ways the timing could not have been worse, as the first consignment of legal-deposit books from Stationers' Hall was about to arrive and the Board had just received an alarming report about the state of the Library roof.

It was clearly pointless to unpack the collection until there was somewhere to store it and so the only case that was opened was the last, number 115, which contained copies of the sale catalogue. These were distributed to each Fellow and professor in the College, to the Erasmus Smith governors and to various other worthies.[22] Five copies of both parts were sent to Richard

[19] Smith Trust, note 1 above, 11 February 1803; MUN/V/5/5, 4 December 1802.

[20] Transcribed in MUN/V/5/5, 24 December 1802; original in Erasmus Smith Trust Archives.

[21] Ernst Braches, 'The first years of the Fagel Collection in Trinity College Dublin', in Susan Roach, ed., *Across the narrow seas: studies in the history and bibliography of Britain and the Low Countries, presented to Anna E. C. Simoni* (London: British Library, 1991), pp. 189–96.

[22] MUN/V/5/5, 26 July 1802; MUN/LIB/2/1, 2 June–5 October 1802 *passim.*

Mercier, four to be bound for the Provost, and 'one to be elegantly bound in morocco for the Lord Lieutenant'.[23] In 1806, Mercier received a further six copies to be bound for Fagel himself.[24]

The obvious location for the new collection was the Long Room, but there was insufficient space for it to be placed together without a major reorganisation and so the location selected was the Manuscripts Room at the east end of the building. This meant that a new home had to be found for the Library's manuscripts, and the Bursar was asked to obtain costs for fitting out a new Manuscripts Room on the floor above.[25] Work started in earnest the following spring. The manuscripts and books of prints were packed up and the carpenter Timothy McEvoy dismantled the bookcases. By September 1803 they had been reassembled in the room above and the manuscripts were unpacked again into their new location.[26]

In the meantime another carpenter, William Chapman, was brought in to convert the old Manuscripts Room. The Board had decided that the room they were now starting to call the 'Fagel library' should be fitted out in a similar manner to the Long Room, and so Chapman's work included '8 oak fluted pilasters . . . and Corinthian capitals' and nine carved seat-ends.[27] (See Figure 10.) Chapman completed the work in August 1803 at a cost of £1,090 2s. 3d., but the shelving provided to house the collection seems to have been insufficient once the books had been fully unpacked and the pamphlets had been bound, as McEvoy, who had been repairing the Library roof, was brought back in 1807 and 1808 to carry out further carpentry work, including the erection of more shelving. The need to accommodate the collection seems to have entailed the removal of some of the seats installed earlier and the blocking-up of two windows so that shelves could be erected across them.[28]

Space was not the only problem. The collection also had to be organised and catalogued. Elrington noted in his diary for August 1802 that arrangements were to be made for cataloguing it, and the following May the Provost reported to the Board that Barrett was working on the catalogue. By early 1804 the unpacking was under way, the books were being placed on the shelves in the new room and pamphlets were being sent to Mercier for binding. The books were checked off against a copy of the sale catalogue, and the Board decided that duplicates would not be kept with the collection but would be placed in the Lending Library.[29] Barrett's *Catalogus Bibliothecae*

---

[23] MUN/LIB/2/1, 16 August 1802. [24] *Ibid.*, 2 July 1806. [25] MS 4960, 8 May 1802.

[26] MUN/LIB/2/1, 7 February, 8 September 1803; MUN/P/2/189/23; MUN/V/57/8, December quarter 1803.

[27] MUN/P/2/187/3. [28] MUN/P/2/193/23, MUN/P/2/194/39 and MUN/P/2/199/3.

[29] MS 4960, 16 July 1803; MUN/LIB/2/1, August–September 1804.

Figure 10 The Fagel library (W. B. S. Taylor, *History of the University of Dublin* (London: Cadell & Cumming, 1845), plate opposite p. 311)

Fagelianae was duly delivered, in six manuscript volumes, to his successor as Librarian, Richard Graves, in November 1807, and the compiler was paid £100 for his work and for 'putting up the books'.[30]

Barrett's first term of office as Librarian ended in November 1806 and Graves set to work with renewed vigour to complete the processing of the collection. The binding programme was revived, students were taken on for

30 MUN/LIB/11/9/5. The catalogue is MS 1707.

the final placing of the books and adjustments were made to the shelving as necessary. The books and pamphlets were sent to several binders as well as to Mercier. These included George Mullen, William Figgis, who submitted an account in April 1808 for binding fifty-two Fagel volumes, and Christopher Lewis, who bound more than ninety in May and June. Mercier organised the numbering of 9,244 volumes and Michael Logan worked throughout the first half of 1808 lettering and numbering 7,963 vellum-bound books. He then moved on to preparing two catalogues, the first a transcription 'from rough copies into one fair volume [of] all the classes of the Fagel Library in alphabetical order', which he then marked up as a concordance between the sale catalogue and the new shelfmarks, and the second the local catalogue in shelf order, which he completed in February 1809.[31] In authorising the bill for payment, Graves noted of Logan that 'all the above work was done and very well done'.[32]

The Board obviously felt that the Fagel Room now required supervision, and towards the end of 1807 Digby Cross, a retired porter, was paid a gratuity of £10 for his attendance. This arrangement was put onto a regular basis with the appointment of John O'Neill, who became designated as the 'Fagel porter' and served until 1816, when he was dismissed for insolence to the Librarian.[33] O'Neill's salary was £50 a year, considerably more than the £20 paid to the regular Library porter or the £15 that the Assistant Librarian received.

Finally, on 1 March 1809, all was ready. The Board ordered that the Fagel library should be opened, and Graves was paid £200 for his work in preparing it for use.[34] The total cost to the Erasmus Smith Trust and the College of acquiring the collection, finding space for it and preparing it for use amounted to at least half as much again as the £8,000 paid to Fagel, but the College had nevertheless acquired something that was to become one of its greatest treasures.

The Fagel collection is essentially a working library, not that of a bibliophile. The Fagels did not seek to acquire books or manuscripts simply because of their rarity or fine bindings; indeed plain vellum and dark-stained calf bindings are the norm and there is only one item stamped with the family coat of arms. The collection certainly contains some magnificent items, but its importance lies more in its scale and broad scope, and, in particular, the

[31] MUN/LIB/11/2/28, MUN/LIB/11/2/29, MUN/LIB/11/2/38; MUN/LIB/11/9/13–
       MUN/LIB/11/9/21; MUN/V/57/8, December quarter 1807 to March quarter 1809.
[32] MUN/LIB/11/10/3.   [33] MUN/V/57/8; MUN/V/5/6, 14 September 1816.
[34] MUN/V/5/5, 1 March 1809.

amount of material relating to foreign exploration, botanical and anthro-
pological investigation by the Dutch and others. It reflects the family's role
as statesmen and politicians, though the breadth of the Fagels' collecting has
been described as 'something more often associated with a royal or national
library than with a family collection'.[35] It has been calculated on the basis of
Paterson's classification that the subjects of history, geography and topogra-
phy (including maps), politics and law represent about half the collection.
This is almost certainly an underestimate, as Paterson noted that, for example, the single entry numbered 7593 in the sale catalogue contained more
than ten thousand pamphlets on the history of every state in Europe. The
section on history and politics is dominated by works on the Netherlands,
and then by books on its allies and enemies, chiefly France, Great Britain
and Germany, but it also covers the ancient world, with works such as Grae-
vius' *Thesaurus antiquitatum romanarum* (Leiden, 1694–9) and Gronovius'
Thesaurus graecarum antiquitatum (Leiden, 1697–1702). Among the Dutch
books is the extremely rare first authorised edition of Carlos Coloma's *Las
guerras de los Estados Baxos desde el año de MDLXXXVIII hasta el de MDXCIX*
(Antwerp, 1624) which came from the library of Constantijn Huygens, a
major figure in Dutch literary history. His collection was broken up and
sold, and the Fagel library contains twenty-three titles, the largest number
of books from Huygens' collection now to be found in one place.[36] There
are also major Dutch periodicals recording current affairs, such as 192 volumes of the *Mercure historique et politique* (1686–1782), *Lettres historiques*
(1692–1725), *Europische Mercurius* (1690–1754) and a complete set of the
Hollantse Mercurius (1650–90). Non-Dutch periodicals include sixty-two
volumes of the *Philosophical Transactions of the Royal Society* (1665–1789).

French historical material ranks second only to the Dutch and the collection has been described as 'a monument to the *ancien régime*', illustrating
both its strengths and the cracks that led to its downfall.[37] It includes a
wide range of printed sources, of which perhaps the most important are
collections of edicts and ordinances, but there are also memoirs, statistics
and a good deal of local history. Among just over a dozen manuscripts relating to eighteenth-century France (MSS 893–909) are thirty-two volumes

[35]   Vincent Kinane, 'The Fagel Collection', in *Treasures*, pp. 158–69 (p. 165). See also Maryvonne
       Vonach, 'Premières recherches sur la collection Fagel conservée à la Bibliothèque de Trinity
       College Dublin' (unpublished dissertation, Université des Sciences Humaines de Strasbourg,
       1991–2).
[36]   Ad Leerintveld, 'Ex libris "Constanter": boeken uit de bibliotheek van Constantijn Huygens',
       Jaarboek voor Nederlandse boekgeschiedenis, 16 (2009), 151–76.
[37]   J. -P. Pittion, 'The Fagel collection', *Hermathena*, 121 (1976), 108–16 (p. 115).

of '*Mémoires concernant plusieurs provinces, villes, etc. de la France*', which comprise reports of the *intendants* from about 1700 and contain a full statistical account of each province and town, with forty large, engraved, coloured maps.

The maps in the collection have been described as 'dazzling' in terms of breadth of territorial coverage and cartographic subject-matter: 'there can have been few map libraries quite so cosmopolitan in the England of 1802 and surely none in Ireland . . . Its subjects embrace virtually the whole world as known to contemporary Europeans, and its imprints cover almost all the major map-publishing centres'.[38] In addition to around ninety volumes of atlases, including Blaeu's *Atlas maior* (Amsterdam, 1662), there are twenty-four portfolios containing 1,631 maps and town plans, mostly dating from the seventeenth and eighteenth centuries and covering not only the whole of Europe but extending to Asia and the Americas.[39] There is also a very rare album of eighteenth-century drawings for the palatial buildings and gardens in St Petersburg.[40]

Literature seems to have been of lesser importance to the family. The classics are well covered, including about fifty volumes of Elsevier editions from Leiden. About a third of the literature is represented by English-language texts, mostly in eighteenth-century editions. In the French section, La Fontaine, Molière and Voltaire appear, but the authors are mainly minor poets and playwrights, and many of the French-language books are of Dutch origin. The representation of Dutch literature is 'quite disappointing', consisting mostly of 'second-rate 18th century authors'.[41]

The section on natural history contains the most visually spectac-ular printed books. These include John Johnston's *Historia naturalis* (Frankfurt am Main, 1650–3), Andreas Cellarius' *Harmonia Macrocosmica* (Amsterdam, 1661) and Maria Sibylla Merian's *Metamorphosis insectorum Surinamensium* (Amsterdam, 1719). Some of the illustrated folios have title pages in gold: examples are Jan Commelin's *Horti medici Amstelodamensis* (Amsterdam, 1697) and Athanasius Kircher's *Mundus subterraneus* (Ams-terdam, 1678).[42] Paterson, not normally given to providing anything more than an unornamented list of titles, was sufficiently excited by the last two to describe each of them as 'a matchless copy!'. The Dutch interest in matters

[38]   J. H. Andrews, 'Maps and atlases', in *Treasures*, pp. 170–83 (p. 177).
[39]   J. R. Bartlett, 'Fagel's maps: the eighteenth-century world', in *Old Library*, pp. 133–48. Abbott, *Manuscripts* includes a list of the Fagel maps.
[40]   Edward McParland, 'A drawing in the Fagel collection', in *Old Library*, pp. 149–50.
[41]   Brummel, note 8 above, p. 232.
[42]   For the latter, see D. A. Webb, 'Athanasius Kircher', *Annual Bulletin*, (1958), 8–11.

botanical is also represented by *Alckmaarse lusthoff van tulpaanen* (MS 1706), a very rare catalogue of a tulip sale at Alkmaar, one of ninety-eight sales recorded for 5 February 1637, the day before the tulip-mania bubble burst. It contains sixty-three watercolour illustrations of tulips, into which have been inserted price lists, both printed and manuscript, of tulips and other bulbs, some bearing the dates 1707, 1708 and 1711. Also among the botanical items is a set of thirty-five red crayon drawings by Nicolas Robert dating from between 1667 and 1683, bound in red morocco and stamped with the arms of Louis XIV's minister, Colbert.[43] Coloured drawings of plants and animals are contained in the only surviving manuscript of a journal kept by Simon van der Stel, Commander of the Dutch East India Company's headquarters at the Cape of Good Hope, during an expedition in 1685 (MS 984). It was placed in the Colonial Archives of the Dutch East India Company but removed at the end of the seventeenth century. How it came into the possession of the Fagel family is not known.[44]

There are only four incunabula, but one, the so-called Agostini Plutarch (*Vitae illustrium virorum* (Venice, 1478)), makes up in quality for the paucity in numbers. It has been described as a 'masterpiece of Italian printing and illumination . . . printed in Venice on fine parchment by the most brilliant of early printers, Nicolaus Jenson, and illuminated by a refined miniaturist, the Master of the London Pliny'.[45] It is a two-volume edition decorated for the wealthy Agostini family of Venice with the frontispiece to each volume magnificently painted in gold and brilliant colours and almost every section decorated with a painted initial.

The Fagel Missal (MS 81), dating from 1459–60, is one of the largest and most elaborately decorated manuscripts made by the canonesses regular of the convent of St Agnes in Delft. As well as the standard missal text, it contains a mass for St Anne, twenty-six illuminated initials and two full-page miniatures, one showing the crucifixion and the other the two patrons of the convent, St Augustine and St Agnes.[46]

[43] C. E. J. Caldicott, 'The drawings of Nicolas Robert in Trinity College Library: a seventeenth-century view of nature', *Long Room*, 20/21 (Spring/Autumn 1980), 7–15.

[44] Gilbert Waterhouse, ed., *Simon van der Stel's journey to Namaqualand in 1685* (Cape Town: Human & Rousseau, 1979); G. Waterhouse, 'Simon van der Stel's expedition to Namaqualand, 1685', *Geographical Journal*, 64 (1924), 298–312.

[45] Lilian Armstrong, 'The Agostini Plutarch: an illuminated Venetian incunable', in *Treasures*, pp. 86–96 (p. 86).

[46] Kathryn M. Rudy, 'The Fagel Missal', in *Old Library*, pp. 65–8; Henri L. M. Defoer, Anne S. Korteweg and Wilhelmina C. M. Wüstefeld, *The golden age of Dutch manuscript painting*, (Stuttgart: Belser, 1989), pp. 192–3.

Though the College played a passive role in the early stages of acquiring the collection, the attention they gave to providing a fitting location for it and the amount they spent on that and on ensuring that the books were bound and catalogued indicates that its members realised the importance of what they had received. The new acquisition became a matter of increasing pride, and from an early date it was drawn to the attention of visitors. In 1805, Sir John Carr noted the, as yet unopened, Fagel Room: 'the books are not yet arranged, some of them are most beautifully illuminated', and the following year the antiquary and book-collector Sir Richard Colt Hoare wrote of the recent acquisition of the library.[47] Twenty-five years later the young French historian Montalembert, on his tour of Ireland, was much impressed by the Library ('*un magnifique établissement*') and particularly by the Fagel ('*la partie la plus précieuse de la bibliothèque*').[48]

As a 'foreign' collection housed in a separate room, the Fagel has always had the air of something slightly 'apart' from the rest of the Library. It has remained surprisingly little known in the Netherlands; indeed, in the 1950s, the Director of the Koninklijke Bibliotheek regretted that 'a valuable and characteristic part of the Dutch cultural heritage' should be 'lost to our country'.[49] In recent years, a number of projects and publications have sought to raise the profile of the collection, and the books are used extensively as part of the normal collections of the College Library.[50]

[47] Sir John Carr, *The stranger in Ireland; or, A tour in the southern and western parts of that country, in the year 1805* (London: Phillips, 1806), p. 88; Sir Richard Colt Hoare, *Journal of a tour in Ireland in 1806* (London: Miller, 1807), p. 8.

[48] Charles de Montalembert, 'Journal de voyage en Irlande, 1830', *Dublin Magazine*, 15/2 (April/June 1940), 44–62 (p. 48).

[49] Brummel, note 8 above, p. 228.

[50] In 2008 an international symposium devoted to the Fagel collection was held at Trinity College. This chapter is an abridged version of a public lecture given as part of the symposium.

Legal deposit

On 2 July 1801 the royal assent was given to the *Act for the further encouragement of learning, in the United Kingdom of Great Britain and Ireland, by
securing the copies and copyright of printed books, to the authors of such books,
or their assigns for the time herein mentioned.*[1] The effect of this Act, the
Copyright Act of 1801, was to extend copyright in printed books to include
Ireland and to place Trinity's Library on an equal footing with those of the
English and Scottish universities in that it was now entitled to receive a
free copy of books published in the United Kingdom. It was fundamental
in determining the development of the Library to the present day. From it
derives much of Trinity's status as one of the great libraries of the world and
from it also derive most of the problems of space and funding with which
the College has had to grapple ever since.

The impact of the legislation was not felt immediately, and in the College
records there is no mention either of the passing of the Act or – for almost a
year – of the deposit of books. There is no evidence that Trinity played any
role in encouraging the extension of copyright protection or the deposit of
books to Ireland, but it is clear that the new Act had a devastating effect on
many areas of the Irish book trade.

The concept of legal deposit dates back to sixteenth-century France and
the Ordonnance de Montpellier of 1537, which required all printers and
publishers in the country to deposit a copy of every newly published book
with the Bibliothèque royale. The purpose of the legislation was that of
censorship. Books had to be deposited to ensure that they did not contain
seditious material before they were more widely distributed. The concept
of building up an archive of the national published record is one that
developed only gradually. In Britain, Sir Thomas Bodley arranged for his
library in Oxford to receive copies of new books under a private agreement
of 1610 with the Company of Stationers. This agreement was superseded
during the seventeenth century by a series of press Licensing Acts, which

---

[1] Copyright Act, 1801 (41 George III, c. 107).

had the explicit purpose of preventing the printing of treasonable books and pamphlets, and which included a requirement that the publishers must deposit a copy of their books with each of three libraries, the Bodleian, Cambridge University Library and the Royal Library.

By the time of the Copyright Act of 1710, the concern of the government was no longer that of censorship but the prevention of pirated editions, and the Act linked the deposit of books with the granting of copyright.[2] It was introduced under pressure from the printers, who wanted legal protection for their work, but their success in obtaining the legislation was mitigated by the fact that the number of copies they were required to deposit was increased from three to nine. The libraries of the four Scottish universities (Aberdeen, Edinburgh, Glasgow and St Andrews) – now in the United Kingdom, following the Act of Union of 1707 – were added to the original three, as were the Faculty of Advocates in Edinburgh and Sion College, the library of the London clergy. Books were to be deposited with the Warehouse Keeper at Stationers' Hall, whose role was to register them for copyright and distribute them to the libraries. The Act had little practical effect on the delivery of books, as the printers took the view that the only titles liable for deposit were those that they chose to register at Stationers' Hall in order to secure copyright protection, and by the end of the eighteenth century the libraries were receiving no more than a handful of books by this means.[3]

In 1737, a Bill was introduced at Westminster that would have had the effect of increasing the number of deposit copies to fourteen by adding the Inns of Court in London. The Bill failed to proceed through Parliament but it did briefly raise in some minds the question of Trinity's position. Edward Southwell, Secretary of State for Ireland, reported to Marmaduke Coghill, MP for the University of Dublin, that some MPs had been considering whether to introduce a motion adding Trinity to this list but that the proposal had been dropped on the grounds that it was unlikely to pass and 'may remind the Parliament here to add some clause in our disfavour'.[4] This 'disfavour' was almost certainly the threat of copyright restrictions on Irish printers, for whom the absence of such legislation had turned the eighteenth century into a golden age of literary piracy. Members of the Irish book trade were free to reprint books first published in London and sell them at prices

---

[2] Statute of Anne, 1710 (8 Anne, c. 19).

[3] Partridge, pp. 33–8; John Feather, *Publishing, piracy and politics: an historical study of copyright in Britain* (London: Mansell, 1994), pp. 97–121; Vincent Kinane, 'Legal deposit, 1801–1922', in *Essays*, pp. 120–37.

[4] NLI MS 876, 22 March 1737.

below those of the English editions. The English printers were, therefore, effectively excluded from the lucrative Irish market and, worse, many of the pirated books either found their way back to England to be sold more cheaply than the original edition or they were sent across the Atlantic to supply the growing American trade.

This situation changed abruptly in 1801 when the Act of Union, which joined the two formerly separate kingdoms of Great Britain and Ireland, was followed by the passing of the Copyright Act later that year. As well as extending publishers' copyright protection to include Ireland, the Act added Trinity and the Dublin barristers' library, the King's Inns, to the nine existing deposit libraries, making a total of eleven. Since the British publishers largely ignored their responsibility to deposit their books at Stationers' Hall, and since the British libraries did not bother to exercise their right to claim them, the deposit aspect of the Act passed largely unnoticed at the time. However the new legislation meant that the mainstay of the Irish printers' business, the reprint trade, was removed at a stroke. It has been estimated that book production in Ireland dropped by 80 per cent and, conversely, that the import of books from Britain increased fourfold, with the result that the book trade in Dublin declined to the level of that in a provincial city and its main business became the retailing of books imported from other centres, chiefly London.[5]

It took some time for the implications of Trinity College Library's new status to become clear, but the Board responded with alacrity to a letter received early in 1802 from the Secretary to the Speaker of the Commons, Charles Abbot, stating that all papers printed by order of the House since the first session of the united Parliament would be delivered regularly to the College if it were to appoint an agent for the purpose. The Board chose the London publishers and booksellers Cadell and Davies for this role and also charged them with the duty of applying every half-year to the clerk at Stationers' Hall for the books that had been entered there and were due to the College. The clerk, George Greenhill, was to be paid 2 guineas a year for this work – though the College failed to pay him until 1815, when he received £29 5s. 2d., representing 12 years' worth of arrears![6]

The first parcel of books from Stationers' Hall arrived in the summer of 1802. The receipt of miscellaneous books of this sort was a situation that the Librarian had not been faced with before and he seems to have been

5   Partridge, pp. 45–73; Vincent Kinane, *A brief history of printing and publishing in Ireland* (Dublin: National Print Museum, 2002), p. 23; M. Pollard, *Dublin's trade in books 1550–1800* (Oxford: Clarendon Press, 1989), p. 31.
6   MUN/V/5/5, 1 May 1802; MUN/LIB/13/3; MUN/V/57/9, March quarter 1815.

uncertain about quite how to deal with them. Some were clearly wanted for the Library and were catalogued. These included scientific and medical works such as Thomas Thomson's *A system of chemistry* (Edinburgh, 1802) and John Cheyne's *Essays on the diseases of children* (Edinburgh, 1801), as well as more general titles like Samuel Burder's *Oriental customs* (London, 1802) and George Mason's *Supplement to Johnson's English dictionary* (London, 1801). Some books were received in sheets and were sent to Mercier for binding. That left a residue which Barrett was unsure about and which the Provost asked to inspect. Quite what happened to them is not clear. Some were returned from the Provost's House with instructions that they should be added to the Library, but in at least one case a book rejected by the Provost was sent to Mercier to be sold and 'credited for to the College account'.[7] In selling a book in this way, Trinity was behaving no differently from Oxford and Cambridge, both of which were accustomed to selling deposited books or disposing of them as waste paper.[8]

Regular deliveries of books from Stationers' Hall to Trinity and the King's Inns represented a new situation that the Irish libraries had to cope with, but in Britain both publishers and libraries continued largely to ignore the terms of the Act. In 1803, 372 books were entered at Stationers' Hall, a much lower number than were actually published but, even of those, fewer than 10 per cent found their way to the libraries.[9] However, this situation was about to change and both libraries and publishers were to be shaken out of their complacency.

In 1805, Basil Montagu, a Cambridge-educated lawyer, having failed to find some law reports in the University Library, published a pamphlet, *Enquiries and observations concerning the University Library*, in which he asked a series of questions about the deposit of books. Montagu had little standing in the University and the publication of his pamphlet passed largely unnoticed, but his questions turned out to be the opening shots in a battle that soon involved much bigger guns in the form of the Downing Professor of the Laws of England, Edward Christian. Christian's approach was a good deal less tentative than Montagu's.[10] He complained about being unable to find certain books in Cambridge University Library because, he had established, the publishers had failed to register them and so the Library

[7] MUN/LIB/2/1, 19 October and 18 December 1802.   [8] McKitterick, p. 408.

[9] Partridge, p. 315; McKitterick, pp. 394–445.

[10] John Feather, 'Publishers and politicians: the remaking of the law of copyright in Britain, 1775–1842. Part 1: legal deposit and the battle of the library tax', *Publishing History*, 24 (1988), 49–76.

had not received them. His reading of the various Acts convinced him that the libraries were entitled to copies of newly published books regardless of whether or not they had been registered at Stationers' Hall. As far as the extension of deposit to Ireland was concerned, he considered that, if publishers continued to avoid their obligations, the Irish libraries were not likely to derive much benefit 'from the learning of the sister kingdoms'. He predicted that the books they would receive during the next century would not fill a single shelf and even those few would be seen as 'an insult, rather than a public benefit'. The grant to Ireland was, he said, 'completely delusive and unavailing'.[11]

Christian proposed that one of the universities should begin an action against a publisher, so that the subject could be openly debated and a judgment pronounced. An attempt in 1808 to have the matter resolved in the Commons was unsuccessful, and so Cambridge followed Christian's advice in 1811 by beginning legal proceedings against the printer Henry Bryer for failing to deposit. The University won and Bryer was fined, but the victory was something of a pyrrhic one as the judgment provided reassurance to the publishers that deposit could be enforced only by individual prosecutions. It also demonstrated the differences of opinion between the libraries and the book trade, differences thrown into stark focus by a petition to the Commons from the London booksellers in December 1812 and a memorial from the University of Glasgow the following month. This led the House to set up a Select Committee to examine the Acts relating to copyright and to make a recommendation on whether any changes should be made. The members of the committee included MPs for the two English universities and William Conyngham Plunket, member for the University of Dublin, with, on the other side, several supporters of the book trade, including Sir Egerton Brydges, the MP for Maidstone. The committee, which sat from March to June 1813, took evidence only from the publishing side, the representatives of which argued that the number of deposit copies should be reduced to five, that copies should be supplied only on demand and not at all if copyright was not sought. To the annoyance of the publishers, the committee ultimately recommended that the provisions of the existing Acts should be retained and a Bill to that effect was brought before the Commons in May 1814. During the committee stage the Bill was subject to several amendments which favoured the trade, and the libraries, led on this occasion by Trinity, finally awoke to the realisation that they had to act

---

[11] Edward Christian, *A vindication of the right of the universities of Great Britain to a copy of every new publication* (Cambridge University Press, 1807), pp. 16, 32.

if their rights were not to be seriously eroded. On 6 June, the Commons received a petition from the College asking to give evidence, and this was followed by representations from the other universities and the Faculty of Advocates.[12] Christian also advised the College to urge the Irish MPs in the Commons to oppose the 'obnoxious clauses' in the Bill.[13] The trade side continued to seek amendments up to the last minute and the Act that finally received the royal assent on 29 July 1814 turned out to be no less ambiguous than those of 1710 and 1801 that it had sought to clarify.[14]

Under the Copyright Act of 1814 all new works had to be registered at Stationers' Hall, either within a month, if published in London, or within three, if published elsewhere in the country. The British Museum copy was to be deposited immediately, and the Warehouse Keeper was to supply the other libraries with lists every 3 months from which they could select the books they wanted, which they must do within 12 months. All eleven libraries retained their deposit status, but modifications made to meet the publishers' demands included an extension of the term of copyright from 14 to 28 years and the introduction of the requirement that the libraries must claim the books they wanted.

The returns submitted to the Commons indicate that most of the libraries chose to take almost everything that was available to them and to decide later what to keep. Of 897 titles entered at Stationers' Hall between July 1814 and June 1815 all but a handful were claimed, and for about half of those the full eleven copies were demanded. Those claimed in a reduced number were mainly devotional publications, music and novels, and from the end of March 1815 the overwhelming majority of items registered were claimed in eleven copies.[15] The booksellers' response to this unexpected level of demand was to revert to their previous practice of failing to register the majority of their titles, and although the number of books entered at Stationers' Hall rose from 350 in 1813 to 1,244 in 1815 the shortfall between the number published and the number registered was still significant. A recent calculation of the output of the five major book-production centres in the United Kingdom suggested that it amounted to four times the number of books registered, and Henry Baber, Keeper of Printed Books at the

[12] House of Commons, *Journals*, vol. LXIX (1813–14), p. 329; MUN/V/5/6, 2 June 1814; Philip Ardagh, 'St Andrews University Library and the Copyright Acts', *Edinburgh Bibliographical Society Transactions*, 3 (1948–55), 179–211.

[13] MUN/LIB/22/19/1.   [14] Copyright Act, 1814 (54 George III, c. 156).

[15] *A list of publications entered at Stationers' Hall, from 29 July 1814 to 10 June 1815*, HC 1814–15 (392), XIII, 37.

British Museum, reported to the libraries in 1816 that of 8,000 publications advertised the previous year only 1,244 had been registered.[16]

With the new Act behind them, the libraries now felt in a stronger position to take action, and their representatives met on 26 March 1816 at Sion College. The four English libraries each sent delegates, while the Scottish institutions were represented by the London solicitor for St Andrews and Edinburgh, and the two Irish libraries by Henry Monck Mason, Librarian of the King's Inns. Monck Mason provided the Provost with a detailed report of the meeting, at which a number of important principles were established, chief of which was that the libraries, recognising their common interests, had agreed to share information and act collectively in future. There was a particular concern about their failure to acquire books published outside London, and it was agreed that the libraries should each take responsibility for informing the others of new publications from Ireland, Scotland and the English provincial cities. In an early recognition of the potential long-term importance of even apparently ephemeral publications, it was agreed that all books should be claimed, 'as the most trivial pamphlets become very frequently important and valuable in the lapse of time'.[17] Novels and school books were exempted from this. The most urgent matter was the issue of evasion, as demonstrated by Baber's figures. It was agreed that the only recourse was prosecution, and the representatives decided that four simultaneous actions should be commenced. In the event, just the threat of prosecution was sufficient to elicit deposit and the planned legal action was abandoned. A printed circular, with an attached record of delivery and receipt, was produced for George Greenhill, the Warehouse Keeper at Stationers' Hall, to send to the publishers, stating that he was authorised to demand copies of their books.[18]

This comprehensive approach to claiming caused consternation among the publishers and there were further attempts to persuade the Commons to amend the Act. They were initially unsuccessful; the publishers continued to complain that the libraries were demanding works that could not be considered as useful to their readers and that the cost to them of supplying eleven copies was excessive. In 1818, Sir Egerton Brydges again took up the case of the book trade but, before his Bill reached the committee stage, the

---

[16] MUN/LIB/13/15; Simon Eliot, ' "Mr Greenhill, whom you cannot get rid of ": copyright, legal deposit and the Stationers' Company in the nineteenth century', in Robin Myers, Michael Harris and Giles Mandelbrote, eds., *Libraries and the book trade: the formation of collections from the sixteenth to the twentieth century* (New Castle, Del.: Oak Knoll Press, 2000), pp. 51–84; Partridge, p. 315.

[17] Monck Mason's report, 10 May 1816, MUN/LIB/13/15.   [18] Reproduced in Partridge, p. 313.

Commons set up another Select Committee to examine the Act yet again. Brydges was one of the members supporting the publishers' side, and for the libraries there were five university members, including Plunket, MP for the University of Dublin, and Robert Peel, who was the member for the University of Oxford and a former Chief Secretary for Ireland. Each of the libraries submitted petitions defending the provisions of the Act, and Trinity made the additional case that the cost to the publishers of having to deposit their books was greatly outweighed by the fact that the Act prevented republication in Ireland of books originally printed in Great Britain.[19] The committee's recommendations on deposit were equivocal and offered the alternative either of a reduction to five deposit libraries, of which Trinity would be one, or of the British Museum being the sole depository, with the other libraries receiving an annual grant in lieu.[20] The House ignored the committee's recommendations and the 1814 Act remained in force, with the book trade nursing its disappointment but unable to arouse any further interest at Westminster until the 1830s.

The question of how comprehensively the libraries should collect is one that has vexed both sides in the legal-deposit debate. The libraries base their stance on the principle that one of the purposes of legal deposit is to preserve the published record of the country, that it is impossible to know which books will be important in the future and that even apparently ephemeral publications are significant as evidence of social or cultural developments. The force of this argument has been demonstrated many times when, for example, novels rejected in the nineteenth century became regarded as classics, or collections of pamphlets became source material for research. Ranged against this case is the claim that it places an unreasonable financial burden on publishers and that there is a substantial cost to the libraries in acquiring, cataloguing, storing and preserving material that receives little use.

Over the next 200 years, policy would evolve, but all the deposit libraries have maintained to a greater or lesser degree the principle of comprehensive collecting, though each has adopted a slightly different approach, either formally or unofficially, some tending more to inclusivity, others to greater selectivity. In his evidence to the Select Committee in 1818 Edward Clarke, the Cambridge University Librarian, confirmed that his agent's instructions were to claim all titles registered, even though they included 'a great quantity of idle trash', and that the books were sorted on receipt into those

---

[19] MUN/V/5/6, 9 May 1818.
[20] *Report from the Select Committee on the Copyright Acts*, HC 1818 (402), IX, 249.

wanted for the Library, those to be kept elsewhere and those to be thrown out altogether.[21] Oxford has traditionally been the most inclusive of the libraries and a later librarian at the Bodleian noted in regard to Cambridge's submission of 1818 that it 'shows a recklessness of rejection which speaks little for the judgement of the librarians . . . the far wiser plan is now carried out in the Bodleian of rejecting nothing'.[22] In its submission in 1818 Trinity pointed out that it did not claim music, novels or school books and that 'a considerable part' of what was received was placed in the Library. The remaining items were either 'imperfect works or such as there occurred some difficulty in determining upon the propriety of placing them in the public library', but they remained in the custody of the Librarian and were never disposed of.[23] Those exclusions were noted by the publishers, but that did not prevent them from asserting that Trinity still took 'the most frivolous works of other descriptions'.[24] In Dublin, as in Cambridge, the attitude towards some of the material being received was an ambiguous one. The official line was to aim at comprehensive collecting but, on a note in the Library minutes book for August 1813 recording the receipt of two large parcels from Stationers' Hall, someone has added in a contemporary hand, 'alias, packs of trash'.[25]

Within a few years of its enactment, the inadequacies of the 1814 legislation became increasingly apparent. As Warehouse Keeper to the Stationers' Company, Greenhill saw his role as essentially a passive one, that of obtaining copies of books registered by the publishers and passing them on to the libraries. The libraries, concerned at the number of books they were not receiving, decided that they needed someone to play a more active role in claiming those books that were not being registered at all. In 1819, the solicitors for Oxford and Cambridge wrote to Trinity and the King's Inns to ask whether the Irish libraries would join them in seeking an alternative agent.[26] The Trinity Board agreed to co-operate, but it was another 2 years before Cambridge appointed Robert Durham, a member of the book trade, to act for the University. Greenhill was retained in his former role, and so there were now two collecting centres for the deposited books. Trinity remained with Greenhill for the time being, even though the Bursar, James Wilson,

[21] *Minutes of evidence taken before the Select Committee on the Copyright Acts*, HC 1818 (280), IX, 257 (p. 334).

[22] William Dunn Macray, *Annals of the Bodleian Library, Oxford*, 2nd edn (Oxford: Clarendon Press, 1890), p. 303.

[23] MUN/LIB/12/20.

[24] 'Claims of public libraries to the gratuitous delivery of books', *British Review*, 13 (1819), 226–47 (p. 241).

[25] MUN/LIB/2/1, 13 August 1813.   [26] MUN/LIB/2/2, 22 February 1819.

had had to remonstrate with him for not claiming books to which the College was entitled.[27] At the Board's visitation of the Library in 1822, however, it was decided to employ Durham to claim books for Trinity as he did for Cambridge. He was to be paid £60 a year and Greenhill was retained at his former salary of £25, to which it had been increased after the passing of the 1814 Act.[28]

Purchases and donations

The acquisition of the Fagel collection and the intake of books from Stationers' Hall were two of the three factors behind the growth of the Library during the first two decades of the nineteenth century. The third was Barrett's increasingly effective implementation of the Board's decision of 1791 to spend more money on acquisitions. From 1797, he began a 'Library accounts' book, in which he recorded the books ordered, by whom they had been recommended, and a note stating if and when they had been received, often with details of prices.[29] The most assiduous proposer of books for the Library was Whitley Stokes, later to become the Regius Professor of Physic. Many of his requests were for continental scientific publications, such as the fifty-five volumes of French medical books, including the *Encyclopédie méthodique: médecine*, which he ordered from Paris in 1803 at a cost of £26 14s. 6d.[30] Expenditure on books and binding fluctuated from year to year, but on occasion significant amounts were spent. In 1820, for example, the Dublin bookseller Richard Milliken was paid £434 15s. 11d. for topographical items, and Italian books costing £109 16s. 6d. were bought from Mullen.[31]

As well as carrying out binding work and supplying requested books and periodicals, Richard Mercier also provided lists of books that he thought the Library might wish to buy, many of them British publications not registered at Stationers' Hall or books published before the Copyright Act of 1801. Barrett marked these up, indicating which titles were required.[32] He also bought foreign books and periodicals from the London bookseller J. C. de Boffe, and his successors Treuttel and Würtz, as well as items from Cadell and Davies, which were often included in the same parcels as those from

[27] MUN/LIB/13/23, 8 January 1821.
[28] MUN/V/5/6, 21 October 1822; MUN/V/57/9, September and December quarters 1822.
[29] MUN/LIB/1/29.   [30] *Ibid.*; MUN/V/57/8, June quarter 1803.
[31] MUN/V/57/9, September and December quarters 1820; MUN/LIB/11/3/12a.
[32] See, for example, MUN/LIB/12/3. Mercier's accounts are MUN/LIB/11/2.

Stationers' Hall. The regular Dublin-based suppliers were Mercier, Milliken, John Archer and James Vallance, whilst some of the periodicals came via the Clerks of the Roads at the General Post Office. On the reverse of an invoice from William Armit at the GPO, dated 1802, is a note in Barrett's hand that the College wished to take regularly the *Monthly Review*, the *Critical Review*, the *Gentleman's Magazine* and the *British Critic*, by 1811, Nicholson's *Journal of Natural Philosophy, Chemistry and the Arts* and the *Philosophical Magazine* had been added to this list, at a total annual cost of £14 2s. 6d.[33]

In the early 1800s the war with France affected the importation of books and the safety of those in transit to Dublin. Cadell and Davies sent a parcel of French titles in 1803, but were obliged to include a list of those 'not to be found in London at present, and which, during the present state of things, it will be impossible to procure from the Continent'.[34] In 1811, a ship carrying a consignment of books from Stationers' Hall was captured by a French privateer and taken to Gravelines.[35] In the same year, de Boffe supplied several volumes of the *Acta Academiae Scientiarum Imperialis Petropolitanae* for various years between 1774 and 1796, but noted in relation to these that 'the Petersburgh Transactions are very scarce and difficult of attainment but you may rely on my utmost endeavours to procure the intermediate deficiencies'.[36] This was one of a number of foreign scholarly journals, especially in classics, science and engineering, to which the Library subscribed from the early nineteenth century.

Sales of private libraries continued to be a source of acquisitions, especially of older books. Among the items bought in 1805 from the collection that had belonged to the late Arthur Browne, Regius Professor of Laws, was a Shakespeare first folio, acquired for 22½ guineas. The following year the sale of the politician John Beresford's books yielded Prynne's *Records* in three volumes for 62 guineas.[37] In 1812, the Board set up a committee to select books to be bought from the library assembled by the Whig politician Thomas Wogan Browne, who had committed suicide, being deeply in debt. They spent £64 8s. 3d. and acquired around 50 titles from the 6,000 in the auction, including several incunabula.[38] Eight years later, £116 17s. 8d. was spent on about a hundred titles bought at the Monck Mason sale.[39]

Oriental literature too, in both printed and manuscript form, arrived from several sources. General Vallancey acted as the conduit between the

---

[33] MUN/LIB/11/7/6; MUN/LIB/12/6.　　[34] MUN/LIB/11/8/2.

[35] MUN/LIB/2/1, 23 January 1811.　　[36] MUN/LIB/13/8a.

[37] MUN/LIB/2/1, 25 November 1805, 10 March 1806.

[38] *Ibid.*, 9 January 1813; MUN/LIB/11/2/53a.　　[39] MUN/LIB/2/2, 19 June 1820.

College and the orientalist Sir William Ouseley, who was trying to establish whether Trinity was interested in buying a collection of manuscripts, mostly in Persian, Arabic and Turkish, that 'a friend' was trying to sell. Ouseley sent Vallancey a list of the manuscripts, noting that the price had been reduced from 110 guineas to 85, 'which to those who know how Persian M.S.S. sell (25 and 30 guineas for a handsome book is not thought high) must appear extremely moderate considering that there are 66 volumes'.[40] The Board was persuaded and the sixty-six volumes and four pictures were received in the Library in April 1808.[41]

Vallancey himself donated four Sanskrit manuscripts in 1802 and they were placed with the earlier donation from La Touche.[42] In 1805, Claudius Buchanan, a Scottish clergyman, who was Vice-Provost of the East India Company's training college at Fort William in Calcutta, donated to Trinity, as well as to Cambridge and Eton College, about sixty volumes of books on oriental subjects, including grammars and translations of literature, as well as Christian scriptures translated into Indian languages.[43] The East India Company also acquired whatever had not already been looted from the library of Tipu Sultan, the ruler of Mysore, who had resisted British expansion in India and was killed in 1799. Some of his manuscripts were given to Oxford and Cambridge, and in 1806 Trinity received a fine Qur'an and a manuscript of the *Shahnamah* by the Persian poet Firdawsi.[44] A decade or so later, these were shown to the Persian ambassador, who is reported to have expressed surprise at the number of Persian manuscripts in the Library and to have valued the Qur'an at a thousand guineas. Its condition must have been something of an embarrassment, however, as George Mullen was brought in to repair the binding a few days after the visit.[45]

In 1806, a volume of what he described as 'affidavits to prove the occurrences of the rebellion of 1798' (MS 871) was donated by Sir Richard Musgrave, who had used them for his virulently anti-Catholic *Memoirs of the different rebellions in Ireland* (Dublin, 1801–2). They remained sealed until 1817. This was the first of several groups of documents relating to the events of 1798 that were to be acquired over the next century.[46]

---

[40] MS 2571.

[41] MUN/LIB/13/7. The manuscripts were shelved with others in the same languages and were allocated various numbers between MSS 1515 and 1622.

[42] MUN/LIB/2/1, 3 July 1802.   [43] *Ibid.*, 27 November 1805.

[44] McKitterick, pp. 376–80; MUN/LIB/1/53, p. 259 (20 September 1806); the manuscripts are now MSS 1539 and 1549.

[45] MUN/LIB/2/2, 16 and 29 November 1819; W. B. S. Taylor, *History of the University of Dublin* (London: Cadell & Cumming, 1845), p. 315.

[46] MS 871, fol. 166; MUN/LIB/2/1, 21 November 1806; MUN/LIB/2/2, 25 September 1817; R. B. McDowell, 'The 1798 Rebellion', in *Treasures*, pp. 143–7.

The outstanding donation of the early nineteenth century, however, was the collection bequeathed by Henry George Quin in 1805.[47] It numbers just 157 volumes, but each one is of bibliographical importance. Quin, educated at Trinity, was the son of a wealthy Dublin doctor and his considerable fortune allowed him to indulge his passion for book collecting. In 1785, he set off to tour Europe, buying books in Paris on the outward journey. He left some, including an Elsevier Cicero, to be bound by Derome and to be collected as he passed again through Paris on his return journey. He travelled abroad at least twice more to attend book sales, first to Amsterdam in 1790, to buy at the sale of the library of Pietro-Antonio Bolongaro-Crevenna, and then the following year to London for James Edwards' sale of the Bibliotheca Parisiana. Among the items he bought in Amsterdam were three incunabula and one of the Mahieu bindings in the collection. His expenditure of £192 10s. 0d. on a 1470 Vindelinus de Spira edition of Virgil, printed on vellum, was the highest price paid at the Crevenna sale and for this he was awarded the auctioneer's gavel, which formed part of his later bequest to Trinity.

In 1805, at the age of 45, Quin shot himself in his bed, leaving a note to say that he was tired of living. In his will he left the bulk of his estate to his brother, but bequeathed to Trinity his 'large mahogany bookcase, together with such of my books and manuscripts as are specified in a catalogue bound in red morocco leather written with my own hand'. He directed that, because of their value, the books should be kept in the Manuscripts Room and that the words 'Bibliotheca Quiniana' be put on the doors of the bookcase. The books were never to be rebound or re-lettered.[48] The bookcase, with its collection, was duly placed in the new Manuscripts Room above the Fagel library. It contained seventeen incunabula, including four Aldines, and sixteen books printed on vellum. Of greater significance even than the editions are the bindings. Several date from the time of Henri II of France, including five of Trinity's eight Grolier bindings and two commissioned by Thomas Mahieu, financial secretary to Henri's queen, Catherine de Medici. As well as the Derome bindings that Quin ordered in Paris, he also placed commissions with several English binders. Those that can be identified with certainty are seven books bearing the tickets used by Christian Kalthoeber, at least six executed by Roger Payne and one each from Staggemeier &

---

47 MUN/LIB/2/1, March 1805–November 1806 *passim*; Veronica Morrow, 'Bibliotheca Quiniana', in *Treasures*, pp. 184–96; Arthur Rau, 'Portrait of a bibliophile, XIII: Henry George Quin', *Book Collector*, 13 (1964), 449–62; T. P. C. Kirkpatrick, 'Bibliotheca Quiniana', *Annual Bulletin* (1946), 6–7.
48 MUN/V/5/5, 16 March 1805.

Welcher, and Edwards of Halifax. One volume of Quin's diary was bought for the Library in 1946.

The manuscripts

In the first decade of the nineteenth century, the government's attention was drawn to the poor conditions in which many Irish public records were being stored and the lack of any guides or indexes to them. This led to the establishment of a Royal Commission in 1810 to examine the repositories, determine the extent of the catalogues and begin the work of creating calendars and indexes.[49] Barrett submitted a detailed return to the Commission, in which he listed the Trinity manuscripts that he considered related to the records and history of Ireland. He stated that the College statutes restricting access to the manuscripts were 'diligently observed' and that the Manuscripts Room was opened only in the presence of the Librarian.[50] In making these statements he was being somewhat economical with the truth, as the entries in the front of Lyon's catalogue attest to the occasional loan of manuscripts before and during Barrett's period of office.[51]

The catalogue of manuscripts that was still in use in the Library was indeed that compiled by Lyon 60 years earlier, on the final pages of which had been added all the manuscripts subsequently received. Barrett recorded his regret that Lyon had failed to provide any concordance between his catalogue and that published by Bernard in 1697, which meant that Bernard's list was of little use and that the only usable catalogue was that in the Manuscripts Room.[52] In the light of these comments, the Commissioners, at their meeting on 16 July 1812, appointed two sub-Commissioners, John Fowler and Henry Monck Mason, to prepare a catalogue of the College manuscripts for publication.[53] Monck Mason borrowed Lyon's catalogue for this purpose and in December he and Fowler visited the Library to inspect the manuscripts, which the Board had agreed could be brought by the Librarian to his room six at a time.[54] Monck Mason undertook the

[49] Margaret Griffith, 'The Irish Record Commission 1810–30', *Irish Historical Studies*, 7 (1950), 17–38.

[50] *Reports from the Commissioners, appointed by His Majesty to execute the measures recommended in an address of the House of Commons respecting the public records of Ireland, 1810–1815*, HC 1812–13 (337), XV, 1 (p. 318).

[51] MUN/LIB/1/53.   [52] Public Records Commission, note 50 above, p. 318.

[53] *Ibid.*, p. 482.   [54] MUN/LIB/2/1, 10 November, 3 December 1812.

cataloguing and relied extensively on Lyon's work, but his entries are more detailed than those of his predecessor. His catalogue is in five volumes and, like Lyon's, is organised in shelf order, covering presses A to M and including manuscripts that had arrived since the 1740s.[55] He gave responsibility for cataloguing those in Irish to the Irish-language scholar Edward O'Reilly, whose entries were later dismissed by E. J. Gwynn in the Preface to his 1921 catalogue as 'usually superficial and frequently incorrect'.[56] One of the Junior Fellows, Edward Hincks, helped with the oriental manuscripts and George Cash, a Trinity graduate who was then a barrister, with the Icelandic ones.

Monck Mason subsequently alleged that he had been shabbily treated by the Commission because, even though he claimed to possess a letter from the Secretary setting out the terms of his engagement, they refused to pay for his work, on the grounds that no minute existed of the original order. He described the circumstances in some detail in the Preface to his catalogue and said that this fact explained what he called its 'want of finish'. Having received neither payment nor 'the credit which I might have drawn from its publication', he had decided not to devote any more time to the work other than to finish the 'essential points'.[57] However, Gwynn maintained that Monck Mason's complaints were not borne out by documents that he claimed to have seen in the Public Record Office.[58] In 1833, on the recommendation of the two Assistant Librarians, Thomas Gannon and James Henthorn Todd, the Board decided that 500 copies of the catalogue should be printed at the College's expense and that Monck Mason should receive 400 of them.[59] This plan was never carried out, and in 1835 Monck Mason sold his catalogue, still in manuscript, to the College for £100.[60]

In 1815, no doubt as a result of Monck Mason's work, the Board ordered a review of the state of the manuscripts. All were to be examined to establish which needed to be repaired, an investigation that would precipitate a major rebinding programme in the 1820s. James Wilson, the Assistant Librarian, was instructed to organise the more recently received manuscripts in presses H to L, putting the Irish manuscripts together with those of the 'northern languages and antiquities' and then the Persian manuscripts. The catalogue was to be corrected and completed, and 'proper marks' were to be applied to the manuscripts themselves. Hincks was to assist with the

---

[55] The catalogue is now MUN/LIB/1/55.   [56] Abbott and Gwynn, p. xix.
[57] MUN/LIB/1/55 (1), pp. 1–3.
[58] Abbott and Gwynn, p. vi. The documents presumably perished in 1922.
[59] MUN/V/5/7, 2 February and 23 March 1833.   [60] MUN/V/57/10, June quarter 1835.

Persian manuscripts and was also asked to produce a separate catalogue of them.[61] This catalogue never materialised and in 1820 Hincks resigned his Fellowship for the seclusion of a country rectory, where he became one of the pioneers in the decipherment of hieroglyphic and cuneiform scripts.

Edward Barwick, book thief

The books now arriving steadily from Stationers' Hall, and those coming as a result of the increased budget for purchasing, all had to be catalogued. The Board's response to this need was to follow its previous practice of employing temporary assistants. On this occasion they selected Edward Barwick, a graduate resident in the College – a decision that turned out to have been unwise in the extreme. Barwick was employed from early 1812, at a salary of £100 a year, to prepare a *catalogue raisonnée*, or subject-catalogue, in which he was to indicate the name of each book and 'its exact place in the Library'.[62] In October, the Board inspected a specimen of his work and declared itself satisfied with it.[63]

Barwick's duties also included acknowledging the receipt of books from Stationers' Hall, and his signature appears on several lists, as well as on those from the College bookseller, Richard Mercier.[64] He was clearly trusted by the authorities. Even though he was only an MA and not a Fellow, the Board appointed him to hold the Library keys when the Assistant Librarian was absent during the summers of 1812 to 1814. Towards the end of 1815 he was paid the balance of the salary due to him for his catalogue, but the Board agreed that he should 'have access to the said catalogue to inspect and amend the same from time to time'.[65]

This trust turned out to have been badly misplaced.[66] In 1815, the London firm of publishers and booksellers Longman, Hurst and Rees distributed the catalogue of their sale of early English poetry, in which was listed Wynkyn de Worde's 1522 printing of *The worlde and the chylde*, described as 'a poetical tract of excessive rarity' and priced at £30.[67] This book is in fact so rare

---

[61] MUN/V/5/6, 13 May 1815.   [62] *Ibid.*, 1 May 1813.

[63] *Ibid.*, 3 October 1812; MUN/LIB/11/11/14 and MUN/LIB/11/11/22; MUN/LIB/11/12.

[64] E.g. MUN/LIB/11/2/48 (24 July 1812) and MUN/LIB/2/1 (18 August 1813).

[65] MUN/V/5/6, 25 November 1815.

[66] Ian Lancashire, 'The provenance of *The worlde and the chylde*', *Papers of the Bibliographical Society of America*, 67 (1973), 377–88.

[67] *Bibliotheca Anglo-poetica; or, A descriptive catalogue of a rare and rich collection of early English poetry* (London: Longman, 1815), p. 412.

that the only known copy was, and is, that in Trinity. The inclusion of it in the sale catalogue was drawn to Barrett's attention by Mercier as part of his role as an adviser on potential purchases. Barrett checked the shelves, discovered that the Library's copy was missing, and in April 1817 Longman was contacted. The firm replied that they had bought the book in July 1814 from a Mr Henry Osborne of Belfast. They sent 'Osborne's' letter and, a few days later, a list of 115 books that they had bought from him. This was followed by a further list of over a hundred books bought from 'Osborne' in May 1815.[68] It must have been clear from the handwriting on the letter that 'Osborne' was in fact Barwick, and Barwick himself must have realised that suspicion would fall upon him once the theft was noticed, and so he wrote a long letter to the Provost stating that he was a collector who bought and sold books. He admitted using the pseudonym Osborne, but claimed that he had done so in order to avoid being approached by booksellers trying to sell their wares. He protested his innocence at length, claimed that the Wynkyn de Worde was not unique and that it was impossible for him to know whether he had sold it, given the 'distance of time and the innumerable volumes I have at various times purchased'.[69] He even suggested that if the book had indeed been taken from the College Library, then it might have been stolen by Casey in 1793.

Barrett had Longman's list checked against the shelves. He discovered not only that the books on the list were missing from the Library but also that in many instances the catalogue had been amended in Barwick's handwriting to disguise their removal.[70] The Board was unimpressed with Barwick's protestations of innocence and ordered that he should be banned from the Library. They also accepted Longman's offer to return the books on payment of £130, the amount that 'Osborne' had received for them, and Mercier was paid £100 for the information he had supplied.[71] The thefts included at least three incunabula and a 1551 edition of More's *Utopia*; over two hundred books, including the Wynkyn de Worde, were recovered.

It was not known whether Longman had been Barwick's only outlet for the stolen books and since, as the person responsible for compiling the catalogue, he had been able to cover his tracks, Barrett decided that only a complete shelf-by-shelf inspection of the Long Room would establish the full extent of the thefts. In 1818, the Library clerks were instructed to carry out such an investigation and produce a detailed record of the missing

[68] MUN/LIB/13/17–MUN/LIB/13/18; MUN/LIB/2/2, fols. 17–21.
[69] MUN/LIB/2/2, fols. 15–16.   [70] MUN/LIB/2/6/5–MUN/LIB/2/6/8.
[71] MUN/V/5/6, 20 September 1817; MUN/V/57/9, September quarter 1817.

books. Their list ran to two volumes, of which only one now remains, and so it will probably never be possible to establish precisely how many books were stolen. The extant volume provides detailed evidence of Barwick's activities. In some cases he had substituted one book for another; in others he had removed a pamphlet from a volume containing several titles and amended the catalogue record accordingly. Typical of the entries in the clerks' report are:

F.7.40: an erasure & substitution. The book substituted has the label carefully scraped off & the reference on the inside written in the suspicious hand

and:

N.8.6–8: The 3 original books are taken away & only 2 books left in their place, but the title of one is so entered in local catal. as to appear to be 2 distinct titles.[72]

A final twist to this story occurred in April 1818 when twenty-six volumes were thrown over the wall into the Provost's courtyard with a note that they had been taken from the Library. From Barrett's report of the incident and the related alterations to the catalogue, it is clear that these, too, were part of the same theft.[73]

There is no evidence that Barwick was prosecuted for his crimes, but in May 1817, at the instigation of Provost Elrington, the Board introduced new regulations to improve the security of the collections. An additional table was provided so that readers, who were no longer to be allowed to read at the desks in the alcoves, could be better supervised. Only Library staff were to have access to the shelves and a system of dockets was introduced to record the ordering of books and their return to the porters. The new regulations did not apply to Fellows, but the Board minuted that it was hoped they would 'show an example in conforming to them except in very particular cases'.[74] William Davenport, Professor of Natural and Experimental Philosophy and a member of the Board, objected to the new regulations, pointing out that the thefts had not been carried out by a reader but by one of the Library staff, who had access at all times and had been employed to catalogue the very books that he had stolen. He also argued that, as the regulations had been changed without the approval of the Visitors of the University (the Chancellor and the Archbishop of Dublin), they contravened the statutes. At the annual visitation of the College the following October, Davenport submitted his objections to the Visitors, who determined that,

---

[72] MUN/LIB/1/30.   [73] MUN/LIB/2/2, 7 April 1818; MUN/LIB/2/6, fol. 7.
[74] MUN/V/5/6, 3 May 1817.

until the Board had resolved its differences, the old regulations were to be applied.[75]

The Board meeting on 31 October 1817 was a fraught one. A motion to replace the regulations from the previous May with more suitable ones was approved, but Elrington insisted that his dissent be recorded, and he spoke at length in support of the regulations that he had introduced in May. He was concerned as much for the preservation of the students' morals as for that of the books. The regulations were, he said, designed to protect the books, 'of which many have been stolen and many mutilated', because readers were allowed direct access to them and read them in the alcoves. It was also necessary 'to preserve the morals of the students, who … protected from observation … have often employed themselves in reading very improper books. I recall magic to have been so studied, and all the Senior Fellows are aware that indecent books have been much read'.[76] He defended his proposed system of dockets on the grounds that it provided evidence of who had used the books if damage was later discovered and he reminded the Board that similar arrangements applied at the British Museum and Marsh's Library.

The Board managed to agree and avoid further involvement of the Visitors. It took the view that, because the alcoves made it impossible for the Library staff to monitor readers properly, further 'depredations' could be avoided by removing the seats and desks and replacing them with a small table in each recess, and by setting up a 'common table' in the centre of the Long Room. It also extended the Library's opening by an hour. The salaries of the Library staff were increased by a quarter to compensate, bringing the Librarian's salary to £125 and that of his assistant to £42. A second porter was also appointed.[77]

The Lending Library

Claudius Gilbert's will had included provision for establishing a lending library for students, who were not allowed to use the main Library. The existence of a 'Lending Library borrowers book' dating from 1762 suggests that this may have been the date when the library opened.[78] The book was organised in a traditional way, with columns showing the date of the loan,

---

[75] MUN/LIB/12/11–MUN/LIB/12/13.   [76] MUN/V/5/6, 31 October 1817.
[77] *Ibid.*; MUN/V/57/9, December quarter 1817. The new hours were 8 a.m. to 10 a.m. and 11 a.m. to 2 p.m.
[78] The book is now MUN/LIB/8/13.

the title of the book borrowed, the name of the tutor borrowing the book, the name of the student on whose behalf the book had been borrowed, and the date of return. To start with, use of the collection was minimal, but it increased gradually. Only eight books were recorded as being borrowed in 1763. Ten years later, the number had risen to twenty-three and in 1783 sixty-five loans were listed, generally, as might be expected, of the same titles being loaned on multiple occasions. The most frequently borrowed were either those in the curriculum, such as John Conybeare's *Defence of revealed religion*, or those likely to be of use to the future Protestant clergyman, like Gilbert Burnet's *Exposition of the thirty-nine articles* and John Pearson's *Exposition of the creed*.

Books were occasionally bought for the lending collection and charged to the main Library account, and Fellows donated copies of their own publications.[79] In 1790, when the Board commissioned the College bookseller to publish an edition of Robert Gray's *Key to the Old Testament*, it took twenty copies for the use of the Lending Library. The Professor of Modern History was also asked to provide a list of books to be bought.[80]

The disposal of Provost Murray's collection after his death in 1799 acted as a catalyst to revitalise the Lending Library. His mathematical and philosophical books, numbering about 130 volumes, many in multiple copies and valued by Mercier at £107 10s. 0d., were presented to the College by Dr William Murray. The Board decided that they should be used to form a Lending Library, 'to be put under new regulations'.[81] The books in the existing Lending Library were moved to the Law School lecture room on the ground floor of the West Pavilion and augmented by those from Murray. To that nucleus were added more books over the coming years. In 1803, duplicates that had arrived with the Fagel collection were transferred, and in 1816 other Fagel books deemed more appropriate for the Lending Library were placed there.[82] Regular additions were made of works by Fellows and former Fellows, usually in multiple copies. In 1802, for example, twenty-five copies of each of Richard Stack's *Introduction to the study of chemistry* (Dublin, 1802) and Matthew Young's *Analysis of the principles of natural philosophy* (Dublin, 1800) were added, followed, the year after, by the same number of Joseph Stock's edition of Isaiah (Bath, 1803).[83]

The Lending Library was placed in the care of one of the Junior Fellows, to be appointed at the annual election of officers and to be paid £30 a

---

[79] MUN/LIB/2/1, e.g. 31 October 1787 and 16 November 1793.   [80] MUN/V/5/5, 10 July 1790.
[81] *Ibid.*, 20 June 1800; MUN/LIB/2/1, 2 December 1800; MUN/LIB/10/222a.
[82] MS 4960, 16 July 1803; MUN/V/5/6, 13 November 1816.
[83] MUN/V/5/5, 27 March 1802, 20 July 1803.

year, that being the interest from Gilbert's bequest. It was specifically noted that this would not reduce the salary of the Assistant Librarian, who had presumably exercised responsibility for the Lending Library up to that point. On 20 November 1800, Thomas Prior was elected Junior Dean and Librarian of the Lending Library, and from then on those two offices were held in tandem by the same Junior Fellow. The Librarian of the Lending Library was required to attend from 1 p.m. until 3 p.m. on Tuesdays and Fridays in term, and for the same hours, on Fridays only, in the vacation. From the outset he was provided with a junior Assistant, paid a salary of £8 a year.[84] The Librarian also had to produce a report within three weeks of his election, listing the books on loan at the time of his appointment and the amount deposited for them, together with details of any losses in the previous year.

The regulations for the use of the Lending Library were stringent.[85] Admission was granted only to those whose names were on the College books and who had taken the Library oath, which meant that undergraduates were excluded from this collection as well as from the main Library. The only exception was made for mathematical and theological books, which could be lent to any students attending lectures in those subjects as long as they produced a certificate from their lecturer indicating that they were 'deserving of such extraordinary indulgence'.[86] The borrowing process was cumbersome. Each borrower had to deposit in advance a sum of money equal to the value of the book or set to which the book belonged. In practice, this seems to have been established at £1 2s. 9d. per volume or multiples thereof, and later at £1 per volume.[87] The money was placed in a sealed envelope in an iron box provided for the purpose and was returned to the borrower when he brought the book back. The loan period was normally one month, and heavy fines were imposed for the late return of books.

These regulations remained in place until 1838. They were described by the Dublin University Commission report of 1853 as 'cumbrous, and, in some respects, vexatious', and had the effect of discouraging use of the collection by the students, very few of whom were even aware of its existence.[88] Members of the Board took a rather different view. The regulations required a committee of the Board to visit the Lending Library in the first week of November each year; the first visitation took place in 1801 and its reports, reproduced annually in the Board Register, were invariably favourable.

[84] MUN/V/58 1–3, *passim.*   [85] MUN/V/5/5, 8 November 1800.   [86] *Ibid.*
[87] MUN/LIB/8/14.   [88] DU Commission, *Report*, p. 78.

Barrett and Prior were the two Senior Fellows who carried out the visitations between 1813 and 1820. In 1819, they reported that 'the students appear to have derived considerable advantage' from the Library and the following year they noted that there had been 'many applications to it for the loan of books' – a somewhat rose-tinted view since in fact only twenty-nine loans were recorded during that year.[89] After Barrett's death, in 1821, the visitations seem to have stopped and the Lending Library ticked over until the 1830s, when new life was breathed into it by James Henthorn Todd.

The building

By the turn of the century, the Library had been in use for 70 years and serious problems with the roof were starting to become evident. A report from the stonemason George Darley and the carpenter Timothy McEvoy was presented to the Board in May 1802, but it was felt to be inconclusive, and so the Bursar and Elrington, then a Senior Fellow, were asked to investigate further.[90] It was another 4 years before decisive action was taken and by that stage major repairs were required. The architect Richard Morrison, who had recently completed Sir Patrick Dun's Hospital, was commissioned to produce plans and estimates, and in April 1806 he was appointed as the College architect (a post that he held until 1831) with immediate responsibility for superintending the repairs to the Library.[91] The old slates were stripped off the roof and replaced with a temporary canvas covering whilst work on the rafters was carried out. This was a major undertaking, with up to seventeen carpenters at a time working throughout the summer of 1806. By the end of the year the new roof was in place but the plaster ceiling, which had also been removed, had to be reinstated. McEvoy made moulds for the plasterers and George Stapleton carried out the plastering and stucco work. His bill included '851 yards of floated and coated ceiling', covering the whole of the Long Room, as well as circular and oval 'stucco ornaments'.[92] These are presumably the ones that remained until the rebuilding of the roof in 1859–60 (see Figure 13), though the Library had to be closed again in the summer of 1823 for him to carry out repairs to the ceiling, and it was repainted again in 1839.[93]

---

[89] MUN/V/5/6, 6 November 1819, 11 November 1820; MUN/LIB/8/14.

[90] MS 4960, 1 May 1802.   [91] MUN/V/5/5, 25 April 1806; MUN/V/57/8, March quarter 1806.

[92] MUN/P/2/191–MUN/P/2/194 (MUN/P/2/194/39).

[93] MUN/LIB/2/2, July–August 1823; MUN/V/57/9, September quarter 1823; MUN/P/2/295/10 and 18; MUN/V/57/11, September quarter 1839.

The total cost of the repairs to the roof exceeded £3,000. That included the price of 72 tons of Portland stone imported by George Darley. There is a note in Barrett's hand to the effect that it had been intended to erect a balustrade around the roof but that the plans had changed, and this led to a dispute between Darley and the College about the ownership of the stone. In the end, some was used at the Dunsink Observatory, but in 1811, 50 tons of Portland stone were reported as still lying around the College.[94]

The sandstone facing on the upper part of the external walls remained in its decayed state. Like Thomas Campbell over 30 years earlier, the writer Anne Plumptre, visiting in 1814, observed that it was 'of such a soft and mouldering nature that though not a hundred years old it seems falling rapidly to decay'.[95]

The two most significant changes inside the Long Room during this period were the replacement of the ceiling and the removal of the seats from the alcoves. The original capacity of the room for the storage of books – about 45,000 volumes – had been reached and the shelves were full. In 1804, the Board asked for an estimate of the cost of installing shelving in the gallery. Timothy McEvoy erected one set of shelves as a sample and quoted £690 for thirty-eight double stalls to match it.[96] These plans caused consternation both inside and outside the College. A visitor wrote that the gallery 'is about to be disfigured by projecting rows, which will spoil the view of the whole, or parallel with the wall, by which means the pillars will be broken. On this momentous question, the Fellows I understand are at present divided.'[97] The division among the Fellows was such that no further action was taken at the time, but the shortage of space became more acute. In 1816, James McEvoy fitted shelving into the 'waste room' above the Librarian's Room in the West Pavilion to create a Reading Room, and the following year the Board agreed that, 'space being now wanted in the Library for new books', the Librarian could transfer books to the Reading Room.[98] McEvoy's samples of bookcases were also removed from the gallery.[99]

Several busts were added during the first two decades of the nineteenth century. The first was that of Edmond Sexton, Viscount Pery, Speaker of the Irish House of Commons during the 1770s and 1780s. The sculptor

---

94 MUN/P/2/195.
95 Anne Plumptre, *Narrative of a residence in Ireland during the summer of 1814 and that of 1815* (London: Colborn, 1817), pp. 20–1.
96 MUN/V/5/5, 15 October 1804; MUN/P/2/190, 19 October 1804.
97 [Anon.] *Ireland in 1804*, with an Introduction by Seamus Grimes (Dublin: Four Courts Press, 1980), pp. 60, 62.
98 MUN/V/5/6, 15 March 1817.   99 MUN/P/2/229 and 236; MUN/LIB/13/20.

was the English artist J. C. Rossi, and the bust is thought to have been put into the Long Room in 1807, shortly after Pery's death, though there is no record of its arrival in the College. In 1812, the Board ordered two busts from the Belfast-born sculptor Peter Turnerelli, who had recently completed busts of the royal family.[100] The two were those of Ernest August, Duke of Cumberland, who had been elected as Chancellor of the University in 1805, and of his father, George III.

Visitors

By the beginning of the nineteenth century the Long Room had become part of the itinerary for many of the increasing number of visitors to the city. During Barrett's tenure of office, however, their delight in the building and its collections was tempered for many by their encounter with the Library's custodian. There are several published accounts of Barrett's treatment of visitors, few of them flattering.[101] The French naval engineer Charles Dupin criticised the restrictions on access not just to Trinity's Library but to others in the city and, although he was granted a tour, Barrett would not allow him to stop anywhere: 'I wished to approach a window from which a tolerably fine prospect was to be enjoyed; but the doctor, who accompanied me, held me back.'[102] The Polish writer Karol Sienkiewicz faced a similar reception: 'I found the Librarian, a little old figure with short shanks, so that his knees seemed to grow from his abdomen. I said that I wanted to see the Library . . . [I] asked only that he would allow me to look at least at the manuscripts catalogue but on this he basely replied to me, with understanding worthy of a barbarian, that in this Library only licentiates had the right to read. Others had not.'[103]

The description that most incensed Barrett himself was that by Anne Plumptre, who was brought to the Library by William Magee, the Dean of Cork and a former Senior Fellow. Plumptre was shown a number of manuscripts and wrote in admiring terms of the 'dignified' appearance of the Long Room and the 'celebrated' Fagel library. In her pen portrait of the Librarian, she acknowledged his scholarship and 'passion for books and

[100] MUN/V/5/6, 8 July 1812.

[101] Peter Fox, '"A library well deserving the notice of the traveller"', in Holland, pp. 135–52.

[102] Charles Dupin, *Two excursions to the ports of England, Scotland and Ireland in 1816, 1817 and 1818* (London: Phillips, 1819), p. 54.

[103] Henry Heaney, '"Quo vadis?": a Polish visitor to TCD in 1821', *Linen Hall Review*, 4/4 (Winter 1987), 13–14.

learning [which] even rises above another very prevailing feature, the love of money'. Barrett, she said, 'never stirs beyond the college walls excepting twice in the year to the bank, which is close by, to receive his half-yearly dividends'. He spent nothing except on books and would have starved 'were not his dinner provided free of expense by the College'.[104] When Plumptre's book arrived in the Library, Barrett tried to prevent it from being added to the collection. He noted in the Library minutes book that he had catalogued the books recently received, 'with the exception of Miss Anne Plumptre's narrative which I hope the board will order to be locked up as too silly and too ill mannered for a public library'.[105] His attempt at censorship was unsuccessful and the book is in the Library with a manuscript copy of this note inside the front cover.

One of Barrett's last public occasions was the visit by George IV in August 1821, the first of several by reigning monarchs and an early example of what was to become the custom by which the Library and its treasures were shown to heads of state and other distinguished visitors to Dublin. However, no other such visit has been attended with quite the same level of extravagance. The Long Room was specially carpeted in crimson, a throne was built at the east end, the busts were rearranged, the empty gallery was used to provide seating for the ladies, and the nobility and gentry filled the main floor 'in all the costumes of the Church, the Law, the University, and the Profession of Arms'.[106] Barrett, in his role as Vice-Provost and Librarian, addressed the King in Latin 'but what small talk, if any, then took place between the First Gentleman of Europe and the most dilapidated scholar of Europe history does not relate'.[107]

* * *

Barrett died in his rooms in the College on 15 November 1821 having amassed a fortune amounting to around £70,000. He left almost all of this to charities for the relief of the 'sick and indigent and poor and naked', with only token annuities to his relatives.[108] However, they successfully persuaded the trustees of his will that their impoverished state, caused in part by Barrett's refusal to support them during his lifetime, made them eligible to benefit under the terms of the will.

[104] Plumptre, note 95 above, pp. 18–21.   [105] MUN/LIB/2/2, 9 September 1817.
[106] *Freeman's Journal*, 31 August 1821; MUN/P/1/1489–MUN/P/1/1502 (documents relating to George IV's visit, including the text of Barrett's speech).
[107] McDowell and Webb, p. 82.   [108] MS 2376 (copy of Barrett's will).

10 | Sadleir, Wall and Todd: 1822–1851

Franc Sadleir

Barrett's death occurred conveniently close to the statutory date for choosing College officers, and so the vacancy for the Librarianship was filled within a week by the election of Franc Sadleir at the Board meeting on 20 November 1821. Sadleir's career was marked more by its administrative competence and his accumulation of College offices than by its academic significance. By the mid 1820s he was simultaneously a Senior Fellow, the Librarian, the Bursar and the Professor of Mathematics, and in 1837 he succeeded Bartholomew Lloyd to the far more lucrative post of Provost. If the diaries that he maintained from the turn of the century until his death in 1851 accurately reflect his main preoccupations, then those were primarily his finances, dining, preaching, his estates, and family matters. The Library featured rarely, and usually only when he recorded the arrival of a distinguished visitor to the Long Room.[1]

In the early years of his Librarianship at least, he did not, however, revert to the practice of treating the running of the Library as a sinecure, as had some of his predecessors. The manuscripts again became the subject of attention. Scholars working on them at the time included Henry Monck Mason, who was allowed to read them in the Librarian's Room, and Sir William Betham, Ulster King of Arms, who borrowed several during the course of 1824.[2] The inspection of the manuscripts for the Irish Record Commission in 1812 was followed in 1825 by another investigation, this time by a committee of the Royal Irish Academy, and for this the manuscripts were transferred in batches to the Fagel Room.[3]

The programme of rebinding, which had been planned after the 1812 inspection, began in earnest during Sadleir's tenure of office. The binder employed on this occasion was George Mullen junior. Mullen's father, also George, had been binding books for the College Library since 1808. Among

---

[1] The diaries are MSS 3337a–3358.
[2] MUN/V/5/6, 25 January 1823; MUN/LIB/2/2, January–March 1824.
[3] MUN/V/5/6, 17 October 1825.

his early commissions were the 'local catalogue' (shelf list) and Barrett's catalogue of the Fagel collection, and by 1815 he had taken over from Richard Mercier as the College binder, receiving regular large consignments of books and periodicals that had arrived from Stationers' Hall.[4] Father and son worked together until Mullen senior's death in 1822, and the younger man established a reputation for producing some of the finest and most distinctive Irish bindings of the nineteenth century.[5]

The main rebinding programme began in 1825, when the Board instructed Sadleir in his role as Bursar 'to have sundry books carefully repaired', and it continued until 1831.[6] Mullen's work on the manuscripts principally involved that half of the collection that had not been touched by Exshaw in the 1740s, but he also replaced Exshaw's bindings on some of the College's treasures, presumably either because the earlier bindings had broken down or because they were not deemed to be fine enough for contemporary taste. He produced sumptuous bindings for the Book of Durrow, the Garland of Howth and the Fagel Missal, the first two in rich brown calf and the last in dark morocco, blind tooled but with gilt lines.[7] Other manuscripts rebound around the same time included the Book of Kells, the *Liber hymnorum* and the Tinnakill *Duanaire*, and in 1831 Sadleir obtained the Board's approval to proceed at his own discretion with further disbinding and cleaning of the manuscripts, as he had reported that they were 'in a state of decay by worms'.[8] The infestation was not confined to the manuscripts, and scores of books from the Fagel collection and the Long Room had to be sent to the College's other binder, Joshua Devoy, because worms had been found in them.[9]

The quality of Mullen's bindings is superb, but the liberties he took with some of the manuscripts themselves are a different matter entirely. Roger Powell, who rebound the Book of Kells in 1953, described Mullen's treatment of it in 1826 as a 'disaster'.[10] Mullen washed it, causing the vellum to shrink unevenly, and then allowed the pages to be pressed together whilst still damp, a process that caused a considerable amount of the colour to be lost.

---

[4] MUN/LIB/2/1 *passim*; MUN/V/57/8 and MUN/V/57/9. Mullen's accounts are MUN/LIB/11/1.

[5] McDonnell and Healy, p. 69; M. Pollard, *A dictionary of members of the Dublin book trade, 1550–1800* (London: Bibliographical Society, 2000), p. 421.

[6] MUN/V/5/6, 17 October 1825.

[7] William O'Sullivan, 'Binding memories of Trinity Library', in *Decantations*, pp. 168–76.

[8] William O'Sullivan, 'Notes on the Trinity *Liber hymnorum*', in John L. Sharp, ed., *Roger Powell: the compleat binder* (Turnhout: Brepols, 1996), pp. 130–3; Anne O'Sullivan, 'The Tinnakill Duanaire', *Celtica*, 11 (1976), 214–28; MUN/V/5/7, 11 June 1831.

[9] MUN/LIB/2/2, June–October 1825, September 1827.   [10] MS 2589, p. 2.

He painted some of the margins with what appeared to be white oil-paint, he filled and tinted the holes in the vellum, regardless of whether this was structurally necessary, and, most unforgivable of all, he trimmed the pages, sometimes by more than a centimetre, in order to produce an even edge that could be gilded, a process that had the effect of cutting off parts of the decoration on certain pages. Mullen was paid £22 15s. 0d. for his work on the Book of Kells.[11] The biblical scholar Samuel Prideaux Tregelles, who worked on Codex Z in 1853, was similarly alarmed at the effect of Mullen's intervention on that manuscript. The pages had been 'unmercifully strengthened' by pasting paper or vellum over the margins; they had been trimmed, so that text that had been read by Barrett around 1800 was now irrevocably lost; and the binder seemed to have assumed that the underlying text of the palimpsest was dirt marks, which he had 'industriously obliterated'. By the application of chemicals (unspecified) Tregelles managed to restore some of the text to legibility.[12]

A more successful commission carried out by Mullen was the production of an elaborately tooled russia binding for a collection of maps that had been assembled by George Carew, Lord President of Munster, at the beginning of the seventeenth century. The maps had formed part of an important collection of manuscripts relating to Ireland, most of which are now in Lambeth Palace Library. It is not known how the maps became separated from the rest of the collection and reached Trinity, though it has been speculated that they may have arrived with Gilbert's library, which was rich in atlases.[13] They were certainly in the College by the 1780s, when they were being borrowed by Charles Vallancey.[14] There are around seventy maps, almost all in manuscript, forming one of the most important collections of Tudor and Jacobean maps of Ireland in existence. They were catalogued in 1821 by James Hardiman, working for the Irish Record Commission, and they became known as the Hardiman Atlas (MS 1209) after being bound by Mullen.[15]

[11] MUN/V/57/10, March quarter 1826.
[12] Samuel Prideaux Tregelles, *An account of the printed text of the Greek New Testament* (London: Bagster, 1854), p. 167.
[13] William O'Sullivan, 'George Carew's Irish maps', *Long Room*, 26/27 (1983), 15–25.
[14] MUN/LIB/1/53, fol. iv r.
[15] James Hardiman, 'A catalogue of maps, charts and plans, relating to Ireland, preserved amongst the manuscripts in the Library of Trinity College Dublin', *Trans. RIA*, 14 (1825), 57–77; J. H. Andrews, 'Maps and atlases', in *Treasures*, pp. 170–83. Hardiman's catalogue is MUN/LIB/1/62. The 'atlas' was disbound in 1982.

James Henthorn Todd

The Library employed too few staff to keep up with cataloguing the books newly received from Stationers' Hall, and, despite the disastrous appointment of Barwick, the practice of appointing recent graduates as clerks resumed from 1816.[16] The clerks normally stayed for only a short time, usually whilst they were completing their MA, and so were unable to develop much expertise in Library procedures. It was obvious to those who used the Library that its staffing, both in terms of quantity and quality, was no longer adequate and from 1831 several newly elected Fellows offered their services as supernumerary Assistant Librarians without salary. The first of these was James Henthorn Todd, who volunteered less than a week after being elected as a Fellow. (See Figure 11.) He was followed by three more new Fellows, as well as by one of the Senior Fellows, Charles William Wall, shortly to be Sadleir's successor as Librarian.[17]

This activity on the part of the Fellows reflected a growing recognition that all was not well with the Library. In 1831, the year of Todd's election to a Fellowship, Samuel Kyle resigned as Provost and was replaced by Bartholomew Lloyd, who immediately set about reforming many aspects of the College's activities. The Library did not escape his attention, and at a Board meeting in July 1834 he openly criticised Sadleir's running of it. Thomas Prior, one of the Senior Fellows present, recorded in his diary, 'much said by the Provost against the Librarian Dr Sadleir and his present assistant [Thomas Gannon]', and Sadleir himself, in a rare diary reference to the Library, noted: 'Board about the Library. Provost spoke about the duty, not being done. This I denied <u>strongly</u>.'[18]

Clearly the Board felt that more was required than simply criticising Sadleir, and so at the same meeting they appointed Todd as an additional paid Assistant Librarian and extended the Library opening hours.[19] Various proposals for longer hours had been discussed over the previous few years, and the elimination in 1831 of the closure between 10 and 11 in the morning meant that the Library was open from 8 a.m. to 2 p.m.[20] In 1834, two hours were added in the afternoon, so that the Library then closed at 4 p.m. However, the 1831 changes had also introduced a closure of six weeks from

[16] MUN/V/5/6, 20 January 1816.
[17] MUN/V/5/7, 23 November 1831, 16 February, 13 July, 9 November 1833.
[18] MS 3369, p. 345 [Prior]; MS 3351, 5 July 1834 [Sadleir].
[19] MUN/V/5/7, 5 July 1834.   [20] *Ibid.*, 10 December 1831.

the beginning of August, an arrangement that proved an inconvenience to many, including Thackeray, who visited the College in the summer of 1842 and found the Library shut. Commenting on the general lethargy of the place, he observed: 'The librarian, I suppose, is at the sea-side.'[21]

Todd's salary was set at £60 a year and his duties included taking 'his third part of the duty of attendance at the Library' (with Sadleir and the other Assistant Librarian), as well as supervising the arranging, classing and lettering of the books and dealing with Robert Durham in London.[22] In fact he applied himself to all aspects of running the Library, and from then on Sadleir was content to remain little more than a titular Librarian, resigning on 22 December 1837, on his appointment to the Provostship. He was succeeded the following day by the Professor of Hebrew, Charles William Wall, whose impact on the Library during his 14 years in office was minimal.

Todd remained as an Assistant Librarian until his election to a Senior Fellowship in 1850. Though by nature a conservative who disapproved of many of Lloyd's changes in the College, he nonetheless addressed his considerable intellect and energy to those areas of the Library that needed to be reformed, and over a period of 30 years he was responsible for turning an inward-looking and rather amateurish institution into a great international library. He extended the range and number of books purchased, he supported the opening up of the Library to undergraduates and, more than a decade before Panizzi adopted a similar approach at the British Museum, he sought to ensure that the College's rights under the Copyright Act were properly enforced. Todd also introduced a new system of cataloguing, which led eventually to the publication of the Printed Catalogue, and he improved the Library's record-keeping, noting for the first time, in 1837, the number of volumes in the collection: 81,721.[23] His reports for the annual visitation of the Library became more detailed, and included statistics of books and manuscripts acquired as well as more general issues that he wished to bring to the Board's attention.

Todd was also to become one of the most distinguished scholars in the field of Irish studies. His work in that area was centred at the Royal Irish Academy, of which he was elected a member in 1833 and in due course became President. The Academy was the principal institution supporting Irish studies, but other bodies such as the Irish Record Commission of 1810–30 and the Ordnance Survey, established in 1824, played an

---

[21] 'M. A. Titmarsh', *The Irish sketch-book*, 2 vols. (London: Chapman and Hall, 1843), vol. I, p. 25.
[22] MUN/V/5/7, 5 July 1834.   [23] MUN/LIB/2/3, August 1837.

Figure 11 James Henthorn Todd, Librarian 1852–69 (MS 4900/8)

important role, as of course did the College Library's own collection of Irish manuscripts.

Soon after his appointment as an Assistant Librarian, Todd turned his attention to those manuscripts, and in 1836 the Board provided a grant of

£50 to pay John O'Donovan to catalogue them.[24] O'Donovan was a member of the recently founded topographical section of the Ordnance Survey, headed by George Petrie and established to determine accurate forms of Irish place-names, based on fieldwork and the examination of documents. O'Donovan's early experience of trying to use the College Library for his topographical work had not been a happy one, and in 1834 he had complained that, despite the help he had received from Todd, 'too much of the monkish secrecy and seclusion yet lingers in that half-ecclesiastical edifice'.[25] The catalogue that he produced was described as 'very minute and accurate' and Todd claimed that O'Donovan had identified among the Fergus manuscripts the Annals of Kilronan, or Loch Cé (MS 1293), which were thought to have been lost.[26]

In 1840, Todd obtained funds from the Board for another Ordnance Survey employee, Eugene O'Curry, to transcribe and translate Irish manuscripts in the Library. For this work O'Curry was paid a salary of £50 a year until 1854 and received an additional £15 for arranging the leaves of the Book of Leinster (MS 1339) for binding. That manuscript had, rather surprisingly, not been bound by Lhuyd when it was in his possession and it had arrived in the Library with the Sebright manuscripts in 1786, still in an unbound state.[27] Through his work on the College's Irish manuscripts, O'Curry developed a comprehensive knowledge of the collection that was described by O'Donovan as 'not equalled by any living scholar'.[28] The two men later collaborated on the transcription and cataloguing of the Irish legal manuscripts in Trinity, the British Museum and the Bodleian for the Brehon Law Commissioners, a body set up at the instigation of Todd and his Trinity colleague Charles Graves.

Purchases and donations

The first half of the nineteenth century was a time of prosperity for the College, with its annual income doubling between 1800 and 1850.[29] Indeed,

---

[24] MUN/V/5/7, 20 February 1836. The catalogue is MUN/LIB/1/61.
[25] Letter from Maghera, 8 October 1834, RIA MS 14.D.21/43.
[26] DU Commission, 'Appendix A: Evidence', p. 175; J. H. Todd, 'Account of a discovery', *Proc. RIA*, 1 (1841), 22–4.
[27] MUN/V/57/11–MUN/V/57/12; MUN/LIB/11/22/9, MUN/LIB/11/22/19 and MUN/LIB/11/22/27; MUN/V/5/8, 31 May 1845; W. O'Sullivan, 'Notes on the scripts and make-up of the Book of Leinster', *Celtica*, 7 (1966), 1–31.
[28] John O'Donovan, *The tribes and customs of Hy-Many* (Dublin: Irish Archaeological Society, 1843), p. 21
[29] McDowell and Webb, p. 509.

a contemporary writer claimed that it was the wealthiest college in Europe and compared the income of the Provost, at £2,000 a year, with those of the heads of house at Oxford and Cambridge, who only earned about £750.[30] That affluence was reflected in the sums spent by the Library on acquisitions. Between 1811 and 1820 the average annual expenditure on books, periodicals and binding was just under £400. By the late 1830s it had risen to almost £1,500, compared to £1,800 at the Bodleian, about £800 at Cambridge and £350 at the University of Edinburgh.[31]

Important individual items were purchased, such as the *Acta sanctorum*, bought from the London booksellers Rivington and Cochran in 1823 for £124 3s. 2d., and nine volumes of the *Flora Danica* (Copenhagen, 1764–83), acquired the following year from Sir Charles Giesecke for £100.[32] But it was the demands of subjects newly introduced into the university curriculum, like geology and civil engineering, and the varied nature of the legal-deposit intake, that dramatically altered the subject-matter of Library acquisitions during this period. Soon after his election to a Fellowship, Todd began to address the Library's purchasing with his customary energy, and Thomas Prior noted in his diary: 'a large number of books not in the library recommended by Mr Todd to be bought'.[33] Books in foreign languages, especially German, were acquired in quantity. To some extent this reflected Todd's interest in Celtic studies, a subject in which Germany was a major centre, but others in the College were also recommending German literature, including both secondary works and the writings of eighteenth- and nineteenth-century poets and dramatists.[34] The secularisation of the German monasteries after the Napoleonic wars brought many items from their libraries onto the market, and in 1841 the College spent £352 11s. 0d. on several hundred German Reformation pamphlets.[35]

Manuscripts were also being bought, especially those of Irish provenance or relating to Irish history. The most important was the small eighth-century

---

[30] Denis Caulfield Heron, *The constitutional history of the University of Dublin*, 2nd edn (Dublin: McGlashan, 1848), pp. 95–101.

[31] I. G. Philip, 'The Bodleian Library', in *The history of the University of Oxford*, 8 vols. (Oxford: Clarendon Press, 1984–2000), vol. VI, pp. 585–97; McKitterick, p. 500; S. M. Simpson, 'The history of the Library, 1837–1939', in Jean R. Guild and Alexander Law, eds., *Edinburgh University Library 1580–1980: a collection of historical essays* (Edinburgh: University Library, 1982), pp. 94–114.

[32] MUN/LIB/11/18/5; MUN/V/57/9, June quarter 1823; MUN/LIB/11/19/8.

[33] MS 3369, 31 May 1834.

[34] Veronika Koeper-Saul, 'The study of German in TCD and the acquisition of German language works by the Library in the nineteenth-century', in *Essays*, pp. 151–66; Roy Stanley, 'Trinity College Library, Dublin', in *German studies: British resources* (London: British Library, 1986), pp. 205–9.

[35] MUN/V/57/11, December quarter 1841.

Gospel book known as the Book of Dimma (MS 59), with its *cumdach* of silver-plated bronze. The manuscript takes its name from a word that appears several times in the text, possibly referring to its scribe or a group of scribes. It was owned by Sir William Betham, who had purchased it from Henry Monck Mason in 1825. Betham later offered it to the English collector Sir Thomas Phillipps for £250, the price he said he had paid Monck Mason for it, but nothing came of that offer. In 1830, it was included in an auction of Betham's manuscripts in London, but those sold poorly and Betham withdrew it. In 1836, the College bought it from him for £150.[36]

The rebellion of 1798 was documented by an important collection of informants' reports on the United Irishmen, letters seized by the authorities, and dossiers of political prisoners (MS 869). These had been collected by Major Henry Sirr, who was Town Major, the head of the Dublin police, between 1798 and 1826, and they were bought by the Library in 1842 from his son Joseph D'Arcy Sirr for £40.[37] In the same year the younger Sirr donated two manuscripts (MSS 2467–8) by the seventeenth-century Church of Ireland Bishop of Meath, Anthony Dopping, writing mysteriously to Todd, 'Don't mention from whom you received them. Let the channel be a profound secret . . . I will try to get the remainder, some of which are of value.'[38]

Two of the Library's finest manuscripts, a fifteenth-century Book of Hours (MS 105) and the fourteenth-century 'Dublin Apocalypse' (MS 64), include notes in Todd's hand that they were donated by Sadleir. The former was certainly received as a bequest at his death in 1851, but Sadleir's own diary shows that his munificence in the case of the latter was not completely altruistic. There he noted that in 1837 he had persuaded the Board to agree to a somewhat curious exchange, that of the manuscript for 'all the old annuals which were not put up in the Library'.[39]

Among the collections of Greek papyri in Irish and British universities, those in the College Library rank second in importance only to those of

---

[36] MUN/V/57/10, March quarter 1836; 'Three opportunities', in A. N. L. Munby, *Essays and papers* (London: Scolar, 1977), pp. 141–50; A. N. L Munby, *The formation of the Phillipps library up to the year 1840* (Cambridge University Press, 1954), p. 59; Raghnall Ó Floinn, 'The shrine of the Book of Dimma', *Éile: Journal of the Roscrea Heritage Society*, 1 (1982), 25–39; R. I. Best, 'On the *subscriptiones* in the Book of Dimma', *Hermathena*, 20 (1930), 84–100.

[37] MUN/V/57/11, December quarter 1842; MS 868, fols. i–ii; R. B. McDowell, 'The 1798 Rebellion', in *Treasures*, pp. 143–7.

[38] MS 2214, fol. 123a.

[39] MS 3352, 9 July 1837; Jennifer Osborne, 'From Paris to Dublin: the Sadleir Hours in Trinity College', *Irish Arts Review Yearbook*, 15 (1999), 108–17; Bernard Meehan, 'A note on the Dublin Apocalypse, Trinity College Dublin MS 64', *Scriptorium*, 38 (1984), 82–3.

the Bodleian. Trinity's acquisition of papyri began, however, not with documents in Greek but in hieroglyphic, hieratic and demotic scripts, in the form of a donation from Lord Kingsborough in the late 1830s. They are mainly extracts from the Egyptian Book of the Dead dating from the thirteenth century BC (MSS 1658–76). They were unrolled and mounted in frames at a cost of £500.[40] Edward Hincks, who had failed to produce a catalogue of the Library's Persian manuscripts in 1815, was by this time writing extensively on the ancient Near East from his rectory in County Down. He found the arrival of these papyri irresistible and in 1843 published a catalogue of them.[41]

Todd's influence can be discerned behind the publication of this catalogue as part of his efforts to make the Library's collections better known. His proposal that the College should publish Monck Mason's catalogue of manuscripts had not been carried out, but in 1839 a catalogue of the collection of coins bequeathed by Claudius Gilbert was published. This was compiled by one of the Junior Fellows, John Adam Malet, who, though without any expertise, had expressed an interest in the coins and as a result seems to have been surprised to find himself designated as the College Numismatist. The coins were hardly ever touched and the publication of Malet's catalogue did little to increase their use, a fact noted by the Dublin University Commissioners, who recommended that the collection should be extended to include modern coins and that the more interesting ones should be put on display.[42] Todd himself turned his attention to the Waldensian manuscripts that formed part of Ussher's library. He published a catalogue of them in five parts in the *British Magazine* in 1841 and began work on a catalogue of the biblical manuscripts, though that project was abandoned because of lack of time.[43]

The Royal Irish Academy was the eventual recipient of two collections of manuscripts that Trinity tried, but failed, to acquire. For several

[40] Abbott, *Manuscripts*, p. iv; MUN/V/5/7, 29 September 1838; MUN/V/57/11, September and December quarters 1840.

[41] Edward Hincks, *Catalogue of the Egyptian manuscripts in the Library of Trinity College Dublin* (Dublin: Milliken, 1843). Hincks was paid £50 for the work (MUN/V/57/11, September quarter 1843).

[42] J. A. Malet, *A catalogue of Roman silver coins in the Library of Trinity College Dublin* (Dublin: Graisberry, 1839), p. iii; DU Commission, *Report*, p. 78; DU Commission, 'Appendix A: Evidence', p. 204.

[43] James H. Todd, 'The Waldensian manuscripts in the Library of Trinity College, Dublin', *British Magazine*, 19 (1841), 393–402, 502–11, 632–7; 20 (1841), 21–5, 185–93. The catalogue was subsequently published as James Henthorn Todd, *The books of the Vaudois: the Waldensian manuscripts preserved in the Library of Trinity College, Dublin* (London: Macmillan, 1865). See also DU Commission, 'Appendix A: Evidence', p. 175.

years the College booksellers, Hodges and Smith, had been collecting Irish manuscripts, and by 1843 they owned over 600 items, in 227 volumes, which they placed on the market for £1,200. The Lord Lieutenant asked the College Board if they would be willing to contribute towards the cost if the government provided a grant, and he also asked whether the Board would provide a lesser sum if the manuscripts were bought for the Academy. Unsurprisingly the Board's response was that it would meet a quarter of the cost if the manuscripts were for the College, but that it had no power to use College funds to benefit the Academy.[44] With the intervention of Sir Robert Peel and support from public subscription the Academy acquired the collection.

The second collection was that owned by the Duke of Buckingham at Stowe, a library that included the Irish manuscripts collected by Charles O'Conor in the eighteenth century. In 1849, the auction of the manuscripts was announced, and Todd was authorised to attend and to spend up to £300.[45] Before the sale could take place, however, one of the great collectors of the time, the Earl of Ashburnham, placed a bid for the whole collection, and though the British Museum had also begun negotiation, dithering by its Trustees meant that Ashburnham's bid was successful. Despite the new owner's reputation for putting difficulties in the way of scholars wishing to use his library, Todd was granted permission to see the Irish manuscripts, and he presented a paper to the Academy on the most important item in the collection, the eighth-century mass book known as the Stowe Missal.[46] In the meantime, however, he had managed to offend the Earl by offering him £500 for these manuscripts. The response was distinctly frosty, Ashburnham saying that he had told Todd that he had no intention of selling them, but that he might be persuaded to part with them by way of exchange: 'if you will send me one of the finest MS now in your possession – for instance the Book of Kells – I will tell you whether I will or will not give my Irish MSS for it. This proposal may . . . be inadmissible – but I beg to say . . . that it is no more so than would be an offer of five times five hundred pounds for my collection of Irish MSS.' Todd reminded Ashburnham that his lordship had declined to allow his manuscripts to be transcribed on the grounds that this would diminish their value. From this he had concluded

---

[44] MUN/V/5/8, 10 February 1844; R. B. McDowell, 'The main narrative', in T. Ó Raifeartaigh, ed., *The Royal Irish Academy: a bicentennial history, 1785–1985* (Dublin: Royal Irish Academy, 1985), pp. 1–92 (p. 43).

[45] MUN/V/5/9, 3 February 1849.

[46] James Henthorne Todd, 'On the ancient Irish missal and its silver box', *Trans. RIA*, 23 (1859), 3–37.

that, since Ashburnham could not read the manuscripts in Irish, he placed no value upon them 'except a pecuniary one' and so he, Todd, would not be guilty of any impropriety if he offered their 'marketable value'. As far as the Book of Kells was concerned, 'nothing would induce' the University to part with it.[47] The correspondence ended at this point, but after the Earl's death in 1878 his son sold the entire collection to the government. The bulk of it was placed in the British Museum, but the Irish manuscripts were separated and deposited in the Royal Irish Academy, where they remain.[48]

Donations of printed books were intermittent and modest. In 1840, the Board was approached by Robert McGhee, the Church of Ireland rector of Harold's Cross, Dublin, asking if the College would accept a collection of books and documents on the 'Roman Catholic controversy', housed in a special bookcase.[49] He had already donated almost identical collections to Cambridge University Library and the Bodleian. The bookcases arrived in each of the libraries bearing a brass plaque with the words 'Documents on the crimes of the Papal apostasy'. Neither Trinity nor the Bodleian had any difficulty accepting the gift, but the Cambridge Library Syndicate insisted on having the wording on the plaque altered to read less provocatively. McGhee submitted to these demands under protest and new plaques were produced, reading simply 'Books and documents on the papacy'.[50] In a letter to the Cambridge University Librarian, McGhee insisted, however, that the original plaques be kept in each of the libraries along with a memorandum explaining the alteration, because, he said, it was his duty to demonstrate by means of the collection 'the apostasy of Rome, and the crimes committed and inculcated by her hierarchy now living in Ireland'.[51]

This period also marked the start of the Library's acquisition of Ordnance Survey maps. Between 1833 and 1846 the Survey published a series of maps of Ireland at the scale of six inches to one mile. They were widely circulated, with Marsh's Library and the Royal Irish Academy receiving copies as well as Trinity, though the distribution of later series was restricted to the legal-deposit libraries. The astonishing scale and detail was a source of wonder

---

[47] MS 2214/161a, MS 2214/167, MS 2214/170.

[48] *Catalogue of the Stowe manuscripts in the British Museum*, 2 vols. (London: British Museum, 1895–6), vol. I, pp. iii–v.

[49] MUN/V/5/8, 29 August, 10 October 1840.

[50] Cambridge University Library, CCA.9.33; McKitterick, pp. 504–6; [R. J. McGhee] *The church of Rome: a report on 'the books and documents on the papacy'* (London: Partridge and Oakey, 1852).

[51] Cambridge University Library, CCA.9.33, No. 33. The TCD bookcase has not survived, but both versions of the plaque are preserved in the Department of Early Printed Books.

for the German geographer Johann Georg Kohl, who described the maps that he was shown in the College Library as 'a truly gigantic work . . . one of the fullest and most faithful maps in the world'.[52]

In 1844, after Todd had been allowed to have his head for 10 years, the Board became concerned at the increasing cost of the Library, which had risen from £1,346 in 1835 to £2,344 in 1843 (plus the salaries of the Librarian, Assistant Librarian and porters, which were charged to general College funds).[53] A committee of Fellows was set up to examine the expenditure, with a view to reducing it, and this led to the establishment for the first time of a Library Committee, which held its initial meeting on 16 April 1845.[54] It consisted of the Librarian (Wall), Todd and three other Fellows, and it met every two or three weeks, principally to consider lists of foreign books for purchase. The Board instructed the committee to reduce expenditure on the Library to not more than £1,000 a year, as a result of which it cancelled seventeen subscriptions to periodicals, mainly the publications of French local academies of sciences.[55] The amount spent with the London booksellers Bossange, Barthès and Lowell, the main suppliers of foreign periodicals and books, dropped from around £550 a year in the early 1840s to about £200 by 1850.[56] The cost of binding was also reduced by using cloth instead of leather for periodicals and by having a contract for the binding of books. Mullen was instructed to quote a price, including 'lettering and classing' for different sizes of volumes.[57]

By these various means, expenditure on the Library was brought back to approximately that of 1835, and although it varied considerably from year to year it remained at about that level until the 1860s. Todd's analysis in his evidence to the Dublin University Commission showed that in the years 1849 to 1851 the amount spent on books and manuscripts varied between £390 and £574 a year (plus £50 for the Lending Library) and that on binding between £147 and £280.[58] The main source of supply, apart from Bossange, Barthès and Lowell, was Hodges and Smith in Dublin.

Having carried out its instructions to reduce expenditure, the Library Committee produced a submission to the Board in January 1851, citing the figures as evidence for what it considered had now become an unsatisfactory level of purchasing. It argued that the lack of any specific provision for

---

[52] J. G. Kohl, *Travels in Ireland* (London: Bruce and Wyld, 1844), p. 288.   [53] MUN/V/58/3.

[54] MUN/V/5/8, 6 July, 12 October 1844. The minutes of the Library Committee are MUN/LIB/3/1.

[55] MUN/V/5/9, 21 January 1851; MUN/LIB/3/1, 23 April 1845.

[56] MUN/LIB/17/3, Response to DU Commission.   [57] MUN/LIB/3/1, pp. 3–6.

[58] DU Commission, 'Appendix A: Evidence', pp. 178–80.

buying books, and the fact that purchases were included with other Library expenditure in the accounts, meant that there could be no regular acquisition of foreign books, and that the Library was unable to take advantage of the opportunities provided by auctions. The Board was asked to allocate a specific sum for the purchase of books, and since the average expenditure in the previous 5 years had been £590, the committee suggested that an allocation of £600 a year would be reasonable.[59] It took the Board 4 years to make a decision.

Legal deposit

Following his appointment to a salaried post in 1834, Todd immediately began to address the failure of the Library to acquire books to which it was entitled under the Copyright Act. Robert Durham was dismissed as the College's agent, with effect from the beginning of 1835, and replaced by Hodges and Smith, the University Bookseller, at a salary of £100 a year. Since they were based in Dublin, the firm had to employ a sub-agent, Mawer Cowtan, of the British Museum's Department of Printed Books, whose task it was to contact the publishers and claim books that had not been received.[60] Todd took a very firm line with the new agent. In April 1835 he sent Hodges and Smith a list of 560 books, of which only about half had been received, and 2 months later he wrote again with a further list, demanding that they produce the books on the list unless they could show that the Library was not entitled to them.[61] Throughout 1835 and 1836 he kept up a regular correspondence, sending similar lists of missing books or issues of periodicals. He also adopted a more comprehensive approach than his predecessors and included novels in the lists of books to be claimed.

By the 1830s, it had become clear to both publishers and libraries that the deposit legislation of 1814 was not working. The publishers regarded the libraries' demands as rapacious; the libraries resented the publishers' failure to deposit many of their titles, which meant that they received the dross but had to buy the books that they needed. In April 1836, James Silk Buckingham, the MP for Sheffield, proposed that legal deposit should be abolished completely, arguing that it restricted, rather than encouraged,

[59] MUN/V/5/9, 29 June 1850, 21 January 1851.
[60] MUN/LIB/2/3, 18 November–1 December 1834; MUN/V/5/7, 29 November 1834; Harris, p. 77.
[61] MUN/LIB/2/3, 8 April, 29 June 1835 and *passim*.

learning because it increased the cost of books. He introduced a Bill proposing that the deposit privilege should be removed from ten of the libraries,
and that the British Museum should be obliged to pay for a copy of every
work it received from the publishers. The libraries would be granted compensation equivalent to the value of the books they had received each year,
on condition that they reported annually to Parliament on how the money
had been spent. This sum was calculated as £500 a year for Oxford and
Cambridge, £300 for Trinity, Aberdeen, Edinburgh and Glasgow, and £200
for the other libraries.[62] Thomas Lefroy, MP for the University of Dublin,
immediately warned that he would resist any attempt to deprive Trinity of
any of its rights.[63] The British Museum complained about having to pay for
the books supplied, Oxford and Cambridge objected on the grounds that
no sum would be an adequate compensation for the loss of such a valuable
privilege, and petitions were also received from the Scottish universities.
Opinion within the institutions was far from unanimous, however. S. P.
Rigaud, Savilian Professor of Astronomy at Oxford, with whom Todd corresponded about the proposed changes to the Act, noted that some of the
Curators of the Bodleian felt that the £500 compensation would be of more
benefit than the 'mass of trash' received from Stationers' Hall.[64] Similar
views were expressed by some who gave evidence to the Royal Commissions
on the Scottish universities.[65] Todd did not share this scepticism and sought
the advice of the former Provost, Samuel Kyle, now Bishop of Cork and
Cloyne. Todd thought that the College should refuse the £300 because it
would only provide an opportunity for 'dragging us before Parliament'.[66]
He told Kyle that Trinity had petitioned against the changes and had asked
its MPs, Lefroy and Frederick Shaw, to try to have the proposed amount
of compensation increased, as it would not be sufficient to purchase more
than about half the books now received, the value of which he estimated at
£800 a year.

Ultimately the publishers achieved a partial success in that, when a new
Copyright Act came into force on 20 August 1836, the number of deposit
libraries was reduced, with the four Scottish universities, Sion College and
the King's Inns losing their right to claim books. In return, they received a
compensatory grant, which in the case of the Scottish universities continued

---

[62] *Copyright Act amendment Bill*, HC 1836 (252), II, 385.
[63] HC Hansard (3rd series), vol. 33, col. 463 (28 April 1836).   [64] MS 2214, fol. 24.
[65] For example: *Evidence, oral and documentary, taken and received by the Commissioners . . . for
visiting the universities of Scotland. Volume I: University of Edinburgh*, [92], 1837, XXXV, 1
(p. 156); *Volume II: University of Glasgow*, [93], 1837, XXXVI, 1 (p. 178).
[66] MS 2214, fol. 28.

to be paid until it was subsumed into the government grant in the twentieth century. The grant to the King's Inns was £433 a year, probably a satisfactory level of settlement given the specialised nature of that library, and it continued to be paid by subsequent British and then Irish governments until 2003, though without any increase for inflation.[67] The five libraries that retained their deposit privilege were Trinity, the British Museum, Oxford, Cambridge and the Faculty of Advocates in Edinburgh.[68]

The passing of the new Act seems to have spurred Todd on to even greater activity. In his evidence to the Dublin University Commission in 1852, he claimed to have achieved a threefold increase in the annual number of legal-deposit books acquired after 1835.[69] He was unsure whether the provisions of the Act covered the current arrangement, whereby Hodges and Smith were employed to claim books on Trinity's behalf, and he sought counsel's opinion on the matter. The College's legal adviser confirmed that the use of an agent was acceptable, but that it would be preferable to have one firm, not two (Hodges and Smith sub-contracting to Mawer Cowtan), and for that agent to be based in London. In his submission to the lawyers, Todd also expressed his concern that the response to claims was sometimes 'vague and unsatisfactory, and in several instances direct refusals'. He referred in particular to John Macrone, a minor publisher of novels, who refused to supply any books and threatened to defend any action brought against him 'with a view to bring the hardship of the law before the legislature'.[70]

These discussions coincided with a visit by Todd to London, where he instructed Greenhill at Stationers' Hall to send a circular to publishers who failed to enter their books, threatening that the College would take legal action to enforce its rights. He wrote from London to the Bursar, Richard MacDonnell, saying that he had been advised not to prosecute Macrone, because the College would be accused of simply trying to obtain novels, and that a better target would be a more 'respectable' firm such as Butterworth, who would be less likely to resort to 'low means of evading the law'.[71] Whilst in London, he also sought a replacement for Hodges and Smith as agent. Robert Cowtan, the son of the agent for the British Museum, was recommended, as he had access not just to his father's expertise but also to the Museum's accessions lists. He was appointed as the College's Copyright

---

[67] Information supplied by Jonathan Armstrong, Librarian of the King's Inns.
[68] Copyright Act, 1836 (6 & 7 William IV, c. 110); Partridge, pp. 74–7; *Report from the Select Committee on Public Libraries*, HC 1849 (548), XVII, 1 (p. 29).
[69] DU Commission, 'Appendix A: Evidence', p. 173.   [70] MUN/LIB/22/19/2.
[71] MUN/LIB/22/20/1.

Agent in April 1837.[72] During his visit Todd planned to call on Bodley's Librarian, reporting proudly to the Bursar that 'the booksellers tell me here that we have got more books than either of the English universities! who appear to have managed their affairs even worse than we have'.[73] This boast is not borne out by the evidence, however, as both Cambridge and Trinity reported roughly the same level of deposit intake in the mid 1830s, a little over 1,400 volumes a year.[74]

The Copyright Act of 1836 was short-lived. It dealt solely with the deposit of books and did not meet the demands of authors and publishers concerned about the protection of their copyright. Each year, Bills proposing changes were introduced into Parliament. Eventually, in 1842, the demands of the publishing community prevailed, and the so-called 'Imperial' Copyright Act was passed, repealing the previous Acts and seeking to regulate copyright legislation throughout the British Empire.[75] As far as legal deposit was concerned, it left intact the rights of the five libraries but defined those rights more precisely. A major change was that books no longer had to be registered at Stationers' Hall for their copyright to be protected. The link between copyright and legal deposit was thus broken, though until the late twentieth century legal-deposit legislation remained enshrined in successive Copyright Acts and the term 'copyright library' continued to be used.

The 1842 Act defined a 'book' to include not just volumes and pamphlets but also periodicals, sheet maps and music, and it distinguished more clearly between the rights of the British Museum and those of the other libraries. A copy of every publication, on the best paper, was to be deposited with the Museum (thus the onus was on the publishers to deposit); the other libraries had the right to claim, within a year of publication, a copy in the form in which the largest number of copies was printed (the onus thus being on the libraries to claim). The employment of an agent for this purpose was specifically permitted and the publishers were given the option of supplying claimed copies either to Stationers' Hall or directly to the libraries. Penalties for non-delivery were also set out. The right of the British Museum to receive copies now extended not just to the United Kingdom but also to books published anywhere in the Empire, and the

---

[72] MUN/V/5/7, 29 April 1837.   [73] MUN/LIB/22/20/1.

[74] *A return of the number of volumes and parts of volumes of printed books received in each year respectively from 1814 to 1847*, HC 1849 (18), XLV, 199; MUN/V/5/9, 4 November 1848, 13 January 1849.

[75] Copyright Act, 1842 (5 & 6 Victoria, c. 45).

same applied theoretically to the other libraries, though this right was never enforced because of the difficulties of establishing what was being published and the length of time it took to communicate with the colonies. This aspect of the Act was rescinded with the passing of the International Copyright Act of 1886.[76]

The deposit provisions of this Act were no more palatable to the publishers than they had been under earlier legislation and they continued to find ways of escaping their obligation or of causing inconvenience and cost to the libraries. In his evidence to the Select Committee on Public Libraries, Edward Edwards of the British Museum asserted that he knew of instances where Dublin publishers, instead of delivering their books directly to Trinity, sent them to Stationers' Hall in order to put the College to the expense of having them shipped back to Dublin.[77]

The new Act stated that deposit copies must be of the same quality as those issued to the public, a requirement that was particularly significant for books published with illustrations. The colouring of engravings was important, especially for botanical and natural history books, and so the agent had previously been instructed to pay to have plates coloured, because the libraries took the view that they were entitled only to uncoloured copies of such books.[78] John Gould, who had received £43 6s. 6d. in 1841 for colouring Trinity's copy of *Birds of Europe*, maintained that even under the new Act he was not obliged to supply his books with coloured plates unless the College paid for the colouring. Todd had to threaten to take legal action if he continued to refuse.[79]

Robert Cowtan was finding his position increasingly difficult. He was under pressure from Todd to claim as many books as possible, he had to deal with recalcitrant publishers and, increasingly, he was engaged in a turf war with Greenhill, who was still employed to collect the books registered at Stationers' Hall. After the passing of the 1842 Act, Cowtan was provided with a letter of attorney, formally appointing him as the College's agent to claim books on its behalf.[80] His father proposed that, as the new Act no longer required books to be registered at Stationers' Hall, the College should retain Greenhill just for those books still being sent there but, beyond that, should sever its links. Greenhill, he said, would resist this, as the fees paid by the libraries provided 'a handsome remuneration for his labour',

---

[76] International Copyright Act, 1886 (49 & 50 Victoria, c. 33).
[77] Select Committee on Public Libraries, note 68 above, p. 30.   [78] MUN/LIB/11/20/14.
[79] MUN/V/57/11, December quarter 1841; MUN/LIB/22/20/38; MUN/LIB/2/3, 24 October 1842.
[80] MUN/LIB/22/19/3.

which he would be unwilling to relinquish.[81] Greenhill not only continued to encourage publishers to deposit their books at Stationers' Hall, rather than with the agent, but even stated that it was illegal not to do so.[82] By December 1844, the College had had enough and decided that the most efficient system would be to revert to its previous arrangement of employing the Warehouse Keeper as their agent, as Cambridge had done throughout. Greenhill was therefore appointed as the College's Copyright Agent with effect from 25 March 1845 and Cowtan was dismissed.[83] He protested to Joseph Dobbs, the Library clerk with whom he dealt on an almost daily basis, saying that he was not surprised at the decision, as he had been long aware that Greenhill was using every possible means 'to induce the heads of the College to avail themselves of his exclusive services'.[84] He claimed that, in 1844, Greenhill had supplied books to the value of £1,040 and that he, Cowtan, had sent additional titles worth £400, most of which the College would not have received if he had not been collecting, since many publications were delivered to the British Museum without being advertised, 'and consequently Mr Greenhill never hears of them'.[85] He offered, at a fee of £10 a year, to continue to send lists of items received at the Museum so that the College could compare them with what it received from Greenhill, but Todd turned down this proposal.[86]

Todd's success in increasing the number of books received by deposit meant, of course, that the shelves of the Library were filling up more rapidly. The Board's concern at this led it to seek counsel's opinion on whether it could save space by selling duplicates, imperfect works and books that were deemed to be 'useless for the purposes of the Library', such as 'ephemeral novels, children's books and other insignificant publications'.[87] The advice received was that, whilst there was nothing in either the College statutes or the Copyright Act to prevent sale, the College ought to exercise its rights with caution, especially as far as legal-deposit books were concerned. The object of the Act was to preserve copies of the works 'in the most important public institutions' and, if the College were to claim books and then sell them, it would lead to 'great clamour' and probably precipitate a change in the law.[88] On the other hand, there was no objection to placing legal-deposit books in the Lending Library or returning to the publisher those not considered suitable for the Library. The sale of duplicates that did not form part of a donation was deemed to be acceptable and so, with

[81] MUN/LIB/22/20/40.   [82] MUN/LIB/22/20/45.
[83] MUN/LIB/2/4, 16 December 1844.   [84] MUN/LIB/22/20/50.   [85] *Ibid.*
[86] MUN/LIB/22/20/52.   [87] MUN/LIB/12/21.   [88] *Ibid.*

the approval of the Visitors, Todd was instructed to select such books for disposal.[89]

The catalogue

Soon after his appointment, Todd addressed himself to the catalogue of printed books, which he found to be in a state of 'deplorable confusion'.[90] The catalogue still in use was the one compiled in manuscript by Edward Hudson in 1737, into which details of newly acquired books had been added over the course of nearly a century. As a result, the pages were crowded, with entries inserted in the margins and other vacant spaces without any strict observance of alphabetical order; and new entries were written in different hands, sometimes not very legibly, and 'frequently displayed the greatest ignorance'.[91] Todd regarded the catalogue as useless for the majority of readers and realised that a different approach was required. He advised the Board that the practice of employing recent graduates as Library clerks was unsatisfactory, as the short-term nature of their employment meant that they were unable to build up much expertise and the quality of their contributions was decidedly variable and inconsistent. The Board was persuaded to appoint two additional clerks on a permanent basis in 1834. From then on, all new books were catalogued on paper slips, following the model of the British Museum and the Bodleian. These slips, conforming to what Todd described as 'a settled rule' for the form of the entries, were filed in alphabetical order in drawers and were available for consultation by readers.[92]

The slip catalogue was undoubtedly an improvement on the old manuscript volumes, but access to it had to be carefully controlled, to prevent slips being removed and misfiled by readers. Todd therefore insisted that it should remain under the supervision of the Assistant Librarian, who would help readers to find the books they wanted. He also provided for readers' use an interleaved copy of the Bodleian printed catalogue, after its publication in 1843; Trinity shelfmarks for the books most commonly requested were added to this in manuscript.[93]

[89] MUN/LIB/13/74; MUN/V/5/8, 23 and 28 October, 11, 18 and 25 November 1843.
[90] J. H. Todd, 'Advertisement', in *Catalogus librorum impressorum qui in Bibliotheca Collegii Sacrosanctae et individuae Trinitatis Reginae Elizabethae juxta Dublin adservantur* [The Printed Catalogue], 9 vols. (Dublin University Press, 1864–87), vol. I, p. iii.
[91] *Ibid.*   [92] *Ibid.*; MUN/V/5/7, 15 October 1834.
[93] Todd, note 90 above, p. iv; MUN/V/5/8, 29 March 1845. The catalogue is MUN/LIB/1/49.

Todd's ultimate aim, however, was the publication of a printed catalogue.[94] In this he was following not just the example of the Bodleian but also that of the British Museum, which had published its catalogue in seven volumes between 1813 and 1819. At its visitation of the Library in November 1835, the Board agreed to obtain an estimate for the cost of a new catalogue, and in 1837 Todd was appointed as its editor. Two hundred pounds was committed towards the printing of it, and the clerks turned their attention to writing slips for the books already in the Library. In March 1837, George Mason began to transcribe the contents of the old catalogue. He left in September, by which time he had reached the letter K, and was succeeded as a Library clerk by Richard Gibbings, at a salary of £50 a year.[95]

Todd persuaded the Board that, with additional staff, he could have the catalogue completed within 2 years. In 1839 he was given permission to appoint four more clerks for the purpose, at a salary of £60 a year each. Within a fortnight of receiving the Board's approval, Todd had already found three new clerks, and Gibbings was promoted to senior clerk at an increased salary of £120. Anxious not to allow the cost of the Library to rise too far, however, the Board insisted as a quid pro quo that, for the 2 years Todd said he would need to complete the catalogue, no foreign books were to be bought without its specific approval.[96] Todd's estimate turned out to be hopelessly optimistic and the work proceeded at a glacial pace. Some of the slips were revised more than once, because previous revisions were deemed to have been unsatisfactory, and in October 1845 Todd reported that the catalogue had made little progress because of the difficulty of 'procuring qualified persons who can devote their whole time to it for the salary offered'.[97]

One of the clerks was the poet James Clarence Mangan, taken on in February 1842 at the request of George Petrie, for whom he had been working at the Ordnance Survey. Mangan was initially responsible for annotating the copy of the Bodleian catalogue with Trinity shelfmarks, and he then moved on to supervise the arranging of the catalogue slips. However, his temperament and his penchant for alcohol and opium did not equip him well for the detailed and accurate work required of a cataloguer. He appears to have been absent for 6 months from September 1844 and to have returned to

[94] Vincent Kinane and Ann O'Brien, '"The vast difficulty of cataloguing": the Printed Catalogue of Trinity College Dublin (1864–1887)', *Libraries and Culture*, 23 (1988), 427–49.

[95] MUN/LIB/2/3, 9 November 1835; MUN/V/5/7, 11 February, 30 December 1837; MUN/LIB/11/20/9; MUN/LIB/11/20/15–MUN/LIB/11/20/16; MUN/LIB/11/21/8; MUN/V/57/11, 1837–.

[96] MUN/V/5/7, 26 October, 2 and 16 November 1839.   [97] MUN/LIB/2/4, 27 October 1845.

work half-time. In 1845, Todd reported in exasperation to the Board that 'no effectual progress can be made until a competent person can be engaged' but, despite his unsatisfactory performance, Mangan remained on the staff until the end of 1846.[98]

By this time, according to Todd, records had been produced for all the books in the Library, but he insisted on checking the slips himself, and it was another 2 years before he was ready to bring a specimen of the Printed Catalogue for approval by the Board.[99] His models for the rules by which the catalogue was to be compiled were those of Bulkeley Badinel's Bodleian catalogue of 1843 and the British Museum's cataloguing rules of 1841, but he subjected both to considerable local amendment. An important difference in policy between the Trinity catalogue and Badinel's was that Todd did not stop adding new entries at the point when the printing of letter A started, as had been decided in Oxford, but included all books in the Library at the point when a particular sheet was sent for printing. Given the length of time it took to publish the entire catalogue, this was probably an unavoidable decision, but Todd was aware that it would not then be possible to include secondary entries for more recently acquired books if they alphabetically preceded the primary entry for the book. Work proceeded slowly, and by the time of Todd's resignation as the Assistant Librarian in 1850, printing of the sheets for the letter A had barely started.

Despite the lack of progress with the printed version of the catalogue, Todd's reorganisation of the Library's procedures for recording and cataloguing new books and periodicals attracted praise from Joseph Power, the Cambridge University Librarian, who visited Dublin and noted with envy the 'accurate and systematic manner' in which those records were kept.[100]

The Lending Library

Todd felt strongly that access to both the main Library and the Lending Library was too limited and that undergraduates and the general public

[98] MUN/LIB/2/3, 14 February 1842; MUN/LIB/2/4, 23 October 1843, 27 October 1845; Jacques Chuto, 'Mangan's "antique deposit" in TCD Library', *Long Room*, 2 (Autumn/Winter 1970), 38–9; Jacques Chuto, 'A further glance at Mangan and the Library', *Long Room*, 5 (Spring 1972), 9–10; Ellen Shannon-Mangan, *James Clarence Mangan: a biography* (Blackrock: Irish Academic Press, 1996), pp. 249–79.
[99] MUN/V/5/9, 23 December 1848, 13 January 1849.
[100] *Report of Her Majesty's Commissioners appointed to inquire into the state, discipline, studies and revenues of the University and Colleges of Cambridge*, [1559], 1852–3, XLIV, 1 ('Evidence' section, p. 58).

should be entitled to use them. In his evidence to the Dublin University Commission he expressed the view that the statutory restrictions on use of the main Library should be removed and that the Board should have the power to determine 'without restriction' who should be admitted.[101] This was a battle for another day, but in 1837–8, when he held the office of Junior Dean as well as that of Assistant Librarian, he was at least able to initiate reforms to the Lending Library, which was still the responsibility of the Junior Dean. It was very little used, and in that year the rules were amended and access was granted to undergraduates. New books were also needed, and for this purpose an initial allocation of £200 in 1838–9 later became an annual grant of £50.[102] The Board decided that use of the collection would be encouraged by the publication of a catalogue, and Joseph Dobbs, the Library clerk who also acted as clerk to the Lending Library, was paid £10 for compiling it. The catalogue was sold for one shilling, with the proceeds accruing to the Lending Library, and every student using the collection was required to buy a copy, of which new editions were published every 3 or 4 years.[103]

The building

The poor condition of the Library's external stonework had been the subject of comment since the 1750s, but no remedial work had been carried out, and even as late as 1825 a visitor was able to describe the building as 'subject to a premature appearance of decay'.[104] Repairs were finally undertaken during 1826 and 1827, when the stonemason Thomas Baker was employed to replace the Scrabo sandstone on the upper part of the walls with 'granite rusticated ashlar', at a cost of about £2,800.[105] The limestone arcades of the ground floor were in good condition and needed no remedial work. The following year the work on the balustrade that had been abandoned at the beginning of the century was carried out, and the old balustrade was replaced with a new one in Portland stone.[106]

During the late 1830s, the range of brick buildings abutting the north side of the West Pavilion was demolished, opening the view from the Front Gate

---

[101] DU Commission, 'Appendix A: Evidence', p. 176.
[102] MUN/V/5/7, 8 December 1838 and 16 March 1839; MUN/V/57/11, December quarter 1838, March quarter 1839.
[103] MUN/LIB/2/3, 27 October 1840; MUN/V/5/8, 6 March, 13 November 1841, 29 January 1842.
[104] J. N. Brewer, *The beauties of Ireland*, 2 vols. (London: Sherwood, Jones, 1825–6), vol. I, p. 74.
[105] MUN/V/58/2, 1826–7; MUN/P/2/288.
[106] MS 3369, 12 and 26 April 1828; MUN/V/5/6, 19 April 1828.

Figure 12 The Old Library from the north side, before the removal in the 1830s of the residences on the right of the picture (*Dublin Penny Journal*, 4, No. 171, 10 October 1835)

to Library Square. The parallel range on the east side of Library Square (the Rubrics) was shortened, creating a space between it and the Library. The removal of these buildings meant that repairs were required to the north side of the East and West Pavilions, and in 1838 Baker was employed again. He restored the stonework and inserted windows on the upper floors to match those of the Long Room, adding three blank windows at ground-floor level. The lower storey was faced in 'best blackstone rusticated ashlar' and the upper floors in granite to match his earlier refacing of the main part of the building. He was paid £360 for the work on the West Pavilion and a further £380 for similar work on the East Pavilion, including the plastering of the exposed end of the Rubrics.[107]

Changes also took place internally but, as few Library records survive for the period between 1826 and Todd's appointment in 1834, it is possible only to speculate on the precise sequence of those changes. The removal of the benches and desks from the alcoves in 1817 allowed shelves to be added to the lower part of the bookcases. The larger volumes were moved down and placed on those, leaving space for new books on the higher shelves. All the books then had to be renumbered, and it is likely that this was the occasion when the shelfmarks were changed from their original format of LETTER/figure/figure (e.g. AA.3.15) to the present LETTER/letter/figure (e.g. AA.c.15).[108] The tables that had been placed in the alcoves in 1817 were

[107] MUN/V/5/7, 10 February, 5 July 1838; MUN/V/58/3, 1838–9; MUN/P/2/288–MUN/P/2/289.
[108] Brendan Grimes, 'The library buildings up to 1970', in *Essays*, pp. 72–90.

still in place when Robert Graham, a Scottish politician, visited in 1835, but they must have been removed soon after that, as the increased capacity provided by the extra shelves proved insufficient, and each table was replaced by a low bookcase.[109] Between 1837 and 1839 the carpenter John Phayre was employed to construct these bookcases, made of oak with scroll ends, and to supply new ladders for access to the books on the higher shelves.[110] The new bookcases were painted and varnished by Henry Hanbridge, who also repainted the ceiling. His detailed bill described the work he carried out: the ceiling itself was in 'distemper Portland stone colour', the moulded frames forming the panels were painted in oil in an oak colour and the sixteen large flowers in the panels were in stone-coloured oil paint, picked out in gold.[111]

The Library was growing at the rate of between 1,500 and 2,000 volumes a year by the 1830s and so the low bookcases in the Long Room alcoves provided only a temporary respite. In 1839, the Board again turned its attention to the storage opportunities presented by the gallery and asked the College architect Frederick Darley to provide an estimate for installing shelves in the window recesses.[112] At its visitation in 1844, it approved a prototype, which consisted of a fixed set of shelves fitted against the wall under the windows, and, in front of it, a second, double-sided, case was added. This had wheels and hinges which allowed it to be swung out, giving a total of three sets of shelves (see Plate 6). The deeper window-recesses in the centre of the building allowed two parallel hinged cases to be inserted, providing five sides of shelving. This ingenious arrangement had the advantage that the shelves were invisible from the Long Room floor, a factor that was doubtless in the minds of those members of the Board who had been Fellows during the furore when gallery cases were proposed in 1804. Todd estimated that these cases would eventually accommodate about 23,000 volumes.[113]

By the time of Graham's visit in 1835, the busts had been moved from their original position on the balustrade of the gallery and placed on tall pedestals on the floor of the Long Room. The College's enthusiasm to commemorate its current and former members during the first half of the nineteenth century led to a considerable increase in the number of busts. About a dozen were added between 1820 and 1850. Seven of them are by

[109] Henry Heaney, ed., *A Scottish Whig in Ireland 1835–38: the Irish journals of Robert Graham of Redgorton* (Dublin: Four Courts Press, 1999), p. 29.

[110] MUN/LIB/11/20/13; MUN/LIB/11/21/1; MUN/LIB/11/21/17a.

[111] MUN/P/2/295/10; MUN/P/2/295/18.

[112] MUN/V/5/7, 25 November 1839.   [113] MUN/LIB/2/4, 21 October 1844.

Thomas Kirk, one of the most popular Irish sculptors of the day. They are the likenesses of the scientist Matthew Young, commissioned in 1827 for £80; William Magee, Archbishop of Dublin and a former Professor of Mathematics; Charles Wall, done in 1840 during his tenure as Librarian but not placed in the Library until 1861; George Miller, who lectured in modern history, donated by his family in 1850; and three former Provosts: Samuel Kyle, Bartholomew Lloyd and Thomas Elrington, the latter bust given by Elrington in 1835, a few months before his death.[114] In the same year a further Vierpyl bust, that of Robert Clayton, Bishop of Clogher and a former Senior Fellow, was received. The Long Room contains two busts by the Irish sculptor Christopher Moore: those of Thomas Lefroy and William Conyngham, Lord Plunket, both former MPs for the University. The second was donated in 1846 by the sitter; the first bears the date 1859 and was presented to the Library after Lefroy's death, by his family.[115] A bust of James McCullagh, Professor of Natural and Experimental Philosophy, was placed in the Long Room in 1849 at the request of his fellow physicist John Jellett, but it has since been moved elsewhere in the College.[116] Two of Trinity's more distinguished alumni were commemorated in busts by the English sculptor William Behnes, who was commissioned to produce a likeness of Edmund Burke in 1822, at a cost of £54 12s. 0d., and one of Oliver Goldsmith in 1827 for £84 15s. 5d.[117]

John Hogan, an Irish sculptor who had settled in Rome, returned frequently to his native land, partly to collect commissions. On one of those visits, in 1840, he undertook to produce for the College a marble relief to commemorate John Brinkley, Professor of Astronomy and the first Royal Astronomer of Ireland. In his sixties, Brinkley had exchanged his Chair for a series of positions in the Church of Ireland, and at the time of his death was Bishop of Cloyne. Hogan's monument records Brinkley's scientific, rather than his ecclesiastical, achievements, including a telescope and a globe beside the sitter, and it is devoid of any spiritual references.[118] It was erected in the hall of the West Pavilion in 1845, where it would have been visible to all who entered the building. Because of changes made to the Library entrance and the creation of a tunnel to the 1937 Reading

[114] MUN/V/57/10, September quarter 1827 [Young]; MUN/V/5/11/2, 12 October 1861 [Wall]; MUN/V/5/9, 28 September 1850 [Miller]; MUN/V/5/7, 3 January 1835 [Elrington].

[115] MUN/V/5/8, 18 April 1846; MUN/V/5/13, 4 February 1871.

[116] MUN/V/5/9, 15 December 1849.

[117] MUN/V/5/6, 21 September 1822; MUN/LIB/11/18/13b; MUN/V/57/10, December quarter 1827.

[118] John Turpin, *John Hogan: Irish neoclassical sculptor in Rome 1800–1858* (Blackrock: Irish Academic Press, 1982), pp. 134–5.

Room it now sits rather incongruously above a stairwell and is seen by few people.

Readers and visitors

The architectural splendour of the Long Room did little to ameliorate the conditions in which readers had to work, and by the 1830s the lack of any form of heating had become a source of complaint. An article in the *Dublin University Magazine* referred to 'this Nova Zembla of letters . . . lighted by upwards of ninety windows, so disposed as to produce fully forty separate through drafts', and the *Freeman's Journal* printed a letter from 'a graduate of T.C.D.' claiming that the Library was almost useless in the winter because it was impossible to endure the excessive cold.[119] The writer recommended the use of hot-air heating, as at the King's Inns. The College had already decided to install such a system, and in 1831 had accepted a proposal from Anthony Meyler, who had provided a hypocaust at Leinster House for the Royal Dublin Society. Meyler was paid £300 and the system was tested the following winter, but introducing warm air into the Library turned out to be more expensive than expected. The system ultimately proved to be a failure and the hypocaust was removed in 1838. Todd was asked to investigate how the Bodleian was heated.[120] The reply to his enquiry has not survived but the hot-air heating that had been in use there since 1821 was described as 'wholly ineffectual'.[121]

In 1839, the Library was again subject to the activities of a book thief. At the Board visitation in November that year, Todd reported that fifty volumes were missing and that seventy more had been recovered from a pawnbroker.[122] The following March he encountered one Robert Harman, a graduate who was now a member of the bar and whom he had long suspected of being the thief. He detained Harman and sent for the pawnbroker, who identified him as the supplier of the books. Todd marched him across to the police office, where he was committed to stand trial. He was found guilty and sentenced to 6 months' hard labour.[123]

---

[119] 'Curiosities of Irish literature: the libraries', *Dublin University Magazine*, 9 (1837), 341–5 (p. 343); *Freeman's Journal*, 14 February 1835.

[120] MS 3369, 4 and 11 February 1832; MUN/V/5/7, 9 July 1831, 8 October 1837, 5 July, 17 November 1838.

[121] William Dunn Macray, *Annals of the Bodleian Library, Oxford*, 2nd edn (Oxford: Clarendon Press, 1890), p. 310.

[122] MUN/LIB/2/3, 25 November 1839.

[123] MUN/V/5/7, 25 November 1839, 24 March 1840; MUN/LIB/2/3, 21 March–15 April 1840.

Mutilation of books, especially the removal of plates, was also a problem. Todd first reported this in 1839, but by 1842 it had reached such a level that the Board set up a committee to advise on security.[124] Two of the existing porters were demoted, on the grounds that they were 'wholly inefficient', and they were replaced by two new men who were required specifically to note where each reader was sitting and especially to watch 'any gentleman who appears to be moving about the Library, and to note the different places where he takes down books'.[125] New regulations approved on 18 March 1843 were almost identical to those that had been introduced and quickly withdrawn in 1817. Only Fellows and professors were allowed access to the shelves without specific permission from the Board. Other readers were obliged to complete dockets for books they required, which would then be fetched for them and returned to the shelves by a porter, and for this the number of porters was increased to six. The Board baulked at the committee's recommendation that brass doors should be fitted across each of the alcoves, but it did order the transfer of all the incunabula from their various locations in the Long Room to the Manuscripts Room.[126]

One result of preventing readers from browsing the shelves was to reduce the numbers using the Library. This was almost certainly unintended, but it is clear from the report of their visitation of the Library in 1844 that the Board did not disapprove, as it had the effect of excluding 'all who came merely to idle or to amuse themselves by turning over books at random'.[127] Readers, on the other hand, felt rather differently. Arguing the case for a public library in Dublin, the nationalist newspaper the *Nation* complained about the restricted rights of access to the College Library and, in particular, about the cold, darkness and the 'system of book-tickets ingeniously contrived to make the library useless for reference and inconvenient for any other purpose'.[128] It returned to this theme the following year in a review of public libraries in Dublin, complaining again about the new regulations, about the lack of heating in the Long Room and about the simultaneous summer closure of all the publicly accessible libraries in the city.[129]

Todd had succeeded in improving the security of the books and he also sought to improve the quality of the Library staff. In 1842, he tried to

[124] MUN/V/5/7, 25 May 1839; MUN/V/5/8, 11 and 18 June 1842.
[125] MUN/LIB/2/4, 18 and 22 October 1842.
[126] MUN/V/5/8, 22 June, 19 November 1842, 23 October 1843; 'Decree . . . for the regulation of the Library', in *Chartae et statuta Collegii Sacrosanctae et Individuae Trinitatis Reginae Elizabethae juxta Dublin* (Dublin: Gill, 1844), pp. 349–51; Lydia Ferguson, '*Custodes librorum*: service, staff and salaries, 1601–1855', in *Essays*, pp. 25–38.
[127] MUN/LIB/2/4, 21 October 1844.   [128] 'The Dublin Library', *Nation*, 25 January 1845.
[129] 'The public libraries of Dublin', *ibid.*, 20 June 1846.

persuade the Board to appoint attendants 'of a better class . . . men of some literary attainments' to replace the porters who, he said, unintentionally gave offence and, 'from having no education of their own', were unable to assist readers.[130] In this he was unsuccessful, but the existing porters were required to sign an oath before a magistrate stating that they would carry out their duties, though these were expressed in terms of custodianship of the collections rather than assistance to readers.[131]

Although a reading room had been created in the West Pavilion in 1816 there is no evidence of how much it was used – indeed, up to 1831 it was taken over at least in part for bookbinding and repairs.[132] In 1843, presumably in response to the complaints about the lack of heating in the Long Room and the failure to find a solution, Darley was asked to assess whether the Divinity School on the ground floor of the East Pavilion would be suitable as a reading room. His proposal, including a plan for heating and ventilation, was approved, and the new Reading Room was opened in March 1848.[133] The average daily number of readers was about fifty, though on occasion it rose to ninety.[134]

The tradition of displaying some of the Library's treasures for the benefit of readers and visitors began in the late 1830s, when a glass case containing twenty-six manuscripts was placed in the Long Room.[135] It is not clear what was on display, but the *Irish Penny Journal* referred to 'beautiful antique manuscripts in glass cases' and in 1843 the Sallust containing the name of Mary Queen of Scots, donated in 1800, was put into the case.[136] Not everyone was in favour of the innovation. The *Illustrated London News* disliked the high stand which, it said, 'injured the general fine effect of the room'.[137] In 1850, green silk blinds were fitted to the case to protect the contents from the light.[138]

As well as the ordinary 'strangers' who were admitted to view the Library in the presence of a Fellow or Master of Arts, there was a steady trickle of distinguished visitors. These included Sir Walter Scott, on the occasion of his being conferred with an honorary degree in 1825; Lord Anglesey, the Lord Lieutenant, in 1832; Prince Esterhazy, the Austro-Hungarian

---

[130] MUN/LIB/2/4, 21 October 1844.
[131] *Ibid.*, 18 January 1845; MUN/LIB/12/60 (signed copies of oaths).
[132] MUN/V/5/7, 17 December 1831.
[133] MUN/V/5/8, 29 April 1843, 25 July 1846; MUN/V/5/9, 18 March 1848.
[134] DU Commission, 'Appendix A: Evidence', p. 177.
[135] MUN/LIB/2/3, report for year ending September 1838.
[136] *Irish Penny Journal*, 1 (1841), 340–2; MUN/V/5/8, 23 October 1843.
[137] *Illustrated London News*, 25 (11 August 1849), 87.   [138] MUN/V/5/9, 26 October 1850.

Ambassador in 1836; and Lord John Russell, the Prime Minister, in 1848.[139] The itinerary for the celebrated eleven-day visit of Queen Victoria and Prince Albert to Ireland in 1849 included the Library. Wall and Todd prepared an extensive display including the Books of Kells, Durrow and Dimma, other manuscripts, papyri, the Brian Boru harp and the Sallust. The Queen and the Prince Consort signed their names on a vellum flyleaf that had been added to the Book of Kells by Mullen when he rebound it in 1826.[140] This became the source of a popular tradition that they had written on one of the original pages of the manuscript, a myth fostered by the Queen herself, who wrote in her journal, 'Dr Todd . . . showed us some very interesting ancient manuscripts and relics, including St Columba's Book (in which we wrote our names)'.[141]

* * *

In 1850, Todd became a Senior Fellow and was therefore required to resign as the Assistant Librarian. Unusually, the Board issued a notice inviting Junior Fellows to apply for the vacancy.[142] Three did, and Benjamin Dickson, a Junior Fellow since 1848, was elected for 5 years.

---

[139] Constantia Maxwell, *The stranger in Ireland* (London: Cape, 1954), pp. 252–4; MS 3350, 17 May 1832; MS 3352, 30 August 1836; *Freeman's Journal*, 7 September 1848.

[140] MUN/V/5/9, pp. 131–2; *The Times*, 9 August 1849.

[141] Queen Victoria, *Leaves from the journal of our life in the Highlands, from 1848 to 1861: to which are prefixed and added extracts from the same journal giving an account of earlier visits to Scotland, and tours in England and Ireland, and yachting excursions*, ed. by Arthur Helps (London: Smith Elder, 1868), p. 182. At that time the Book of Kells was still believed to have been written by St Columba. The leaf was removed in 1953 and is now MS 58**.

[142] MUN/V/5/9, 2 and 16 March 1850.

11 | The Library in 1850

In 1850–1, three Royal Commissions were set up to enquire into the state of the universities of Oxford, Cambridge and Dublin (the Scottish universities having been the subject of a similar commission two decades earlier). Unlike Oxford and Cambridge, where recommendations for far-reaching reforms were proposed, Trinity and its Library emerged relatively unscathed, and the Commission's recommendations regarding the Library generally coincided with the views expressed by the less conservative members of the College community. All three reports covered the university libraries in some detail. Those for Dublin and Cambridge provided statistical information, but that for Oxford contained few figures about the Bodleian.[1]

The total number of volumes in Trinity was about 105,000, which made it larger than Edinburgh and Glasgow (both of which had around 70,000) but considerably smaller than Cambridge (170,000) and the Bodleian (220,000).[2] The libraries were reported as growing at significantly different rates, the Bodleian at between 6,000 and 7,000 volumes a year, Cambridge at about 5,000 and Trinity at only 1,500 to 2,000. The figure quoted for Trinity is initially puzzling, as the number of items received from Stationers' Hall was considerably larger than that, comprising about 3,500 'articles', as Todd described them; in addition, approximately 750 volumes a year were acquired by purchase or donation. Although many of the 'volumes' received by legal deposit were pamphlets, which were eventually to be bound together, often more than twenty to a volume, and would subsequently be counted as a single item, there is still a considerable discrepancy between the two figures. Todd explained this as being due partly to the cataloguing backlog that he had inherited and partly to those legal-deposit books 'deemed too insignificant to be placed in the Library'.[3]

---

[1] DU Commission; *Report of Her Majesty's Commissioners appointed to inquire into the state, discipline, studies and revenues of the University and Colleges of Cambridge*, [1559], 1852–3, XLIV, 1; *Report of Her Majesty's Commissioners appointed to inquire into the state, discipline, studies and revenues of the University and Colleges of Oxford*, [1482], 1852, XXII, 1; Anne Walsh, 'The Library as revealed in the Parliamentary Commission Report of 1853', in *Essays*, pp. 138–50.

[2] Peter Freshwater, 'Books and universities', in *Cambridge history*, vol. II, pp. 345–70.

[3] DU Commission, 'Appendix A: Evidence', p. 172.

It is clear from answers to questions from the Commission that the College drew a distinction between legal-deposit books regarded as being of academic importance and those that were not. At Cambridge, a similar distinction was made, with books in the latter category becoming known as the 'Upper Library', receiving minimal cataloguing and being shelved according to the date of receipt. In Dublin, the distinction was more pronounced. Though Todd was assiduous in pursuing publishers to ensure the deposit of their books, only about 70 per cent of those acquired were actually catalogued and placed in the Library. The Library minutes book recorded that the value of books and periodicals received from Stationers' Hall in 1836 was about £740, of which those not added to the Library were valued at £214.[4] The categories regarded as unsuitable were principally children's and school books, what were described as 'the inferior class of novels', and 'insignificant publications' of various kinds.[5] They were listed and, for the most part, retained within the Library building – admittedly in a not very easily accessible manner, in chests and boxes. However, they were not deemed to be part of the Library, were not included in the statistics until the mid twentieth century and were not considered to be subject to the regulations that prevented lending. Todd informed the Commission that the Library statutes 'expressly prohibit' the borrowing of printed books. This statement was factually correct, even though in 1845 the Board, in reaffirming the regulation that books were not to be lent, had agreed that Fellows and professors could borrow 'those that are laid aside by the Librarian as not to be put into the Library'.[6] This arrangement was confirmed in the new regulations approved in 1849.[7] Some of the titles recorded in the loan registers, however, suggest that even books ultimately destined for the Library could be borrowed, provided they had not yet been catalogued. The facility was well used, with some Fellows regularly borrowing half a dozen or more titles each month, many in two or three volumes, and a careful note was kept of their return.[8]

The Library was open from 10 a.m. until 3 p.m. between 20 November and 20 February and from 9 a.m. until 4 p.m. for the rest of the year.[9] Admission was still restricted to graduates and to external readers recommended to

---

[4] MUN/LIB/2/3, January 1837.   [5] DU Commission, 'Appendix A: Evidence', p. 173.

[6] MUN/V/5/8, 25 January 1845.

[7] MUN/V/5/9, 17 November 1849. Up to six volumes could be borrowed, until the following 21 March or November.

[8] MUN/LIB/6/14–MUN/LIB/6/16.

[9] In 1837, the opening hours had been changed, from 8 a.m. to 4 p.m. all year round, to 9 a.m. to 4 p.m. in summer and 9 a.m. to 3 p.m. in winter; in 1850 the winter opening time moved to 10 a.m.: MUN/V/5/7, 8 April 1837; MUN/V/5/9, 23 March 1850.

the Board by two Fellows.[10] Undergraduates were expected to find the Lending Library adequate for their needs, but there was increasing pressure for them to be allowed to use the main collection as well. Formally the situation was the same in Trinity as in Oxford and Cambridge, though a more liberal interpretation of the statutes meant that Oxford undergraduates had little difficulty obtaining access to the Bodleian and undergraduates were admitted to Cambridge University Library for the last hour of opening each day.[11] All three universities were to open their libraries to undergraduates within the following decade.

At Trinity there were just over twelve thousand reader visits in a year, which translated into an average of forty-seven readers a day. Professors and Fellows had direct access to the shelves, but other readers were required to complete a docket for each book they wished to see. The average daily number of dockets was forty-one. The Commissioners commented on the comparatively low level of use, saying that, 'considering the extent and value of the Library . . . the small extent to which it is used is certainly remarkable'.[12] They urged that the restrictions placed on access to the Library should be reduced, particularly in the case of undergraduates.

Dublin possessed several important libraries by the middle of the nineteenth century, but access to most was far from straightforward and they offered little to the general reading public. The Royal Irish Academy and the King's Inns were restricted to members, and Marsh's Library was open to graduates and gentlemen, but its collections were primarily of antiquarian interest. There were a few subscription or circulating libraries. Trinity was commended in the 1849 report of the Select Committee on Public Libraries as being accessible to the public 'on certain easily-performed conditions' and was compared favourably with the university libraries of Oxford, Cambridge, Glasgow and Aberdeen.[13] Despite the alleged ease with which they could gain admission to Trinity's Library, the number of external readers admitted between 1838 and 1853 never in fact exceeded twenty in a year and in some years was as low as two.[14] The nearest the city had to a public library was that of the Royal Dublin Society, which contained about nineteen thousand volumes and recorded around ten thousand visits a year from members of the public. The Select Committee recommended that the Society's library should be extended and made more accessible, but its collection was eventually to become the nucleus of the National Library of Ireland rather

---

[10] MUN/LIB/12/22b.   [11] Oxford, Report, note 1 above, p. 119; McKitterick, p. 615.

[12] DU Commission, *Report*, p. 75.

[13] *Report from the Select Committee on Public Libraries*, HC 1849 (548), XVII, 1 (p. v).

[14] MUN/LIB/2/4, fol. 37v.

Figure 13 The Long Room in 1859, before the alterations by Deane and Woodward (MUN/MC/29a)

than a public library for the city.[15] Although various Public Libraries Acts were passed, Dublin had to wait until 1883 for the establishment of a municipal library.

---

[15] Gerard Long, 'The foundation of the National Library of Ireland', *Long Room*, 36 (1991), 41–58.

Physically, the College Library in 1850 had changed in only relatively minor respects since 1750. It was now a free-standing building, no longer attached to residences on its north side, and the stonework had been repaired. Internally the main changes were the construction of a new Manuscripts Room following the receipt of the Fagel collection, the removal of the seats and desks from the alcoves of the Long Room, and the introduction of a central table for readers. An article published in the *Dublin University Magazine* described the Long Room, the decrepit state of the eighteenth-century catalogue, which was still in use, and the central table,

at which readers sit, and occasionally write, with demoralized ink, and pens of the most extraordinary truculency, deteriorated by age . . . Along the green surface of this table, flatly repose in brown and leathern recumbency, some dozen of large square volumes, containing the catalogue of the library . . . venerable with senility, dogsears, and decay . . . tattered and difficult of decipherment.[16]

The busts, of which there were now about thirty-five, had been moved down from the gallery and placed on pedestals at Long Room level, with four of them in niches at the ends of the room. The original bookcases were full, as was the low shelving that had been added in the alcoves. Space for new acquisitions was provided by the hinged bookcases that were being erected against the walls of the gallery. In 1852, they contained about 4,500 volumes and Todd estimated (more optimistically than when he had first proposed them in 1844) that they would eventually hold 35,200 volumes.[17] The ground floor of the East Pavilion had recently been converted into a Reading Room, and the corresponding room at the west end contained the Lending Library, but was also still used for lectures in law.

In 1852, the Lending Library contained around 2,700 titles and served a student population of 1,500. The number of books lent each year was about 2,800. Its Librarian regarded the mathematics, engineering and divinity sections as well stocked but the collections in law and medicine as 'deficient'.[18] In comparison to aspects of the main Library, the Commissioners expressed themselves very satisfied with the operation of the Lending Library which, they said, had become a 'most useful and efficient establishment'.[19]

The staff of the Library had increased considerably and now numbered ten, including a Reading Room attendant, three porters and the two additional assistant clerks appointed in 1849.[20] In his evidence to the

[16] 'Patrick Delany, D.D.', *Dublin University Magazine*, 52 (1858), 578–86 (pp. 578–9).
[17] DU Commission, 'Appendix A: Evidence', p. 172.
[18] DU Commission, 'Appendix A: Evidence', p. 193.
[19] DU Commission, *Report*, p. 79.   [20] MUN/V/5/9, 29 September 1849.

Commission, Todd listed the staff and their salaries. The Librarian was paid £115 8s. 0d. and the Assistant Librarian £60, but these figures represented only part of their income. In 1850, Wall was simultaneously Librarian, Vice-Provost and a Senior Fellow, with total emoluments of almost £400, and Dickson, the Assistant Librarian, was also Greek Lecturer and a Junior Fellow, earning a further £100 a year, to which were added in both cases payments for teaching and other duties.[21] The head clerk, Thomas Fisher, on a salary of £150, was responsible for preparing the catalogue for printing, and the second clerk received £80 for cataloguing new books. The assistant clerks earned £60: one managed the Lending Library under the Junior Dean and the other examined publishers' catalogues and sent Greenhill lists of books to be claimed.[22]

The funding of the Library was a complex matter, as even Todd had to admit. It consisted of three elements. There was a Library Fund of about £500 a year, which was derived from fees paid by students and charges for proceeding to a degree. To this was added a grant from the Board, which varied each year and was used to meet the difference between the Library Fund and the actual expenditure. In 1850, for example, the Library Fund of £512 was supplemented by a Board grant of £938. Todd maintained that the Library Fund had originally been intended solely for the purchase of books and manuscripts (which varied from £364 to £574 between 1849 and 1851), but by 1850 it was also used to meet the salaries of the Library clerks, the cost of binding and the annual grant of £50 to the Lending Library. The third element, covering repairs, miscellaneous charges and the salaries of all staff except the clerks, was met from the general College accounts.[23]

---

[21] DU Commission, 'Appendix A: Evidence', p. 179.   [22] MUN/LIB/2/4, fol. 27.

[23] DU Commission, 'Appendix A: Evidence', pp. 178–9. Income and expenditure of the Library Fund is recorded in MUN/V/58.

12 | Todd as Librarian: 1852–1869

On 7 February 1852, Wall resigned as Librarian, though he was allowed to retain a set of Library keys and have exclusive use of the Librarian's Room for a further 5 years.[1] He remained a Senior Fellow and, until his death 10 years later, continued as Vice-Provost, an office he had held simultaneously with that of Librarian since 1847. There could be only one successor – the man who had effectively run the Library for the previous 20 years. James Henthorn Todd, elected Librarian for an initial period of 5 years from the date of Wall's resignation, was then 47 and the Professor of Hebrew and Senior Lecturer at Trinity, as well as Secretary of the Royal Irish Academy and a founder of both St Columba's College, Dublin, and the Irish Archaeological Society. (See Figure 11.)

Though the Library had been without Todd's involvement for only 2 years, it was already showing signs of a lack of direction, and the report that he produced for the Board during his second year in office was a depressing one. The books in the gallery were 'in very great disorder'; there was a substantial backlog of cataloguing (though the appointment of an additional Library clerk had already started to reduce this); the shelf-lists were not properly written up and contained 'perplexing irregularities'; one of the Library clerks had been dismissed for neglect of duty; one of the cleaners had stolen some books; and, finally, a 'want of room' was being felt, because the carpenters had been slow in installing bookcases in the gallery – and even when those were completed they would provide space for only about a further 4 years' intake.[2] Cataloguing and space were to dominate Todd's tenure of office.

The catalogue

The backlog of books awaiting cataloguing was a problem that he began to tackle immediately after his appointment. Within a month, he presented

---

[1] MUN/V/5/10, 7 February 1852.   [2] *Ibid.*, 28 January 1854.

a report to the Board indicating that the arrears, of 5,000 volumes, would take 2 years to clear with the existing level of staff, and by that time a further 6,000 volumes would have arrived. The Board agreed to his request for an additional Library clerk, at an annual salary of £60, to clear the arrears of cataloguing, and a second Assistant Librarian, also at a salary of £60. Todd proposed that the Assistant Librarian's salary should be met by a reduction of the equivalent amount in his own salary, provided he also held the office of Senior Lecturer or Bursar, which would provide him with a sufficient income. William Lee was appointed to the second post, his appointment to terminate at the same time as that of Dickson, the other Assistant Librarian already in office.[3] Todd's measures had the desired effect, and by the time of his report to the Board at the beginning of 1854 the cataloguing backlog had been reduced by two-thirds and the services of the additional temporary clerk were no longer required.[4]

The Printed Catalogue had made considerably less progress, however. By mid 1852 only twenty-six sheets of the letter A had been printed and it was the end of the following year before A was completed, almost 5 years since Todd had started the printing. Thomas Fisher, who had been appointed as a Library clerk in 1843, was the head clerk responsible for preparing the slips for the catalogue.[5] Both Todd and Fisher were aware that many major libraries were wrestling with the question of what the precise nature of a catalogue should be. Should it be simply a finding-list, with brief author–title information and shelfmarks, or should it contain full bibliographic descriptions for each book in the library? Todd sought external advice by consulting the heads of several large libraries, including Anthony Panizzi, Keeper of Printed Books at the British Museum.[6] Fisher kept a commonplace book in which, under 'Rules to be observed in the catalogue of printed books in the Library of Trinity College, Dublin', he not only codified the rules he was applying but listed reference books on the subject and made notes on general cataloguing issues, including those raised in the report of a Select Committee on the British Museum.[7] The resulting Printed Catalogue is something of a compromise, in that the entries fall

[3] *Ibid.*, 6 and 13 March 1852; DU Commission, 'Appendix A: Evidence', p. 177.
[4] MUN/V/5/10, 28 January 1854.
[5] MUN/V/5/8, 28 January 1843, 25 October 1845; Vincent Kinane and Ann O'Brien, ' "The vast difficulty of cataloguing": the Printed Catalogue of Trinity College Dublin (1864–1887)', *Libraries and Culture*, 23 (1988), 427–49; Vincent Kinane, *History of the Dublin University Press, 1734–1976* (Dublin: Gill & Macmillan, 1994), pp. 188–92.
[6] DU Commission, 'Appendix A: Evidence', p. 175; A. H. Chaplin, *GK: 150 years of the General Catalogue of Printed Books in the British Museum* (Aldershot: Scolar, 1987), p. 67.
[7] MUN/LIB/4/2; *Report from the Select Committee on British Museum*, HC 1836 (440), X, 1.

short of being a complete bibliographical description but are more detailed than those in a simple finding-list.

If printing of the letter A had been slow, B was even slower, taking a decade to complete (though it did include that bête noire of all cataloguers, the Bible entry). In a futile attempt to reduce the inconvenience to readers, Todd published a list of books added to the Library in the year to November 1853.[8] In the 'Advertisement' to that volume he commented on the problem of the lack of currency of printed catalogues and the fact that the Bodleian catalogue was 8 years out of date when it appeared. He suggested that the publication of annual supplements might reduce the inconvenience, but this approach was abandoned after the single issue for 1853. It took until May 1864 for the first volume of the Printed Catalogue, containing the letters A and B, to be published, and no further volumes appeared before the deaths of Fisher in 1867 and Todd 2 years later.

Legal deposit

In 1849, the British Museum Trustees had given Panizzi responsibility for enforcing legal deposit. By dint of warnings, followed by writs and then by prosecutions, he had brought the London publishers to heel and, as he reported in a letter to *The Times*, he had increased the level of deposit with the Museum from 9,871 in 1851 to 13,934 in 1852.[9] He extended his activities to include publishing houses in Oxford and Cambridge, and in September 1852 visited Dublin and Cork in pursuit of recalcitrant publishers there. He found many books available in Dublin which had not been deposited at the British Museum and of whose existence he was unaware, a situation similar to that which he found in Wales and Scotland and in cities in the English Midlands and North. During his Irish visit, he arranged for a list of new publications to be sent to him on a quarterly basis.[10]

Even if many Irish publications were escaping the net of the British Museum, Todd was doing his utmost to ensure that they were claimed for Trinity. One of the Library clerks was responsible for checking advertisements in newspapers and compiling lists of books to be demanded from Irish publishers.[11] However, Panizzi does not appear to have met Todd during

---

[8]   *Catalogus librorum quibus aucta est Bibliotheca Collegii SS. Trinitatis Reginae Elizabethae, juxta Dublin, anno exeunte Kal. Novembr., MDCCCLIII* (Dublin University Press, 1854).

[9]   *The Times*, 2 February 1853; Harris, pp. 218–20; McKitterick, pp. 566–7; Partridge, pp. 84–6.

[10] British Museum, Central Archive, Officers' Reports, 7 October 1852, 16975.

[11] One such list for the period 1850 to 1858 contains over 1,000 Irish-published items, including both periodicals and monographs: MUN/LIB/22/12.

his visit, and it does not seem to have occurred to Todd to keep the other deposit libraries informed of the books he was able to obtain.

Panizzi's success was noted by the other libraries, who realised the extent of the material that they were failing to obtain. The main problem for them was the inefficiency of their agent, Joseph Greenhill, who had taken over as Warehouse Keeper on his father's retirement in 1849. At Cambridge's request, he supplied a list of publishers who were not depositing their books; this included several of the major houses such as Collins and the legal publishers Wildy and Sons. Both Todd and Joseph Power, the Cambridge Librarian, wrote letters threatening prosecution, but their success was minimal, partly because of inaccurate information supplied by Greenhill. Todd continued to send Greenhill lists of books that he wished to have claimed, but it was clearly time to act in consort with the other libraries.[12]

On 31 May 1859, Todd and representatives of Oxford, Cambridge and the Faculty of Advocates met at the British Museum. Panizzi was asked for his advice and proposed that the four libraries should 'act together in protecting their rights' by appointing an agent based at the British Museum (and thus – like Cowtan in the 1840s – with access to its list of accessions). The agent would send a monthly list to Greenhill, so that those books that had not been received could be claimed by the latter.[13] This approach was agreed, though Todd would have preferred to have had an agent independent of the Museum, to avoid the risk of divided loyalties. Greenhill was informed of the decision and of the fact that his salary would be reduced to £25 a year from each of the four libraries. He objected strongly to this significant loss of income and enlisted the support of the Stationers' Company, with the result that the decision to relieve him of his duties of claiming was not implemented immediately. However, the Faculty of Advocates soon lost patience with his continued inefficiency and dismissed him as their agent, replacing him with Gregory Eccles, a member of staff at the British Museum. Todd wrote to Henry Wellesley, the representative of the Bodleian Curators, complaining about Greenhill and proposing that, if a book were not delivered and no reason given, his salary should be stopped until the book was produced or a satisfactory explanation provided.[14]

Pressure from the libraries seems to have increased Greenhill's vigilance on behalf of his three remaining clients and for a time the number of books supplied by him increased. Trinity even issued him with a power of attorney

---

[12] MUN/LIB/22/20/63; MUN/LIB/2/4, 10 April 1855; McKitterick, pp. 569–82; Craster, pp. 61–4.
[13] MUN/V/5/11/2, 21 May 1859; British Museum, Central Archive, Officers' Reports, 9 June 1859, 459.
[14] MUN/LIB/2/4, 21 March 1860.

to enable him to instigate legal proceedings against defaulting publishers on behalf of the College.[15] By 1863, however, Cambridge had had enough and followed Edinburgh in asking Eccles to act as their agent.[16] Eccles then wrote to Oxford and Trinity describing the service he could offer and pointing out that it would be more efficient and less troublesome to have one agent claiming on behalf of all four libraries. His entreaties were successful, and he was appointed as agent for the College from September 1863 at a salary of 60 guineas a year, the same as he was receiving from each of the other libraries.[17] Greenhill continued as Warehouse Keeper and contrived to make life as difficult as possible for Eccles by delaying the delivery of books received at Stationers' Hall and even sending out circulars to publishers implying that he was still the agent for the libraries.

In 1864, Adam Black, the Edinburgh publisher, sought to have the legislation on copyright amended to provide increased protection for publishers and authors. He proposed no alterations to the legal-deposit legislation, but Eccles saw this as an opportunity to circumvent Greenhill by having the libraries' agent designated as the place of deposit rather than Stationers' Hall.[18] The Select Committee set up to consider the application for new legislation recommended that there should be no change, and so the unsatisfactory situation between Eccles and Greenhill continued.

A shortage of space in the British Museum meant that Eccles had to set up his office at premises in Bloomsbury Square. This effectively marked the beginning of the Copyright Agency, whereby Oxford, Cambridge, the Faculty of Advocates and Trinity employed staff in London and used bibliographic data from the British Museum as a basis for their claims. Todd even suggested that the libraries should collaborate with each other and with the British Museum to share the burden of cataloguing legal-deposit books – a proposal that was a century ahead of its time.[19]

All this activity in the 1860s represented a further step by the libraries towards an understanding of legal deposit as it is perceived today. They were gradually coming to recognise that all books were significant, both as far as the law was concerned and from the perspective of current and future generations of readers. This principle was enunciated in a letter from Todd to the Ordnance Survey, in which he stated his view that the purpose of the Act was to require the Library to obtain and preserve all the publications to which it was entitled, 'and I do not allow the question of the utility or the

---

[15] MUN/V/5/11/2, 9 March 1861.   [16] MUN/LIB/22/20/69.
[17] MUN/LIB/2/4, 1 and 6 July 1863; MUN/V/5/12, 4 July 1863.
[18] MUN/LIB/22/20/90.   [19] McKitterick, p. 576.

merit of a publication to interfere with our right to it'.[20] In this particular instance it was a statement that he may have regretted making, as it had the effect of eliciting a deposit of some 14,000 Ordnance Survey maps of England and Scotland from the Secretary of State for War.[21] Printed music was also being sent regularly by the late 1850s, with over three hundred items received in October 1859, and five hundred the following year. Music had been deposited intermittently since at least 1811, though it had not been claimed, and there is no evidence that it was retained during the first half of the century.[22]

Staff, readers and visitors

In March 1855, the terms of office of the two Assistant Librarians, Dickson and Lee, came to an end and Todd took the opportunity to persuade the Board to change its policy of appointing from among the Junior Fellows. This allowed him to promote Thomas Fisher to be the senior Assistant Librarian and appoint as the junior Assistant Rudolf Siegfried, a graduate in comparative philology of the University of Tübingen, who had entered Trinity to learn Irish.[23] Fisher retained his salary of £150 and Siegfried was to receive £100 a year, a considerable increase on the sum paid to previous Assistant Librarians, to reflect the fact that they were not in receipt of Fellows' emoluments. Fisher remained in charge of the Printed Catalogue, and Siegfried was responsible for cataloguing new books and supervising the work of the clerks. These Assistant Librarians did not have teaching or other responsibilities in the College as had the previous incumbents as Fellows, which meant that, for a short period at least, all those working in the Library, except the Librarian, were full-time staff rather than annually elected academics or temporary clerks. Todd put Siegfried's knowledge of Sanskrit to good use by having him catalogue the Sanskrit and Hindustani manuscripts, but this skill proved too much of a temptation to the College, and his full-time commitment to the Library turned out to be a brief one.[24] Candidates for the Indian Civil Service were now expected to have a knowledge of Sanskrit, and Trinity responded quickly to the demand for graduates with that language by appointing Siegfried as a lecturer in 1858

[20] MUN/LIB/2/4, 11 February 1863.   [21] *Ibid.*, 21 August 1863.
[22] MUN/LIB/22/16–17; Roy Stanley, 'Music collections at Trinity College Dublin', *Brio*, 39/2 (Autumn/Winter 2002), 32–7.
[23] MUN/V/5/10, 1 March, 30 April, 7 June 1855; McDowell and Webb, pp. 232–4.
[24] MUN/V/5/10, 17 November 1855.

and as the first Professor of Sanskrit and Comparative Philology 4 years later. He held the offices in tandem with his post of Assistant Librarian, but died in 1863 at the age of 33. He was succeeded both as Professor of Sanskrit and Assistant Librarian by his countryman Carl Friedrich Lottner, whom Todd had appointed as a Library clerk in 1861.[25]

This was a period of considerable turnover of staff. Thomas French replaced Lottner as a Library clerk.[26] Fisher died in 1867 and was replaced as the senior Assistant Librarian by William Brownrigg Hunt.[27] At the same time, the Board also decided to revert to its previous practice of appointing a Junior Fellow as an Assistant Librarian and selected Benjamin Dickson, who had already held the post a decade earlier.[28] For about 2 years, therefore, there were three Assistant Librarians, Lottner, Hunt and Dickson, but only Hunt was full-time, Dickson holding assistant lectureships in divinity and Hebrew, and Lottner the Chair of Sanskrit. In 1869, Lottner was granted leave of absence and Todd died before he could replace him in the Library.[29]

The theft of around fifty medical books in 1862 gave Todd the opportunity to plead for better supervision of the Library. He claimed that at least one porter was almost always absent 'on the pretence of ill health' and that two men were insufficient to fetch books for readers as well as to police the Long Room and the Fagel Room. It was not possible to return used books at the end of a day, which encouraged readers to hide them. He suggested that 'a higher class of attendants' might replace some of the porters at a lower cost, as 'there are men of high educational attainments who would gladly accept such a situation at a very moderate salary'.[30] The Board failed to act, and in October 1865 Todd submitted a memo declaring that he intended to suppress a vacant post of porter and appoint an attendant with 'some literary attainments'. There was, he said, no other library 'of such magnitude' that was left in the hands of 'illiterate attendants'.[31]

Todd told the Dublin University Commission that he believed the Library should be open to undergraduates and to members of the public, though he recognised that this was a view not shared by all. The main objections, he noted, were that undergraduates might spend their time in 'useless reading, or in the perusal of pernicious books'.[32] In 1849, it had been proposed that senior undergraduates and scholars should be allowed access, and in 1851 the scholars themselves wrote to the Board seeking permission to use the Library. They were told that the Board was 'favourably disposed' to the

[25] MUN/V/5/11/2, 21 September 1861; MUN/V/5/12, 14 February 1863.
[26] MUN/V/5/12, 14 February 1863.   [27] MUN/LIB/2/4, 17 January 1867.
[28] MUN/V/5/12, 2 March 1867.   [29] *Ibid.*, 1 May 1869.   [30] *Ibid.*, 20 December 1862.
[31] MUN/LIB/12/25.   [32] DU Commission, 'Appendix A: Evidence', p. 176.

request, and Todd was asked to consider what changes would be necessary to the statutes to remove the restriction and other 'obsolete or objectionable clauses'.[33] Pressure was also applied by the Commissioners themselves, who made the specific recommendation that the statutes be changed to give the Board the power to grant admission to the Library to whatever categories of reader it thought fit.[34]

In 1855 and 1856 new regulations were approved, replacing the Library oath with a declaration to be made in the presence of the Provost or Vice-Provost, and allowing the Librarian to admit undergraduates who had passed the senior freshman examinations.[35] Graduates of the universities of Dublin, Oxford and Cambridge were entitled to 'permanent or life' admission and external readers, whose application still had to be approved initially by the Board, were given tickets for 6 months, which could subsequently be renewed by the Librarian.[36] From then on, the Board minutes regularly recorded the names of those approved for admission to the Library. At the same time, the Lending Library became a department of the College Library, under the supervision of the Librarian. The £30 a year interest from Gilbert's bequest, which had hitherto been paid to the Junior Dean as Librarian of the Lending Library, was to form half the salary of the junior clerk responsible for that Library, but the level of the Junior Dean's salary was preserved.[37] Though borrowing was not permitted from the College Library, loans to Fellows and professors from the books not yet catalogued or not destined for the main collection were extensive, and in 1857 Todd introduced a 'Light-reading Book' in which those loans were recorded.[38]

By the 1850s, the Library had become one of the sights on the itinerary of many a visitor to Dublin, but access was still not straightforward, the intending visitor being warned by a contemporary guidebook that the Library could be seen only with an introduction by one of the 'college authorities'.[39] To meet the expected influx of visitors to the city for the Irish Industrial Exhibition of 1853 the Board agreed to allow 'strangers' to visit without prior arrangement during the summer vacation. One member of

---

[33] MUN/V/5/9, 8 December 1849, 12 April 1851. [34] DU Commission, *Report*, p. 76.

[35] Letters patent, 18 Victoria (31 January 1855), *Chartae et statuta Collegii Sacrosanctae et Individuae Trinitatis Reginae Elizabethae juxta Dublin*, 3 vols. (Dublin University Press, 1898), vol. II, pp. 59–110; Decree of Board and Visitors, 13 February 1856, *ibid.*, pp. 122–3. See also Appendix 3. The Librarian's authority was extended to cover all undergraduates in 1875 (MUN/V/5/13, 17 April 1875).

[36] MUN/V/5/10, 20 December 1855; MUN/LIB/12/24. [37] MUN/V/5/10, 19 December 1855.

[38] MUN/LIB/6/15–MUN/LIB/6/17.

[39] William F. Wakeman, *Dublin: what's to be seen, and how to see it*, 2nd edn (Dublin: Hodges & Smith, 1853), p. 41.

each party was required to sign a book at the entrance, giving his address and the number of people in the party. Between May and October, 18,675 people were recorded, the greatest number on one day being 519 on 30 August, just after Queen Victoria's arrival in the city to visit the exhibition.[40] This simplified procedure for the admission of visitors continued in force, and a record of visitor numbers became a standard component of the Librarian's annual report. The figure was normally between 3,000 and 4,000 a year, though in 1865, the year of the Dublin International Exhibition, it increased to a staggering 51,041 and then dropped the following year to 4,679.[41]

Raising the roof

The question of library space occupied the minds of those appointed to each of the three Royal Commissions of the early 1850s. The reports for Oxford and Cambridge recommended that a new reading room should be provided in the Bodleian, and additional book storage and reading rooms at Cambridge.[42] In 1862, the Bodleian acquired the Radcliffe Camera as a reading room and in 1867 a wing was added to Cambridge University Library. Trinity's new reading room in the East Pavilion had recently been completed and Todd convinced the Commissioners that space was not a priority for him. The completion of the gallery shelving, the move of the Manuscripts Room and proposals that he had made for changes to the Fagel Room would, he said, provide accommodation for over fifty thousand new books.[43] At the then current rate of intake, that represented between 15 and 20 years' growth.

Todd's written evidence to the Commission was dated July 1852, but in his report to the Board for 1853 he adopted a considerably less positive tone and warned that the completion of the gallery bookcases would provide accommodation for only 4 more years' accessions. He recommended that the shelving in the Fagel Room should be altered in the same way as had been done in the Long Room, by removing the seats and desks between the shelves and replacing them with low bookcases. Even that, however, would provide space for only a further 17,000 volumes. He also identified the need

---

[40] MUN/LIB/2/4, fols. 38–40.   [41] MUN/V/5/12, 11 November 1865, 28 November 1866.

[42] *Report of Her Majesty's Commissioners appointed to inquire into the state, discipline, studies and revenues of the University and Colleges of Oxford*, [1482], 1852, XXII, 1 (p. 118); *Report of Her Majesty's Commissioners appointed to inquire into the state, discipline, studies and revenues of the University and Colleges of Cambridge*, [1559], 1852–3, XLIV, 1 (p. 132).

[43] DU Commission, 'Appendix A: Evidence', pp. 172–3.

for better access to the gallery, as the number of books housed there was growing and the only route from the Long Room was by the stairs at the west end. He pointed out that the attendant, based at the east end of the Long Room, had to travel the whole length of the room four times to retrieve a book at the east end of the gallery and a further four times to replace it. He made several proposals for providing access to the gallery from the east end.[44]

At the Board visitation in November 1855 Todd drew attention yet again to the shortage of space and urged that his plans for alterations to the Fagel Room be carried out.[45] The spacing of the shelves was changed to provide accommodation for an additional 5,000 volumes, but by the time of the following visitation more pressing matters relating to the building had begun to occupy the attention of the Board and the Librarian.

The minute of the Board meeting on 15 November 1856, instructing the clerk of works to examine the state of the timbers in the roof, gave no indication of the scale of the crisis that was about to unfold. At the meeting a week later, Todd (who was Bursar that year as well as Librarian) read the report of the clerk of works, in which he described the state of the roof as 'insecure'. Advice was sought from Sir Thomas Deane and the College architect John McCurdy.[46] Deane and McCurdy were rivals in matters of architecture in Trinity, particularly since McCurdy had won the competition for the Museum Building but had then seen the work carried out by the firm of Deane and Woodward, on his ground plan but to Woodward's design.[47] Each architect offered different solutions to the problem of the Library roof and during the course of 1857 proposals were discussed by the Board without any conclusion being reached.

By the end of the year a Building Committee had been set up. Its concerns were no longer just the stability of the roof but also the provision of more accommodation for books. It was presented with two very different approaches.[48] McCurdy proposed to support the roof by inserting iron trusses into the void between it and the existing ceiling of the Long Room, and to lay a new floor in the roof-space to allow bookcases to be constructed there. From the outset, Deane, working with his partner Benjamin Woodward, made it clear that his preferred option was to replace the roof with a new one but, having been instructed by the Board to retain the existing roof,

---

[44] MUN/V/5/10, 28 January 1854.   [45] *Ibid.*, 17 November 1855.
[46] MUN/V/5/11/1, 15 and 22 November 1856.
[47] Anne Crookshank, 'The Long Room', in *Treasures*, pp. 16–28; Frederick O'Dwyer, *The architecture of Deane and Woodward* (Cork University Press, 1997), pp. 349–55.
[48] MUN/V/5/11/1, 17 January, 7 February, 16 December 1857.

the firm produced two proposals. The first was to block the gallery windows, place bookcases parallel to the walls and illuminate the room from above. This, they admitted, would be unsightly and expensive, involving either a new roof or new skylights in the present roof. The alternative was to run bookcases at right-angles to the walls and support the roof on these, thereby removing the weight from the walls, which, they claimed, were no longer in a very secure condition. They also raised doubts about the state of the Long Room floor and proposed to replace it with a new one which, they asserted, would not only be fireproof but would permit heating to be introduced safely. They concluded by holding out the prospect that, if a new roof 'be deemed advisable, the room could be made one of the handsomest libraries anywhere'.[49]

The Building Committee preferred Deane and Woodward's plans to those proposed by McCurdy but, to satisfy itself about the state of the floor, the Board decided to call in the builder Gilbert Cockburn, who had been employed on work in the College since the 1830s.[50] McCurdy, supported by Cockburn, stated that the floor timbers were in as good a state of preservation as when first laid. Deane and Woodward disagreed and proposed to insert a series of arches to support the floor.[51] To resolve the matter, the Board summoned all the parties to appear before it. Deane and Woodward were represented by Benjamin Woodward and Thomas Newenham Deane, the son of Sir Thomas, who was now in poor health. McCurdy brought along Robert Mallet, an engineer and iron-founder, and the hapless Cockburn was there to hold the ring. All now agreed that the floor of the Library was perfectly sound, but views on the condition of the roof were not unanimous. Mallet and McCurdy maintained that the timbers were unsound and could not be relied upon to support the roof in the way proposed by Deane and Woodward. Cockburn considered the timbers to be sound, except at the ends which rested on the walls. Mallet, the iron-founder, strongly advocated the introduction of iron trusses and the removal of all the timber, and claimed that this could be done without touching the slates or lead of the roof and without damaging the ceiling.[52] The meeting resolved nothing in relation to the main issue, the roof. Deane and Woodward, having had to concede on the state of the floor, continued to advise against the use of iron in the roof. Mallet produced drawings and an estimate for his proposed iron trusses which, he said, would provide sufficient strength to support a floor to hold books within the roof space. Lighting would be

---

[49] MUN/P/2/355.   [50] MUN/V/5/11/1, 2 January 1858.
[51] *Ibid.*, 6 and 9 January 1858.   [52] *Ibid.*, 13 January 1858.

provided by the installation of skylights in the upper part of the roof.[53] (See Plate 7.)

There the matter stalled. Todd was becoming increasingly concerned about space, and his report for September 1858 stated that 2,000 volumes, for which there was no room in the Library, were arranged in the clerks' room and entered in the catalogue in red ink.[54] Then, in October, he noticed additional cracks in the ceiling of the Long Room. He dispatched McCurdy to investigate and brought his alarming report straight to the Board. McCurdy wrote that the sagging was 'so manifest since my last inspection that I would deem it prudent not to lose a day in having the ceiling shored up'.[55] This was done and a collapse narrowly averted. A three-man committee, including Todd, was set up to advise on the various conflicting plans for resolving the problem.

During the spring and summer of 1859, Deane and Woodward attended a number of Board meetings, at which they presented their plans. These involved the installation of bookcases in the gallery, the removal of the plaster ceiling and its replacement by a barrel-vaulted ceiling clad with oak. The plans were approved, and on 17 September the seal was put to a contract with Cockburn to carry out the work, at a cost of £7,250.[56] As the work progressed, the architects discovered that some of the beams holding the gallery floor had rotted because they had been inserted into a damp wall, and so they revised their original plan to rest the roof beams on the bookstacks in the gallery. Instead, they proposed to support the roof on timber columns within the bookstacks, and these columns would then rest on new granite pillars to be inserted into the open arcades below the Long Room.[57] This, too, was approved and the work continued through 1860, with the building protected from the elements by a canvas roof and from other dangers by a night-watchman – though two porters were fined £2 each for leaving the Library keys at the gate for the workmen to let themselves in.[58]

Even at this stage the project attracted controversy. Matthew Good, ship-builder and Surveyor to the Board of Trade, wrote to condemn Deane's use of white Canadian oak on the grounds that it was subject to decay and would be dangerous for use in a roof. McCurdy weighed in behind him.

[53] *Ibid.*, 16 January, 24 April 1858; Mallet to Board, 21 April 1858, Irish Architectural Archive, 79/17.58/5.

[54] MUN/V/5/11/2, 19 November 1858.   [55] *Ibid.*, 16 October 1858.

[56] *Ibid.*, March–September 1859 *passim*; MUN/P/2/360.

[57] MUN/V/5/11/2, 15 April 1860. For a cross-section of the structure, see Brendan Grimes, 'The library buildings up to 1970', in *Essays*, pp. 72–90 (p. 81).

[58] MUN/V/5/11/2, 12 and 19 May, 19 September 1860.

Figure 14 The Long Room in about 1890, after the alterations to the ceiling and installation of gallery shelving by Deane and Woodward in 1860–1. The stained glass window donated by Charles Graves can be seen in the Fagel Room at the far end (MS 4897/1)

Deane enlisted the support of various timber merchants, who produced testimonials to the suitability of the oak, and the Board ordered the work to proceed.[59] Just as it seemed that these expensive repairs were reaching a conclusion, it was discovered that the timbers of the flat roofs in the East and West Pavilions were unsound and in a dangerous condition. Deane and Woodward proposed to extend their new roof to cover both pavilions. This too was agreed and Cockburn was contracted to carry out the work at an additional cost of £900.[60]

Deane and Woodward's transformation of the Long Room replaced Burgh's horizontal lines with the verticality of a medieval cathedral. It is not clear how far the architects might have been influenced by other recent university library buildings, in particular William Playfair's at Edinburgh and Charles Cockerell's at Cambridge, both of which have galleries and vaulted ceilings, though in a more neo-classical style, or perhaps Johan Daniel Herholdt's neo-gothic university library in Copenhagen, built between 1857 and 1861. It has also been suggested that Wren's church of St James,

[59] *Ibid.*, 2–18 June 1860; MUN/P/2/364–MUN/P/2/373.
[60] MUN/V/5/11/2, 23 July and 25 October 1860, 9 and 16 February, 3 April 1861; MUN/V/58/5, 1860–2.

Piccadilly, close to Deane and Woodward's London office, might have been a source of inspiration.[61] The installation of gallery bookcases and the replacement of Burgh's flat plaster ceiling with oak barrel-vaulting was an act of extraordinary boldness and self-confidence. It is widely admired today as an unusually successful example of Victorian intervention in an older building. As one critic has put it, 'what had been superb, they made sublime'.[62] The response at the time was more mixed, however. The *Dublin Builder*, though generally supportive of the change, noted that it had 'evoked some personal correspondence in the daily journals, wherein the architects are accused of Vandalism and unnecessarily tampering with the present edifice'.[63]

The work was completed by May 1861, and the Librarian was authorised to close the Library so that the books could be cleaned and arranged.[64] This was no small task. Most of the hinged bookcases had been removed from the gallery to permit the installation of the new high shelves, and so almost all the 24,000 volumes housed there had to be reshelved. The annual stocktaking had to be abandoned 'in consequence of the confusion resulting from the removal of the books in the gallery'.[65]

In his evidence to the Dublin University Commission, Todd had set out three schemes to create more space for books: the rearrangement of the shelves in the Fagel Room; the completion of the hinged bookcases in the gallery; and the removal of the manuscripts from the room above the Fagel. By the mid 1850s, when the roof problems started to become apparent, the first of these had been achieved and the second was about to become unnecessary. The opening of the Museum Building, constructed between 1854 and 1857, provided the opportunity to implement the third part of the plan. The Law School was transferred from the West Pavilion of the Library to the Museum Building, and the Engineering School was also moved to the Museum Building, vacating its temporary accommodation between the Public Theatre and the Library.[66] This created space in the now vacant Engineering Building for the Lending Library. The room in the West Pavilion, hitherto the Law School and Lending Library, could then be converted into a new Manuscripts Room. The move of the manuscripts in turn released the room above the Fagel to accommodate printed books. It is not clear precisely when these moves took place but 1860 can be assumed, as presses were built in the new Manuscripts Room that summer and a

61 O'Dwyer, note 47 above, p. 355.
62 Edward McParland, 'Trinity College Dublin – I', *Country Life*, 159 (6 May 1976), 1166–9 (p. 1169).
63 *Dublin Builder*, 2 (1860), 196.   64 MUN/V/5/11/2, 4 May 1861.
65 *Ibid.*, 3 February 1861; MUN/V/5/12, 27 October 1862.   66 McDowell and Webb, p. 184.

Board minute of March approved the removal of the Lending Library, and the transfer of the papyrus case into the new Manuscripts Room, as soon as the 'present alterations' had been completed.[67] The result of all these moves was that the West Pavilion now accommodated the Manuscripts Room on the ground floor, the Librarian's Room on the first floor and the Clerks' Room on the second floor. The East Pavilion contained the Reading Room on the ground floor, the Fagel Room above it and the new room for printed books (which became known as the Upper East Room) above that.

During the 1860s, two busts were added to those in the Long Room. The first to be produced was a posthumous one of Rudolf Siegfried, sculpted by Joseph Kirk and dated 1864, and in 1868 the College commemorated its great mathematician Sir William Rowan Hamilton by buying a bust of him from the sculptor John Henry Foley.

Purchases and donations

A fixed allocation for purchasing, which had been requested by the Library Committee 4 years earlier, was finally approved by the Board in 1855. However, instead of the £600 a year that the committee calculated would allow a reasonable number of foreign books and journals to be bought, only £560 was provided, to cover not just purchases but also binding for both the College Library and the Lending Library.[68] This meant that subscriptions to about forty of the more expensive foreign journals had to be cancelled, including *Bibliothèque universelle de Genève*, *Natuurkundige verhandelingen van de Hollandsche Maatschappij der Wetenschappen te Haarlem*, *Annales de la Société Linnéenne de Lyon* and *Bulletino archeologico napoletano*.[69] This retrenchment in the Library was part of a more general attempt to reduce the College's expenditure. Its finances had been depleted both by the economic problems following the famine and by the cost of the Museum Building; the rebuilding of the Library roof was about to become another burden.[70]

The establishment of a purchasing budget and the cancellation of these probably little-used periodicals did, however, allow Todd to continue to acquire other material, including manuscripts relating to Irish history. In

---

[67] MUN/V/5/11/2, 17 March 1860; MUN/V/57/12, June and September quarters 1860; William O'Sullivan, 'The new Manuscripts Room', *Annual Bulletin* (1958), 12–13.

[68] MUN/V/5/10, 15 December 1855. The allocation was subsequently increased to £600: MUN/V/5/12, 20 November 1867.

[69] MUN/LIB/17/13.   [70] McDowell and Webb, pp. 537–8.

the 1850s he bought manuscripts of Archbishop King and his contemporaries from the bookseller John O'Daly, and a memorandum book in the
hand of Archbishop Ussher for £7. He spent £10 on three volumes of printed
maps by the eighteenth-century Huguenot mapmaker John Rocque.[71] This
is a mixed bag of maps and plans covering areas ranging from Dublin,
Kilkenny and County Armagh through England and Paris to North America and including town plans, gardens and the seraglio in Constantinople.
The papers on the 1798 rebellion that were already in the Library were augmented by a large collection of letters and other documents bought in 1865 at
one of the sales of material from Richard Robert Madden's library. Madden,
born in 1798, was a historian of the United Irishmen and had gathered information from a wide range of sources, often by sending out questionnaires
to descendants of those involved in the rebellion. Some of the questionnaires, with their answers and Madden's notes, form part of the collection
(MS 873).[72]

At the sale, in 1858, of the library belonging to William Monck Mason,
Todd bought two manuscripts, the Book of Fermoy and the Life of Red
Hugh O'Donnell, and offered them to the College for the price he had
paid. The Board declined to buy them and both are now in the Royal Irish
Academy.[73]

As well as manuscripts of Irish interest, Todd also bought examples
of Irish printing, the most substantial being the 106 volumes, containing
about 1,300 pamphlets, purchased at the auction of the library of Joseph
Singer, Bishop of Meath, in 1866. In 1853, Frederick Conway, owner and
editor of the *Dublin Evening Post*, died leaving a substantial library, the sale
catalogue of which ran to almost eight thousand lots. Among them were
many incunabula, which clearly tempted the College, as Abbott's catalogue
lists some thirty-one items in the Library marked *Bibliotheca Conoviana*,
which were acquired for about £30.[74]

It was during this time that the Library received one of its most important
early Irish manuscripts, the Book of Armagh (MS 52). Written about the
year 807, it contains some unique texts relating to St Patrick and the only
complete copy of the New Testament to survive in Ireland from that period.
It is also the only Irish manuscript of the time that still possesses its original
binding boards. These were found inside the medieval leather satchel in
which the manuscript was kept, itself one of only a handful of such satchels

[71] MUN/LIB/11/24/11–MUN/LIB/11/24/12; MUN/LIB/11/32/19; MUN/LIB/11/32/15.
[72] R. B. McDowell, 'The 1798 Rebellion', in *Treasures*, pp. 143–7.
[73] MUN/V/5/11/1, 28 April 1858.
[74] Abbott, *Incunabula*, p. 224; MUN/LIB/5e/2 (March and June quarters 1854).

known to have survived from the Middle Ages.[75] The acquisition of the manuscript by the College was a protracted affair. In the early nineteenth century it was owned by the Brownlow family of Lurgan and was described in detail by Sir William Betham in 1827.[76] In 1831, it was put up for sale and viewed by hundreds of people at Edward Maguire's Dublin sale room. Because of the level of interest and public concern that it would be sold abroad, its former owner, Francis Brownlow, had second thoughts, outbid the dealers and bought it back, for £390. He later placed it on deposit in the library of the Royal Irish Academy. After Brownlow's death it was offered to Sir Thomas Phillipps, but he was unable to afford it at the time, and it appeared on display at the Irish Industrial Exhibition in 1853, with a notice stating that it belonged to William Brownlow (Francis' son) and was for sale. Seeing this notice, the antiquary William Reeves urged the Archbishop of Armagh, Lord John George Beresford, to buy it. Beresford, believing the price to be £500, declined, and Todd, who was staying with Beresford at the time, decided that it was beyond the College's means.[77] Reeves wrote to Brownlow to ask the price and, to avoid the risk of its being lost to the country, offered him the requested amount of £300.[78] His offer was accepted.

Todd, a close friend of Reeves, was concerned that he, a mere curate, could ill afford this amount and suggested that the archbishop might be prepared to part with £300 for it. He was right and the sale took place successfully, with Reeves being reimbursed the price he had paid Brownlow and the Primate acquiring the manuscript. There were two conditions attached to the transaction: first, that Reeves could retain the manuscript until he had prepared it for publication and, second, that it was then deposited in Trinity College Library, which both Reeves and Beresford regarded as a safer and more accessible library than that in Armagh. The University *Calendar* recorded the date of the donation to the Library as 7 July 1854, the date of the sale to Beresford, noting that the manuscript was to remain in Reeves' hands until he had published it. In fact, Reeves placed it in the Library before he started work, possibly as early as 1854. It was certainly in there in 1883, when a new iron safe was provided to house it along with the Book

---

[75] Bernard Meehan, '"A melody of curves across the page": art and calligraphy in the Book of Armagh', *Irish Arts Review Yearbook*, 14 (1998), 90–101; Bernard Meehan, 'Book satchels in medieval Ireland and Scotland', in Anne Crone and Ewan Campbell, eds., *A crannog of the first millennium AD* (Edinburgh: Society of Antiquaries of Scotland, 2005), pp. 85–92; MS 2589 (lecture by Roger Powell, March 1961), p. 3.

[76] Sir William Betham, *Irish antiquarian researches: part II* (Dublin: Curry, 1827).

[77] Lady Ferguson, *Life of the Right Rev. William Reeves* (Dublin: Hodges, Figgis, 1893), pp. 32–5.

[78] MSS 2770–2774/559a.

of Kells and the Book of Durrow, and it was rebound the following year by
C. J. Bigger, a Library porter who had trained as a bookbinder and whose
duties included the binding and repair of books.[79] In 1889, the manuscript
was handed over to Reeves, who was now ready to prepare an edition of
it.[80] In a paper read in April 1891 to the Royal Irish Academy, of which he
was then President, Reeves set out in detail the history of the manuscript
and its purchase, noting that it was now in his possession 'with a view to
publication'.[81] He died the following January and his work was continued by
the Regius Professor of Divinity, John Gwynn, whose edition was published
in 1913.[82]

An even more extraordinary history surrounds the acquisition of around
seventy volumes of Roman Inquisition documents covering a period from
the late Middle Ages to the eighteenth century and forming one of the
largest collections of such documents anywhere.[83] In the first decade of the
nineteenth century, Napoleon set out to create in Paris a central archive
of documents from the countries that he had conquered, and to that end
over three thousand crates of records were taken from Rome and the Holy
See. After Bonaparte's fall, there was a chaotic attempt to return some of
the documents to Rome, whilst others, deemed to be of insufficient importance to justify the transport cost, were destroyed or sold. Some of them
fell into private hands, and a collection of about fifty volumes eventually came to the attention of George Montagu, Viscount Mandeville. In
1841, Robert McGhee (who had recently donated records of the 'Roman
Catholic controversy' to the Library) was commissioned by Mandeville to
travel to Paris to buy the Inquisition documents. McGhee shipped them
to Kingstown and then to Mandeville's residence at Kimbolton Castle,
near Huntingdon. Whilst in Kingstown they were seen by Richard Gibbings, who had worked in the College Library as a clerk and was now
rector of Killcleagh, County Meath. Gibbings later asked Mandeville if he
would either sell them or make them available for publication, and it was
agreed that Gibbings could offer them to Trinity for £300. The offer was
declined by the College and so Gibbings bought them for himself. He discovered another twenty volumes still with the shippers, and in July 1854 again
tried to interest the College. In a later letter, Gibbings described how the

[79] MUN/LIB/2/4, 12 December 1883 and fol. 4; MUN/V/5/14, 4 December 1884.
[80] MUN/V/5/15, 19 October 1889.
[81] William Reeves, 'On the Book of Armagh', *Proc. RIA*, series 3, 2 (1893), 77–99 (p. 97).
[82] John Gwynn, ed., *Liber Ardmachanus: the Book of Armagh* (Dublin: Hodges, Figgis, 1913).
[83] John Tedeschi, 'A "queer story": the inquisitorial manuscripts', in *Treasures*, pp. 67–74; MS
3216 is an account by J. G. Smyly of their acquisition.

manuscripts were brought to Dublin on the roof of a coach 'and this was a marvellous adventure, but I would not lose sight of my treasures'.[84] Wall, the former Librarian, agreed to buy the whole collection and donate it to the Library. It consisted of three groups of documents, now bound in sixty-seven volumes. The first thirteen volumes (MS 1223) are Papal letters and bulls from the Roman Dataria dating from 1389 to 1787; the second group (MSS 1224–42) consists of nineteen volumes of Italian trial records and sentences from the sixteenth and seventeenth centuries; and the third group of thirty-five volumes (MSS 1243–77) contains details of proceedings for witchcraft, heresy, blasphemy, etc. from Italian provincial courts in the sixteenth, seventeenth and eighteenth centuries. They are an important source of information on early jurisprudence, censorship, the spread of the Reformation in Italy and other aspects of early modern history.

The Reformation in neighbouring Switzerland and the history of Geneva is the subject matter of another collection of manuscripts received about the same time. In 1857, Charles, comte de Meuron, of Malahide, County Dublin, presented fifteen volumes of letters, minutes of meetings, chronicles, memoirs and trial reports written in French, Latin, Italian and English and dating from the sixteenth and seventeenth centuries. They are now MSS 1145–59.

Throughout the rest of his tenure, Todd's spending remained within the budget that had been set in 1855. Between 1861 and 1868, expenditure on books varied between about £350 and £450 and the binding bills amounted to about £100 or less.[85] Mullen had died in 1848 and Frederick Pilkington had been appointed as the College binder.[86] Todd frequently had to complain about the time that Pilkington took to bind books and the unsatisfactory quality of some of the work. In 1852, he demanded that all books be returned, whether finished or not, and instituted 'an entirely new arrangement respecting our binding'.[87] Three years later he had to complain again that the binding of some books was taking up to 6 months.[88] Despite the dissatisfaction, Pilkington continued to bind books for the Library until at least 1880, though complaints surfaced again from time to time. In 1878, he was threatened with dismissal if the number of binding errors was not reduced. The College did not act on its threat, but repeated it more than once in the following 2 years because of damage caused to plates, and 'gross neglect' in the case of Bunting's *Ancient music of Ireland*.[89]

---

[84] MS 3791.   [85] MUN/LIB/2/4, fol. 109.   [86] MUN/V/5/9, 21 October 1848.
[87] MUN/LIB/2/4, 23 October 1852.   [88] *Ibid.*, 15 June 1855.
[89] MUN/LIB/3/1, 27 February 1878, 17 June 1879, 9 June 1880; MUN/V/5/14, 14 June 1879; MUN/LIB/13/70–MUN/LIB/13/71.

* * *

Todd died on 28 June 1869. His legacy, not just to the Library, but to Irish scholarship in general, and especially Irish studies, was outstanding. He collected Irish manuscripts, sometimes buying them with his own money for the Library (and sometimes having his purchases rejected by the Board), procured transcriptions of manuscripts in continental libraries for the Royal Irish Academy, edited manuscripts himself and encouraged others to do the same, and wrote the first modern life of St Patrick. His meticulous attention to detail, so valuable in his scholarly work, proved a hindrance to the progress of the Printed Catalogue but, despite the fact that only one volume had been published after 30 years' work, it was he who recognised the need to transform the Library's cataloguing procedures from those of the eighteenth century and to embrace modern techniques. He developed the collections in both scale and breadth, through his enforcement of the provisions of the Copyright Act and through assiduous purchasing, particularly of continental publications. When he was appointed as an Assistant Librarian the Library contained around eighty thousand volumes; at his death it was twice that size. He also brought order to many other aspects of the Library's work, maintaining records of acquisitions, clarifying the duties of the clerks and Assistant Librarians, and making a conscious effort to appoint staff with some level of competence. His obituary noted that the Library was 'not all that it might' be but did not lay the blame for this at Todd's feet: he made it 'as useful both to the University and the public as the radical defects in its construction and the very limited funds placed at his disposal would permit'.[90]

---

[90] *Irish Times*, 29 June 1869. See also G. O. Simms, 'James Henthorn Todd', *Hermathena*, 109 (1969), 5–23.

13 | Malet and Ingram: 1869–1886

John Adam Malet

The Board did not immediately fill the vacancy left by Todd's death, but appointed the Assistant Librarian, Benjamin Dickson, to be the acting Librarian.[1] With the summer intervening, it took several months before the process of appointing a new Librarian began in earnest. When it did, Dickson put his name forward, as did Richard Gibbings, now Professor of Ecclesiastical History, and William Reeves, now rector of Tynan, County Armagh, and librarian of the Diocese of Armagh.[2] Interest in the filling of the post was not confined to the College community. The *Irish Times* published a lengthy editorial in which it compared the relative merits of Dickson and Reeves, whom it regarded as the principal candidates. It claimed that the Library was better supplied 'with ancient than with modern books', and in a clear reference to Dickson said that what was needed was a Librarian 'conversant with the latter department'.[3] In the end the Board selected none of those candidates and again chose to appoint one of its own members, John Adam Malet, a Senior Fellow, elected Librarian on 27 November 1869.[4]

Malet's career to date had been singularly undistinguished, his only publication having been the catalogue of the Library's Roman coins compiled 30 years earlier, though he is credited with having discovered and identified the oldest record of the College, known as the Particular Book, in what was described as a 'waste-paper-basket store' in the Library.[5] As Librarian, his relationship with the Board and with other Fellows was an uneasy one, and his tenure of office was characterised by apparently impetuous decisions, several of which subsequently had to be reversed. His dealings with Dickson were problematical from the start. Having been passed over for the Librarianship, Dickson had been invited to continue as the Assistant Librarian, initially for 5 years, at a salary of £100, and had agreed. The

---

[1] MUN/V/5/12, 3 July 1869.   [2] *Ibid.*, 15 and 20 October 1869.
[3] *Irish Times*, 18 November 1869.
[4] MUN/V/5/12, 27 November 1869. Since the new regulations of 1855, the office of Librarian was no longer restricted to Fellows, but it was not until 1965 that the first non-Fellow was appointed.
[5] *Freeman's Journal*, 8 April 1878.

Library minute book records his appointment as the Assistant Librarian, but includes a note by Thomas French that Malet had 'obliged' him to write this, even though Dickson had actually been appointed by the Board to be the 'Second Librarian'.[6] The University *Calendar* for 1870 follows French in listing Dickson as the Second Librarian and Hunt as the Assistant Librarian.

Within a month of Malet's appointment, Dickson complained about 'the removal of certain books by the Librarian'. He was summoned before the Board to hear Malet's explanation, and on that occasion the Board supported its new Librarian and noted Dickson's acceptance that his letter had been written 'under a misapprehension'.[7] Malet's explanation for the alleged removal of books is not recorded, and so it is unclear whether Dickson's complaint was justified or whether it was an act of vindictiveness by a disappointed candidate. Malet's accident-prone career continued, however. The following year he dismissed the Copyright Agent, a foolish decision that had to be reversed after a few years of unsatisfactory service from the man he appointed as a replacement, and in 1873 he resigned from the Library Committee – a decision that the Board immediately ordered him to rescind.[8]

In 1874 came a more serious challenge, this time to the fact of his appointment, on the grounds that he had been an undischarged bankrupt when elected. The case was brought by J. W. Barlow, Professor of Modern History, a difficult man who managed to quarrel with the Provost, the Archbishop of Dublin and many of his Trinity colleagues.[9] Barlow argued that the words '*vir frugi*', used in the statutes to refer to the qualities required of the Librarian, described a man of 'thrift and prudence', and a bankrupt could not be considered as such. The Visitors were consulted and ruled that the fact of the bankruptcy might be a matter to take into account in the election of the Librarian but it did not absolutely disqualify someone who, in the opinion of the electors, had the other qualities that were required.[10]

Malet survived that attack, but he was less fortunate later the same year when the Board was informed that he had taken the Book of Kells to the British Museum for rebinding, without seeking approval in advance. He was ordered to bring it back without delay. He prevaricated and asked for further instructions by telegram. A furious Board demanded the immediate

---

6 MUN/V/5/12, 27 November 1869; MUN/LIB/2/4, same date.
7 MUN/V/5/12, 22 December 1869.   8 MUN/V/5/13, 5 April 1873.
9 McDowell and Webb, p. 300.
10 *Opinion delivered on the 23rd February 1874, by the Vice-Chancellor, on the 'dubium' submitted, as to the interpretation of the statutes that relate to the office of Librarian* (Dublin: Gill, 1874); MUN/V/5/13, 31 January, 4, 7 and 14 February, 7 March 1874.

return of the manuscript.[11] Three days later, Malet reported that it was still with the British Museum, and so the Board, its patience exhausted, dispatched J. H. Nunn, the College's law agent, to London 'with authority to receive the book and restore it to the College Library'.[12] In removing the manuscript Malet may have chosen to ignore the statutes or thought he was acting within their provisions, which had been a matter for discussion only the previous year, when the Royal Irish Academy had asked to borrow the Book of Leinster, so that Robert Atkinson could work on it for the edition he was preparing.[13] The Academy's request had been referred to the Vice-Chancellor, who proposed a decree recognising that the statutes of 1734 made no provision for the loan of books or manuscripts, other than to state that the Librarian was prohibited from allowing their removal from the Library, except for binding or repair. As far as 'omitted cases' were concerned, he advised that requests for loans 'to public bodies or eminent scholars for purposes of reference or comparison' be considered by the Board and, if approved, that a precise loan period be stated and that a bond of not less than £50 be required.[14] The Academy was duly allowed to borrow the Book of Leinster for a year against a bond of £100.[15] It could be argued that this left the matter unclear as to whether the Librarian required the approval of the Board to remove a manuscript for rebinding but, during the fracas over Malet and the Book of Kells, the Board eliminated any question of doubt by resolving that 'no manuscript be removed from the Library, on any account, without the authority of the Board, given at a formal meeting'.[16]

The Library Committee, which had ceased to function during Todd's tenure of office, was revived. Its members included a future Provost, J. P. Mahaffy, and two future Librarians, J. K. Ingram and T. K. Abbott, and from April 1872 it resolved to meet monthly.[17] However, it became deeply involved in the increasingly acrimonious dispute between the editors of the Printed Catalogue and, probably as a result of members' distaste for this unpleasantness, many of the meetings had to be cancelled because they were inquorate. The quorum was reduced to four, and even then seven of the fifteen scheduled meetings in 1873–4 did not take place, with only Dickson, Ingram and Abbott – and not, it might be noted, the incumbent

---

[11] MUN/V/5/13, 24 October–7 November 1874 *passim.*   [12] *Ibid.*, 31 October 1874.

[13] Robert Atkinson, ed., *The Book of Leinster: sometime called the book of Glendalough* (Dublin: Royal Irish Academy, 1880).

[14] MUN/V/5/13, 4 October 1873.   [15] *Ibid.*, 19 June and 10 July 1873; MUN/LIB/12/27(2).

[16] MUN/V/5/13, 28 October 1874.

[17] *Ibid.*, 24 February and 2 March 1872; MUN/LIB/3/1, 9 April 1872.

Librarian – attending more than half of these.[18] By the end of 1876, Dickson was described as being unable to attend to his duties in the Library, perhaps because of the onset of the health problems that were to lead to a mental breakdown.[19] Hunt took over much of his work, but died the following February and was replaced as the senior Assistant Librarian by Thomas French.[20] At Malet's suggestion, French received an additional £20, to be deducted from the salary of Dickson who, Malet observed acidly, continued to receive £100 a year 'for doing nothing'.[21] With Dickson's second period of office due to expire in November 1879, the Board obtained legal opinion that they were not obliged to fill the vacancy. The post created for Dickson, confusingly entitled either Assistant Librarian or Second Librarian, was suppressed, with Thomas French remaining as the Assistant Librarian and running the Library on a day-to-day basis until his death in 1889.[22]

Readers

Humphrey Lloyd, elected Provost in 1867, took the opportunity, after Todd's 35 years at the helm, to review the Library and consider how its 'utility' could be increased. He was keen to improve the facilities for readers and, though his amendment to the opening hours represented the reduction of an hour a day for most of the year, the six-week-long summer closure (plus another week for cleaning) was shortened in 1876 to two weeks.[23] This closure had long been the subject of complaints, especially from readers outside the College, for whom the long vacation had less relevance. The *Irish Times* described it as a 'serious loss to literary men', and a committee set up to review the Library regulations agreed that it was excessive compared to that of other libraries.[24]

The Reading Room in the East Pavilion was open until 6 p.m. but books could not be fetched to it after the Long Room closed, and by all accounts it was not a pleasant place to work, being overcrowded and poorly ventilated.

18   MUN/LIB/3/1, 11 March 1874, 13 January 1875.
19   MUN/V/5/13, 9 December 1876; McDowell and Webb, p. 262.
20   MUN/LIB/2/4, 16 February, 24 March 1877.
21   MUN/LIB/13/67; MUN/V/5/14, 4 July 1878.
22   MUN/LIB/12/31; MUN/V/5/14, 6 December 1879; MUN/LIB/2/5, 12 August 1889.
23   MUN/V/5/12, 26 February 1870; MUN/V/5/13, 21 November, 19 December 1871, 2 March 1876. From December 1871 the Library was open from 10 a.m. to 3 p.m. between 1 November and 31 January, and until 4 p.m. for the rest of the year.
24   *Irish Times*, 10 September 1873 and 4 August 1874; MUN/LIB/2/4, 7 February 1876.

In 1872, the Provost announced that he wanted to seek plans from the two firms of Deane and McCurdy, former rivals over the Library roof, for a new reading room near the east end of the building and connected to it by a bridge.[25] John McCurdy, now in partnership with William Mitchell, proposed three schemes, all of which involved demolishing the Rubrics. His preferred option (the most expensive, at almost £50,000) was to erect 'an important building' containing physical laboratories, a lecture room and a reading room, which was to be linked by a bridge to the first floor of the East Pavilion.[26] Thomas Newenham Deane produced a design that he said would not cause the Reading Room to 'sink into insignificance' and would 'neither clash with the severity of the Library, or be so ornate as the Museum [Building]'.[27] In the end, the members of the Board abandoned the idea altogether, almost certainly on cost grounds, and possibly also because they baulked at the idea of demolishing the Rubrics. They turned to the possibilities presented by the west end of the Library, and the same two firms were asked to produce designs for a single-storey reading room between the Library and the Public Theatre. The plans were exhibited at the Royal Institute of the Architects of Ireland in January 1874. According to the *Irish Builder*, Deane's proposals (now lost) were 'as usual, original and picturesque', but not easily reconciled with 'the staid *genius loci* of T.C.D.', whilst McCurdy's were classical, 'with that "neo-Grec" feeling which finds favour at Munich'.[28] (See Plate 8.) Nothing came of any of these schemes and they became the first in a growing heap of abandoned plans to build a reading room separate from Thomas Burgh's library, a vision that was not finally realised until 1937.

Conditions in the Reading Room, however, remained unsavoury. The *Freeman's Journal* complained that its poor ventilation and the 'olfactory manifestation' of the few oil lamps created a 'chronic atmosphere [that] defies all health-conditions'.[29] Malet admitted as much in a letter to the newspaper and blamed it at least in part on the increase in usage.[30] At the Board's visitation of the Library in 1878, the need for a new reading room was again discussed and Deane produced a further plan. Recognising that the Library required not just more reading space but also accommodation for books, he offered a scheme that would 'supply the deficiency at little cost'. He proposed to create a reading room in the Museum Building and link it to the East Pavilion of the Library at first-floor level, thus facilitating the

---

[25] MUN/V/5/13, 2 November 1872.   [26] MUN/P/2/385/1.   [27] MUN/P/2/385/2.
[28] *Irish Builder*, 16 (1874), 32.   [29] *Freeman's Journal*, 5 September 1876.
[30] *Ibid.*, 3 April 1877.

transfer of books from one building to the other along a passage supported on 'a row of graceful arches'. (See Plate 9.) To turn the Library into what he claimed was always intended, 'an emporium for books', he proposed to install transverse cases 3 metres high and 3½ metres wide across the centre of the Long Room. Lest anyone should question the aesthetic impact of such an intrusion, he added reassuringly, 'their effect will not injure the room'.[31] Mercifully this proposal went no further, but it was to be another decade before plans to deal with the inadequacies of the Reading Room were again seriously discussed.

Following the review of the Library after Malet's appointment, the Lending Library was transferred from the temporary building previously occupied by the Engineering School to the Museum Building, though it continued to have very restricted opening hours: 9–10 a.m. on Tuesdays and Thursdays.[32] It was briefly put into the charge of the Junior Fellow holding the office of Censor, though that arrangement lasted only until 1876, when responsibility was transferred back to the second Assistant Librarian.[33] A budget of £50 a year was allocated for buying books, and duplicates continued to be transferred from the main Library. Provost Lloyd was a great supporter and donated many books, especially in mathematics, bequeathing more at his death in 1881.[34] In 1882, Ingram, by then Librarian, proposed that the Lending Library should be developed and that restrictions should be placed on junior undergraduates using the main Library. The Board received the latter proposal without enthusiasm, but supported an attempt to publicise the lending collection. A printed notice was placed at the College gate, the opening times were extended to 3 days a week, and copies of the catalogue were given to the two main student societies, the Philosophical Society and the Historical Society.[35] Members of the Library Committee were encouraged to supply lists of books to be bought and a new borrowing register was started.[36] From an undergraduate body of a little over a thousand, about 180 loans were recorded in 1882, a figure that had almost doubled by the end of the decade.[37]

In the provision of library facilities, medical students were particularly favoured, as they were not only allowed to borrow from the library of the Royal College of Physicians of Ireland, which had moved to Kildare Street in 1864, but also had their own reference library in the Anatomy

---

[31] MUN/P/2/399c.   [32] *DU Calendar*, 1873, p. 341.
[33] MUN/V/5/12, 5 March 1870; MUN/V/5/13, 19 December 1871, 2 March 1876.
[34] MUN/V/5/12, 15 January 1870; MUN/V/5/14, 5 February 1881.
[35] MUN/V/5/14, 25 February 1882, 16 February 1884.
[36] MUN/LIB/3/1, 8 February 1884.   [37] MUN/LIB/8/21.

House – a precursor of the departmental libraries that were to proliferate in the College after the turn of the century.[38]

The Printed Catalogue

Soon after its establishment, the newly formed Library Committee revisited the outstanding issue of the unfinished (indeed, hardly started) Printed Catalogue. In April 1872, Dickson was asked to produce a report on the cataloguing methods in use at the British Museum and the Bodleian, and to make recommendations for catalogues of both manuscripts and printed books at Trinity. His report on a catalogue of manuscripts was considered, but no further action was taken. As far as the printed books were concerned, he estimated that there were about 250,000 slips that would form the volumes yet to be printed (letters C to Z) and that the editorial work would take no more than forty weeks. The printing and revision of the estimated 1,250 sheets, on the other hand, would take the University Press more than 10 years, at a cost that Michael Gill, its manager, estimated would be £6,250.[39]

The Library Committee was divided on whether a full-time editor would be needed to complete the work in a reasonable time, and Dickson also raised the question of whether the slips should be printed or left in manuscript form. The committee's deliberations reflected the debates that were under way elsewhere. In 1837, when the Board had originally approved the undertaking, the British Museum's catalogue had recently been published and that of the Bodleian was in progress, and so a printed catalogue of the type envisaged by Todd seemed an obvious approach to adopt. Thirty-five years later, the position was far less clear-cut. The main advantage of a printed catalogue was that it could be made available in multiple copies within the library and could be circulated to other institutions, so that a potential reader could check the holdings of a library without having to visit it first. The obvious drawback was that such a catalogue was out of date as soon as it was published and required regular supplements to record later acquisitions. The Bodleian catalogue, for example, appeared in three volumes in 1843, but covered acquisitions only up to 1834, and a further volume, covering 1835–47, appeared in 1851. The Curators realised that if they continued in this way they were committing themselves to the continual printing of supplements, which would soon become larger than the original

[38] *DU Calendar*, 1873, p. 341; MUN/V/5/14, 6 December 1879.
[39] MUN/LIB/3/1, 9 April–19 June 1872.

volumes, rendering the catalogue impossible to use.[40] In North America, card catalogues were well established by the 1870s, but in the United Kingdom librarians favoured catalogues in volume form. These were usually so-called 'guard-book' catalogues, consisting of blank sheets onto which slips of paper for each catalogue entry were pasted, in such a way that they could be moved easily to accommodate new entries, and, as the sheets were held in place by pegs, new pages could be inserted without difficulty. By the 1870s this form of catalogue had been adopted by Oxford, Cambridge and the British Museum and, at the Conference of Librarians held in London in 1877, John Winter Jones, Panizzi's successor as Principal Librarian of the British Museum, rejected the concept of a printed catalogue for a library that is adding books, on the grounds that it was impossible to keep it up to date: 'the best answer to the call for a printed catalogue is the fact that so few printed catalogues exist, and that some which have been commenced have been discontinued'.[41] Trinity, however, chose to complete Todd's project as it had originally been envisaged. The man who was to be appointed editor later acknowledged that, even though 'the scientific art of cataloguing' had moved on, to abandon publication now meant that the work on Volume One would have been wasted and that the slip catalogue for letters A and B would have had to be reconstructed.[42] It was, however, decided that the catalogue would contain entries only for books published up to the end of 1872.

The Library Committee decided that a full-time editor was needed to continue Todd's work. The post was advertised widely in the Dublin and London newspapers, and the qualifications specified were of a high order: 'an adequate knowledge of Greek, Latin, French, and German, and . . . some experience in the arrangement and cataloguing of libraries'. The salary offered was £300 a year and, with an optimism that proved to be unfounded, the College stated that the work was expected to be completed within 3 or 4 years.[43]

Forty-two applications were received and from them the committee selected as the most suitable candidates Henry Dix Hutton, a Dublin barrister, and Jan Hendrik Hessels, a Dutch scholar who had worked briefly as

[40] Craster, p. 51.

[41] John Winter Jones, 'Inaugural address', in Edward B. Nicholson and Henry R. Tedder, eds., *Transactions and proceedings of the Conference of Librarians held in London, October 1877* (London: Chiswick Press, 1878), pp. 1–21 (p. 18).

[42] Henry Dix Hutton, 'Preface', in *Catalogus librorum impressorum qui in Bibliotheca Collegii Sacrosanctae et individuae Trinitatis Reginae Elizabethae juxta Dublin adservantur* [The Printed Catalogue], 9 vols. (Dublin University Press, 1864–87), vol. IX, p. iii.

[43] Advertisement in, for example, *Freeman's Journal*, 26 July 1872.

a cataloguer at Cambridge University Library and had been described by its Librarian as 'a man of rare energy'.[44] Hutton's qualifications were, according to the committee, 'of the nature of general linguistic and literary knowledge, with proved habits of industry', whilst Hessels' were 'of a special kind, comprising, in addition to an extensive knowledge of languages, previous actual work in the preparation of catalogues'.[45] The Library Committee was unable to choose between the two and left the decision to the Board. It selected Hutton, but also appointed Hessels as his assistant, at a salary of £200 a year. In making what appeared to be an eminently sensible decision to benefit from the diverse skills of the two men, the Board had unwittingly sown the seeds of a dispute that was to last 6 years and become ever more acrimonious.

Hessels' role was to abbreviate the catalogue slips and submit them to Hutton, who was then to check them and prepare them for printing. From the beginning, Hessels showed himself to be a perfectionist, unwilling to compromise and constantly undermining the authority of the senior editor, whom he regarded, probably with justification, as a less able, and certainly less painstaking, cataloguer. Hutton, on the other hand, was obliged to adopt a more pragmatic approach, as he was under pressure from the Board to work quickly, even if that meant less than total accuracy. The two men were simply incompatible and unable to collaborate, a matter that became apparent even within the first month of their appointment, when the Board asked them to produce a joint plan for the catalogue. Hutton refused to work with Hessels on the plan and said that he would prepare it alone, as 'to undertake it conjointly with my assistant would be likely to cause serious difficulties and delays'.[46] Hessels declined to draw up a separate plan and, even though he had been working on the slips for less than a week, he said that he was already convinced that 'I shall never agree with him [Hutton] as to the mode of cataloguing books. Or rather, I shall have to correct and to amend so much, that the catalogue would be more my work than his.'[47]

Hutton produced a detailed proposal for the catalogue, in which he enunciated two principles: 'my work should be executed in the shortest time possible, consistently with its being done in a careful and creditable manner [and] the existing slip-catalogue is to form the basis of my work. I must therefore as a general rule assume that the slips truly represent the titles.'[48]

[44] [J. E. B. Mayor] *Statement made to the Syndics by the Librarian* (Cambridge: Palmer, 1866), p. 9; McKitterick, pp. 630–1.
[45] MUN/LIB/3/1, 25 October 1872.   [46] MUN/LIB/15/180.   [47] MUN/LIB/15/179.
[48] MUN/LIB/15/182.

Books would be examined only in exceptional cases. He commented that Todd's catalogue had taken so long because 'probably too much time was given to incidental points of literary research; for example the authorship of anonymous books; the identity of authors'.[49]

By early 1873, the Library Committee had defined the work to be carried out and signed an agreement for the printing of 250 copies of the catalogue by the University Press.[50] The initial target was 5 sheets, or about 900 slips, a week.[51] As time passed, the disagreements between the two editors grew. In February 1873, Hutton complained to the Library Committee about the poor quality and slowness of Hessels' work and the fact that Hessels would take instruction only from the Library Committee, 'as interpreted by himself'.[52] The following month Hessels was asked to increase his productivity and had to be reminded that he was required to 'take general directions' from Hutton.[53] For the Board visitation in December 1873, Hutton produced a report showing that just over two sheets a week were being completed, and he was asked to increase this to at least three by, if necessary, abridging titles to a greater extent.[54] By the time of the visitation the following year, Hutton could report that the letter C had been completed, but the average rate of production was still only two and a quarter sheets a week. He estimated that the work would take 10 years from the start of printing in May 1873, but at least he was also able to report that Hessels was now following instructions.[55] Despite this more positive picture, the Board was not satisfied, and its members were becoming increasingly alarmed at the cost that they were incurring. Hutton was instructed to abridge the slips even more, and was told that the whole question of the completion of the catalogue would have to be reconsidered when the current period of employment of the two editors expired in November 1875.[56] In June, the Bursar reported that the editing and printing of letters C and D had cost £1,943, which meant that the total cost of the catalogue was likely to be four times what had been expected.[57] When November came, Hutton reported that work was proceeding according to his estimate, and the Library

---

49 *Ibid.*

50 Vincent Kinane and Ann O'Brien, ' "The vast difficulty of cataloguing": the Printed Catalogue of Trinity College Dublin (1864–1887)', *Libraries and Culture*, 23 (1988), 427–49; Vincent Kinane, *History of the Dublin University Press, 1734–1976* (Dublin: Gill & Macmillan, 1994), pp. 188–92.

51 MUN/LIB/3/1, 12 and 19 December 1872; MUN/V/5/13, 5 April 1873.

52 MUN/LIB/15/202. See also MUN/LIB/3/1, 12 February–26 March 1873.

53 MUN/LIB/15/207.   54 MUN/LIB/3/1, 3 December 1873, 14 January 1874.

55 MUN/LIB/15/229; MUN/LIB/3/1, 25 November 1874.

56 MUN/V/5/13, 11 November 1874.   57 *Ibid.*, 19 June, 7 July 1875.

Committee recommended that he and Hessels be retained for a further year. The Board 'reluctantly' agreed, on condition that an average of three sheets per week was maintained and, if possible, increased.[58]

By the end of 1876, relations between Hutton and Hessels had deteriorated again. Hessels had reached the letter I, which he claimed marked the end of Fisher's revision of the slips, and that, as a result, he would no longer be able to produce three sheets a week. He asserted that many of the slips were 'merely in a preparatory state' and sometimes did not even include a title. He wrote to the Library Committee criticising the project as a whole, alleging that the sheets that had already been printed contained 'wholesale errors and omissions'. The catalogue was being distributed across the world, and so these errors were being spread far and wide: 'why should the College continue to inflict this calamity on the literary world? The catalogue as it is now being printed can only be a nuisance and it must inevitably cover the College with ridicule.'[59] Hutton was asked for his comments and, needless to say, disagreed with Hessels about the state of the slip catalogue. He also complained that Hessels had supplied only 803 slips in the previous 2 months instead of the required 3,700. Hessels responded that 'proper arrangement and bibliographical accuracy' seemed to have been of no concern to the College and followed this with an attack on 'the incompetency of the so-called editor', as a result of which 'the catalogue has become at once a farce, and a literary tragedy'.[60] He proposed that the printing should stop until the slips had been properly revised. The criticism of Hutton continued. Hessels produced a detailed list of errors, which he categorised as 'Blunders, Absurdities, Inaccuracies . . . I am bound to say that the blunders are exclusively those of MR. HUTTON'.[61] A sub-committee was set up to investigate the complaints. It found that both editors were responsible for errors, but did not discover enough of them to justify any changes to the procedures. Hessels was provided with an assistant to fetch the books he needed, so that his rate of production would not fall below five sheets a fortnight. He was also reprimanded for his 'unmeasured language' towards Hutton, and to avoid further recrimination a permanent sub-committee was established to supervise the work.[62]

In his report for the year to October 1877, Hutton still maintained that his estimate of the final completion date was accurate, Volume Four (H to K) having now been completed, but Hessels again said that, although a printed catalogue might be valuable in itself, one compiled from the present slips 'would not only be of no value but would be productive of mischief'.[63] He argued that for internal library use the guard-book system used by the British Museum and Cambridge was satisfactory, but for a printed catalogue that was to be distributed to the public the books needed to be recatalogued from scratch. He also enlisted the support of Robert Atkinson, a member of the Library Committee, who wrote to the Board saying that he had not changed his former view that the catalogue was 'a complete mistake in its original conception, and it is not in its execution likely to be of the slightest use'.[64] If the next 10 years were to be as 'productive' as the past, by the time of its completion there would be at least 50,000 modern books in the Library of which 'the catalogue will give no hint'.[65] He proposed that the slips should simply be transcribed into a 'finding-catalogue' as they were. The Board ignored these objections and decided that the work should continue as before.[66]

By now, relations between the two editors had completely broken down. Hessels was reprimanded for refusing even to open letters from Hutton, he was absent on a number of occasions and declined to account for his absences and he complained that the Library Committee had surrounded him with a 'network of resolutions'.[67] In yet another letter he asserted that before coming to Trinity he had been warned at Cambridge by someone acquainted with the College that 'he did not envy any man who came to have the privilege of working under the auspices of the authorities of this institution'.[68] For the committee, that was the final straw and the Board dismissed him with effect from the end of that year's engagement.[69]

Hessels was replaced in October 1878 by Thomas Keenan, the junior Assistant Librarian, who proved more amenable to editorial policy, though he was no more productive than his predecessor. The output of sheets continued at between two and three a week and the Bursar continued to complain about the cost, noting in his review of the financial state of the College in November 1878 that expenditure on the Library had risen from £1,187 in 1869 to £2,600 in 1878 as a result of the cost of the catalogue.[70] Hutton was at least able to report with relief that 'the excellent understanding' between himself and his assistant had enabled him to devote more attention to his editorial duties.[71] Despite the Bursar's concerns, Hutton was reappointed each year until 1887, when the final

[63] MUN/LIB/15/242.   [64] MUN/LIB/3/1, 2 November 1877.   [65] *Ibid.*
[66] MUN/V/5/13, 3 November 1877.   [67] MUN/LIB/15/243.   [68] MUN/LIB/15/256.
[69] MUN/V/5/14, 12 October 1878.   [70] *Ibid.*, 26 October, 18 November 1878.
[71] MUN/LIB/3/1, 12 November 1879.

volume was published. This was a supplementary volume containing entries beginning with A and B for books published between the printing of Volume One and the closing date of 1872, as well as other addenda and corrigenda. Forty-eight copies of the whole catalogue were bound and sent to major libraries in the United Kingdom, North America and continental Europe, and copies were later made available for sale.[72]

Despite its undoubted flaws, the Printed Catalogue has been justifiably described as 'a significant monument to the nineteenth-century concern for bibliographic systematization', and Hutton was invited to speak about it at the seventh annual meeting of the Library Association of the United Kingdom held in Dublin in 1884.[73] Until the retrospective conversion of the Library's catalogues that began in the late twentieth century, it remained the principal means of access to printed books that had been received up to 1872.

Unlike the catalogue of printed books, that of the manuscripts made little progress. In December 1874, Dickson sought funding to compile a new catalogue, prompted by John Gilbert's criticism in his reports to the Royal Commission on Historical Manuscripts.[74] The Commission, established in 1869, had appointed Gilbert, the Librarian of the Royal Irish Academy, as the Inspector of Manuscripts in Ireland with responsibility for searching out and documenting collections throughout the country. In his review of the College collection (which he described as 'the chief repository of MSS in Ireland') he noted that the absence of a complete catalogue meant that he had felt obliged to deal with them 'in a compendious manner', and his reports were in effect a shelf-list of the majority of manuscripts that the Library possessed.[75] The collection at the time occupied fourteen presses, lettered from A to N, but Gilbert's lists, which included lengthy transcriptions from some of the manuscripts, extended only as far as press G.

In March 1876, it was agreed that Thomas Connellan, who had been employed as a Library clerk to insert shelfmarks into the catalogue of printed books, could assist Dickson with the catalogue of manuscripts.[76] He began to compile a card index to Monck Mason's catalogue of 1814,

[72] MUN/V/5/15, 12 February 1887; MUN/V/6/1, 26 February 1891.
[73] Kinane and O'Brien, note 50 above, p. 446; Henry Dix Hutton, *Impressions of twelve years' cataloguing in a great library: address delivered at the seventh annual meeting of the Library Association of the United Kingdom, 1884* (London: Chiswick Press, 1886).
[74] MUN/V/5/13, 19 December 1874.
[75] HMC, *Fourth report, Part I: report and appendix*, [C. 857], 1873, XXXV, part I, 1 (p. 588); HMC, *Eighth report: report and appendix (Part I)*, [C. 3040], 1881, LV, 1.
[76] MUN/LIB/3/1, 3 November 1875; MUN/V/5/13, 11 March 1876; MS 2417.

but the project was abandoned after 12 months when a sub-committee, appointed to examine the slips that had been produced, decided that their 'fragmentary nature and general inaccuracy' rendered them useless when a catalogue of manuscripts came to be prepared for printing.[77] Connellan's initial appointment to transcribe shelfmarks, and his subsequent transfer to the manuscripts catalogue, were both decisions made by Dickson. Within a month of the report on the manuscripts slips, Connellan complained that he had not yet been paid for his work on the shelfmarks, and Hutton also wrote to the Library Committee to say that Dickson's decision to transfer Connellan had begun to cause delay to the Printed Catalogue. The Bursar objected to paying Connellan at all, on the grounds that his appointment had never been sanctioned.[78] Though he was eventually reimbursed for his work on the printed books, Connellan had to write to the Provost in 1881 to complain that he had given up a salary of £80 a year to work on the manuscripts, that he had not been paid for this and that, whenever he raised with Malet the matter of the payment to which he was entitled, the Librarian failed to provide him with a satisfactory answer.[79]

Legal deposit

One of Malet's first acts on taking up office was to dismiss Gregory Eccles as the College's Copyright Agent, a move not followed by the other three deposit libraries. Malet's objections to Eccles are not recorded, but a sub-committee of the Board supported the Librarian when Eccles appealed.[80] The Dublin bookseller Samuel Figgis was appointed in July 1870 as his replacement, but this arrangement was clearly unsatisfactory and Malet travelled to London early in 1872 to look for a new Agent. The Board authorised him to pay up to 120 guineas a year, which was twice the amount that Eccles had been costing the College.[81] Malet appointed Thomas Gray, a former Dublin curate whom he had presumably known as a student in Trinity, but this arrangement proved equally unsatisfactory and in 1877 Mahaffy, on behalf of the Library Committee, wrote to the other libraries to ask whether their agent obtained 'nearly all the books to which the universities are entitled'.[82] Henry Coxe, at the Bodleian, replied that Eccles

[77] MUN/LIB/3/1, 28 March 1877. Connellan's incomplete card index is MUN/LIB/1/56.
[78] MUN/LIB/3/1, 18 April 1877; MUN/V/5/13, 21 April 1877.
[79] MUN/LIB/13/72–MUN/LIB/13/73.   [80] MUN/V/5/12, 5 and 12 March, 28 May 1870.
[81] MUN/LIB/2/4, 1 July 1870; MUN/V/5/13, 17 February, 6 April 1872.
[82] MUN/LIB/3/1, 7 March 1877.

was a very efficient agent, especially because of his links with the British Museum. He could think of nobody better qualified, and added: 'I had always thought that, in rejecting Mr Eccles as your Agent, your authorities acted (if I may so speak) very injudiciously.'[83] Mahaffy proposed that Eccles should be reappointed, and so the College had to overturn Malet's earlier decision and offer Eccles his old job back on the same terms as before. He accepted, and restarted on 22 June 1877 at a salary of £70 a year, with Trinity also sharing the other costs of the Agency with Oxford, Cambridge and Edinburgh. Gray was dismissed with effect from the same date.[84]

After 30 years of relative peace since the passing of the Act of 1842, the question of copyright and, inevitably, legal deposit came under scrutiny again, with the appointment in 1875 of a Royal Commission to review the working of the various Copyright Acts.[85] Several witnesses called by the Commission suggested that registration at Stationers' Hall should be abolished and that the processes of registration and deposit at the British Museum should be combined. The Museum objected to this proposal because of the extra administrative work that would be involved. Unsurprisingly, several witnesses from the publishing community took the opportunity to complain about the financial burden placed upon them by the requirement to deposit five copies, especially of expensive books printed in small numbers. The Commissioners wrote to each of the libraries to ask how many books they received and what they estimated was their monetary value.[86] Malet stated that Trinity received between three and four thousand books a year, valued at about £1,500. The Advocates provided similar figures, but the Bodleian estimated that it received over five thousand volumes and Cambridge failed to reply.[87] No further evidence was sought from the libraries and they had no representation among over fifty witnesses who were called. It was hardly surprising, therefore, that the Commissioners sided with the publishers, expressing the view that the libraries were 'possessed of considerable means and . . . well able to purchase any books which they may require'.[88] They recommended that the deposit privilege be abolished for all the libraries except the British Museum.

[83] MUN/LIB/22/20/94.
[84] MUN/V/5/13, 22 March–18 April, 30 June 1877; MUN/LIB/22/19/4.
[85] Copyright Commission, *The Royal Commissions and the report of the Commissioners*, [C. 2036], 1878, XXIV, 163; Partridge, pp. 92–102; Harris, p. 344; McKitterick, pp. 750–2; Craster, pp. 63–4.
[86] MUN/LIB/22/20/93.   [87] Copyright Commission, note 85 above, pp. 408–9.
[88] *Ibid.*, p. xxvii.

The report was published in the summer of 1878 and the libraries reacted angrily, complaining that they had not been called to give evidence. Coxe, opening the first annual meeting of the Library Association in Oxford that October, spoke against the proposal on the grounds that the preservation of one copy was insufficient protection against loss, and that deposited books should be available in other cities as well as London. He was supported by Malet, there as a Vice-President of the Association, and by the representatives of the Faculty of Advocates and the British Museum.[89] Cambridge sent a high-level delegation, including the High Steward, the Vice-Chancellor and the University's two MPs, to see Lord John Manners, the Chairman of the Commissioners and a Cambridge graduate. The Faculty of Advocates prepared a lengthy printed statement noting that its library and that of Trinity were the only institutions outside England 'in which every new book might be expected to be found' and that it was now 'proposed to deprive Scotland and Ireland of the privilege which the peoples of these kingdoms enjoy, of having a complete public library in their own country'.[90] In Ireland a public campaign began in which, as in Scotland, the national element was emphasised. Articles appeared in the *Freeman's Journal* and the *Irish Times* defending Trinity's position.[91] The Board drew up a 'remonstrance' and directed that Malet, Mahaffy and the University's two MPs should form a deputation to present this to Manners. In it they stressed that Trinity was not just a university library but that, 'being situated in the capital of Ireland, and accessible to a large reading public, it ministers to the wants of those who pursue serious studies in Ireland – a steadily growing class, as may be inferred from the fact that the number of readers in our Library is increasing largely every year'.[92] They concluded by pointing out that the privilege enjoyed by the libraries imposed no burden on the state. After the return of the Trinity delegation from London, the *Freeman's Journal* reported that Manners had initially concluded that the libraries were not interested in the deposit privilege, because he was under the mistaken impression that they had failed to respond to an invitation to give evidence when in fact no such invitation had been issued.[93] He was convinced by the libraries' case, and the

---

89   Henry R. Tedder and Ernest C. Thomas, eds., *Transactions and proceedings of the first annual meeting of the Library Association of the United Kingdom, held in Oxford, October 1878* (London: Chiswick Press, 1879), p. 122.

90   *Statement by the Faculty of Advocates in regard to the recommendation of the Royal Commissioners on copyright as to repealing the statutes requiring that a copy of every new book be deposited in public libraries in the United Kingdom*, 17 March 1879, CUA ULIB/7/2/27.

91   *Freeman's Journal*, 18 February, 1, 7 and 11 March 1879; *Irish Times*, 12 March 1879.

92   MUN/V/5/14, 8 March 1879.   93   *Freeman's Journal*, 17 March 1879.

Bill he introduced in July 1879 to amend the law on copyright left their rights intact.[94] After all this effort, however, the Bill failed because of pressure of other business, but the work was not entirely in vain, as some of the petitions were to be dusted off again the next time a threat arose, in 1911.

John Kells Ingram

In April 1879 Malet died, and Thomas French was appointed as the acting Librarian. Gibbings applied again for the post, but the Board selected the Regius Professor of Greek, John Kells Ingram, who had established a considerable scholarly reputation and was to become internationally renowned in a range of fields from literature and Irish archaeology to economics and mathematics.[95] (See Figure 15.)

The mid nineteenth century marked the birth of the modern library profession. The report of the Select Committee on Public Libraries in 1849 and the Public Libraries Acts of 1850 and 1855 had begun the development, albeit a slow one to begin with, of the public library system. Edward Edwards' *Memoirs of libraries* of 1859 was in part the first modern textbook of library administration and management, and in it he argued for the creation of a professional organisation of librarians.[96] The challenge was taken up by Edward Nicholson, Librarian of the London Institution, who wrote to *The Times* proposing a conference of librarians, with John Winter Jones, Librarian of the British Museum, as its President and the other legal-deposit librarians, including Malet, as Vice-Presidents.[97] The conference took place in 1877 at the London Institution, and during the meeting the Library Association of the United Kingdom was established. Malet was elected *in absentia* as one of its three Vice-Presidents (Henry Bradshaw, the Cambridge University Librarian, had declined the invitation) and he participated in the following conference, the first annual meeting of the new Association, which was held in Oxford. This involvement with the Library Association was continued by Ingram, and in September 1884 the organisation held its

---

[94] *Copyright (no. 2). A bill to consolidate and amend the law relating to copyright*, HC 1878–9 (265), II, 3.

[95] Sean D. Barrett, 'John Kells Ingram (1823–1907)', *Hermathena*, 164 (1998), 5–30.

[96] Edward Edwards, *Memoirs of libraries: including a handbook of library economy*, 2 vols. (London: Trübner, 1859), vol. II, pp. 937–8; W. A. Munford, *A history of the Library Association, 1877–1977* (London: Library Association, 1976), pp. 8–32.

[97] *The Times*, 16 February 1877.

Figure 15 John Kells Ingram, Librarian 1879–86 (MS 4900/3)

seventh annual meeting in Dublin, with Ingram as its President, the only Trinity Librarian ever to hold that office.[98] In preparation for the meeting, the Book of Armagh was rebound and several of the other manuscripts

[98] 'The Library Association at Dublin', *Library Chronicle*, 1 (1884), 161–2.

were repaired.[99] In his opening address to the conference, Ingram noted not just the imminent completion of the Printed Catalogue but also the deliberations about the form that its successor catalogue would take.[100]

Purchases and donations

Todd's extensive personal library of books and manuscripts was sold by John Fleming Jones in November 1869.[101] Dickson, as the acting Librarian, was authorised to spend up to £200, but he far exceeded his authority, committing over £250 to the purchase of manuscripts and a further £450 for a copy of Harris' 1745 edition of Ware's *Works*, which had been heavily annotated by Todd.[102] The Board refused to countenance expenditure at prices that even Todd's brother Charles, who had put the collection up for sale, regarded as 'absurdly too high'.[103] In the Library's copy of the sale catalogue, which Dickson annotated with a list of all the purchasers and the prices paid, those entries ascribed to Trinity have been crossed through and a note added: 'These books were not purchased, as stated here, by Trinity College Dublin.'[104] The College returned them all to Todd's brother, who then offered them to Henry Bradshaw at Cambridge. Bradshaw, a close friend of Todd, had been a major competitor at the sale, bidding both for the University Library and to add to his own extensive collection of Irish material, but he had failed to obtain many of the items that he wanted. He bought everything that Trinity had returned and subsequently donated his collection to Cambridge University Library.[105]

During the 1870s the amount spent on purchases and binding remained close to the figure of £560 a year approved by the Board in 1855.[106] Acquisitions were mainly routine, but included a few items of significance. In 1870, £100 was spent on manuscripts from the library of the recently deceased Edward Hincks; the following year a thirteenth-century manuscript of

---

[99]   MUN/LIB/2/4, May 1884; MUN/V/5/14, 4 December 1884.

[100] John K. Ingram, *The Library of Trinity College, Dublin, being an address delivered at the seventh annual meeting of the Library Association of the United Kingdom, September 30, 1884* (London: Chiswick Press, 1886).

[101] *Catalogue of the valuable library of the late Rev. James H. Todd . . . to be sold by auction by John Fleming Jones* (Dublin, 1869).

[102] MUN/V/5/12, 13 November 1869; TCD MSL–1–847 (annotated copy of sale catalogue).

[103] Charles Todd to Bradshaw, 11 August 1870, Cambridge University Library, MS Add. 8916/A70/46.

[104] TCD MSL–1–847.   [105] MUN/V/5/12, 23 April 1870; McKitterick, pp. 682–6.

[106] MUN/LIB/3/1, 13 February 1878.

French religious legends (MS 951) was bought; and in 1876 the Library paid £180 for Migne's *Patrologia latina*.[107] In 1879, Ingram purchased seven volumes of correspondence of the antiquary Joseph Cooper Walker, which included letters from Edward Ledwich, Charles O'Conor and Charles Vallancey (MS 1461).[108] The Librarian's freedom of action was, however, severely constrained, as Board approval was required before he could spend more than £5 on the purchase of books.[109]

Donations were also thin on the ground. In 1872, Whitley Stokes, a prominent member of the Indian colonial administration, gave two copies of a manuscript containing the quatrains of Omar Khayyám in Persian (MSS 1571–2), and in 1877 Samuel Haughton, the Professor of Geology, presented a Buddhist *mani* stone from Tibet.[110] Haughton had also built up a collection of illustrated reference books for his department, and this was transferred to the Library in 1879.[111] Following the death in the same year of Sir Thomas Larcom, formerly of the Ordnance Survey and then Under-Secretary of State for Ireland, the Library received fifty-seven volumes of papers, mainly dealing with religious affairs and sectarian disputes of the mid nineteenth century (MS 1710), as well as a further seventy-six volumes of pamphlets dealing with similar subjects.[112] A much larger collection of Larcom's administrative papers was bequeathed to the National Library of Ireland.

The largest donation of the period was the bequest in 1881 from Aiken Irvine, a retired clergyman from Celbridge, County Kildare. This collection was particularly strong in controversial theology, and Ingram selected about a thousand volumes of books and pamphlets dating from the sixteenth to the nineteenth centuries, including eight incunabula and a similar number of manuscripts.[113] One gift that was not accepted was an American edition of Walt Whitman's *Leaves of grass*, which on examination was deemed to be 'of an obscene and immoral character' and unfit to be placed in the Library. The Librarian was instructed to return it to the donor and not to claim the English reprint then being issued.[114]

The medieval ivory charter-horn of the Kavanagh family of Borris, County Carlow, was thought to have been in the College since it was deposited for safe-keeping when Borris House was attacked in 1798. It had been on display in the Long Room for some years when Arthur

---

[107] MUN/V/5/12, 26 March 1870; MUN/V/5/13, 28 October 1876.
[108] MUN/LIB/4/7, 3 December 1879.   [109] MUN/LIB/3/1, 12 November 1879.
[110] MUN/LIB/4/7, 6 February 1872; MUN/LIB/13/60, 2 May 1877.
[111] MUN/LIB/3/1, 3 December 1879.   [112] MUN/LIB/1/32, 1 November 1879.
[113] MUN/V/5/14, 9 December 1881.   [114] *Ibid.*, 11 February 1882.

Macmurrough Kavanagh requested its return in 1882. This caused the Board to investigate the various Irish antiquities in the College. It was agreed that the charter-horn should be returned to the Kavanagh family but that the other Irish antiquities that were in the Library should be retained there, whilst those in the College Museum were to be presented to the Royal Irish Academy and the ethnological items to the National Museum of Ireland.[115]

The building

By the end of the 1870s, space for books was becoming a problem again. The carpenter John Bain was commissioned to provide shelving for the former Manuscripts Room, following the same layout as that of the Fagel Room directly beneath it. This meant that the room would be able to accommodate about thirty thousand volumes, but the work required the strengthening of the foundations of the East Pavilion. All the Fagel books had to be removed and placed on the floor of the Long Room for the summer of 1880, and the books from the Reading Room on the ground floor were stored in a temporary wooden shed in the arcades under the Long Room. The books were returned at the end of August and even the *Freeman's Journal*, never slow to criticise the Library, admitted that Thomas French's organisation of the moves had enabled the building to remain open to readers and that its 'summer *habitues*... were scarcely conscious' of any disturbance.[116]

The display of manuscripts in the Long Room appears to have been removed during the 1850s. A guidebook of 1853 refers to the 'precious collection of manuscripts, chiefly Irish' kept in a separate room, and an article of 1858 describes in detail the appearance of the shelves in the Long Room, the busts and the central table for readers, referring to the Irish manuscripts as being in the East Pavilion, as does a German visitor's account of the same year.[117] It was not until 1881 that, at Ingram's instigation, a glass case was again placed in the Long Room to exhibit the Book of Kells and other manuscripts.[118] It was crammed, not just with the Books of Kells, Dimma, Mulling and Armagh but also a Qur'an, a volume of

---

[115] *Ibid.*, 4 and 18 February 1882; MUN/LIB/2/4, 23 February 1882.

[116] MUN/V/5/14, 20 March 1880; MUN/LIB/2/4, 17 June 1880; MUN/LIB/4/3, 17 June 1880; MUN/LIB/12/31a; *Freeman's Journal*, 22 July 1880.

[117] William F. Wakeman, *Dublin: what's to be seen, and how to see it*, 2nd edn (Dublin: Hodges & Smith, 1853), pp. 40–1; 'Patrick Delany, D.D.', *Dublin University Magazine*, 52 (1858), 578–86; Julius Rodenberg, *Die Insel der Heiligen: eine Pilgerfahrt durch Irland* (Berlin: Janke, 1860), p. 49.

[118] MUN/LIB/4/3, March, October 1881.

the Inquisition documents, Barrett's Codex Z and a range of printed books including a Caxton and the Sallust thought to have belonged to Mary Queen of Scots.[119]

For distinguished visitors, specially selected items continued to be put out on display. The year 1877 was a particularly busy one, with the Emperor of Brazil Dom Pedro II, the Archbishop of Canterbury Dr Archibald Tait, the Chinese ambassador and William Ewart Gladstone, the Prime Minister, all paying their respects.[120] Gladstone appears to have approved of the new bookcases in the gallery, citing the Long Room, where 'the bookcases ascend very high, and magnificent apartments walled with books may in this way be constructed', as being superior to Wren's Library at Trinity College, Cambridge.[121]

During this period the only bust to be added to the Long Room, in May 1885, was that of James Whiteside, a former Lord Chief Justice, by the Belfast-born sculptor Patrick MacDowell.[122]

---

[119] *Freeman's Journal*, 20 October 1881.
[120] MUN/LIB/2/4, 8 July, 23, 28 August, 22 October 1877.
[121] W. E. Gladstone, 'On books and the housing of them', *Nineteenth Century*, 27 (1890), 384–96 (p. 391).
[122] MUN/V/5/15, 11 December 1885.

On Christmas Eve 1886, Ingram resigned as Librarian and took up office as the Senior Lecturer.[1] He was later elected Vice-Provost of the College and President of the Royal Irish Academy, and he remained active in research and publication for more than a decade. He was succeeded as Librarian on 29 January 1887 by Thomas Kingsmill Abbott, a Junior Fellow. (See Figure 16.) Abbott resigned as Professor of Biblical Greek at the end of 1888, but he retained his other Chair, that of Hebrew, alongside the Librarianship, until 1900.[2] He quickly began to address the problems of storage that were again becoming acute, and during his tenure of office he immersed himself in the Library's collections, compiled catalogues and greatly expanded the collection of objects on display in the Long Room. The day-to-day running of the Library was left largely in the hands of the senior Assistant Librarians.

The first of those, Thomas French, died in 1889 and the Board again considered whether he should be replaced by a Junior Fellow, for whom the post could be seen as an apprenticeship for the post of College Librarian. Abbott wrote a lengthy memorandum against the proposal, arguing that the management of the Library between the time of Barrett and that of Todd, when the Assistant Librarian had been a Junior Fellow, provided no justification to follow that example. Indeed, he said, the Library was still suffering 'from the perfunctory manner in which some of the Librarians of that time performed their duties'. He conceded that, though Todd – the exception to his criticism – had been both a Junior Fellow and the Assistant Librarian, he was 'only nominally so; he was really Acting Librarian and owed nothing to training under his Chief'.[3] The Board was persuaded and Thomas Keenan, the junior Assistant Librarian, succeeded French. Samuel Brambell, a Library clerk, was promoted to be the junior Assistant Librarian and Alfred de Burgh, who had graduated from Trinity a decade earlier, was appointed as a second junior Assistant Librarian.[4]

[1] MUN/LIB/2/4, 24 December 1886.   [2] MUN/V/5/15, 29 January 1887.
[3] MUN/LIB/2/5, 17 October 1889.
[4] MUN/V/5/15, 26 October 1889; MUN/LIB/4/3, 20 November 1889.

Figure 16 Thomas Kingsmill Abbott, Librarian 1887–1913 (MS 4900/1)

The salaries and duties of the various officers were determined at the Board's annual visitation of the Library in December 1889. Keenan was to receive £300 a year to catalogue foreign books and periodicals and to assist Abbott with the catalogue of manuscripts; Brambell, earning £200, was responsible for 'finding places for books in the Library', as well as the opening and closing of the building and the issuing of admission tickets; de Burgh, on £150, was in charge of English periodicals and pamphlets; and Robert French, the Library clerk, on a salary of £100, wrote slips for the English books and took charge of the Reading Room from 4 p.m. to

Figure 17 Alfred de Burgh, Assistant Librarian 1896–1929 (MS 5861/10)

6 p.m.[5] Hutton, still compiling the catalogue of printed books, was regarded as a supernumerary member of staff. In 1896, Keenan resigned on grounds of ill health and was succeeded as the senior Assistant Librarian by de Burgh.[6] (See Figure 17.)

Catalogues

By the 1870s, as work proceeded on the Printed Catalogue, attention had turned to the cataloguing of books published and received in the Library since the end of 1872. Slips for these books were produced and, from 1878, brief entries were transcribed in rough alphabetical order into a handwritten

[5] MUN/LIB/12/38.   [6] MUN/V/5/16, 20 June 1896.

catalogue for the use of readers.[7] By 1884, the catalogue had grown to three volumes but, as more and more entries were squeezed onto the pages, it was becoming difficult to use and almost impossible to establish whether or not a book was in the Library. It was clear that these volumes could form only an interim solution and that a long-term decision on a catalogue of post-1872 books had to be made. Addressing the Library Association that year, Hutton rejected the notion of printing any supplementary volumes to the Printed Catalogue and proposed instead that the existing manuscript slips should be used as copy for printed slips, which would then be cut up and pasted into guard-books, following the Cambridge model. In his presidential address to the same meeting, Ingram expressed agreement with with this view.[8] The main question to be resolved was whether the final slips should be printed, as was the case at the British Museum and St Andrews, as well as Cambridge, or whether the Bodleian model of inserting handwritten slips should be followed. Ingram produced a detailed report for the Board strongly recommending the use of printed slips, a recommendation that was accepted.[9]

Following the publication of the final volume of the Printed Catalogue in 1887, Hutton was reappointed to edit the slips for the post-1872 catalogue and to organise the printing of them by the University Press.[10] In 1890, he reported that entries for about two-thirds of the books received since 1873 had been printed and that this retrospective work would be completed within 2 years. It would then be possible to calculate how many volumes would be needed to allow the slips to be spaced in such a way as to allow the insertion of new entries with the minimum need for later rearrangement.[11] Blank volumes for the catalogue were ordered in batches of fifty over the next decade and Hutton remained responsible for the work until his retirement in 1903.[12] This catalogue became known as the 'Accessions Catalogue', and it was actively maintained until 1963.

[7] MUN/V/5/13, 2 March 1876; MUN/LIB/2/4, 15 July 1876; MUN/LIB/4/3, 14 June 1879.

[8] Henry Dix Hutton, *Impressions of twelve years' cataloguing in a great library: address delivered at the seventh annual meeting of the Library Association of the United Kingdom, 1884* (London: Chiswick Press, 1886), p. 6; John K. Ingram, *The Library of Trinity College, Dublin, being an address delivered at the seventh annual meeting of the Library Association of the United Kingdom, September 30, 1884* (London: Chiswick Press, 1886), p. 15.

[9] MUN/V/5/15, 11 December 1885.

[10] *Ibid.*, 13 May 1887; Vincent Kinane, *History of the Dublin University Press, 1734–1976* (Dublin: Gill & Macmillan, 1994), p. 240.

[11] MUN/V/6/1, 13 October 1890.

[12] MUN/V/5/16, 28 November 1894, 27 November 1895; MUN/V/5/17, 13 January 1900, 30 May 1903.

Both the Printed and Accessions Catalogues were essentially author catalogues, offering readers almost no access by subject. Hutton planned to remedy this by using additional copies of the printed slips in a separate sequence of volumes organised under subject headings. Between 1895 and 1899, twenty-six volumes for subjects beginning with the letters A to C were produced, but in 1902 it was estimated that a card-based subject catalogue would cost only about one-tenth that of a guard-book and the scheme was terminated.[13] After Hutton's retirement, de Burgh and William Butler, the third Assistant Librarian, began to revise the subject slips, de Burgh noting ruefully in his annual report for 1903–4 that 'Mr Hutton's non-observance of his own rules made it necessary to revise every entry.'[14] This catalogue, which became known as the 'Secondaries Catalogue', was also maintained until 1963, but as it was never transferred to anything more secure than the slips (which were stored in hundreds of envelopes), access to it was restricted chiefly to the Library staff, who used it to carry out subject-searches for readers.

Plans for a catalogue of manuscripts, which had been abandoned in the 1870s, were revived at the end of 1883, and it was agreed that Robert Atkinson, Professor of Romance Languages and Sanskrit, would assist Ingram in compiling it.[15] After Ingram's resignation as Librarian, the work seems to have come to a halt until Abbott took it over again in 1890.[16] His catalogue was published in 1900.[17] As the first printed catalogue of the College's manuscripts since that in Bernard's *Catalogi* of 1697 and Gilbert's incomplete lists in his reports to the Historical Manuscripts Commission, it represented a major advance in the provision of access to the collection, and even today it remains the main source of information for many of the manuscripts that it includes (MSS 1–1691). Abbott abandoned the system that had been adopted by Lyon, of identifying manuscripts by shelfmark, and he reclassified the entire collection in a single numerical sequence. He tried to place manuscripts with a similar subject content together but, apart from broad language divisions like Irish, Icelandic and oriental, this subject arrangement was inevitably haphazard. All manuscripts added to the Library since 1900 have been numbered according to Abbott's scheme.

The catalogue included several indexes and, most importantly, it provided a concordance between Abbott's new numbering system and those used by Bernard and Lyon. Rather oddly, it also included a catalogue of the maps

---

[13] MUN/LIB/4/8, July 1902.   [14] MUN/LIB/17/131; MUN/LIB/4/8, 11 June 1903.
[15] MUN/V/5/14, 27 November, 1 December 1883, 12 January, 31 May 1884.
[16] MUN/V/6/1, September 1890.   [17] Abbott, *Manuscripts.*

and plans in the Fagel collection, even though most of those are printed. Abbott described it as a summary catalogue and acknowledged his debt to earlier cataloguers, noting also that some of the older volumes that contained several distinct manuscripts deserved fuller examination, 'but to have waited for this would have been to postpone the publication indefinitely'.[18] Though it was an enormous improvement on the situation hitherto, the catalogue has not received universal approbation. Writing in the 1920s, the medievalist Mario Esposito considered that it brought '*assez peu honneur*' both to the author and the College because of its summary nature.[19] Esposito's comments were perhaps not entirely objective, as in 1912, the year he graduated from Trinity, he had sought £100 from the College to publish his own catalogue of the Library's medieval manuscripts, but the Board had turned down the request and the catalogue never materialised.[20] Half a century later, the errors were again noted by the author of a new catalogue of medieval Latin manuscripts, Marvin Colker, who recorded textual inaccuracies, wrong dating and misclassification in Abbott's work.[21]

The most extensive criticism was reserved for Abbott's treatment of the Irish manuscripts, for which he had relied on the earlier descriptions by O'Reilly and O'Donovan. In his evidence to the Royal Commission of 1906–7, Eoin MacNeill, a representative of the Gaelic League, criticised the status of Irish in the College and subjected the Irish section of Abbott's catalogue to a blistering attack, saying that with its blunders and typographical errors it resembled more the work of an auctioneer than that of a university, and that the work appeared 'to have been entrusted to a half illiterate and wholly unscholarly scribe'.[22] The Commission's final report commented on the Library's alleged neglect of its Irish manuscripts, and this stung Abbott to write to *The Times* to complain that no effort had been made to check the 'erroneous impression' given by that statement.[23] Nonetheless, he started to compile a new catalogue of the Irish manuscripts, but died before it could be completed, and the work was taken over by E. J. Gwynn. The first 176 pages had already been printed, and so they were published as Abbott had

---

[18] *Ibid.*, p. vii.
[19] Mario Esposito, 'Inventaire des anciens manuscrits français des bibliothèques de Dublin', *Revue des bibliothèques*, 31 (1921), 374–80 (p. 374).
[20] MUN/V/5/20, 19 October 1912.
[21] M. L. Colker, 'The recataloguing of the mediaeval Latin manuscripts', *Long Room*, 1 (Spring 1970), 13–16.
[22] *Royal Commission on Trinity College Dublin and the University of Dublin, Appendix to the final report: minutes of evidence and documents*, [Cd. 3312], 1907, XLI, 87 (pp. 309–10).
[23] *Ibid., Final report of the Commissioners*, [Cd. 3311], 1907, XLI, 1 (p. 59); *The Times*, 1 February 1907.

left them, with the remainder being either prepared from Abbott's notes or revised from his catalogue of 1900. The catalogue was published in 1921 under the names of both Abbott and Gwynn.[24]

Several lists covering sections of the manuscripts collection, such as the papyri, the Icelandic and the Syriac manuscripts, have been published since then, but the only printed catalogue of major significance has been that of the medieval Latin manuscripts, compiled by Marvin Colker and published in 1991.[25]

As well as his work on the manuscripts, Abbott also published a catalogue of the Library's fifteenth-century books.[26] It lists 606 incunabula in Trinity and Marsh's Library, together with a few from other collections, and contains indexes of printers, places, watermarks, former owners and dates of publication. This catalogue was more positively received, an internal Library report of the 1920s noting that, unlike the summary approach of the catalogue of manuscripts, it was 'a work of minute detail'.[27]

Enclosing the Colonnades

Between 1886 and 1913, the number of volumes recorded as being acquired each year more than doubled, from about 2,800 to 6,000. Most of this increase was attributable to legal-deposit receipts. The Copyright Agent, Eccles, reported that in the 1880s he had been sending thirty-four boxes a year to each library, but by 1909 the number had risen to sixty-three.[28] He received an increased allowance to enable him to appoint an assistant, J. G. Bradford, to help with the additional work, and in 1890 Edward Nicholson, Bodley's Librarian, supported his request for a further increase, so that he could pay more to Bradford, upon whom much of the work was falling.[29] Eccles, said Nicholson, was an Agent 'whom it would be very difficult to better'.[30]

At this time it was Nicholson who took the lead in resisting attempts to reduce the privileges of the libraries. In 1890, the Incorporated Society of Authors suggested that the right to claim books printed in fewer than 250 copies should be removed, and as part of their justification they claimed

[24] Abbott and Gwynn.
[25] For these catalogues, see the list on pp. 369–71. The online catalogue of manuscripts, MARLOC, is gradually superseding the printed catalogues and the handlists in the Library.
[26] Abbott, *Incunabula.*   [27] MUN/LIB/9/10, p. 9.   [28] MUN/LIB/22/20/286.
[29] MUN/V/5/14, 2 June 1883; MUN/LIB/22/20/101–MUN/LIB/22/20/103.
[30] MUN/LIB/22/20/102.

that this would save space in the libraries. Nicholson firmly rejected that argument and asserted that the correct course was not to abandon deposit but 'whenever we build fresh rooms, to build them so that they may contain the greatest number of volumes'.[31] Abbott also wrote to the Society, citing the use made of the deposit libraries by authors, and arguing that Trinity was a national library in all but name, though it received no public funding.[32] In 1898, Nicholson gave evidence before a Select Committee set up to review copyright, and was again in the vanguard of the libraries' successful campaign to ensure that no changes were made to their rights.[33]

The policy of claiming as much as could be acquired was pursued with varying degrees of vigour by the four libraries, and within each of the institutions views differed as to the wisdom of comprehensive claiming. Even in Oxford, Nicholson's approach was called into question, and in 1895 the Bodleian Curators, concerned at the threat of being swamped with books – and despite their Librarian's protest – felt obliged to contact the other libraries to try and reach an agreement to limit the number of claims. It turned out to be impossible to find common ground.[34]

In Trinity, the burden of processing, cataloguing and housing the growing intake of books, periodicals, maps and music was already becoming a problem, and over the next half-century what had begun as an inconvenience worsened into a crisis and threatened to overwhelm the Library's resources. The policy of selecting from the legal-deposit books those to be included in the Library, and those to be rejected, remained in force. Books in the former category were catalogued, but a report from Alfred de Burgh noted that 1878 had been the last year in which there were no arrears of cataloguing.[35] By the end of the century, the backlog was about 16,000, representing roughly 3 years' intake of books, though de Burgh regarded these figures as inflated, because they included 'many volumes not really added to the Library', such as trade directories.[36] He attributed the cause of the backlog to the increase in the number of items received from the Agent and the fact that Abbott's policy had been to accept books which in former times would have been rejected.

This two-tier approach – deciding whether books should be added to the Library or not – continued to be applied also at Cambridge, where the books selected as insufficiently academic for the main collection were given

[31] MUN/LIB/2/5, 23 May 1890.   [32] *Ibid.*, 2 June 1890.

[33] MUN/LIB/22/19/9; *Report from the Select Committee of the House of Lords on the Copyright Bill and the Copyright (Amendment) Bill; together with the proceedings of the committee, minutes of evidence, and appendix*, HC 1898 (393), IX, 231.

[34] Craster, p. 173.   [35] MUN/LIB/17/120.   [36] MUN/LIB/17/123.

minimal cataloguing and shelved according to date of receipt. However, in Cambridge they were at least catalogued and findable. In Trinity, on the other hand, the arrangements for dealing with this type of material became increasingly unsatisfactory, and space to store it was a more urgent problem even than the lack of resources needed to process it.

In June 1885, a committee was set up to examine a scheme produced by John McCurdy for enclosing the arcades under the Long Room to provide additional space for books and an enlarged reading room.[37] Thomas French, the Assistant Librarian, was becoming increasingly desperate for space, describing the Library as 'choke-full'.[38] In his report in 1886, he asked the Librarian to 'direct the attention of the Board to the fast failing space'. Unless something were done to resolve the problem of parliamentary papers and patent specifications, he said that the Library would soon be 'completely blocked'.[39] A floor was installed in the attic of the West Pavilion to provide a temporary respite but within 3 years it had become a 'huge mass of waste paper', unsorted music and rejected books.[40]

In 1888, Abbott told the Board that there was space left for only 3 years' accessions. He proposed to increase the height of the shelving in the Fagel Room and the Upper East Room and also suggested that sliding bookcases could be installed along the front of the fixed cases in the same rooms, and even in the Long Room if necessary.[41] These would be merely palliatives to deal with an increasingly desperate situation, however, and it was obvious that a more long-term solution was required.

McCurdy had died in 1885, but his plans to enclose the arcades were examined again. Two specimen windows were erected on the south side of the building to allow the Board to judge their effect, and early in 1889 the architect Thomas Drew was asked to produce plans to enclose the whole of that side.[42] He responded enthusiastically, saying, 'it can hardly be questioned that the Library would be improved as an architectural work by some filling in of the "void" arches of the sub-structure... A massive superstructure such as this standing, as it were "upon legs" is not satisfactory architectural composition.'[43] He estimated that the south Colonnade could accommodate about 45,000 volumes, a figure that would double if both the north and south sides were enclosed. A capacity of 90,000 volumes was roughly that of the Long Room or its gallery. The Board approved his plan

[37] MUN/V/5/14, 13 June 1885.   [38] MUN/V/5/15, 11 December 1885.

[39] *Ibid.*, 17 December 1886.   [40] *Ibid.*, 15 October 1887; MUN/LIB/9/10, p. 4.

[41] MUN/LIB/12/34.   [42] MUN/V/5/15, 25 February, 10 March 1888, 19 January 1889.

[43] MUN/P/2/403.

Figure 18 The Reading Room in the Colonnades, *c.*1892 (Charles Hubert Oldham, *Trinity College pictorial* (Dublin: Thom, 1892), p. 146)

and by April 1890 the enclosing of the south side of the Colonnades had been completed.

Abbott also proposed that the room in the attic of the East Pavilion should be converted for storage as had been done with the equivalent room in the West Pavilion.[44] Drew advised against, because of the fire risk and because some of the floors were already under strain. For the latter reason he also rejected the College's suggestion that the granite pillars installed under the Long Room by Deane and Woodward might be removed. Burgh's central spine-wall, on the other hand, now served no purpose and could be dismantled to allow a full-width reading room to be built if the arcades on the north side were enclosed in the same way as those on the south side had been. This would in turn allow the existing Reading Room in the East Pavilion to be converted into storage space for books.[45] The plans were approved, the north side was enclosed and the new Reading Room was opened in April 1892, in time to be seen by visitors attending the celebrations to mark the College's Tercentenary. (See Figure 18.) It occupied eight bays at the west end of the building, a little over one-third of the Colonnades, with

[44] MUN/V/5/15, 15 March 1890.   [45] MUN/P/2/404–MUN/P/2/405.

the remaining two-thirds allocated for shelving, to be installed as required. Wooden bookcases were erected gradually over the next 20 years until, in 1913, a decision was made to complete the work using steel shelving, rather than wood.[46] The construction of the Reading Room meant that the door from the arcades to the West Pavilion could no longer be used as the main entrance to the Library as it had been for many years, and the west door, facing the Public Theatre, was brought back into use to provide access both to the Reading Room and to the stairs leading to the Long Room.

Deane and Woodward's intervention in the Long Room in 1859–60 was controversial at the time, but it is now widely applauded by architectural historians. The enclosure of the arcade has suffered the opposite fate, being now considered to detract from Burgh's design, whereas the contemporary press regarded the replacement of the open arches by 'handsome windows' and the conversion of the 'dark and somewhat dreary passage' into a well-lit and effectively ventilated reading room as 'nothing short of some transformation under the magician's wand'.[47]

Whatever their architectural merits, the new Colonnades provided the Library with welcome storage space for those books deemed suitable for cataloguing and adding to the collection. There remained the problem of what to do with 'rejected' books and other items, such as maps, for the processing of which there was simply insufficient staff time. In 1896, the West Attic was cleared and what was described as 'waste paper' was sold, though how much of that was actually legal-deposit material must be open to speculation. The sheet music was roughly sorted and placed on shelves, pamphlets were arranged into subjects, some of the 'rejected' books were moved to the Colonnades, some were catalogued for the Library, and others 'of no importance', along with elementary textbooks and patent specifications, were piled in subject groups in the basement of the Museum Building.[48] In 1899, the West Attic became a store for calendars and directories, but was described as 'the dirtiest place in the Library owing to the smuts which are driven by the westerly winds through the joints of the slates'.[49] Periodicals also threatened to overwhelm the Library's resources. Some journals in scientific subjects were transferred to academic departments and new titles were simply left uncatalogued.[50] Newspapers created an even greater storage problem. Those deemed worthy of retention were stored with the

---

[46] MUN/LIB/9/10, p. 1.   [47] *Irish Times*, 19 April 1892.
[48] MUN/LIB/9/10, pp. 4, 16; MUN/LIB/2/7, 21 September 1896 and 19 October 1897; MUN/LIB/4/8, 30 January 1902.
[49] MUN/LIB/9/10, p. 4.
[50] Typed report: 'Library shelving', 25 February 1913, MUN/LIB/15, Box I.

parliamentary papers in the former Reading Room in the East Pavilion, renamed the Newspaper Room, but having started down the disposal route the College could not resist the temptation to do the same with unwanted newspapers. In this case, at least, there was a worthy recipient, the National Library of Ireland, which in 1899 received a van load, including issues of the *Daily Graphic*.[51] At the same time as little-used newspapers were being discarded, others were being sought assiduously. After a lengthy correspondence, lawyers for *The Times* agreed to deposit the paper, though without conceding that they were under any obligation to do so.[52]

In 1892, the War Office donated a collection of eighteenth- and early nineteenth-century maps of Ireland.[53] Abbott also persuaded the Ordnance Survey to deposit both their revised series of Irish maps and the coloured geological series.[54] On arrival in 1890 these were divided into two categories. The first and second editions of the six-inch survey of Ireland were bound county-by-county and an attempt was made to do the same with the large-scale maps of England and Scotland, but this was abandoned after about eighty-five volumes because of the cost and the space required to store the bound volumes. Unbound maps were piled unsorted in the Upper East Room, and by 1900, when they were moved to the Colonnades and sorted into counties, the cumulative height of the piles had reached over 15 metres.[55] Recognising that this was an unsatisfactory way of dealing with important material, de Burgh visited the British Museum's Map Department in 1904 and reported on how maps were stored there and at the National Library, but it was another 80 years before serious action was taken to start sorting the maps and providing some of them with adequate storage.[56]

A new building?

When the enclosure of the Colonnades was completed in 1892, the number of catalogued volumes in the Library was about 226,000. By 1910, it had reached 321,000, an increase in excess of the 90,000 that Drew had estimated would be the capacity of the shelving in the Colonnades. The Library was facing a storage problem yet again and it was clear that Thomas Burgh's building had now reached its full capacity. The Reading Room

---

[51] MUN/LIB/9/10, p. 14; MUN/LIB/4/8, 17 February 1899.
[52] MUN/LIB/17/26; MUN/LIB/2/5, fols. 41, 67.   [53] MUN/LIB/1/34, p. 96.
[54] MUN/LIB/2/5, fols. 39–40.
[55] MUN/LIB/2/7, 3 March 1896; MUN/LIB/9/10, pp. 12–13; MUN/LIB/17/130.
[56] MUN/LIB/4/8, 17 August 1904.

in the Colonnades was also too small for the numbers of readers now using it.

An approach was made to Andrew Carnegie for funding towards the building of an extension, but unlike the Scottish university libraries, which had been able to call on the Carnegie Trust for the Universities of Scotland, Trinity was told that in Ireland only municipal libraries were being funded.[57] Nonetheless, action had to be taken. The Board began to discuss plans for a new reading room, which would release the remainder of the Colonnades for book storage.[58]

In February 1912, Abbott was asked to consult Sir Thomas Manly Deane, the next generation of the family firm, for advice on extending the Library and providing suitable accommodation for readers.[59] The College's proposal was for a new reading room to be built outside the Library and connected to it by a covered passage. The space vacated by the existing Reading Room would then provide book-storage for 30 years, or more if rolling stacks were used. An alternative suggestion was that a new store, to be built by excavating below the Fellows' Garden, could accommodate the books in the Colonnades, and the whole of that space could then become a reading room. The first option was the firm preference in the Library, particularly if the wooden shelves in the Colonnades were converted to rolling steel stacks, as a new reading-room building would also be able to contain basement rooms for unpacking and sorting books, 'work that is now quite improperly carried on in the entrance hall and Long Room'.[60]

Deane's response was that a building to the east of the Library would 'destroy' both it and the Museum Building, and that 'the suggested subterranean chamber' was out of the question.[61] In his opinion, the only two possible sites available were the Fellows' Garden on the south side of the Library, or between the Library and the Public Theatre. He submitted three designs, for an octagonal building linked to the centre of the south side of the Library, for a similar building roughly where the 1937 Reading Room now stands and for a rectangular building in the same location.

The outbreak of the First World War prevented these plans from progressing any further, but space still had to be found for books. Despite Drew's earlier warning about the floor loading, the attic in the East Pavilion was shelved as a store for periodicals and the Ordnance Survey maps were moved to the former Magnetic Observatory in the Fellows' Garden.[62] (See

[57] MUN/V/5/20, 5 December 1910 and 21 January 1911.   [58] MUN/LIB/2/7, 20 May 1911.
[59] MUN/V/5/20, 24 February 1912.   [60] MUN/P/2/434/4/1.   [61] MUN/P/2/434/4/11.
[62] MUN/LIB/17/57; MUN/LIB/9/10, p. 5; MUN/V/5/20, 4 May 1912.

Figure 19 The Magnetic Observatory in the Fellows' Garden, used from 1912 as a map store and then as the Manuscripts Room. It was demolished in 1971 and moved to University College Dublin (Irish Architectural Archive, 45/70 XI, 2)

Figure 19.) It was also decided that the remaining shelving in the Colonnades would be completed using steel rather than wood, and that the existing wooden shelving would be replaced by steel, as this would provide more storage space and reduce the fire risk. W. Lucy and Company of Oxford, who had recently installed steel shelving in the Bodleian and Cambridge University Library, were employed to carry out the work but, after more than two-thirds of the conversion had been completed, this too came to a halt in 1917 because of the war.[63]

Legal deposit – a new Act

The early years of the twentieth century were marked by a growing hostility in Ireland to Trinity, which was regarded by many as incorrigibly Protestant, anti-national, conservative and out of touch.[64] This attitude was exemplified

[63] MUN/V/5/20, 8 March 1913; MUN/V/6/5, pp. 79, 84; MUN/LIB/15/443– MUN/LIB/15/516; MUN/LIB/17/66.
[64] McDowell and Webb, pp. 363–79.

by organisations like the Gaelic League and by publications such as the
Leader, a nationalist newspaper which in 1900 carried a number of letters
complaining about the difficulties placed in the way of external readers
wishing to use the Library. These letters elicited a response from Douglas
Hyde, founder of the Gaelic League, in which he described the inadequate
resources of the National Library as a scandal. He claimed that Trinity,
Ireland's only 'decent library', buried away the books it received and that
it should either be thrown open to the public or its legal-deposit rights
transferred to the National Library.[65] The *Irish Times* leapt to Trinity's
defence, arguing that access to the College Library was 'a trifling formality'
and criticising the suggestion that the role of the two libraries should be
changed so that they would in effect be in competition with each other.[66]

At the same time, Irish university education came under the scrutiny of
two Royal Commissions, established to try and meet Catholic demands for
a university that would accommodate their religious principles. In evidence
that was submitted to the Commissions, Trinity was subjected to considerable criticism, but, apart from the comments about the Irish manuscripts
that have already been noted, very little was said about the Library and,
unlike their predecessors in the 1850s, the Commissioners showed little
interest in it. The most dangerous proposal made in evidence to the second
Commission – the one dealing specifically with Trinity – was a revival of
the demand that the legal-deposit privilege should be transferred to the
National Library of Ireland, but this was ignored and the final report was
silent on the matter.[67]

The question of copyright lay dormant for a few years until, in 1910, a
Bill was introduced into the Commons with the purpose of establishing a
uniformity of practice across the Empire. It did not reach the discussion
stage but a similar Bill was introduced the following year. Both left the
legal-deposit provisions of the libraries untouched, except for a proposal
to reduce from a year to 3 months the period within which a claim had to
be made.[68] Before the libraries could react to this suggestion, the governors
of the recently created National Library of Wales sent a memorandum
to the President of the Board of Trade arguing that it should become a

---

[65] *Leader*, 10 November 1900.   [66] *Irish Times*, 13 and 21 November 1900.

[67] *Royal Commission on Trinity College Dublin and the University of Dublin, Appendix to the first
report: statements and returns furnished to the Commission in July and August, 1906*, [Cd. 3176],
1906, LVI, 607 (p. 760); Royal Commission, Final report, note 23 above.

[68] *A bill to amend and consolidate the law relating to copyright*, HC 1910 (282), I, 239; *A bill to
amend and consolidate the law relating to copyright*, HC 1911 (149), I, 533; Partridge,
pp. 107–14, 335–45.

legal-deposit library, on the grounds that the lack of a first-class library in Wales restricted intellectual activity there, and that the existing deposit libraries had shown little interest in collecting Welsh publications. The governors claimed that the value of legal-deposit books delivered to each of the libraries in England, Scotland and Ireland was about £2,000 a year and that Wales was being deprived of this.[69] The proposal was received sympathetically and the amended version of the Bill, printed on 13 July 1911, added the National Library of Wales to those institutions entitled to receive free copies of books.[70]

The publishers were incensed at the prospect of an increase in the number of copies to be deposited, and the Publishers' Association submitted a strongly worded memorandum claiming that the cost of supplying the current five copies was already equivalent to a tax of three pence in the pound and that the addition of another library would increase that burden proportionately. They pleaded that not only should there be no increase in the number of deposit libraries but also that the existing institutions should revert to what they asserted was the intention of the Act, by which they meant that only those books that were 'of value in academic libraries' should be claimed.[71] John Murray added, in a letter to *The Times*, that, although the publishers smarted under the present imposition, they would not have raised any protest if the government had left things as they were, 'instead of embodying this late Welsh afterthought in their Bill'.[72]

The libraries responded to this challenge to their rights, fearing that they might lose them altogether. Nicholson, though still in office at the Bodleian, was seriously ill and it fell to Cambridge, in the person of its Librarian, Francis Jenkinson, to lead the campaign. The University produced a memorandum addressed to the House of Lords, to which the debate had now passed. It argued that the revised Bill, which proposed that just one copy of a book should be deposited at the British Museum, was unacceptable on the grounds that one copy was insufficient, both for the convenience of users in different parts of the country and because of the risks posed by wear and tear, fire and theft.[73] Scores of letters and telegrams were dispatched to peers and others, and Jenkinson conducted a spirited exchange with John Murray and William Heinemann in the correspondence column

[69] David Jenkins, *A refuge in peace and war: the National Library of Wales to 1952* (Aberystwyth: National Library of Wales, 2002), pp. 174–7.

[70] *A bill [as amended by Standing Committee A] to amend and consolidate the law relating to copyright,* HC 1911 (296), I, 563.

[71] *The Times*, 13 November 1911.   [72] *Ibid.*, 18 November 1911.

[73] CUA ULIB/7/2/31; reprinted in *The Times*, 20 November 1911.

of *The Times* throughout November 1911. Oxford rallied support in the Commons through its MP, Sir William Anson, and in the Lords through its Chancellor, Lord Curzon. The Faculty of Advocates reprinted and circulated its *Statement* from 1879.[74] Trinity submitted a memorandum to Lord Ashbourne, an Irish peer who had formerly been MP for the University, explaining in detail the College's approach to legal deposit. It also made the case that the Library was not just a College asset but one for the whole of Ireland, and that nobody wishing to use it was turned away. It was 'a great national institution accessible to Irishmen who have not opportunities of using British collections'.[75] Ashbourne duly spoke in support of the libraries' case, especially that of Trinity.[76]

In the end, the libraries won the day and the Copyright Act of 1911 was passed, leaving all their rights intact and adding the National Library of Wales to the legal-deposit list, though initially with more limited privileges than those of the other institutions.[77] As far as printed publications are concerned, the legal-deposit provisions have remained fundamentally unaltered in all subsequent British legislation, though changes were made to the Irish Acts in the years following independence. The 1911 Act specified that a copy of the best edition of every new book published in Britain and Ireland must be deposited with the British Museum within a month of publication, and that the other five libraries were entitled to claim a copy within a year. The copies for the other libraries did not have to be supplied from the best edition but from that of which the largest number was printed. 'Book' was defined to include pamphlets, sheet music and maps, and, in the case of serial publications such as newspapers and periodicals, a claim for one issue was regarded as sufficient to cover all future issues.

As the Bill was proceeding through Parliament, changes were afoot at the Copyright Agency. Eccles had retired from the British Museum in 1900 but remained as the Agent for the other libraries, continuing to have access to the Museum's lists of new books.[78] In July 1911, he retired from the Agency and was replaced by his assistant, Bradford. The junior Assistant, Frederick Osborne, was promoted to be the Assistant Agent.[79] The following year,

---

[74] H. F. Stewart, *Francis Jenkinson, Fellow of Trinity College Cambridge and University Librarian: a memoir* (Cambridge University Press, 1926), pp. 70–5; *Statement by the Faculty of Advocates in regard to the recommendation of the Royal Commissioners on copyright as to repealing the statutes requiring that a copy of every new book be deposited in public libraries in the United Kingdom,* 17 March 1879 [reprinted 1911], CUA ULIB/7/2/27.

[75] MUN/LIB/22/19/11.

[76] HL Hansard (5th series), vol. 10, col. 470 (4 December 1911).

[77] Copyright Act, 1911 (1 & 2 George V, c. 46).   [78] MUN/V/5/17, 12 and 19 May 1900.

[79] MUN/V/5/20, 1 July, 10 October 1911.

Bradford appealed for an increase in his salary, pointing out that he was receiving the same amount for full-time work as Eccles had been paid for 'a small portion of his'.[80] The libraries agreed to increase the sum paid to him from £430 to £500, a figure that was intended to meet the salary and other costs of the Agency.[81]

Purchases and donations

By the turn of the century, the Library's allocation for purchasing and binding had risen to £800, and in the decade before the First World War the average amount spent on books each year was £530, sufficient to buy between 130 and 180 new foreign titles, as well as antiquarian items.[82]

Following the death, in 1892, of the antiquary William Reeves, a small committee was set up to select books and manuscripts from his library that would be suitable for the College, and £100 was placed at the committee's disposal.[83] The resulting purchase was a huge collection of historical documents, some of them originals but most of them transcriptions made or obtained by Reeves during his extensive researches into Irish history and antiquities (MSS 1059–1142, 1188). They included a nineteenth-century transcription of the *Liber hymnorum* (MS 1130) and ninety letters to William King, Archbishop of Dublin, which were subsequently incorporated into the King correspondence (MSS 1995–2008).

The sales of Sir Thomas Phillipps' vast library, which began in 1885 and continued for decades, yielded a number of manuscripts. At the auction in March 1895 the Library bought two fifteenth-century manuscripts, a copy of Seneca (MS 928) for £10 15s. 0d. and a Propertius and Catullus (MS 929) for £32, followed, in 1898, by a fifteenth-century Plautus (MS 1486) for £40.[84] Three volumes of papers formerly belonging to Sir Robert Southwell and his son Edward, relating to affairs of state in Ireland in the seventeenth and early eighteenth centuries (MSS 1179–81), were also bought, the £16 cost being met by the sale of some duplicates from a bequest of 800 volumes from Henry Sheares Perry in 1892.[85]

After a fallow period for donations, several significant gifts arrived during Abbott's tenure of office. By far the most important was the library of the

---

[80] MUN/LIB/22/20/334.   [81] MUN/V/5/20, 30 November 1912.   [82] MUN/V/6/5, p. 29.

[83] MUN/V/5/16, 12 November 1892.

[84] *Ibid.*, 25 May 1895; MUN/LIB/17/35; M. Esposito, 'Classical manuscripts in Irish libraries, part I', *Hermathena*, 19 (1922), 123–40.

[85] MUN/LIB/17/34.

Figure 20 The Lecky Library in the Council Room, Museum Building
(MUN/MC/159/10)

great historian W. E. H. Lecky, which contained over six thousand volumes
and was particularly rich in history and cognate subjects. Lecky died in
1903 and his widow proposed that, after Abbott had selected books for the
College Library, the remainder would be designated as 'The Lecky Library'
and would be available for loan to members of the academic staff and
to students recommended by them. It would be under the control of the
Librarian of the Lending Library.[86] To save burdening the College with
books that it did not want, she sent a list, which Alfred de Burgh marked up
for the future Lecky Library and separately indicated those books, mainly
volumes of pamphlets, that Abbott had chosen for the College Library.[87]
In May 1912, shortly after the books had been shipped from her home in
London, Mrs Lecky died, leaving all her husband's papers to the College
(MSS 1827–1933).

The Board decided that the Lecky Library should be housed with the
Lending Library in the Council Room in the Museum Building. (See
Figure 20.) The lending collection had again fallen into neglect, with fewer
than a hundred books borrowed in 1911, and the arrival of the Lecky books

---

[86] MUN/V/6/5, p. 38; MUN/V/5/20, 12 March 1910.   [87] MS 1931a.

provided an opportunity to weed it.[88] The relatively few titles that were still used by students were retained; the remainder were either given to members of the academic staff for their departments, stored or sold. By this means the collection was reduced from between five and six thousand volumes to about five hundred.[89] Joseph Hanna, one of the Library clerks, was paid £20 for arranging the Lecky books, and in 1913 was designated as Lecky Librarian, at a salary of £20 a year, with the responsibility of attending for half an hour each day to lend books.[90]

The important status of the Library's collection of papyri is based upon those that began to arrive in the 1880s. The first to be received were the documents acquired by Charles Graves at Luxor, but the majority of the several thousand papyri now in the collection were the result of Flinders Petrie's excavations. Petrie had been advised that J. P. Mahaffy, then Professor of Ancient History, was the best person to edit them, and so he sent them to Trinity. Mahaffy published them in three volumes, of which the third was mostly the work of J. G. Smyly, the future Librarian. The publication of these papyri, and those now in the British Museum, was instrumental in raising the status of papyrology, making it a recognised area of classical scholarship. It also encouraged others to seek more papyri.[91] The College later subscribed to the work of the Egypt Exploration Fund and received donations between 1907 and 1915 of a share of the fragments found at Oxyrhynchus.[92]

In the late 1880s the Royal Geological Society of Ireland was in terminal decline, and its library of books and journals was transferred to the College, which accepted a commitment to maintain subscriptions to the journals.[93] Other donations of the period included a large collection of William Rowan Hamilton's books and papers, given in 1890 by Charles Graves' brother Robert, Hamilton's biographer.[94]

Until the late nineteenth century, music played little part in either the College curriculum or the Library's collections.[95] The Chair of Music was

[88] MUN/LIB/8/21.   [89] MUN/V/5/20, 3 February 1912; MUN/V/6/5, p. 64.
[90] MUN/V/5/17, 24 March 1900; MUN/V/5/20, 11 May 1912, 7 June 1913.
[91] B. C. McGing and H. W. Parke, 'Papyri', in *Treasures*, pp. 29–37; W. B. Stanford, 'Towards a history of classical influences in Ireland', *Proc. RIA*, C70 (1970), 13–91; J. P. Mahaffy and J. G. Smyly, eds., *The Flinders Petrie papyri*, 3 vols. (Dublin: Royal Irish Academy, 1891–1905).
[92] *DU Calendar*, 1907–8, 1915–16.   [93] MUN/LIB/12/63; MSS 2784–5.
[94] MUN/V/6/2, fol. 102r.; MS 2505 (Graves' list of Hamilton books).
[95] Eimear Saunders, 'The music in the Library', in *Old Library*, pp. 286–300; Roy Stanley, 'Music collections at Trinity College Dublin', *Brio*, 39/2 (Autumn/Winter 2002), 32–7; G. H. P. Hewson, 'The music collection in the Library of Trinity College Dublin', in A. Fleischmann, ed., *Music in Ireland: a symposium* (Cork University Press, 1952), pp. 310–11.

founded in 1764, but lapsed after 10 years and was revived only in 1845. For the first 50 years after the passing of the 1801 Copyright Act, music was specifically excluded from the items being claimed; by the 1860s it was being received in the Library, though little appears to have been retained. From the 1880s there are references to piles of sheet music in various locations in the College, but systematic cataloguing began only in the 1950s. No attempt was made to develop the collection until 1910, when Mahaffy organised an appeal to raise £500 to buy the library of Ebenezer Prout, the College's Professor of Music, who had died suddenly the previous year. Over £300 was provided by subscriptions from members of the University and the general public, and the Board supplied the rest. The collection contains Prout's working library of about five hundred books, about three thousand copies of printed music, including complete editions of many major composers, a number of rare early items and manuscripts of his own works.[96] It filled some of the serious gaps in the Library's holdings of music and was placed in the Long Room in a bookcase specially designed to interfere as little as possible with the view of the room.[97] The only evidence for music being bought specifically for students was the expenditure in 1906 of £16 11s. 6d. on vocal scores of Wagner for the use of candidates for music degrees.[98] Other musical material acquired at the time included four volumes of Irish traditional music (MSS 3194–7), containing 2,000 melodies collected and copied by James Goodman, Professor of Irish, and deposited in the Library after Goodman's death in 1896.[99]

In 1882, Arthur Macmurrough Kavanagh had successfully persuaded the College to return the Kavanagh charter-horn to his family. A decade later, his son Walter asked for the Book of Mulling, which had also belonged to the family and which he said had been in the Library with the charter-horn since the late eighteenth century. The status of the manuscript was disputed, the College claiming that it was unclear how or when it had arrived, and the family maintaining that it had been deposited in Trinity for safe-keeping and was therefore theirs to recover.[100] In 1894, Kavanagh changed his request and asked for the return of the silver *cumdach* in which the manuscript was kept. The Board challenged him to produce satisfactory evidence that it

[96] MUN/LIB/2/7, 7 September 1910; Rosemary Firman, 'Ebenezer Prout in theory and practice', *Brio*, 41/2 (Autumn/Winter 2004), 15–34.

[97] MUN/LIB/17/56.   [98] MUN/V/5/18, 1 June 1906.

[99] MUN/LIB/2/7, 24 February 1897; Hugh Shields, ed., *Tunes of the Munster pipers: Irish traditional music from the James Goodman manuscripts, 1* (Dublin: Irish Traditional Music Archive, 1998).

[100] MUN/LIB/2/5, fols. 61–4.

had been deposited and not presented to the College. If he could prove his ownership, it would be returned; if not, the College would not part with it, as 'the Library seemed the most fitting place for both the Gospels and the case'.[101] It was impossible to confirm the precise status of these items, and so in 1895 the Board accepted a compromise by which the shrine was given back to the family in return for their agreement that the manuscript was the College's property.[102] The matter did not end there, however. In 1969, the Macmurrough-Kavanagh Trust proposed to deposit the shrine of Mulling in the College if Trinity agreed that the manuscript also belonged to the Trust, a proposal that was unacceptable because it potentially allowed the Trust to remove and sell the manuscript if it chose to do so. The Board directed that the College's ownership of the manuscript, as recorded in 1895, be upheld, and the shrine remained with the family until 2001, when it was placed on loan in the National Museum.[103] The manuscript itself had not been bound whilst it was in its silver shrine, but the return of the shrine to the Kavanagh family and the removal of the manuscript from it meant that a binding was required. The historian Hugh Lawlor, who examined and collated it, described it as consisting of five unbound fascicules of vellum leaves and several loose pages.[104] A binding was supplied at the British Museum in 1894, but in 1910 it was disbound again and the leaves were rearranged according to Lawlor's collation, after which it was rebound in the Library by the Dublin bindery of Alexander Thom.[105]

Readers and visitors

In 1892, when the Reading Room in the Colonnades opened, the number of readers using the Library was about 17,300 a year (an average of 68 a day). By 1914, the figure had increased to 24,700 (97 a day) plus a further 3,000 a year using the Library between 7 p.m. and 10 p.m., after evening opening was introduced in 1900.[106] These readers were almost all current or former members of the College as, despite the regular assertions that were made about the Library's national role, use by external readers was minimal, with an average of only nineteen 'strangers' admitted each year between 1897 and 1900.[107]

---

[101] MUN/V/5/16, 20 October 1894.   [102] *Ibid.*, 25 May 1895; MUN/LIB/2/5, 11 October 1895.
[103] MUN/V/6/14, p. 30; MUN/V/5/36, 30 April 1969.
[104] H. J. Lawlor, *Chapters on the Book of Mulling* (Edinburgh: Douglas, 1897), p. 7.
[105] MS 7398/1e; MUN/LIB/17/30; MUN/LIB/2/7, 7 July, 1 November 1910.
[106] MUN/V/5/17, 8 and 15 December 1900; MUN/LIB/17/28; MUN/V/6/5, p. 79.
[107] MUN/LIB/4/8, June 1900.

Borrowing of uncatalogued novels by Fellows and other College officers remained a common practice, and some of them – or their families – were avid readers. Provost Bernard, for example, borrowed ninety books in a single year.[108] Some Fellows failed to return the items they had on loan. After the death of the Vice-Provost, Joseph Carson, in 1898, two shelves of 'old novels with the Library stamp' were recovered from his rooms.[109] In 1908, Abbott imposed some order on this process by reviving the borrowers' book, which had fallen into disuse after Todd's death.[110] Other uncatalogued novels were treated in a manner that was highly questionable. They were simply given away. In 1897, 150 novels were donated to the North Dublin Union workhouse and in 1902 two boxes were sent to soldiers fighting in South Africa.[111] Gifts of novels to hospitals and troops, including the garrison in Bermuda, continued to be made until the beginning of the First World War, when the trickle turned into a flood.[112]

Around the turn of the century, several manuscripts were sent on loan to University College Liverpool for the use of Kuno Meyer, one of the leading figures in the revival of interest in Celtic studies. These included volumes of the brehon laws and MS 1337, which formed the basis of Meyer's edition of the ninth-century story of Liadain and Curithir.[113]

Although the number of visitors to the Library had not grown over the previous decades and was still around three thousand a year, Abbott enthusiastically began to increase the quantity and range of objects on display in the Long Room. He added not only items from the Library's collections but plaster casts of inscriptions, and photographs of manuscripts held in other libraries, such as the Lindisfarne Gospels, which were placed beside the Book of Kells.[114] He sought advice from the British Museum on the best way of displaying coins, photographs and reproductions of sculptures. Photographs of the Book of Kells were taken and arrangements were made to have them printed and sold in collaboration with the South Kensington Museum.[115] At the time of the College's Tercentenary in 1892, some leaves of the manuscript, which had become loose, were put on display before it was rebound, in 'antique morocco', by Galwey and Company in 1895.[116] Abbott also had a case made to exhibit the Tercentenary addresses

[108] MUN/LIB/6/18.   [109] MUN/LIB/4/8, 6 April 1898.   [110] MUN/LIB/6/18.

[111] MUN/LIB/2/7, 8 July 1897, 18 March 1902.   [112] *Ibid.*, 1904–18 *passim*.

[113] MUN/LIB/4/8, 1899 *passim*; Kuno Meyer, ed. and trans., *Liadain and Curithir: an Irish love-story of the ninth century* (London: Nutt, 1902).

[114] MUN/LIB/2/5, 1888–9 *passim*.

[115] *Ibid.*, 15 October 1888, 13 December 1889; MUN/V/6/2, fol. 131r.

[116] MUN/LIB/17/31; MUN/LIB/4/8, 3 October 1895; Bernard Meehan, 'Bindings: documentary evidence', in *Kells facsimile*, pp. 193–5.

sent to the College from other universities.[117] By the early years of the new century there were fourteen cases in the Long Room, displaying a wide range of material from manuscripts and printed books to seals, medals and Roman coins.[118] In 1906, a new case was provided for the Book of Kells. A number of artists, including Mrs Helen D'Olier, had been allowed to make drawings of the manuscript, and some of Mrs D'Olier's copies (now MS 4729) were framed and placed on display. The removal of the manuscript from its case for copying had caused inconvenience to visitors, 'especially Americans', and so it was decided that any future copying would have to be carried out whilst it was on display in the Long Room.[119] Despite this ruling, Abbott had to complain to the Fellows about the number of requests to remove the Book of Kells for viewing, and asked them 'to exercise discrimination' because of the risk of damage and the demands that these requests placed on staff time.[120] Concern at damage from a different source provoked alterations to the Kells display case in 1913, when the College received warnings that 'malignants among the suffragettes' were contemplating an attack on the manuscripts on display.[121]

Several additions were made to the collection of busts. In 1891, William Magee, a Trinity graduate who was about to become Archbishop of York, offered the College a bust of himself by the Irish sculptor Joseph Watkins. The Board decided that it should be placed in the Long Room next to that of his grandfather, the former Archbishop of Dublin, though it has since been moved.[122] Abbott tried to obtain a likeness of the late Provost, Humphrey Lloyd, of whom a bust had been made by Albert Bruce Joy during Lloyd's lifetime. He was initially unsuccessful but in 1892 Lloyd's widow presented a later copy by the same sculptor.[123] Also in 1892 came a bust of the Duke of Wellington by Sir Francis Chantry, donated to the city of Dublin by Daniel O'Neill of Birmingham, and in 1905 there arrived a bust of James O'Brien, Bishop of Ossory, by Blanche Stack, the only female sculptor represented in the Long Room.[124] Charles Graves, Bishop of Limerick, donated a stained glass window portraying symbolical figures of religion and science, to be placed in the Fagel Room 'to remedy the eyesore caused by the rectangular patch of light' which was visible on entering the Library

---

[117] MUN/LIB/2/5, fols. 62, 69.
[118] *Ibid.*, fol. 83 (list of the contents of each case); *List of selected Roman bronze coins exhibited, also Greek and miscellaneous coins* [compiled by T. K. Abbott] [Dublin: University, 1894].
[119] MUN/LIB/2/7, 8 January 1906.   [120] MUN/LIB/15/590.
[121] MUN/LIB/2/7, 28 March 1913.   [122] MUN/V/5/16, 17 and 24 January 1891.
[123] MUN/LIB/2/5, March 1888, 4 July 1892.   [124] MUN/LIB/17/28; MS 8427.

at the opposite end.[125] (See Figure 14.) The window, which was received in 1889, was removed during the twentieth-century remodelling of the East Pavilion.

* * *

Abbott died in December 1913 at the age of 84. Mahaffy is said to have described him as the most learned man in Europe, though a more considered recent assessment noted that his publications did not reflect the depth of his learning as a scholar, and that 'he was better at absorbing knowledge than at diffusing it'.[126] His work in the Library nonetheless produced a significant legacy in the form of catalogues of manuscripts and incunabula which, though they have been criticised, remained indispensable for a century and are only now gradually being superseded by online catalogues. A well as his theological and philosophical writings, he also published editions of the manuscript known as *Usserianus primus* (MS 55) and a new edition of Codex Z (MS 32), the text discovered by Barrett.[127]

---

[125] MUN/LIB/13/86; MUN/LIB/2/5, 21 March 1889; *Irish Times*, 31 March 1890.

[126] McDowell and Webb, p. 305.

[127] T. K. Abbott, ed., *Evangeliorum versio antehieronymiana ex codice Usseriano (Dublinensi)* (Dublin: Hodges Figgis, 1884); T. K. Abbott, ed., *The Codex rescriptus Dublinensis of St. Matthew's Gospel (Z): first published by Dr Barrett in 1801* (Dublin: Hodges, Foster and Figgis, 1880).

15 | Smyly: 1914–1948

On 24 January 1914, the Board elected Josiah Gilbart Smyly as the next Librarian. (See Figure 21.) He was the Professor of Latin and one of the few Fellows at the time to have published anything of significance.[1] Within months, Europe had descended into war. The College and its Library could not fail to be affected by this and by the rising of 1916, but the long-term impact of those events paled in comparison to the political and financial implications of Irish independence in 1922. Throughout that turbulent period Smyly, who relinquished the Chair of Latin in 1915 for the Regius Chair of Greek, which he held alongside the Librarianship until 1927, spent most of his time deciphering papyri and left the Library in the care of the senior Assistant Librarian.

The post of senior Assistant Librarian was held by Alfred de Burgh from 1896 until his death in 1929.[2] Readers were largely unaware of his presence behind the scenes, attempting to impose some order on the flood of material arriving from the Copyright Agency, handling staff matters and dealing on an almost daily basis with Sir Thomas Manly Deane during the planning of the 1937 Reading Room. A contemporary College newspaper described his daily routine: 'every morning at ten o'clock he appeared, a thin, black-clad figure, rapidly crossing the Fellows' Garden, vanished into the upper regions of the Library, and was seen no more, until, on the stroke of four, he recrossed the Garden, always with the same intent and preoccupied air, and disappeared through the Nassau Street gate'.[3] (See Figure 17.)

De Burgh's successor, Joseph Hanna, was a man of a very different calibre.[4] Though hard-working and conscientious, he had started as a Library clerk in 1900 and was inadequately fitted to be the effective head of a major academic library. Responsibility for the deplorable state of the Library by the end of the Second World War was not his; it was that of the man

---

[1] As well as editing the third volume of the Petrie papyri (see above, p. 251), Smyly was also a joint editor of Bernard P. Grenfell *et al.*, eds., *The Tebtunis papyri*, 4 vols. (London: Frowde, 1902–76). McDowell and Webb, p. 398.

[2] MUN/LIB/2/7, 5 September 1929.   [3] *TCD: a College Miscellany*, 24 October 1929, p. 8.

[4] MUN/LIB/2/7, 19 October 1929.

Figure 21 Josiah Gilbart Smyly, Librarian 1914–48 (MS 4900/7)

who accepted the salary but undertook few of the duties of the Librarian, particularly in latter years. It was a sign of things to come that in November 1914, almost a year after Smyly's appointment, Falconer Madan, Bodley's Librarian, who had been trying since 1912 to arrange a meeting to discuss the implementation of the new Copyright Act, wrote in some exasperation to Francis Jenkinson at Cambridge wondering 'who is the T.C.D. Librarian'.[5]

The First World War

Between 1914 and 1918, activities in the College were increasingly curtailed. The number of students fell from 1,250 to 700, many of the staff left to join the forces and academic development came largely to a halt.[6] Use of the Library fell from 27,700 reader visits in 1914 to 12,700 in 1918 and, not surprisingly, the number of visitors dropped even more, from 4,500 to 1,600. The intake of books also declined dramatically, from 5,000–6,000 a year at the beginning of the war to 2,000 in 1918.[7] Despite an increase in the cost of materials, the installation of steel shelving in the Colonnades continued, but this was stopped in 1917, and in the same year it was decided that the binding of books should also cease, 'as it was not thought right to use paper boards and leather in the present shortage'.[8]

The war also brought about staff changes. The Library minute book noted that in 1915 a woman was employed for the first time on regular staff duties, and when one of the attendants retired in 1918 the Board decided that his successor should be either a woman or a discharged soldier.[9] Miss Ruby Jackson, a graduate of the College, was appointed as Superintendent of the Reading Room, and at the Copyright Agency the place of the Assistant Agent was taken by Osborne's wife whilst her husband was in the Royal Naval Air Service and the office boy was replaced by an office girl.[10]

During the Easter Rising of 1916 the College, in its strategic position in the centre of Dublin, was closed and guarded by members of its Officers Training Corps. The Library did not reopen until 8 May, when the danger had passed.[11] However, during the hostilities many of the buildings close to the General Post Office were destroyed, including Thom's bindery in Middle Abbey Street, which at the time contained 230 volumes belonging to the Library. Many of those were periodical parts awaiting binding or already bound, and volumes that had been sent as patterns. The most serious losses were *Faulkner's Journal* for 1803 and parts of Hely-Hutchinson's notes for a history of the College. Other items could be replaced: the proprietors of the *Irish Times* supplied missing copies of the newspaper and the Royal

---

[5] CUA ULIB/7/2/27, 30 November 1914.   [6] McDowell and Webb, p. 420.

[7] MUN/V/6/5, p. 79; MUN/LIB/17/67.   [8] MUN/LIB/17/66.

[9] MUN/LIB/2/7, 29 November 1915; MUN/V/5/21, 26 January 1918.

[10] MUN/LIB/2/7, 23 March 1918; MUN/LIB/22/20/514.   [11] MUN/LIB/2/7, 8 May 1916.

Dublin Society provided the lost numbers of the *Daily Express* and the *Freeman's Journal*. A claim was lodged with the Commission on Damages and eventually the College received compensation of £213.[12]

In June and July 1922, when there was again fighting in Dublin, including the siege of the Four Courts, the Library was closed intermittently, depending upon the perceived level of danger and the ability of the staff to travel to and from work.[13]

Legal deposit – an independent Ireland

Following the armistice, the situation at the Copyright Agency in London returned to something approaching normality. Osborne was demobilised in 1919 and expressed a wish to return to his old post of Assistant Agent, but he said that, because of high inflation during the war, the salary was no longer sufficient, even though Mrs Osborne had persuaded the libraries to increase it from £100 to £150. The Librarians, anxious to retain him, agreed to a further allocation of £50 and then another in March 1920, bringing his salary to £250. The stipend of the Agent, Bradford, was also increased, to £420. These and other costs meant that between 1900 and 1920 the Agency's budget had doubled, from £404 to £800 a year.[14]

At the end of 1921 Bradford retired and Osborne was appointed as the Agent. The Librarians, who were concerned about a growing backlog in the processing of material, concluded that larger premises were required. The University of Cambridge purchased a building in Great James Street, London, and leased the ground floor to the Agency. The increased rental, Bradford's pension and Osborne's new salary of £300 brought the total cost of the Agency to £1,105 a year, of which Trinity's quarter share was £276, a figure that alarmed the new Bursar, who was aware of the College's serious financial situation. He refused to meet the higher cost without the approval of the Board but, given that Oxford, Cambridge and Edinburgh had already agreed, the Board was left with no choice but to acquiesce.[15]

Meanwhile, Trinity's legal-deposit status was about to be exposed to a more fundamental threat than any it had faced since 1801. Preparations for establishing the Irish Free State in 1922 raised the question as to whether the legislation that entitled the College to receive copies of books published

---

[12] MUN/V/6/5, p. 29; MUN/LIB/17/66.   [13] MUN/LIB/2/7, 28 June–8 July 1922 *passim*.

[14] MUN/LIB/22/20/514–MUN/LIB/22/20/521, 532–7, 557.

[15] MUN/V/6/5, p. 120; MUN/V/5/22, 18 April 1922.

in the United Kingdom and required Irish publishers to deposit their books with British libraries still applied. The Board sought counsel's opinion and was advised that the legislation could be changed only by special provision in the proposed Dominion Act, and that this was 'most unlikely'.[16] The same question was asked by Sir Frederic Kenyon, Director of the British Museum, who also suspected that the National Library of Ireland would claim to be 'the representative library of Southern Ireland'.[17] He, too, was told that the situation could change only when the Free State had determined which existing laws were to continue.[18] Not surprisingly, the Publishers' Association assumed that once the Irish Free State had been legally constituted it would no longer be necessary for their members in the United Kingdom to send books to Trinity. It sought clarification from the Cabinet Office, which again confirmed that the existing legislation would continue in force until it was specifically repealed.[19]

The passing of the Irish Free State Act on 31 March 1922, which provided for the transfer of powers to Dublin, revived the question again, this time on the Irish side.[20] The Controller of the Irish Stationery Office asked for instructions from the Ministry of Finance on whether copies of his publications should now be sent only to Trinity and not to the British libraries.[21] The view of the Ministry was that there was no longer any legal liability under the 1911 Act to continue this distribution, but proposed that the matter should be settled by 'friendly agreement', by which it meant that both the Irish and British Stationery Offices should maintain the existing arrangement. Sir Frederick Liddell, Parliamentary Counsel in London, disagreed with the official Irish view, stating that the Irish Free State Act did not alter the obligation of any publishers, but the British Treasury decided that, until the situation became clear under the Free State constitution, it would be less confrontational to accept the proposed fudge rather than insist on adherence to the letter of the law.[22]

In November, the Publishers' Association pressed the Colonial Office to amend the legislation that covered Trinity's right to receive books, and they were assured that this would be borne in mind in connection with the Irish Free State (Consequential Provisions) Bill then before Parliament. This encouraged some publishers to take matters into their own hands. Osborne reported that, first Methuen, and then Allen and Unwin, were

---

[16] MUN/V/6/5, p. 119.   [17] TNA T 161/160 S.14806, 20 February 1922.
[18] *Ibid.*, 1 March 1922.
[19] Publishers' Association, *Members' Circular*, 4 (1922), 107 and 116–17.
[20] Irish Free State (Agreement) Act 1922 (12 George V, c. 4).
[21] TNA T 161/160 S.14806, 5 May 1922.   [22] *Ibid.*, 16 May, 30 June 1922.

refusing to deposit the Trinity copy of their books at the Agency, and the Publishers' Association helpfully brought this information to the attention of its members.[23] After the College had reminded the recalcitrant publishers that the Copyright Act was still in force and had threatened legal action, the supply of books was resumed 'under strong protest'.[24] In the case of Allen and Unwin, the skirmish marked the start of a 40-year campaign waged by Stanley Unwin against legal deposit in general and Trinity's rights in particular. Protest was not confined to the British side. A major Dublin publisher, the Talbot Press, also failed to deposit its books. Samuel Brambell, the junior Assistant Librarian, visited the firm's offices and received an assurance that copies would be supplied to the Agency, but they failed to materialise.[25] Not all publishers adopted this negative approach. Frederick Warne, for example, wrote to Osborne to say that having received 'definite information re the position of sending free copies to Trinity College Dublin [they had] pleasure in sending a copy of the book requested'.[26]

The question of copyright and legal deposit was also exercising the mind of the Irish Parliamentary Draftsman. He recommended that a short Act be passed, adopting the provisions of the British Copyright Act of 1911, but with a modification that removed the right of the British libraries to receive copies of books published in the Free State whilst leaving those of Trinity intact.[27] This recommendation, which would certainly have resulted in the removal of the College from the British Act, was not pursued. No doubt unaware of what was being considered by the Irish authorities, Trinity sought to pre-empt any change to the British legislation by issuing a memorandum, which it sent to the Prime Minister, Bonar Law, and Sir John Ross (who had been Lord Chancellor of Ireland until that office was abolished at the end of 1922) stressing the Library's role as 'the only great library in Ireland'. To withdraw the supply of free publications would, it said, 'inflict a grave injury upon the Irish Free State and its citizens generally' and would risk the possible repeal of copyright legislation in Ireland with the consequence that British publishers might again be subject to piracy, as had been the case in the eighteenth century.[28] This was not idle speculation, as one Irish publisher, acting as though the Copyright Act had been repealed in the Free State, had already been sued for infringement of copyright by a British publisher. In the face of this, it is not surprising that the Publishers' Association was

[23] Publishers' Association, *Members' Circular*, 4 (1922), 183–4; 5 (1923), 8.
[24] MUN/V/5/23, 25 October 1923.   [25] MUN/LIB/22/20/712 and 736.
[26] MUN/V/5/23, 25 October 1923.   [27] NAI 2002/14/591, November 1922.
[28] MUN/LIB/22/19/23; MUN/V/5/22, 13 January 1923.

concerned when Trinity threatened to initiate legal proceedings against one of its members for their failure to deposit books. The Association maintained the pressure from its side, complaining to the Colonial Office about the delay in remedying a matter that it said was causing 'considerable irritation'.[29]

In March 1923, the British government confirmed to the College and the Publishers' Association that it was not prepared to use the Irish Free State (Consequential Provisions) Act 1922 to make any changes to the legal-deposit legislation, unless the Irish Parliament chose to do likewise.[30] Nonetheless, the first draft of the Irish Free State (Adaptation of Enactments) Order contained a proposal to remove Trinity from the British Copyright Act, but this was struck out at the request of the Board of Trade, keen to retain the mutual obligation on publishers on both sides of the Irish Sea. The file note by Sir Frederick Liddell contained the ominous sentence, 'if the Irish government . . . refuse to enforce the obligation of their publishers to send copies of works to the British libraries, the British government will probably wish to reconsider the question, and relieve their publishers of the obligation to send copies of works to the Irish library'.[31] This was becoming a real danger, with complaints from the British legal-deposit libraries not only that the Talbot Press, and its associated firm the Educational Book Company, were refusing to deposit but, more seriously, that the Stationery Office in Dublin was failing to supply copies of Irish government publications.

At first, the Treasury tried to keep the matter at an unofficial level, leaving the British Museum to negotiate directly with the Irish publishers, but this had little effect. In February 1924, J. H. Thomas, the Secretary of State for the Colonies, was forced to send a dispatch to the Governor General, Tim Healy, passing on complaints from the British Museum and the Faculty of Advocates.[32] In the absence of any satisfactory response, Thomas sent a further, rather more terse, dispatch in May, asking Healy to point out to his ministers that British publishers were still required to deposit with Trinity and that the number of books sent to Dublin was considerably in excess of the number of Irish books deposited with the British libraries. He referred to 'frequent representations' received from British publishers asking to be relieved of their obligation and reiterated that the British government was, for the present, not willing to depart from the status quo.

[29] Publishers' Association, *Members' Circular*, 5 (1923), 12–13.
[30] *Ibid.*, 5 (1923), 22–3; MUN/V/5/22, 20 March 1923.
[31] TNA T 161/160 S.14806, November 1923.   [32] *Ibid.*, December 1923 to April 1924.

He ended, however, with the threat that, if the Irish ministers were unwilling to co-operate, 'His Majesty's Government will feel compelled to reconsider their attitude in this matter'.[33] The correspondence ended with a reply from Healy confirming that the supply of publications from Ireland would be resumed.[34]

The Industrial and Commercial Property (Protection) Bill was introduced into the Oireachtas, the Irish Parliament, in 1925. It contained a number of controversial provisions, including the proposal that the National Library of Ireland should replace Trinity as the recipient of British publications and that, if the other British libraries were to receive Irish books, then British publishers should in return supply four further copies to Ireland, for Trinity and the three colleges of the National University.[35] Trinity was invited to be represented at a meeting on 28 July 1925, at which the provisions of the Bill were to be discussed between the Minister for Industry and Commerce, Patrick McGilligan, and publishers, librarians and authors. The Library was closed and both Smyly and de Burgh were on holiday. It fell therefore to the Vice-Provost, Louis Claude Purser, and W. E. Thrift, the TD for the University, to attend. Purser dreaded the prospect of the meeting, writing to Smyly, 'I feel sure it will be a very unpleasant one, and that we shall get the worst of the matter.'[36] It seems that he was right, as he later reported to Smyly that the meeting 'was rather a difficult one owing to very hostile publishers, a rather hostile minister, and some ultra-patriots – not to speak of somewhat grasping librarians'.[37] Purser and Thrift did, however, succeed in removing the proposal to transfer the British legal deposit from Trinity to the National Library, because the Irish government realised that by pursuing this approach they would probably lose the right altogether. So many changes were made to the Bill that it was withdrawn and reintroduced in a revised form the following year.[38] In the first version of the new Bill, the number of libraries entitled to receive copies of Irish publications was seven: the six specified in the British Act of 1911, plus the National Library of Ireland, but at a later stage the three colleges of the National University of Ireland (Cork, Dublin and Galway) were added.

The Bill became the Industrial and Commercial Property (Protection) Act, 1927, and most of the legal-deposit legislation mirrored that of the 1911 Act, except that Irish publishers were required to deposit, within one month of publication, six copies of their books (defined as in the 1911

[33] *Ibid.*, 26 May 1924.   [34] *Ibid.*, 21 August 1924.
[35] *Dáil Éireann Debates*, vol. XI, cols. 2316–7, 26 May 1925.   [36] MUN/LIB/22/19/21.
[37] MUN/LIB/22/19/22.   [38] *Dáil Éireann Debates*, vol. XVI, col. 2116, 6 July 1926.

Act to include periodicals, sheet music and maps). The recipients of these were the National Library of Ireland, the British Museum, Trinity and the National University for its three constituent colleges. The other four British libraries were entitled to claim a copy within a year.[39] For publishers in the United Kingdom this meant no change to their current practice. For Irish publishers, the place of deposit was transferred from the Copyright Agency to the College for those books destined for Trinity, and those claimed from them for the four libraries in Britain were to be delivered to an address in Dublin, not London. For that purpose the booksellers Eason and Son were appointed, with instructions to forward books to the London Agency for onward distribution to the libraries.[40]

Though British publishers were unaffected by the new legislation, the deposit of ten copies placed a considerable burden on Irish publishers, most of which were small. A number harboured resentment at having to supply free books to Trinity, which was identified with the *ancien régime*, at having to send them to libraries in what was now a foreign country and at the extension of legal-deposit status to the libraries of the National University, which was seen as an opportunistic move by their librarians to avoid paying for books. A vociferous and determined objector was W. G. Lyon, one of the founders of the Talbot Press.[41] Before the implementation of the new Act, the Talbot Press' deposit of books with the Copyright Agency had been at best intermittent, and in August 1926 Lyon wrote to Osborne to complain that it was unfair to expect a small Irish publisher to supply free copies to 'wealthy institutions' in Britain. He would, he said, send books to Trinity, but would not do the same for the British libraries unless titles were specifically requested. Moreover, he would not meet blanket claims.[42] After the new Act had been passed, Lyon sent letters to the newspapers complaining about what he called 'unfair taxation', noting that the publishers had not objected to the proposal for two deposit copies, which had been in the first draft of the Bill, but that to levy ten was 'unjust'.[43] Retaliation came from an unlikely source, the National Library of Wales, which for a time refused to supply its own publications to Trinity on the grounds that some Irish publishers had adopted a policy of 'passive resistance'. Once 'our Irish friends adopt a more reasonable attitude', they said, the supply would be resumed.[44]

[39] The four British libraries were now Oxford, Cambridge, the National Library of Wales and the National Library of Scotland, which had been founded in 1925 and to which most of the legal-deposit rights of the Faculty of Advocates had been transferred.

[40] MUN/LIB/22/20/868.   [41] MUN/P/54/14/9.   [42] MUN/LIB/22/20/819.

[43] *Irish Independent*, 24 November 1928.   [44] MUN/LIB/22/20/857.

In Britain, Unwin maintained his opposition to the principle of deposit. Osborne reported first that the publisher would give no definite reply to claims, then that he had stopped responding altogether and that he threatened to make the working of the Copyright Act as difficult as possible.[45] Unwin also wrote to *The Times* to complain about the principle of depositing more than one copy, especially in the case of books sent to Trinity, some of which were then banned by the Free State government.[46]

Censorship was indeed a new phenomenon for the College authorities. The stated purpose of the Censorship of Publications Act, 1929 was 'to make provision for the prohibition of the sale and distribution of unwholesome literature', by which was meant not just books of an indecent nature but also those advocating contraception. The Censorship Board's enthusiastic interpretation of its remit meant that, over the coming years, the growing list of banned publications included works by Proust, Hemingway, Robert Graves, H. G. Wells and Sean O'Casey, as well as unlikely titles such as *Exchange and Mart.* By the 1930s, the number of new books banned in Ireland each year was between 100 and 150. The customs authorities, responsible for noting dubious books as they entered the country, proved to be the most prolific source of material for the Censorship Board, and the Library had to establish a procedure for dealing with such works.[47] The lists published in *Iris Oifigiúil*, the official state gazette, were checked and permission then had to be sought from the Ministry of Justice either to import the book, or to retain it if it had already arrived. The book was placed in a special press in the Librarian's Room and a reader was allowed to see it only with the Librarian's permission.[48] (See Figure 22.)

Descent into chaos

In November 1919, a public meeting had been held to discuss the building of a war memorial in the College. The committee charged with deciding the form it might take invited proposals from two architects, Sir Thomas Manly Deane and Richard Caulfeild Orpen. Deane proposed that a Hall of Honour should be attached to the octagonal reading room that he had proposed in 1913, to be located between the Library and the Public Theatre. Orpen's plan was similar, but he included passages at ground-floor level

---

[45] MUN/LIB/22/20/764 and 875.   [46] *The Times*, 20 December 1932.

[47] MUN/LIB/22/20/1104; Michael Adams, *Censorship: the Irish experience* (Dublin: Scepter Books, 1968), pp. 171, 243.

[48] MUN/LIB/15/572–MUN/LIB/15/588.

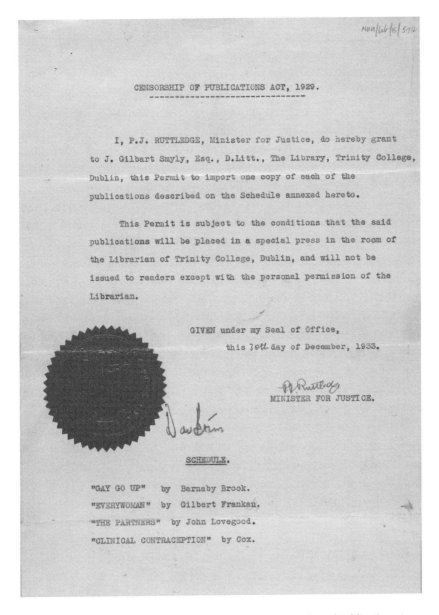

Figure 22 Permit to import books banned under the Censorship of Publications Act (MUN/LIB/15/572)

to both the Public Theatre and the Library. Deane's scheme was preferred, because it retained open space and because the height of Orpen's building would, it was felt, bring it into competition with the two adjacent structures. The Board agreed to proceed with Deane's plans for a Hall of Honour and a 200-seat reading room, with space below to sort and process incoming books.[49] This would then release the existing Reading Room space in the Colonnades for book storage.

Before either the Hall of Honour or the new Reading Room could be built, however, funding had to be found and the Library was only one of the College's post-war financial problems. There had been high inflation during the previous decade and Trinity, along with Oxford and Cambridge, was in a serious financial situation. All three universities were forced to approach the government for help. Two Royal Commissions were set up in 1920, one for the two English universities and the other for Trinity, and both recommended that support be provided from public funds. The Commission on the University of Dublin proposed a capital grant of £113,000, plus £49,000 a year. It recognised the Library's urgent need for more space, but favoured the conversion of the whole of the Colonnades into a reading room and the building of a cheap new store, at a cost of £12,400, rather than the construction of the proposed reading room, at £30,000. The report also recommended an increase in staff salaries, to be met, like the new building, from the proposed state funds.[50] Though the Library staff reacted with disfavour to the Commission's preference for a new store, as it would require the removal of all the books placed in the Colonnades since 1893 and would be 'all loss', the prospect of new funding was an exciting one.[51] During 1921 several Board meetings were devoted to planning how to allocate the expected state grant to the College and its Library, but this, and the Commission's enthusiasm for a book-store, became an irrelevance as Irish independence approached. The College received some ad hoc funding from the British government up to 1923, but none of that could be used for development. The inclusion of an annual grant to Trinity was dropped from the Government of Ireland Act and with that the College's prospects of state support evaporated. After the settlement of an outstanding claim in respect of land purchase, discussions with the Dublin government on the subject of financial assistance ceased until 1946.

For the Library, the need to find accommodation for books had again become urgent, and the problem was worsening year by year. Despite the reduced intake towards the end of the war, around 32,000 volumes had been added between 1912, when Abbott first approached Deane about a new building, and 1920, when Smyly presented a report to the Board

---

[49] MUN/P/2/424; MUN/V/5/22, 21 June 1921.
[50] Royal Commission on the University of Dublin (Trinity College), *Report of the Commissioners*, [Cmd. 1078], 1920, XIII, 1189; MUN/LIB/15/593; McDowell and Webb, pp. 425–9.
[51] MUN/LIB/15/402.

indicating that space was running out.[52] The installation of steel shelving in the Colonnades resumed in 1920, and it was estimated that, when completed, it would provide storage for 12 years' accessions. However, this was an over-optimistic figure, as it was based upon the depressed annual intake of the immediate post-war years. In fact, publishing recovered quickly, and by the late 1920s legal-deposit books were arriving in numbers that were far beyond the capacity of the Library building to accommodate, or the staff to process. Between the wars, the number of books noted as being received each year more than doubled, from 2,913 in 1920 to 6,427 in 1939. The total recorded bookstock rose from 365,784 in 1920 to 450,623 in 1939, but, as will become evident, that figure ignored the large numbers of books that were simply not counted.

The Colonnades contained only those books and periodicals that could be catalogued and were deemed suitable for addition to the Library, and from at least the turn of the century those had represented a minority of the total intake. Most major libraries have backlogs of material awaiting cataloguing, and as long as that material is stored or recorded in a way that makes it findable, the delay is inconvenient but usually tolerable for readers. In Trinity, during and after the First World War, such material was either stored without any records being created and in an increasing state of disorder, or, worse still, it was disposed of.

Following the outbreak of war, the practice that been adopted for over a decade of alleviating the Library's shortage of space and lack of processing capacity by giving away novels had become a regular procedure. Every few months, handcarts full of books were taken to the post office for transmission to the navy or to the troops, sometimes those fighting abroad, sometimes those stationed in Ireland or in hospitals there.[53] A box of 'educational books', consisting of duplicates and uncatalogued textbooks, was sent to London in 1917 for dispatch to British prisoners of war in Germany, where 'they proved to be acceptable and useful in the classes organised by the prisoners'.[54] At least two thousand books were sent to the armed forces over the course of the war. Unwanted material for which no obvious recipient could be found was simply pulped. In 1917, Smyly tackled the unsorted music, retaining the full scores but sending sacks full of separate parts and 'music-hall rubbish' to the waste-paper merchant.[55] The following year, 778 volumes of patent specifications stored in the basement of the Museum Building were also sold as waste paper, the report noting that 'scarcity of

52 MUN/LIB/15/401.   53 MUN/LIB/2/7, 1914–20 *passim*; MUN/LIB/17/66.
54 MUN/LIB/9/10, p. 16.   55 MUN/LIB/17/157.

paper in war-time greatly increased the price of waste'.[56] It had been agreed with the Patent Office in 1902 that no more patents would be supplied to the Library. The justification offered for their disposal was that there was a complete set in the National Library and that they were never asked for – hardly surprisingly as they were described as 'inaccessible, piled without order in the cellars'.[57] In 1917 and 1918 over 10 tons of 'useless matter' was sold as waste paper.[58]

The annual reports up to the 1920s show that valiant attempts were made to maintain some order among the material that was retained but not added to the Library, and an increasing number of places around the College were pressed into service as storage areas. (See Plate 10.) In 1914, books that had been set aside as not suitable for the Library 'but which it is desirable to keep temporarily' were collected from various locations, sorted and put into the basement of the Museum Building.[59] A similar exercise took place again in 1921, when the legal-deposit books piled in the Colonnades were sorted. 'Rubbish' which had accumulated was removed, those books to be retained were rearranged and shelved, and 'doubtful books' were transferred to the Museum Building.[60] The lofts in the Provost's stables were strengthened to accommodate those newspapers that had been piled on the floor of the Newspaper Room for want of space.[61] Indian government documents found a home in the former Herbarium in the Regent House, over the Front Gate, and from 1933 they were joined by novels.[62] Two huts formerly used by the Officers Training Corps, as well as part of the Corps' former headquarters in Campus House at the east end of the College, were given to the Library and were used to store uncatalogued material displaced from the Colonnades. This included large quantities of pamphlets in boxes, 'magazines of lesser importance' and 'things which could be postponed'.[63] There was even a proposal to convert Number 22, that section of the Rubrics closest to the East Pavilion, for use as an extension to the Library, but this was not pursued.[64]

A concept that gained increasing currency was that of 'postponed books', that is, books whose cataloguing it was thought could be postponed temporarily. The idea of processing most of this material was a matter of wishful thinking, as there was no prospect of dealing with it in the foreseeable future. Few novels, apart from sets of the standard titles, were catalogued and added

---

[56] MUN/LIB/17/158.   [57] MUN/LIB/2/7, 30 January 1902, 25 July 1918.
[58] *Ibid.*, 21 November 1918.   [59] MUN/LIB/17/150.   [60] MUN/LIB/17/161.
[61] MUN/LIB/9/10, p. 14.   [62] *Ibid.*, p. 17; MUN/LIB/4/16, 14 November, 19 December 1933.
[63] MUN/LIB/9/10, p. 2; MUN/V/5/23, 21 March, 16 May 1925; MUN/LIB/4/10, 18 May 1925.
[64] MUN/V/5/23, 23 January 1926.

to the Library; those that had 'gained any reputation' were stored in a room opening off the ante-chamber of the Board Room, where they were retained for further consideration in the future.[65] The justification for postponing any action was that they had to be kept 'in a state of limbo to be sifted by the test of time' and thus earn their place in the Library.[66]

After the end of the First World War, the extensive disposal of novels ceased but, in a letter to Smyly before Purser and Thrift's meeting in July 1925 with the Minister for Industry and Commerce, de Burgh conceded that some books were still being given to hospitals and to the staff and Fellows at Christmas, even though they were no longer being donated to schools for prizes or to clergymen 'for their local needs'.[67]

The upshot was that, whether disposed of or simply postponed, the majority of books received in the Library did not find their way to the shelves and thus to the readers. In 1920, Oxford and Cambridge each recorded a legal-deposit intake of about 10,000 volumes. As the same books were sent from the Copyright Agency to Trinity, which recorded only 3,000, it is clear that less than a third of what was received was being counted and added to the Library. The proportion had changed little by the late 1930s, when Trinity was recording new accessions of about 6,000 volumes a year, while the equivalent figures for Oxford and Cambridge were around 16,000.[68]

The response of some of the academic departments to the growing inadequacy of the College Library was to establish their own departmental collections along the lines of those that had become common in many of the older British universities. Such libraries were most extensive in Oxford and Cambridge, but Edinburgh and Glasgow had also accrued a large number of collections separate from the main library.[69] Arguments about the benefits and drawbacks of departmental libraries exercised librarians and academics throughout much of the twentieth century. University teachers tended to favour them as a means of building up a collection of books or journals in their department in order to save themselves and their students from having to visit the main library. However, unless a university were able to commit revenue to extensive duplication, an unplanned and uncoordinated dispersal of its book resources could lead to a wasteful use of funds and to difficulties for those working in interdisciplinary subjects.

[65] MUN/LIB/9/10, p. 15.   [66] MUN/LIB/15/402   [67] MUN/LIB/22/19/20.

[68] 'Annual report of the Curators of the Bodleian Library', *Oxford University Gazette, passim*; 'Annual report of the Library Syndicate', *Cambridge University Reporter, passim*.

[69] Peter Hoare 'The libraries of the ancient universities to the 1960s', in *Cambridge history*, vol. III, pp. 321–44.

The phenomenon was one from which Trinity had been largely immune until the First World War, but from the 1920s departmental libraries began to proliferate. As the pattern of library use differed markedly between the humanities and the sciences, so too did the role of the departmental library. For the humanities subjects in Trinity, especially modern languages, the driving factor was the failure of both the College Library and the Lending Library to meet the needs of undergraduates. Modern-language departments began to obtain funding from the Board for the purchase of books and periodicals. From 1910, an annual grant was made to the German departmental library and 10 years later, the French Department had also acquired a library. This was followed in 1928 by a combined Spanish and Italian library, and in 1937 by one for the Department of Sanskrit and Comparative Philology.[70] In 1941, books belonging to the late Provost and Celtic scholar E. J. Gwynn came onto the market, and the Professor of Irish was allocated £200 to buy books from the collection in order to start a library for his department.[71] In the same year, library grants were made to the Law School and the School of Education.[72]

For science and medicine, the priority was to have journals easily accessible, and from early in the century several departments began to receive titles transferred from the College Library.[73] This arrangement suited many, but not all, and the proliferation of small collections in departments became a matter of frustration for younger academics, especially those who had seen how other universities ran their libraries. In 1925, James Gatenby, Professor of Zoology and Comparative Anatomy, who had worked at Oxford and University College London, wrote to the Provost asking for a separate scientific library. He compared Trinity's situation with that of Oxford, which had the Radcliffe Science Library, and London, where separate departmental libraries were discouraged. In Trinity, he said, where each department had a small library consisting of books purchased by staff, received for review, transferred from the College Library, or bought from departmental funds and external grants, 'all is chaos!'[74] He complained that there was no separate scientific section in the College Library and asked for a thorough investigation of the Library as a whole, noting that 'there is forming in Trinity College a body of younger men who are quite dissatisfied with

---

[70] MUN/V/5/20, 20 December 1910; MUN/V/5/22, 31 January 1920; MUN/V/5/23, 14 January 1928; *Irish Times*, 27 February 1937.
[71] MUN/V/5/25, 7 June 1941.   [72] *Ibid.*, 19 February, 5 November 1941.
[73] MUN/LIB/4/8, 7 October 1902; Trinity College Library, *List of current and recent foreign periodicals, &c., 1906* (Dublin, 1906).
[74] MUN/LIB/15/411.

the present policy of drift'.[75] The Board avoided the wider Library issue raised by Gatenby and referred the specific matter of scientific periodicals to the Vice-Provost, Louis Claude Purser, a man not known for decisive action.[76] Not only did Purser fail to resolve the periodicals question, but the Board minutes of the late 1920s and 1930s record increasingly frequent requests for the transfer of journals from the College Library to scientific departments.[77]

The 1937 Reading Room

By January 1924, de Burgh was becoming desperate for space. He urged the Board to proceed with the Reading Room, or, failing that, with the 'catacomb' behind the Hall of Honour that could eventually form the basement of the Reading Room.[78] The response was sympathetic, but it was clear that no further building could be contemplated whilst the College's annual expenditure exceeded its income. For the same reason, the War Memorial Committee decided to postpone construction of the Hall of Honour. The appeal for this had barely reached an adequate amount, and the hoped-for surplus, that could be applied towards the cost of the Reading Room, had not materialised.[79] The Provost, John Bernard, travelled to the United States and Canada to try to raise funds, but ill-health forced him to curtail his visit and return home.[80]

In the meantime, the academic staff, including the Junior Fellows, joined the clamour for improved library facilities. Many of their demands involved the establishment of specialist libraries. There was, they said, a need for a science library, an economics library, a medical reading room; and the Lecky and Lending Library should receive history books from the main Library until a special history library could be created. These complaints finally provoked some decisive action. In November 1925, a Library Facilities Committee, chaired by Provost Bernard, was set up to consider the state of the Library.[81] The following February, Bernard managed, with some difficulty, to persuade the Board to agree to start building the Hall of Honour and at the same time to lay the foundations for the Reading Room, according to Deane's plan. A committee consisting of the Provost, Bursar

---

[75] *Ibid.*   [76] MUN/V/5/23, 28 April 1925; McDowell and Webb, p. 423.

[77] E.g. zoology (25 February 1928), experimental science (16 November 1929), chemistry (4 May 1932), MUN/V/5/24: physics (10 October 1934), physiology (4 March 1936), MUN/V/5/25.

[78] MUN/V/6/6, p. 29.   [79] MUN/V/5/23, 2 February, 8 March 1924.

[80] MUN/LIB/2/7, 29 April, 13 June 1925.   [81] MUN/LIB/15/398a and 406.

and de Burgh was set up to plan the new Reading Room, in consultation with Deane and the War Memorial Committee. The Dublin building contractors J. & P. Good were appointed to construct the Hall of Honour, a tunnel leading from the Library to the basement of the new building and rooms in that basement for storage. The War Memorial Committee met the full cost of the Hall of Honour, and in 1927, having survived the earlier financial crisis, the Board agreed to commit up to £2,000 a year towards a fund for the Reading Room, provided there was a surplus of income over expenditure of at least that amount.[82] Work on the Hall of Honour started in April 1927 and it was officially opened on the eve of Armistice Day, 10 November 1928.[83] Externally it was a copy of Frederick Darley's Magnetic Observatory of 1838–9, 'a routine little pastiche' in the opinion of one architectural historian.[84] Even with the bulk of the 1937 Reading Room behind it, its scale is diminutive compared to that of the other buildings of Front Square.

De Burgh recognised that the space to be released in the Colonnades by the construction of a new reading room would not provide a long-term solution to the Library's storage problems. In his report of January 1924 he had suggested that, when the Colonnades were full, a store could be built between the front range of the College and the Provost's House, connected by an underground passage to the planned reading room. Such a building, he said, would be 'a magazine rather than an edifice, and would be relatively quite cheap'.[85] This suggestion was not pursued, but the Board recognised the validity of de Burgh's case and decided to investigate the feasibility of building an underground store, along the lines of that constructed for the Bodleian in 1912. The committee set up for the purpose presented its report in February 1929.[86] The evidence from Oxford was not promising. The new Provost, E. J. Gwynn, had visited the Bodleian's store and reported that water had entered through a crack in the concrete, that ventilation was a problem and that the books showed the effects of damp. A. F. Scholfield, the Cambridge University Librarian, also advised rejection on the grounds that 'no architect would guarantee that his building would infallibly remain watertight'.[87] The scientists and engineers took a different view. John Joly,

[82] MUN/V/5/23, 6 and 13 February 1926, 23 April, 8 October 1927.
[83] MUN/LIB/2/7, 11 April 1927, 10 November 1928.
[84] E. J. McParland, 'The College buildings', in Holland, pp. 153–84 (p. 176).
[85] MUN/V/6/6, p. 29.
[86] *Ibid.*, p. 127. MUN/LIB/9/10 is a volume of typed memoranda prepared for this committee, which provides a detailed account of the state of the Library at the time.
[87] MUN/V/6/6, p. 127.

Professor of Geology, argued that underground structures were common in London and could be built much more cheaply than a building above ground that was 'in any sort of harmony with the existing Library'.[88] He was supported by Sir John Griffith, President of the Institution of Civil Engineers. Henry Jeffcott, another engineer, considered that a building above ground would not necessarily be more expensive, but that storing books below ground was 'so obviously a brain-wave suited to the surroundings that it is worthy of every consideration'.[89] At the Board meeting Smyly followed the lead set by his librarian colleagues and argued strongly against an underground store because of the risk of flooding, but the committee took the view that the problems at Oxford seemed to have been caused by a failure to repair the leak. It recommended that such a construction 'was feasible under conditions generally similar to those of the Trinity College site'.[90] Deane submitted an alternative proposal, the construction of a single-storey extension to Burgh's Library running the whole length of the south side and extending to the equivalent of half its width. The stonework and windows at ground-floor level would match those of the existing building and there would be a stone balustrade and flat roof at first-floor (Long Room) level.[91] (See Plate 10.) It was perhaps fortunate that the College's finances were in such a parlous state that none of these options could be anything more than a pious hope for the future, and in any case funding even for the Reading Room was still not fully secured.

Deane had estimated the total cost of the new building at about £25,000 and the Board, recognising that putting aside £2,000 a year was insufficient, increased its annual allocation and resumed its approach to external sources. An appeal to graduates was discounted on the grounds that it would yield little, but in 1931 Provost Gwynn applied to the recently established Pilgrim Trust. His application covered not just the planned reading room but also drew attention to the Library's longer-term needs and the options for a book-store either above or below ground. It also expressed the hope that, 'if financial assistance on a larger scale were within the range of possibility', departmental libraries could be created next to the reading room, more staff could be appointed and more books and journals in foreign languages could be purchased.[92] This ambitious proposal came to nought.

By 1934, however, sufficient funding was in place for Gwynn to feel confident about proceeding with the reading room. Deane had died in 1933 and so Orpen was asked if he would be willing to act as architect to

[88] *Ibid.*   [89] *Ibid.*   [90] MUN/V/5/24, 2 February 1929.
[91] MUN/MC/47.   [92] MUN/P/2/434/6/13.

construct the building on the basis of Deane's design. Gwynn described the plans as 'elaborate drawings' made on Deane's own initiative that were neither ordered by the Board nor accepted by it, but they were felt to be suitable. Orpen agreed, confirming the price as £25,000, and excavations began in July 1935.[93]

At the suggestion of the Vice-Chancellor, Sir Thomas Molony, it was decided that a tablet would be placed in the new reading room recognising the role played by Michael Moore in protecting the Library in 1689. Molony had noted recent attacks on Trinity in the press and felt that 'a simple tribute to a Catholic priest' would be regarded by the opponents of the College as a 'kindly generous act'.[94] His views were not shared by the more conservative Fellows. An eye-witness reported the reaction of the Public Orator, Sir Robert Tate, when asked to devise the wording of an inscription for the plaque: 'we were in the porch of the Dining-Hall, and I thought the fierceness of his indignation would blast everybody out of sight'.[95] Wiser counsels prevailed, however, and the opportunity to extract political capital from the occasion was not lost. W. E. Thrift, who had succeeded Gwynn as Provost in May 1937, invited the President of the Irish Free State's Executive Council, Éamon de Valera, to open the building and unveil the plaque in honour of Moore, 'a priest of your Church . . . who saved the Library and our manuscripts'.[96]

The opening ceremony took place on 2 July 1937. The event, and particularly the involvement of President de Valera, were widely covered in the press, the *Irish Times* musing, in a lengthy editorial, on Trinity's potential role as a force for Irish unity and urging it to become more conspicuously involved with the government of the new nation.[97] The Catholic press was less sympathetic. The *Catholic Bulletin* thundered that what it regarded as half-hearted recognition of Michael Moore was simply a cynical attempt to draw Catholic students into 'the Elizabethan fortress of Protestant England'.[98]

The Library was closed for three weeks, rather than the usual two, to allow books to be transferred from the old Reading Room to the new one, and readers were admitted for the first time on 26 July.[99] Access was from

---

[93] MUN/LIB/15/414–MUN/LIB/15/416; MUN/V/5/25, 14 November 1934; MUN/LIB/2/7, 18 July 1935.

[94] MUN/LIB/15/430.   [95] MUN/LIB/15/431.

[96] MUN/LIB/15/434; Liam Chambers, *Michael Moore, c.1639–1726: Provost of Trinity, Rector of Paris* (Dublin: Four Courts, 2005), pp. 14–15.

[97] *Irish Times*, 3 July 1937; Kenneth C. Bailey, *A history of Trinity College, Dublin, 1892–1945* (Dublin University Press, 1947), pp. 64–6.

[98] Sean Moran, 'Michael Moore of Paris', *Catholic Bulletin*, 27 (1937), 609–15 (p. 614).

[99] MUN/LIB/4/19, 26 July 1937.

Front Square through the Hall of Honour. The Reading Room and its surrounding gallery, which was raised about a metre above the main floor, contained 160 seats, rather fewer than the 200 that had originally been estimated. Natural light came from the clerestory windows and through a glazed dome in the centre of the ceiling. One of the perimeter rooms below the gallery was designated for the use of academic staff, where a table was also reserved for women readers.[100] The exterior of the building was constructed in Irish granite, with window and door facings of Portland stone, and the basement formed a book-store which was henceforth referred to as 'the Catacombs'. An electric conveyor-belt was installed to transfer books from the Colonnades through Deane's tunnel from the West Pavilion and supply them to the readers in the new building.[101] Legal-deposit books arriving from the Agency were delivered to the basement under the Hall of Honour for processing, and the old Reading Room in the Colonnades was converted into storage space by the installation of more steel shelving.[102]

The College had finally acquired its Reading Room but, as de Burgh had warned over a decade earlier, it had not solved the Library's long-term storage problems. Trinity's modest approach to building during the 1930s differed significantly from that of the other two university legal-deposit libraries, both of which had been facing similar space problems. The 1937 Reading Room had cost £25,000, almost entirely found from Trinity's own resources, whereas Cambridge built a massive new University Library building, at a cost of £500,000, and Oxford spent £850,000 on the construction of the New Bodleian and changes to the existing library buildings. Both of those were supported by the Rockefeller Foundation, which provided half of Cambridge's costs and three-fifths of Oxford's.[103] Had Trinity been able to find a similar level of matching funding the Library's future might have been very different.

Purchases and donations

During the inter-war years the Library's reliance on legal-deposit books to sustain its modern collections became almost total, and the number of new

---

[100] MUN/V/5/25, 5 July 1937; *Irish Builder and Engineer*, 79 (1937), 819.
[101] MUN/LIB/2/7, 1 January 1938.
[102] MUN/LIB/4/13, 22 May 1929; MUN/LIB/2/7, February 1938.
[103] Craster, p. 327; Christopher Brooke, 'The University Library and its buildings', in Peter Fox, ed., *Cambridge University Library: the great collections* (Cambridge University Press, 1998), pp. 211–27.

books bought each year was risible. In 1923–4, for example, 3,071 books were added to the Library, but of these only 36 were foreign purchases and 18 were second-hand.[104] This was a pattern that continued for two more decades. In 1933–4 only 38 new foreign books were bought and in 1945–6 the figure was 31.[105] In the same period the Bodleian and Cambridge University Library were each acquiring between 1,500 and 2,000 new foreign books every year. Trinity Library's budget was similarly out of step with those of its sister institutions. In 1936, the allowance for purchasing and binding was increased from £800 to £1,000, of which probably a half went on binding and the bulk of the remainder on subscriptions to foreign journals.[106] The Bodleian and Cambridge spent between £2,000 and £4,000 a year on foreign books and periodicals and almost as much again on binding.[107]

External sources occasionally provided additional funds. The College's Educational Endowment Fund, established in 1927 by a group of graduates, gave £200 in 1934 for the purchase of foreign books and periodicals, in 1942 a donation from American graduates to mark the College's 350th anniversary was used for the purchase of books for the Library, and in 1946, at the instigation of Oliver St John Gogarty, the US State Department offered to provide American publications from the 1920s and 1930s.[108]

Despite the prevailing financial stringency and the minimal number of modern foreign, especially American, books bought, the Library did make a number of important purchases of antiquarian material. In 1919, the Lyons Collection, comprising about two thousand letters of Archbishop William King, were bought from P. E. O'Donnell, a Limerick solicitor, for 10 guineas, and the same year ten further King letters were bought for £3 16s. 6d. at the Sotheby's sale of manuscripts from Sir Thomas Phillipps' library.[109] The Lyons Collection became the nucleus of the College's King correspondence and Edward Phelps, one of the Library clerks, sorted these letters, and others that had been acquired at different times, into a single chronological sequence (MSS 1995–2008).[110]

In 1921, the library of the Provençal scholar William Bonaparte-Wyse was offered to the College by his grandson. It consisted of about 1,250 items

[104] MUN/LIB/17/164.   [105] MUN/LIB/17/174 and 186.

[106] MUN/V/5/25, 29 January 1936.

[107] *Oxford University Gazette; Cambridge University Reporter*, see note 68 above.

[108] MUN/V/5/25, 9 May 1934; MUN/V/5/26, 30 May 1942; MUN/P/54/14/154– MUN/P/54/14/158.

[109] MUN/LIB/17/68.   [110] MUN/LIB/17/159.

of Provençal and Catalan literature from the second half of the nineteenth century. The Board allocated £100 to Thomas Rudmose-Brown, Professor of Romance Languages, to buy it for the French Department library, and it was later transferred to the College Library.[111] After Rudmose-Brown's death in 1942 a considerable number of foreign-language books from his own library were bought for the Modern Languages library and a rather smaller number in classics and history for the College Library.[112]

Donations were few, but there were some of significance. In 1923, Katherine Maxwell, the great-grand daughter of Wolfe Tone, bequeathed a collection of Tone's diaries, notebooks, letters and other papers (MSS 2041–50), together with his death mask and a marble bust by Terence Farrell. Further Tone papers were given in 1964 by Katherine Dickason, his great-great-grand daughter (MSS 3805–7).[113] A regular donor in the first quarter of the century was Samuel Tickell, who sent annual consignments, including incunabula and some rare sixteenth-century imprints, that eventually cumulated to over eight hundred items.[114]

During the First World War, recruiting posters played an important role in disseminating the British government's message, and from 1915 an increasing number was aimed specifically at the Irish population. The largest known collection of these, numbering just over two hundred, is now in the Library, thanks to a donation in 1919 by Captain Rupert Magill of the army administration.[115]

In 1932, Albert Bender of San Francisco presented a collection of books 'of outstanding typographical excellence', mainly printed by private presses in California.[116] Bender was the son of a Dublin rabbi and had made his fortune as an insurance broker. As well as fine printing, he collected works of art, some of which he gave to the National Museum of Ireland and the San Francisco Museum of Modern Art. In 1935, he sent the College 100 guineas to provide suitable shelving for his books, which were to be known as the Philip Bender Collection, in memory of his father. An oak display case was made and this formed part of the exhibition in the Long Room for

[111] MUN/V/5/22, 22 January 1921; Mina Kelly, 'The Bonaparte-Wyse collection', *Hermathena*, 121 (1976), 117–20.

[112] MUN/V/5/26, 1 July 1942.

[113] MUN/V/5/23, 25 October 1923; *Irish Times*, 3 February 1925; R. B. McDowell, 'The 1798 Rebellion', in *Treasures*, pp. 143–7.

[114] MUN/LIB/17/114, p. 1; H. W. Parke, *The Library of Trinity College Dublin: a historical description* (Dublin: Trinity College, 1961), p. 12.

[115] MUN/LIB/17/68; Mark Tierney *et al.*, 'Recruiting posters', in David Fitzpatrick, ed., *Ireland and the First World War* (Dublin: Lilliput Press, 1988), pp. 47–58.

[116] MUN/V/6/6, p. 163.

many years. Bender donated more books to the Library at intervals until his death in 1941, after which the Book Club of California, of which he was a founder member, added its own publications to the Bender Collection for another decade, as they appeared.[117] The collection now numbers about five hundred volumes.

The Lecky donation had provided a collection that to some extent served as a departmental and lending library for historians, though its value for undergraduates was limited. In 1935, academic staff in the departments of History and Economics proposed the creation of a library for students in those subjects, to be housed in the rooms of the new History Society. They sought an annual grant from the Board, arguing that 'a well-stocked departmental library of this sort would greatly relieve the present congestion in the reading room of the College Library'.[118] Law was added to the subjects covered, and the Joint Library for Economics, History and Law was established. As well as its grant, it also attracted donations. In 1939, Walter Alison Phillips, on his retirement from the Lecky Chair of Modern History, made a substantial donation of historical books from his own library, and in 1941 part of the income from the bequest of John Good, a Dublin businessman who had encouraged the establishment of Trinity's School of Commerce, was assigned to the purchase of books in economics and commerce. In 1945, the library of around two thousand books belonging to the late C. F. Bastable, former Regius Professor of Laws, was accepted by the Board, most of it for the Joint Library, though a few books found their way to the College Library.[119]

Readers, visitors and staff

After the end of the First World War, use of the Library rose rapidly, from 22,000 reader visits in 1921 to around 42,000 in the mid 1930s, with a jump to about 60,000 following the opening of the 1937 Reading Room. There was then an inevitable decline during the war years, but by 1948 the figure had climbed again to over 67,000.

In 1922, the regulations were changed to allow the Librarian to issue admission tickets to all undergraduates and to others approved by the Provost.[120] The Library declaration still had to be made in the presence

[117] MUN/V/5/25, 23 January 1935; MUN/V/5/26, 11 March 1942; MUN/V/6/7, p. 36.
[118] MUN/V/6/7, p. 27.   [119] MUN/LIB/1/48; MUN/LIB/15/605; MUN/V/6/7, p. 159.
[120] MUN/LIB/6/6, p. 7.

of the Provost or Vice-Provost, but in 1937 the Registrar, W. A. Goligher, proposed that all admission arrangements should be in placed in the hands of the Librarian, and that the Provost and Vice-Provost should be spared 'this great inconvenience'. He recommended that the declaration should simply be signed and that what he described as an 'objectionable feature', the clause in the declaration stating that a reader would inform the Librarian or the Provost of the name of anyone he saw breaching the rules, should be removed. This, said Goligher, required the applicant 'to act as a common informer – contrary to Irish sentiment' and he argued that no candidate for admission had 'the slightest intention of keeping this promise'.[121] The Board agreed to remove the offending words but the requirement for the declaration to be made in person to the Vice-Provost remained.[122]

In 1925, it was agreed that steel bookcases would be erected against the balustrade in the gallery of the Long Room to accommodate newly received books and periodicals before they were catalogued, and that they would be available on one month's loan to Fellows and professors.[123] J. L. Synge, the newly appointed Professor of Natural Philosophy, persuaded the Board that this right should be extended to all teaching staff on the grounds that the Library 'is not, and cannot become, without radical alterations, an efficient instrument, but such assistance as it can afford should be utilised to the full'.[124]

Women had been first admitted as undergraduates in 1904, and the Second World War led to a relaxation of the rule requiring them to be out of the College by 6 p.m. The women had complained that they were being discriminated against because 'under war conditions' many of the books they needed were not available outside the Library; the Board accepted their case and agreed that they could use the Reading Room until 8.45 p.m.[125]

During both wars the number of visitors to the Long Room declined, but they recovered quickly. In the early 1920s there were just over 2,000 a year, roughly the same as at the turn of the century, but by the late 1930s the number had risen to 7,000. The College gradually began to present a more welcoming front. It participated in the Dublin Civic Week programme in 1927, with demonstrations in various scientific and medical departments, and the Long Room was open to the public, with two plainclothes detectives

[121] MUN/LIB/15/608.
[122] MUN/V/5/25, 12 January 1938. For the text of the declaration see Appendix 3.
[123] MUN/LIB/2/7, 26 November 1925.   [124] MUN/V/6/6, 29 November 1926.
[125] MUN/P/54/14/114; MUN/V/5/26, 25 February 1942.

on duty. De Burgh gave a slide lecture about the Library and the Book of Kells, which had to be repeated the following day because of the level of demand.[126] Dublin Civic Week took place again in 1929, and again Trinity participated, with Gilbert Waterhouse, the Professor of German, publishing a guide to the College, which was sold in the Long Room.[127] De Burgh's lecture was on the programme again, but he died 2 days before the celebrations began and Joseph Hanna had to be drafted in at the last minute to read it. Other events during the 1930s brought the Library to the attention of a wider public. A record number of visitors attended during the Eucharistic Congress in 1932, and in 1936 W. B. Stanford broadcast a series of lectures about the Book of Kells on 2RN, the predecessor of Radio Éireann.[128]

As war again approached, with a greater danger of air raids than in 1914, the safety of the country's manuscript treasures became a matter of concern. The Cabinet Committee on Emergency Measures sought advice from the Irish Manuscripts Commission about the protection of state papers and other records in Dublin institutions such as Trinity, the National Library and the Royal Irish Academy.[129] In the end no government action was forthcoming, but the College moved its most valuable manuscripts to various locations considered safer than the Library itself.[130] In May 1945, all the manuscripts were returned and the Book of Kells was put on daily display again.[131]

Four busts were added to the Long Room between the end of the First World War and the end of the Second. The first was that of Wolfe Tone, donated in 1923 with his papers, and in January 1925 the busts were rearranged into chronological order, with the Tone in its correct place.[132] In 1926, Kathleen Smith, the great-grand daughter of a former Lord Chancellor of Ireland, Sir Maziere Brady, gave a bust of him done by Christopher Moore in 1846.[133] The following year Captain Cyril Beresford Mundey presented a bust of his ancestor Myles John O'Reilly by Thomas Kirk. Then, in 1945, a bust by John Edward Jones of the former Librarian, J. A. Malet, was given by Mrs Malet Hicks, but as it was in plaster, not marble, it was not deemed suitable for the Long Room.[134]

---

[126] MUN/LIB/4/11, 17–25 September 1927.

[127] *A handbook to Trinity College* (Dublin: Hodges, Figgis, 1929); MUN/LIB/2/7, 19 August 1929.

[128] MUN/LIB/2/7, 20 June 1932; MUN/LIB/4/18, September 1936.

[129] Michael Kennedy and Deirdre McMahon, *Reconstructing Ireland's past: a history of the Irish Manuscripts Commission* (Dublin: Irish Manuscripts Commission, 2009), p. 79.

[130] MUN/LIB/2/7, 19 June 1939, 6 July 1940, 12 February, 30 June 1941.

[131] *Ibid.*, 10 May 1945; MUN/LIB/15/628.   [132] MUN/V/6/6, p. 98.

[133] MUN/V/5/23, 5 June 1926.

[134] *Ibid.*, 25 June 1927; MUN/LIB/2/7, 28 June 1945; MUN/LIB/15/534.

Growing discontent

During the Second World War, the Junior Fellows became increasingly disillusioned with the archaic and inefficient administration of the College and, in particular, with the role of the Senior Fellows, who controlled the Board and thus dictated such decision-making as took place. The running of the Library attracted much of the criticism and, though Smyly could be relied upon to resist proposals for change, the state of the institution could no longer be ignored.[135] A committee, chaired by E. H. Alton, the Vice-Provost, was set up in February 1942, 'to inquire generally into the Library administration'.[136] It took a year to produce recommendations, but the outcome was the establishment of a permanent Library Committee, chaired by the Provost, to which office Alton had in the meantime succeeded.[137] The need for such a committee as a channel for suggestions and criticism – and as a means of eliciting a response from the Library – was expressed by the new Vice-Provost, R. M. Gwynn: 'at present I'm afraid the Librarian (and Mr Hanna) may be trusted to regard suggestions as the whim of an individual "grouser"! I may add that my enquiries reveal wide-spread discontent on the staff, especially junior, re the Library'.[138]

The first meeting of the new Library Committee took place on 7 July 1943 and in his briefing paper Gwynn set out the College's dilemma. The Library was, he said, 'perhaps our greatest asset and pride; it is also a responsibility and trust, embarrassing by reason of our slender resources. External criticism is frequent and not seldom unfavourable, coming alike from Irish scholars and members of English universities. We should be ready to give an account of our stewardship, and if so we must be prepared to spend more in building up a more adequate staff with more efficient methods.'[139]

The committee sought the views of academic staff and students on the improvements required.[140] The list was lengthy, but it revolved mainly around the selection and arrangement of books, and above all the number and quality of the staff. The inadequate management of the Reading Room in particular was a recurring theme: the reference books were out of date and the staff were unequal to their duties, too junior, ill-educated and unable to deal with enquiries. One user demanded that 'the little boys at the desk . . . should be supervised by someone with more sense and competence'.[141] It was a widespread view that a graduate

---

[135] McDowell and Webb, pp. 480–90.   [136] MUN/V/5/26, 11 February 1942.
[137] *Ibid.*, 5 July 1943.   [138] MUN/P/54/14/118.   [139] MUN/P/54/14/124.
[140] MUN/LIB/3/3, 7 July 1943.   [141] MUN/LIB/15/623.

Superintendent was needed for the 1937 Reading Room and that the ultimate goal should be for the Library to be administered by a trained Librarian with graduate Assistant Librarians.

Smyly dissented from many of these views and managed to prevent the appointment of a graduate Superintendent whilst he was in office. He also resisted the proposal that books should be borrowable after they had been catalogued and that borrowing rights should be extended to all staff. A compromise was reached whereby Fellows, professors and lecturers of more than 2 years' standing could borrow books both before and after cataloguing, against a bond of £150 to cover loss or damage.[142]

At the beginning of 1944, Smyly, now aged 76, was due for re-election at the end of his third ten-year term of office. He had just become the Vice-Provost, and the Board obtained the approval of the Visitors to reappoint him as Librarian at its discretion and for only one year at a time, instead of the statutory minimum of ten.[143] Nonetheless, despite the criticism levelled at him, the Board continued to reappoint him each year until his death in 1948.

Alton was anxious to find ways of providing more support to the Library and in 1944 he proposed the establishment of a Friends of the Library, along the lines of the Friends of the Bodleian. This was inaugurated the following year with the object of 'providing an income for the purchase of additional books and manuscripts, and also of promoting an interest in the general welfare of the Library'.[144] The organisation continues to this day and has made funds available for purchases, as well as encouraging donations of books and other materials.

Difficulties with publishers surfaced again during the Second World War. In the 1920s and 1930s, Stanley Unwin's case had been based upon the 'injustice of taxing British publishers for the benefit of a self-governing republic'.[145] He repeated that complaint in 1941, but the following year changed the focus of his attack. After being told that Trinity did not retain the books sent to it, he compiled a list of titles supplied by various publishers and asked a reader to request them in the Library – without apparent success.[146] This appeared to confirm his suspicion that Trinity disposed of

---

[142]   MUN/LIB/3/3, 19 November 1943, 18 February 1944; MUN/V/5/26, 8 March 1944.

[143]   MUN/V/5/26, 26 January 1944.

[144]   *DU Calendar*, 1946–7, p. 427; MUN/LIB/3/3, 19 May 1944–18 May 1945 *passim*; 'Report of the Honorary Secretary', *Annual Bulletin*, (1946), 4–5 and leaflet enclosed therein.

[145]   Sir Stanley Unwin, *The truth about a publisher: an autobiographical record* (London: Allen & Unwin, 1960), p. 337.

[146]   Letters to *The Times*, 6 February 1941, 23 January 1942.

some of the books it received and, what was worse, he became convinced that the College was in league with a bookseller, who provided a list of titles to be claimed, so that he could then acquire them for sale.[147] More letters to *The Times* followed. Unwin quoted Hanna's figure that 6,000 new books were added to the Library each year and compared it to the figures for the other deposit libraries. To each of his letters, either Smyly, the Provost or the Vice-Chancellor replied and, as Unwin failed to produce any evidence to support his claim that Trinity was selling legal-deposit books, they were able to rebut the more extreme of his accusations whilst managing to avoid the main issue of the state in which the Library found itself. Unwin eventually accepted that those books not accounted for were not sold or disposed of, but merely 'buried'.[148] His diatribe gained little support among British publishers, with even the trade journal the *Bookseller* dismissing his 'rash accusation' and quoting a letter from another publisher in which he said that he had 'a lot of worries that keep me awake at night...but I cannot honestly say that free books to Dublin has ever been one of them'.[149]

Some other London publishers objected to sending books to Trinity because of Ireland's neutrality during the war, but the College usually managed to deal with those by pointing out how many of its graduates were serving in the British forces.[150] Nicholson and Watson refused to deposit in 1944, claiming a 'lack of reciprocity'. Alton, supposing that the refusal was actually a protest against Irish neutrality, asked Lord Harmsworth, a Trinity graduate, to explain the reciprocal arrangements and try to persuade them to change their mind, as he wanted to avoid having to take legal action. Harmsworth appeared to have succeeded, as the firm agreed to resume sending books to the College 'without prejudice', but Osborne later reported that only three copies were arriving at the Agency instead of the four that were required.[151]

This dispute, together with the establishment of the Friends of the Library and its appeal for support, provided Unwin with another opportunity to renew his campaign. He wrote to Nicholson and Watson to ask whether the matter had been resolved and was told that they had been advised against

[147] RUL, Records of Chatto & Windus Ltd, CW 91/22.

[148] Letter to *The Times*, 10 February 1942. For the remainder of the correspondence see *The Times*, 23, 26, 29, 30, 31 January, 3, 6 February 1942 and MUN/V/5/26, 4 February 1942.

[149] *The Bookseller*, 19 February 1942, pp. 116–17.

[150] See, for example, correspondence in the *Daily Telegraph*, September–October 1945; MUN/V/6/7, p. 154.

[151] MUN/P/54/14/84– MUN/P/54/14/101.

action, because it could lead to the repeal of the 1911 Copyright Act, and that this could damage the interests of British publishers if pirated editions of their books started to be published in Ireland. Nicholson and Watson also raised the matter of Trinity's failure to catalogue the books it received and wondered whether the Publishers' Association might pursue the matter.[152] Unwin seized on this, and in January 1946 he persuaded the Association to write asking the College either to catalogue the books it had claimed, return them or refrain from claiming books which it did not intend to catalogue.[153] The College asserted that it did catalogue the 'vast majority' and that the others, 'judged to be of little value', were kept in alphabetical order and, though uncatalogued, were readily available if wanted.[154] This equivocal response did not satisfy the publishers and they asked for a more definite indication that books would either be catalogued or returned.[155] The Board relented and issued an instruction to this effect, a resolution which satisfied the Association and permitted Unwin to claim victory in a letter to *The Times*.[156]

The establishment of the Friends of the Library allowed some of the younger members of the academic staff to become involved in Library matters, with a view to breathing some life into the institution, though it would become clear that this was the last thing that Smyly wanted. Chief among the malcontents were Herbert Parke, the Professor of Ancient History, and David Webb, who became the Secretary of the Friends and was co-opted onto the Library Committee. The Friends' first exhibition, on Swift in late 1945, caused those involved to reflect upon the suitability or otherwise of the Long Room as an exhibition venue. Parke submitted to the Library Committee a lengthy document on the subject, including questions about what, if anything, should be displayed there.[157] A sub-committee, of which he and Webb were members, was set up to consider the issue further. Its report recommended a reduction in the amount of material on display, a general tidying up of the exhibits, new labels and a rearrangement of the busts. Smyly was absent from the Library Committee meeting at which the proposals were accepted, but at the following one he expressed his disapproval of most of the proposed alterations.[158]

[152] RUL, Records of George Allen & Unwin Ltd, AUC 232/11.
[153] Publishers' Association, *Members' Circular*, 22 (1946), 8; MUN/LIB/15/529; MUN/V/5/26, 30 January 1946.
[154] Publishers' Association, *Members' Circular*, 22 (1946), 21.   [155] MUN/LIB/15/526.
[156] MUN/V/5/26, 24 April, 8 May 1946; Publishers' Association, *Members' Circular*, 22 (1946), 56; *The Times*, 5 July 1946.
[157] MUN/P/54/14/131; MUN/LIB/3/3, 16 November 1945.
[158] MUN/LIB/3/3, 15 February, 19 March 1946.

The display in the Long Room was a minor issue in the context of the over-all state of the Library, but this was the point at which the Library Committee began to flex its muscles and challenge Smyly's intransigence. T. W. Moody, the Professor of Modern History, was added to the sub-committee on the Long Room. Another report was produced, to which Smyly again objected, and so it was submitted directly to the Board, on which Parke served as a representative of the Junior Fellows. The Library Committee asked for the reference books on the open shelves of the Reading Room to be regularly updated, a proposal again rejected by Smyly because of the staff time that he said would be involved in altering the catalogues.[159] Other problems with the running of the Library were also being openly discussed by the commit-tee and the decision of the government to provide state funding to Trinity in 1947 offered an opportunity to consider some improvements. In its sub-mission requesting government support, the College had included the need for an additional £1,000 a year for book purchases as well as increases to salaries.[160] The salary increases were applied from mid 1947, an additional Library Assistant was appointed, the Library was granted an additional £500 a year for purchases and the grants for departmental libraries were increased.[161]

The Board also asked the Library Committee to report on various pro-posals that had been made for further expenditure on the Library. A sub-committee, which included Parke, Webb and Moody, was empowered to report directly to the Board without further consultation with the Library Committee, thus giving Smyly fewer opportunities to object. Its recommen-dations repeated those made before: more staff were needed to reduce the cataloguing arrears, and improved superintendence of the Reading Room and updating of the reference collection were both required. The report noted that these were just the most pressing needs and that a larger scheme would be proposed in due course.[162]

Smyly was now ailing, and he died on Christmas Day 1948 at the age of 81. The chaotic state of the Library by the end of the 1940s resulted from a combination of chronic underfunding and Smyly's failure to provide any leadership. As a result, there had been no planning or prioritisation, merely muddling through. De Burgh had had some success in maintaining a semblance of order, but Hanna was overwhelmed. It was an extraordinary situation. When other major universities employed senior academic figures as their full-time librarians, Trinity's Librarian played almost no role in the

---

[159] *Ibid.*, 14 February, 21 May 1947; MUN/V/5/26, 14 June 1947.   [160] MUN/V/6/7, p. 177.
[161] MUN/V/5/26, 11 June, 2, 5 July 1947.   [162] MUN/LIB/3/3, 14 November 1948.

administration of the Library, but left it to an Assistant who had started work straight from school as a Library clerk. Smyly's lack of commitment had become worse as the years passed, and his intransigence had gradually turned into a refusal to countenance almost any change. At the Board, where he might have made a difference by arguing for more resources, there is hardly any record that he spoke for the Library except to read the Assistant Librarian's report once a year. It was clear that, despite the College's financial constraints, a new approach to the management of the Library was urgently needed.

16 | The Library in 1950

When Todd responded to the enquiries of the Royal Commission in 1852 he was able to show that the Library was generally well run and, though not heavily used, could meet the needs of its readers. The same could not be reported a century later by Herbert Parke, Smyly's successor as the College Librarian.[1] (See Figure 24.)

In 1950, the Library officially occupied two buildings: the 1937 Reading Room and what was to become known as the Old Library. Books stored in the latter were transferred to the Reading Room for readers' use by means of a conveyor belt through a tunnel from the West Pavilion. The annual number of reader visits was about 73,000, a figure that was showing a steady increase each year and was almost three times that in 1912 when the size of the Reading Room had been determined. As a result, the room was overcrowded, even though seats for an additional 32 readers had been added in 1949 after complaints from the students.[2] It was open from 10 a.m. until 10 p.m. on Mondays to Fridays, except during July and August when it closed at 6 p.m., and on Saturdays throughout the year from 10 a.m. until 1 p.m. Because of the pressure on space, some first-year undergraduates were given 'restricted admission', which meant that they could use the Reading Room only after 6 p.m. and in the vacation.[3] The Catacombs in the basement were used for storage, but the area was prone to damp.

After the transfer of the Law School from the West Pavilion in the 1850s, the whole of Thomas Burgh's building had been occupied by the Library. The manuscripts were stored on the ground floor of the West Pavilion, with the Librarian's Room above it and the Clerks' Room above that, whilst the East Pavilion contained the Newspaper Room, the Fagel Room and the Upper East Room. The Long Room was open from 10 a.m. until 4 p.m. on Mondays to Fridays, except between November and January when it closed at 3 p.m. (there was still no artificial light), and on Saturdays it was open throughout

---

[1] Parke produced three reports during his first five years in office, setting out in detail the state of the Library. They are now MUN/LIB/17/113 and MUN/LIB/17/114 (December 1949 and December 1951) and MUN/V/6/8, p. 184 (June 1954); unless otherwise indicated they form the basis of the statistical information in this chapter.

[2] MUN/LIB/3/3, 7 March, 20 May 1949. [3] *DU Calendar*, 1950–1.

Figure 23   Overcrowding in the 1937 Reading Room, *c.*1960 (H. W. Parke, *The Library of Trinity College Dublin: a historical description* [Dublin: Trinity College, 1961], p. 11)

the year from 10 a.m. until 1 p.m. By 1950, Parke had begun to implement the changes in the Long Room that had been so firmly resisted by Smyly. The contents of the exhibition cases had been rearranged and newly labelled, and much of the clutter, such as the plaster casts and photographic reproductions that had been there since the time of Abbott, had been removed. The room was also the venue for temporary exhibitions, an initiative of the Friends of the Library. The whole of the Colonnades contained steel shelving for books and periodicals, and newly catalogued material was still being added to the shelves there. This material represented only a minor part of the Library's intake, however, the remainder of which occupied six other locations in the College, including the former Officers Training Corps huts and several basements. Most of these were not satisfactory even as stores – and their contents were far from readily accessible.[4]

As well as the College Library in its various locations, both official and unofficial, there was also a range of departmental collections and three other libraries important enough to warrant separate entries in the University *Calendar*. The Lecky Library, in the Museum Building, was a collection of books from which historians could borrow, and the Lending Library in the same building served a similar purpose for students of classics, theology,

[4]   MUN/LIB/17/115.

mathematics and civil engineering, but its opening hours were extraordinarily limited: 2–2.30 p.m. on Mondays in term. The Economics, History and Law Joint Library, which had been established in 1935 in Number 25, was a source of books for students in those subjects. None of those libraries was under the control of the College Librarian.

It was obvious to all who knew the Library that many books were not being catalogued, but it is unlikely that anyone, perhaps not even those on the Library staff, was aware of the scale of this until Parke investigated. His report makes depressing reading. Since it acquired the right of legal deposit, the Library had rarely attempted to catalogue all of its acquisitions, especially those deemed insufficiently academic, but from the late 1880s this policy was applied to an ever greater proportion of the intake. Parke calculated that by 1950 less than 5 per cent of the novels, children's books and 'pamphlets' (i.e. paperbacks) had been catalogued, and only 6 per cent of the poetry and plays. School textbooks, guidebooks, maps and music were not catalogued at all, and books in series were given a single series-entry, with the result that all the titles in the Everyman series, for example, were subsumed under one entry in the catalogue. The number of 'postponed books' had risen to about 10,000; scientific textbooks were simply discarded when a new edition was received; and most of the recently received older books, especially donations, were not catalogued. It was now clear why the Library's more recent reports showed an annual intake of around 7,500 volumes a year, whereas the actual number received was close to the 16,000 recorded by the other legal-deposit libraries. Parke estimated that the total number of volumes in the Library was not the 550,000 that appeared in the reports but was in reality about 800,000.[5]

As far as periodicals were concerned, some of those received were catalogued and shelved in the Colonnades, but many were not. Parke was unable to find any issues of the uncatalogued titles dating from before 1942, and so he assumed that they must have been pulped. Parts received after that date had been stored in the Catacombs below the Reading Room, initially in a vague alphabetical order, but often the boxes had collapsed or the piles of periodicals had fallen, leading to a state of complete disarray.

Parke acknowledged that a lack of space had contributed to this situation, but that the main problem was a severe shortage of staff. There were eighteen members of staff in 1950, compared to about a hundred in both the Bodleian and Cambridge University Library. The calibre of the staff was also an issue. He noted that, 'though hard working [they] had not sufficient scholarly

[5] MUN/LIB/15/105c.

equipment. Too many of them had been drawn from our Honors School of History. Most of them had taken to work in the library because they could get nothing better elsewhere'.[6] They were led by Hanna, most of whose library experience was limited to working under Smyly. He seems to have developed an astonishing degree of complacency – or perhaps denial – or simply knew nothing better. In a report to the Registrar in 1949 he said that the arrangements for handling legal-deposit materials were working 'satisfactorily'. Most categories of books were, he said,

catalogued as expeditiously as possible. Exceptions are novels and children's books [which] are delayed for later consideration . . . Important pamphlets are catalogued. Unimportant pamphlets are not catalogued. They used to be kept under subjects, and are now kept in alphabetical order. They are easily turned up on request. Unimportant periodicals . . . are at present kept in alphabetical order in the basement of the reading room or in the Museum Building.[7]

This was a scenario that was utterly different from that perceived and described by Parke.

Although Smyly could have acted to mitigate the effects of the Library's underfunding, it was to some extent inevitable given the College's precarious financial position until the provision of the state grant at the end of the 1940s. Between 1914 and 1948 the Library's budget remained at around 3.5 per cent of the College's expenditure, but that expenditure had been severely constrained because it was dependent upon the interest from endowments, which had fallen sharply after 1914.[8] This meant that Trinity was trying to handle the same legal-deposit intake as Oxford and Cambridge on a budget that was far smaller than that of those libraries. Its financial position vis-à-vis its sister institutions had worsened dramatically over the previous 70 years. In the mid 1870s the budgets for the three libraries were broadly comparable, with Trinity's set at £2,500, Cambridge University Library's at £2,800 and the Bodleian's at £3,600. By 1912, Trinity was spending about £3,000 a year on its Library, compared to £7,500 at Cambridge and £15,000 at Oxford, but it was in the period following the First World War when the differences became extreme. Throughout the 1930s and the early 1940s library expenditure at Trinity remained static, at around £4,000 a year. By 1950, the Bodleian's budget had risen to £84,000 and Cambridge's to £64,000, and though Trinity's more than doubled after the allocation of the state grant in 1947 and then Parke's appointment, this still brought it to

---

[6] MUN/LIB/3/3, 10 November 1950.   [7] MUN/V/6/8, p. 41.
[8] McDowell and Webb, pp. 472–3, 509–15.

only £9,200. Of that, £5,400 was spent on salaries, compared to £40,000 at Cambridge and £47,000 at Oxford. Both the other libraries spent between £8,000 and £10,000 a year on foreign books and periodicals, whilst Trinity's figure was only about £1,700.[9]

Comparisons with other Irish or British university libraries are less relevant, as none is as large as the three deposit libraries and none receives a large proportion of its acquisitions in the same way. The information available from other institutions for 1950 is piecemeal, but it is clear that Trinity's library budget compared poorly, not just to those of Oxford and Cambridge, but to those of other major libraries. Edinburgh and Manchester, for example, spent more than Trinity's total budget of £9,200 on acquisitions alone (about £12,000–£13,000), and at Glasgow, where the expenditure on acquisitions and binding was £8,500, the staff costs were over £14,500. Even University College Dublin, which served a student body of something over 3,000 compared to about 2,400 at Trinity, was spending more than Trinity on a much smaller library: £5,000 a year on acquisitions and £4,800 on staff. It had sixteen library staff, only two fewer than Trinity's eighteen, for an intake of books that was about one-third of Trinity's.[10]

[9] MUN/LIB/15/47; 'Annual report of the Library Syndicate', *Cambridge University Reporter, passim*; 'Annual report of the Curators of the Bodleian Library', *Oxford University Gazette, passim.*

[10] Figures supplied from their archives by the university libraries cited.

17 | Parke: 1949–1965

After Smyly's death, the Board was evenly divided on whether the vacancy should be advertised externally but, since those against such a radical departure from tradition included a majority of the Senior Fellows, they carried the day.[1] An advertisement was, however, distributed within the College, the Board stating its intention to elect the Librarian from among its Fellows or MAs, the salary to be £900 a year, reduced to £400 if the successful candidate were a salaried lecturer or professor, or £300 if a Fellow.[2]

Two members of the academic staff who had been closely involved with the Library, Herbert Parke and David Webb, applied for the post. In their applications both acknowledged that they had no experience of library administration, but Webb, the scientist, stressed the need to make the Library more accessible and to resolve the issue of cataloguing legal-deposit books once and for all, whilst Parke, the classicist, emphasised the desirability of comprehensive collecting.[3] Parke was successful and was appointed with effect from 22 June 1949.[4] (See Figure 24.) Though incomparably more committed to his responsibilities in the Library than his predecessor, Parke nonetheless continued the College tradition of retaining his academic duties alongside those of the Librarian. He remained as Professor of Ancient History throughout his tenure as Librarian and in 1952, when he became a Senior Fellow, added the office of Vice-Provost.

The Augean stables

Parke's first task was to try and impose some order on the chaos that he had inherited. He began in the Librarian's Room, where he found papyri and other manuscripts in the drawers of Smyly's desk, eighteenth-century broadsheets relating to Swift, and uncatalogued pamphlets from the Fagel collection in parcels marked 'duplicates'. Simply by walking around the Library he unearthed caches of uncatalogued material, including Fagel books, and

---

[1] MUN/V/5/27, 2 February 1949.   [2] MUN/LIB/3/3 (advertisement, 28 April 1949).
[3] MUN/P/54/14/141–MUN/P/54/14/142.   [4] MUN/V/5/27, 22 June 1949.

Figure 24 Herbert Parke, Librarian 1949–65, Curator of the Library 1965–73 (left), with Dr F. H. Boland, Chancellor of the University, at the reopening of the Long Room on 12 May 1970 (*Irish Times*)

incunabula given by Samuel Tickell, whose donations had remained uncatalogued since 1918.[5]

5 MUN/LIB/17/113–MUN/LIB/17/114.

During the interregnum before Parke's election, the Library Committee had pressed the Board to proceed with the appointment of a Superintendent of the Reading Room, a post so implacably opposed by Smyly. The committee said that it was 'unacquainted with any great library other than ours where such inadequate supervision is provided'. It was undertaken by 'a boy who supplies readers with books, and generally looks after their wants as well as his limited education allows [but is] incapable of giving intelligent answers to the kind of questions readers in a library are likely to ask'.[6] The Board agreed, and William O'Sullivan, a Trinity History graduate who had worked for the Irish Manuscripts Commission, was appointed, to start on 1 July 1949.[7] O'Sullivan's puzzlement at the state of the reference collection in the Reading Room is palpable from the commonplace book in which he recorded his impressions and plans, noting that the books were arranged not in any comprehensible subject-order but according to size, and that they were there simply because they had been moved from the old Reading Room more than a decade earlier.[8] On Parke's instructions, he prepared a card index of the reference books and circulated sections to academic departments so that the collection could be weeded and brought up to date.

In October 1948, the first annual conference of the legal-deposit libraries had taken place in Oxford, with Hanna as the Trinity representative. Aware of his own lack of experience of running a library, Parke took the opportunity of the second conference, in Cambridge the following year, to visit the University Library, the Copyright Agency and other libraries. He was shown Cambridge's approach to the cataloguing of 'non-academic' books and realised that it offered a potential solution to Trinity's arrears of uncatalogued material. At Cambridge, novels were not normally included in the general catalogue but were listed in a separate card catalogue. Parke saw this as a 'defensible procedure' that would allow him to clear the backlog. The undertaking that the College had given to the Publishers' Association in 1946, that all novels would be catalogued or returned, had been honoured more in the breach than the observance. Some books had been returned and some catalogued, but most novels received in the previous 4 years remained untouched. He estimated that it would cost £200 to employ one typist for a year to list the 10,000 novels received since 1945.[9] The Board authorised him to proceed, the cost to be borne by the Library.[10] The typist remained on the staff until June 1951, by which time she had produced cards for over

---

[6] MUN/P/54/14/144.   [7] MUN/V/5/27, 16 February, 25 May 1949.   [8] MUN/LIB/4/22.
[9] MUN/LIB/32/51, 14 October 1949.   [10] MUN/V/5/27, 26 October 1949.

forty thousand novels, including individual titles that had previously been subsumed within series entries.

Having started to make progress with the novels, Parke proposed to adopt a similar approach for the 'pamphlets' (which included substantial literary works published in soft covers) that had been arriving since the late nineteenth century and had not been catalogued. In October 1951 he persuaded the Board to provide a grant of £1,000 for a year to reduce the arrears of cataloguing, arguing that the Library was vulnerable to charges that it contained quantities of legal-deposit material of which it had no record.[11] This grant was renewed annually, and by 1954, Parke's approach to cataloguing and card-indexing had begun to make serious inroads into the backlog of uncatalogued books. Entries for several thousand plays and books of poetry were now in the catalogue, and over 100,000 cards had been produced for novels, children's books and the 'pamphlets'. He estimated that within 4 years the cataloguing of all books received by legal deposit would be up to date.[12]

A card catalogue of music was also started, but the maps and large numbers of periodicals remained to be tackled, and the problems of over-crowding in the Reading Room had become acute.[13] (See Figure 23.) In October 1949, shortly after his appointment, Parke had suggested that, as an interim measure to alleviate this pressure, the Magnetic Observatory should be converted into a periodicals reading room, with current issues of journals on display. The maps stored there would be moved to the Museum Building and the Geography Department. His proposal had the support of the Library Committee but the Board postponed the plans on the grounds of economy.[14]

The shortage of space in the Reading Room meant that manuscripts had to be read in the Long Room, which exposed their users to disturbance by visitors and to the difficulties of working in a room with no artificial lighting or heating. Parke was also conscious that there was no member of staff with any expertise in manuscripts. In 1950, he brought over from Oxford the Reader in Documentary Papyrology, Colin Roberts, to advise on the preservation of the papyri, and in 1953 he sent William O'Sullivan to the British Museum for training in the administration of a manuscripts

[11] MUN/LIB/15/52–MUN/LIB/15/53.   [12] MUN/V/6/8, p. 184.

[13] Roy Stanley, 'Music collections at Trinity College Dublin', *Brio*, 39/2 (Autumn/Winter 2002), 32–7.

[14] MUN/LIB/32/51, 29 October 1949; MUN/LIB/3/3, 18 November 1949; MUN/V/5/27, 11 January 1950.

collection.[15] On his return, O'Sullivan was transferred from the Reading Room to become Assistant in Charge of Manuscripts, and the room on the ground floor of the West Pavilion, where the manuscripts were stored, was additionally pressed into service as a manuscripts reading room.[16] Parke regarded this as only a temporary expedient and, having failed to obtain permission to convert the Magnetic Observatory into a periodicals reading room, he now revived his plan to transfer the maps to the Museum Building, this time with the intention of converting the Observatory into a manuscripts store and reading room. (See Figure 19.) A. A. Luce, one of the Senior Fellows, objected strongly to the proposal to place the manuscripts in 'a lonely little building within twenty yards of a public thoroughfare in an . . . unpatrolled part of College'.[17] The Board, however, approved Parke's plan and the new Manuscripts Room, used for both the storage and reading of manuscripts, in what became known as 'the Temple', was opened by the Taoiseach, Éamon de Valera, on 3 June 1957.[18] The space in the West Pavilion vacated by the manuscripts was converted into an office for the Deputy Librarian and a room for the receipt of incoming material.

Parke recognised that it was unrealistic to expect the Library's budget to be increased to a level approaching that of Oxford or Cambridge, but even the National Library of Ireland, with a much smaller intake of books, had more staff than the College Library. In 1951, he requested two additional Library Assistants, as well as improvements to the salaries of the existing staff, proposals that would increase the staff costs from about £4,600 a year to £6,600. He also asked for the non-pay expenditure to be doubled from £1,500 (plus £600 for the Copyright Agency), especially as the increase provided in 1947 had been largely eliminated as a result of the devaluation of the pound. Two years later he was still pleading, and the only relief he had received was a continuation of the grant of £1,000 a year to reduce the cataloguing backlog.[19]

Provost Alton, though a supporter of the Library, was faced with a government that was antipathetic to everything that Trinity represented. At a meeting with the then Taoiseach, John Costello, and the Minister for Finance in 1951, the Provost argued that the Library should be staffed at least at the same level as the National Library, and he described the remuneration of the

---

[15] MUN/LIB/17/114.

[16] MUN/V/5/27, 18 February 1953, 26 June 1954; Bernard Meehan, 'William O'Sullivan', *Long Room*, 46 (2001), 16–17.

[17] MUN/LIB/3/3, 16 October 1953.

[18] MUN/V/5/27, 30 June 1954; W. O'Sullivan, 'The new Manuscripts Room', *Annual Bulletin*, (1958), 12–13.

[19] MUN/LIB/3/3, 19 January 1951; MUN/LIB/15/47d, MUN/LIB/15/51 and MUN/LIB/15/67.

current staff as 'quite unreasonably low'.[20] The Minister, the same Patrick McGilligan who had been so hostile to Thrift and Purser in 1925, was intransigent, saying that Trinity could not expect to receive state funding on the same basis as University College Dublin, as it was not a public institution, catering as it did for only 7 per cent of the population and having many students whom he described as 'immigrants from Britain'.[21] A change of government later that year and the return of de Valera as Taoiseach led to a more sympathetic approach to Trinity's financial plight, and in November 1951 the government was sent a memorandum on the College's needs, which included a request for more Library staff, an increase in salaries and a larger acquisitions budget.[22] In 1952, A. J. McConnell succeeded Alton as Provost. He was determined to redress Trinity's former isolation and restore the College's position in Irish public life, a strategy that was facilitated by the need to have regular contact with ministers about the government grant and by his own personal friendship with de Valera.

For the Library, this new relationship bore fruit in the form of consistent state funding, first for more staff and a more generous budget for general running costs, and eventually for a new building. Parke was allowed to appoint an additional Library Assistant and to advertise for a Deputy Librarian to replace Hanna, who was due to retire.[23] Robert Dougan, the City Librarian of the Scottish city of Perth and the first professionally qualified librarian to join the staff, was appointed from 1 September 1952. Hanna retired the same month, after 52 years' service.[24] Dougan held office for 6 years, until his appointment as Librarian of the Huntington Library at Pasadena, California, and on 1 May 1958 he was replaced as Deputy Librarian by another public librarian, John Hurst, from Manchester Central Reference Library.[25]

Having tolerated inadequate salaries for years, the Library staff expressed their dissatisfaction in 1953 and complained again 2 years later.[26] This led to a general staffing review, and new grades of Assistant Librarian and senior Assistant Librarian were created. Plans for a new staff structure were also drawn up, with Departments of Manuscripts and Printed Books, each headed by a Keeper, to be implemented when adequate funding became available.[27]

---

[20] NAI, Department of the Taoiseach, S13962 B/1, report of meeting, 19 March 1951.

[21] *Ibid.*　[22] *Ibid.*, 'Memorandum on the needs of Trinity College Dublin, November 1951'.

[23] MUN/V/5/27, 1 October 1951, 13 February 1952.　[24] *Ibid.*, 21 May 1952.

[25] MUN/V/5/28, 29 January, 12 March 1958; F. J. E. Hurst, 'Mr R. O. Dougan', *Annual Bulletin* (1958), 16.

[26] MUN/LIB/15/66 and MUN/LIB/15/72–MUN/LIB/15/77.

[27] MUN/V/5/27, 4 May, 25 June 1955; MUN/V/6/8, p. 224.

Legal deposit

The threat to the Library's legal-deposit status continued to lurk just below the surface. The constitutional relationship between Ireland and the United Kingdom had been left deliberately vague by de Valera in 1937, when the new Irish constitution was ratified, but by 1948 the Costello government decided that the position must be clarified. The proposed repeal of the Executive Authority (External Relations) Act, 1936, alarmed the College, but assurance was received from the Taoiseach that the position of the legal-deposit libraries on both sides of the Irish Sea would be unaffected by any constitutional changes.[28] The passing of the Republic of Ireland Act in Dublin at the end of 1948 provided for the establishment of a republic the following year and the departure of Ireland from the Commonwealth.

This gave Sir Stanley Unwin the opportunity to make another attempt at stirring the legal-deposit pot, but a letter from him to *The Times* was not published, and support from the Publishers' Association was lukewarm.[29] Nonetheless, he wrote to the *Observer* complaining that 'Eire has secured her complete independence from Britain, but British publishers have not secured their independence from Eire' and said that it was time for 'this now completely indefensible taxation' to be removed from Westminster legislation.[30] His demands were brought to the attention of the British government's working party which was preparing the Ireland Bill. It had been agreed by both British and Irish ministers that the legislation confirming Irish independence would not affect reciprocal trade preferences and that neither country would treat the other or its citizens as 'foreign'. The working party consulted various government departments in London and received a clear indication that Unwin's wishes should be ignored, as the policy of regarding Ireland as 'not foreign' meant that as many as possible of the special links were to be maintained.[31] The Commonwealth Relations Office sent a firmly worded response, making the point that the obligation was reciprocal and not particularly onerous for British publishers, and that the chief sufferer would be Trinity, which was 'actually and traditionally particularly well disposed towards this country'.[32] The Ireland Act, passed at Westminster in 1949, duly left the existing legislation on legal deposit unchanged.[33]

---

[28] MUN/V/6/8, p. 32.
[29] RUL, Records of George Allen & Unwin Ltd, AUC 428/7; Publishers' Association, *Members' Circular*, 25 (1949), 12.
[30] *Observer*, 20 February 1949.   [31] TNA, T 233/240.   [32] TNA, T 233/240/8.
[33] Ireland Act, 1949 (12, 13 & 14 George VI, c. 41).

Scarcely had one threat receded, however, than another emerged. Following the revision, in 1948, of the International Convention for the Protection of Literary and Artistic Works, the British government recognised that the copyright provisions of the 1911 Act needed to be reviewed. The Copyright Committee (the 'Gregory Committee'), set up to carry out this task, was not formally established until April 1951, but the manoeuvring began a year earlier. In April 1950, Unwin wrote to the Board of Trade, which was responsible for the review, to ask for the position of the deposit libraries, especially Trinity, to be reconsidered.[34] At the Copyright Libraries Conference in September 1950 it was agreed that the libraries would argue for the legal-deposit provisions of the 1911 Act to be retained without change, but the united front presented by the four belied a divergence of views behind the scenes. Unknown to Trinity and the National Library of Scotland, Cambridge and the Bodleian had prepared a memorandum setting out the policy that they would pursue in the event of a revision to the Act. H. R. Creswick, the Cambridge Librarian, told his colleagues at the Bodleian that Oxford and Cambridge were 'on a different footing' from the other two libraries, 'Edinburgh having different grounds on which to fight, and Dublin having a poor case anyhow'.[35]

The Copyright Libraries Conference the following year approved a memorandum to the Gregory Committee on behalf of all four libraries. It argued that they performed a national service, that the present system worked well and that no grounds had been adduced for any changes. Furthermore, in response to claims that some libraries failed to preserve or catalogue books received, it stated 'categorically that none of the libraries alienates any book claimed by it . . . and that all such books are kept so that they are available to readers and are made so available at the earliest practicable moment'.[36] Parke and the Vice-Provost, A. A. Luce, were appointed to give evidence on Trinity's behalf before the committee, but before they left for London they were summoned to the Taoiseach's office, where de Valera expressed his support for the deposit libraries, especially Trinity, and urged them to make every effort to persuade the committee not to recommend any changes to the 1911 Act. He also agreed to support any protest, should the outcome be unfavourable. Parke and Luce went armed with a statement that Trinity was fully conscious of its obligations and that it had the resources to meet them.[37]

[34] RUL, note 29 above, AUC 438/2.   [35] CUA ULIB/7/2/26/1, June 1950.

[36] *Ibid.*, Memorandum, 27 September 1951.

[37] MUN/LIB/15/614; MUN/LIB/3/3, 9 November 1951; MUN/V/5/27, 8 October 1951.

Unwin resumed his correspondence with *The Times*, referring back to his campaign of 1942 and demanding to know whether Trinity had now catalogued all the legal-deposit books it had received.[38] He also wrote to Creswick and the Cambridge Vice-Chancellor saying that he would have responded positively to the libraries' memorandum to the committee had it applied just to Oxford and Cambridge, but he was 'shocked' at the others' 'reckless defence' of Trinity.[39]

The Gregory Committee presented its report in October 1952.[40] It acknowledged that the Act placed a burden on publishers but considered that this was comparatively small, and in view of its long-standing nature the committee did not recommend any change to the legislation. In a separate paragraph on Trinity it noted Unwin's objections and the fact that his assertions about the cataloguing situation in the Library had been refuted by the College. It concluded that, as the intention of the Ireland Act was to alter the relationship between the United Kingdom and the Republic as little as possible, the removal of Trinity's right of legal deposit would be a retrograde step of little benefit to the publishers but of great cost in other ways. So the College could breathe again.

Unwin was not the only publisher who objected to the deposit legislation. Throughout the 1950s the Cork firm, Mercier Press, sought to avoid its obligations. It not only failed to deposit with the Copyright Agency but in 1953 also refused to supply books to the National Library of Ireland, which was forced to ask the Irish government to take legal action.[41] This seems to have had little long-term effect, as minutes of the Copyright Libraries Conferences for the next decade recorded the publisher's continued intransigence. In the end, the Irish government again took action, and in 1958 Mercier was successfully prosecuted.[42] After that, the firm deposited books intermittently, though for a time John Feehan, its Managing Director, insisted that communications from the Copyright Agency in London would be answered only if they were written in Irish.[43] In a letter to the *Irish Times* he objected to what he described as the forcible acquisition of private property by the state and made the interesting assertion that the provisions of the Copyright Act 'strike at the very fundamentals of Christian teaching and flatly contradict the teachings of the Papal Encyclicals'.[44] In a later autobiographical book

---

[38] *The Times*, 19 and 23 November 1951.   [39] CUA ULIB/7/2/27, 12 November 1951.
[40] Board of Trade, *Report of the Copyright Committee*, [Cmd. 8662], 1951–2, IX, 573.
[41] CUA ULIB/7/2/27, 28 August 1953.   [42] *Irish Times*, 9 December 1958.
[43] CUA ULIB/7/2/26/3, Minutes of Copyright Libraries' Annual Conferences, 1956–64.
[44] *Irish Times*, 13 December 1958.

he devoted a whole chapter to the iniquity of legal deposit and to what he regarded as Trinity's anomalous position.[45]

A tongue-in-cheek piece by A. P. Herbert in the *Spectator* in 1960 mocked legal deposit as a 'shameless attempt ... [at] statutory robbery' and repeated Unwin's allegation that Trinity sold books that had been deposited.[46] This elicited a robust response from Provost McConnell, who described the article as 'unhelpful' when the College was trying to raise funds to build a new Library. Herbert wrote a conciliatory piece in the *Spectator* and sent a cheque for the appeal, and the President of the Publishers' Association visited the Library when he was in Dublin. He confirmed that all books supplied by publishers were now being 'assiduously catalogued'.[47] Herbert's article roused not only Unwin but also Feehan, who demanded the removal of legal deposit from the Irish Act, which was about to be revised. A new Irish Copyright Act was approved in 1963 and, despite an attempt in the Dáil to remove the legal-deposit provisions, they continued as before, except that St Patrick's College, Maynooth, was added to the list of Irish deposit libraries, bringing the total number of libraries that had to be supplied by Irish publishers to eleven.[48]

The New Library

The College's memorandum to the government in December 1946, which had resulted in the provision of a state grant, had not mentioned the Library among its capital needs, but 2 years later a similar memorandum warned that an extension would soon be required. It noted Trinity's national role, the overcrowding in the Reading Room, the need for storage and the fact that more staff were required, but pointed out that, even if the salaries could be funded, it would be difficult to find space for additional staff to work. A building to rectify the problems would cost at least £100,000, and the College was placing this need on record, though not requesting 'such a large sum' at present.[49]

---

[45] John M. Feehan, *An Irish publisher and his world* (Cork: Mercier Press, 1969), pp. 85–98.

[46] A. P. Herbert, 'Cheap literature', *Spectator*, No. 6863 (8 January 1960), 37–8.

[47] Publishers' Association, *Members' Circular*, 36 (1960), 100.

[48] *Spectator*, Nos. 6864–6 (15, 22 and 29 January 1960); RUL, Records of George Allen & Unwin Ltd., AUC 872/1; NAI, Department of the Taoiseach, S3641 C/61; *Dáil Éireann Debates*, vol. CLXXXVIII, cols. 1385–7, 2 May 1961; Copyright Act, 1963.

[49] MUN/V/6/8, p. 33.

The Gregory Committee's confirmation of Trinity's legal-deposit status in 1952 meant that books would continue to pour into the Library from the Agency, and so it was now a matter of urgency to make provision for storing them. In October that year Parke proposed three options for discussion. His preferred solution was a large new building close to the Old Library. Because of its sensitive location, such a building would have to be 'an imposing piece of architecture', which would cost more than the College could afford from its own resources, and so funding would have to be sought from the government or a philanthropic source such as the Rockefeller Foundation. A second option would be to erect a book-store at the east end of the College. This would be cheaper and could be designed in such a way that additional floors could be added as needed. A third possibility, which might prove more attractive to the government, would be to build a joint store with the National Library. This could be outside the city centre and, whilst Trinity's ownership of its collection would not be surrendered, the National Library might be allowed to 'borrow' the College's books for the use of its own readers.[50]

The concept of sharing resources between Trinity and the National Library was not a new one. In 1943, R. J. Hayes, the Director of the National Library, had proposed such a scheme to Provost Alton. He predicted that the government would have to provide a new building for the National Library after the war and suggested that 'some kind of link' with the College Library might be considered, whereby the collections could be used for the benefit of each library's users.[51] In 1945, Aubrey Gwynn, a historian at University College Dublin and a nephew of the former Provost, went even further by suggesting to Alton that 'a handsome building', which would serve as a link between the College Library and the National Library, should be erected at public expense, on a site adjacent to Nassau Street. This would not only solve the storage problems of the two libraries but, if combined with co-ordinated purchasing, could release money to buy foreign books, especially those from the USA. His proposal was politely rejected by Alton, who said that although he wanted to build another reading room and a proper book-store he did not think it would be possible for the College to spare any land for 'a general public library'.[52]

After considering Parke's paper of October 1952, the Board set up a committee, chaired by the Provost, which recommended that the College should adopt 'an ambitious scheme' to construct a building as large as the Old Library, located at its south-east corner, to accommodate book-storage,

---

[50] MUN/LIB/17/115.   [51] MUN/LIB/15/438.   [52] MUN/LIB/15/440–MUN/LIB/15/441.

reading and administration space. A less desirable smaller option would be to create a new science library and thus release space in the existing Library buildings. The Board chose the more comprehensive proposal, which the committee calculated would provide library accommodation for more than 150 years and would cost £500,000.[53] Even though that figure already represented a five-fold increase in the projected cost of the new library since the submission to the government in 1948, planning for the building over the next decade was characterised by an unrealistic appraisal of the College's future development and the size of library that would be required to provide adequate accommodation for both readers and books. Financial constraints were a major limiting factor and it would have been impossible to imagine the full extent of the growth both in the size of the College and the number of books being published, but each stage in the planning process was marked by an over-optimistic view of how far the new building would meet the College's needs.

Work on a fundraising strategy began in March 1953. R. B. D. French, a lecturer in English, wrote the text for a well-designed and finely printed hardback booklet setting out the case for support from 'all lovers of learning' and expressing the hope that the booklet would 'succeed in persuading some foundation or generous benefactor to come to our assistance'.[54] A University of Dublin Educational Trust was established to encourage donations from the USA, but a request for some of the Marshall Aid being given to Ireland was turned down by de Valera on the grounds that the building of a library was outside the scope of the scheme.[55]

The campaign was opened by Provost McConnell in October 1954 with a target figure of £450,000, of which Lord Iveagh, the Chancellor of the University, had pledged one-tenth.[56] A Library Extension Fund was established, and by the end of 1956 a further £40,000 had been added to Lord Iveagh's pledge of £45,000.[57] A collecting box was put into the Long Room in an attempt to attract donations and an appeal to graduates was launched in 1957. Progress was slow, but as the momentum gradually increased the Library Extension Committee was reconstituted, with an executive consisting of the Provost, Bursar, Registrar and Librarian, to which reported an

[53] MUN/V/6/8, p. 122; MUN/V/5/27, 3 December 1952, 11 March 1953.
[54] R. B. D. French, *The Library of Trinity College Dublin: a great library and its needs* (Dublin: Three Candles, 1954).
[55] MUN/V/5/27, 27 January 1954; NAI, Department of the Taoiseach, S13962 B/2, 9 and 22 February 1954.
[56] *Irish Times*, 15 October 1954.
[57] MUN/V/5/27, 26 October, 9 November 1955; MUN/V/5/28, 10 October 1956.

appeal section (which included R. B. D. French) and a building section (of which Dougan and the College Architect, Ian Roberts, were members). To relieve Parke of having to direct the project, John Luce, a lecturer in classics, was appointed as Executive Officer.[58]

Parke produced a draft specification for the new building that included storage for the books and other materials currently located all over the College, specialist reading rooms for users of periodicals and maps, together with administrative offices and working space for Library staff. The building would be linked to the Old Library via the ground floor of the East Pavilion, where the Newspaper Room would be converted into a reading room for postgraduates and academic staff.[59] Ian Roberts was appointed to work with the Librarian on the details, calculating the space required and the options for allocating it among the various activities.[60] They recommended that the new Library should be designed in such a way that it could be built in self-contained sections with, in the first phase, space for 100 readers, storage capacity for not less than 50 years' intake and the possibility of expansion to take at least a further 100 years' acquisitions.[61]

On 15 July 1958, with £100,000 now donated or pledged, the appeal moved into a more public phase, with a reception in the Long Room, attended by both the President, Seán T. O'Kelly, and the Taoiseach, Éamon de Valera, at which the campaign was launched, with a new target of £500,000.[62] The appeal booklet stressed the position of the library at the heart of a university and drew the analogy – a somewhat unexpected one from a neutral country – that universities were the 'common defences for the preservation of learning and fair thinking. Efficient defences cost money. Two modern fighter aircraft now cost half a million. And that is exactly the figure for which we are asking'.[63] The booklet was widely circulated to businesses and other organisations in Ireland immediately after the launch. A film, *Building for books*, had been commissioned, with a script by French and direction by Vincent Corcoran. After its première at the 1958 Cork Film Festival, when it was awarded a certificate of merit, it was distributed by the Rank Organisation for showing in public cinemas. A separate committee was established to run the British campaign, which was launched a few months later with a showing of the film.[64]

[58] MUN/V/5/28, 29 May, 13 November 1957; J. V. Luce, *Trinity College Dublin: the first 400 years* (Dublin: Trinity College Dublin Press, 1992), pp. 162–7.
[59] MUN/LIB/3/3, 9 March 1955.   [60] MUN/LIB/15/540–MUN/LIB/15/541.
[61] MUN/LIB/32/58; MUN/LIB/32/40, May 1958.   [62] *The Times, Irish Times*, etc., 16 July 1958.
[63] *Trinity College Dublin: Library extension appeal* [1958], TCD EPB 147.c.42, No. 3.
[64] J. V. Luce, 'A report on the progress of the Library extension appeal', *Annual Bulletin* (1958), 14–15.

At this point discussions resumed with the National Library, where Hayes was still seeking a solution to that institution's space problems. In February 1959, he discussed with de Valera a proposal to erect a building on Trinity's Nassau Street frontage, to contain the National Library and the extension to the College Library. It would have separate reading rooms for the two libraries and the collections would remain distinct, but books from each would be available to both libraries' readers. He listed the advantages: the scheme would double the research material that was 'freely available to the Irish people', including the technical and industrial publications of the United Kingdom; the National Library would acquire 'a perfect site'; and money would be saved in the long run because both libraries would seek to avoid future duplication of acquisitions.[65]

The civil servants recognised that the proposal was potentially political dynamite that would require very careful handling and, if it became public, 'sharp criticism' could be expected from both University College Dublin and the Catholic hierarchy, neither of which was favourably disposed towards Trinity.[66] The Archbishop of Dublin, John Charles McQuaid, had already declared it a mortal sin for parents in the Dublin archdiocese to send their children to the College without his permission. In the face of the expected opposition, and following de Valera's resignation as Taoiseach on his election to the presidency, the matter was allowed to lie until it was raised again by Provost McConnell, who sought a meeting with the new Taoiseach, Seán Lemass, in March 1960. McConnell conveyed Trinity's support for Hayes' proposal as being of national importance, and he expressed the College's view that the government should give it very serious consideration, as 'the opportunity of implementing such a scheme will not arise again'.[67] He sought to circumvent the inevitable objections from the hierarchy by stating expressly that readers would be able to enter the National Library's reading room from Nassau Street without passing through Trinity at all.[68]

Hayes was asked to recast his proposal in a form that Lemass could discuss with the archbishop. He removed Trinity's name from the title, emphasised the advantages of the scheme to the National Library and sent his revised version to Maurice Moynihan, the Government Secretary, with the comment:

---

65 NAI, Department of the Taoiseach, S13795 B/61, 'Proposed heads of agreement between the Government of Ireland and Trinity College, Dublin'. See also John Bowman, '"The wolf in sheep's clothing": Richard Hayes' proposal for a new National Library of Ireland, 1959–60', in Ronald J. Hill and Michael Marsh, eds., *Modern Irish democracy: essays in honour of Basil Chubb* (Dublin: Irish Academic Press, 1993), pp. 44–61; Brendan Grimes, '"Will not be heard of again": a proposal to combine the resources of the National Library and Trinity College Library', *Long Room*, 46 (2001), 18–23.
66 NAI, Department of the Taoiseach, S13795 B/61, 12 August 1959. 67 *Ibid.*, 11 March 1960.
68 *Ibid.*, 15 March 1960.

'I enclose the wolf in sheep's clothing.'[69] The scheme now had Moynihan's support and that of Tarlach Ó Raifeartaigh, Secretary of the Department of Education, though the latter expressed concern at the 'extrinsic aspects of the matter', by which he meant McQuaid's likely opposition.[70] Lemass sent the proposal to the archbishop, with a request for a meeting. The outcome was hardly unexpected. McQuaid stated that the bishops were unanimous in opposing the plan, because of the 'undesirability' of suggesting that the government regarded Trinity 'as the most important centre of higher education in the state . . . The chief university institution in a mainly Catholic community should manifestly be a Catholic institution.'[71] In the face of this response from the hierarchy, Lemass decided that the scheme should be dropped, but sweetened the pill when he relayed the news to McConnell by suggesting that a government grant for the new library might be forthcoming.[72]

By late 1959, the College Board recognised that insufficient progress was being made with the fundraising and that professional help was needed. The public-relations firm of Brewster Owen was appointed to advise on the appeal in Britain. Their proposals to breathe life into the campaign included a suggestion that Samuel Beckett might be asked to compose 'a masque' related to the Library.[73] French, who had maintained contact with the writer since the time he had been a student at Trinity, passed on the request, and though Beckett felt unable to produce a masque to order, he supported the appeal by donating a year's worth of royalties from the North American performances of *Krapp's last tape*, which was playing to full houses on Broadway.[74] A professional fundraiser was also appointed to plan the North American campaign, which culminated in a visit to several cities by the Vice-Chancellor, Lord Rosse, in 1959, though a proposal to take the Book of Kells across the Atlantic was dropped because of government opposition.[75] In June 1960, a scheme was launched whereby members of the public donating at least one guinea to the Library Extension Fund could ask for a bookplate bearing their name to be inserted into a book already in the Library.[76]

The most ambitious part of the campaign was an exhibition held at the Royal Academy of Arts, Burlington House, London, between January and March 1961. As well as the Library's manuscript treasures, several of which had never before left Ireland, the exhibition included pictures and silver

[69] *Ibid.*, 18 March 1960.   [70] *Ibid.*, 21 March 1960.   [71] *Ibid.*, 4 and 5 May 1960.
[72] *Ibid.*, 9 May 1960.   [73] MUN/V/5/28, 1 October 1959; MUN/LIB/32/26, 12 October 1959.
[74] MS 9795/2/2–7; *Guardian*, 11 April 1960.   [75] MUN/V/6/9, p. 49.
[76] *Irish Independent*, 6 June 1960.

from the College collection and busts from the Long Room, as well as the Lindisfarne Gospels, lent by the British Museum and placed beside the Book of Kells. An associated programme of lectures included George Otto Simms and Françoise Henry on the Irish manuscripts and Roger Powell on his rebinding of them. About sixty thousand visitors, including the Queen Mother, attended the exhibition.[77]

Meanwhile, in November 1959, the Board had given approval for an international architectural competition to be organised.[78] Conceptually the new building was no longer regarded as an extension to the Old Library but a new library to which Burgh's building was to be a 'functional extension'.[79] The entrance to the Old Library would in future be at the east end of the building, and the architect would therefore be asked to design modifications to the East Pavilion to facilitate movement between the Old and New Libraries. The specification for the New Library had been revised considerably, mainly as a result of the growth in student numbers to about three thousand and a perceived obligation to provide facilities for the general public following the success of the public appeal in Ireland. The building was now to contain 320 reader places, and it was assumed that the 1937 Reading Room, the Lecky and the newly created Regent House Library would continue in use, thus providing a combined total of 775 seats, a ratio of one seat to every four students, which was the average of that in British universities. The total cost was to be limited to £500,000 and the storage capacity was to be 1,200,000 volumes, which was calculated as 60 years' intake at the current rate.[80] That estimate was absurdly optimistic, as the annualised figure of 20,000 volumes barely covered the number of monographs being received and took no account either of periodicals and other materials or of the fact that the intake of books had been rising each year for several decades, a trend that showed no sign of coming to an end.

The competition was launched on 15 June 1960, with a closing date of 1 March 1961. The documents sent to competitors described in romantic tones the setting into which the building had to fit: 'the prevailing colours are greys – the white-grey of lead, the purple-grey of slate, the sparkling silver-grey of granite walls – relieved by the brilliantly green lawns,

[77] *Treasures from Trinity College Dublin, Burlington House, London W1, 12 January–5 March 1961* ([Dublin: Trinity College] 1961); MS 2589 (text of Powell's lecture); *The Times*, 12 January 1961; *Irish Times*, 10 January, 8, 15 February, 7 March 1961.

[78] MUN/V/5/28, 4 November 1959.

[79] F. J. E. Hurst, 'Trinity College Dublin proposed new library', *Library Association Record*, 63 (1961), 45–8 (p. 46).

[80] MUN/V/6/9, p. 90; MUN/V/5/29, 27 January 1960.

sooty-black tree-trunks, and the sharp white of window sashes and rain-washed Portland stone. Over the whole of this washes the light of Dublin, clean, soft, pellucid'.[81] Competitors were given freedom of choice as far as materials were concerned and, as to style, the competition rules stated, 'while it is obviously desirable to establish a harmony with the old buildings, the promoters hope that the design for the new building will represent the twentieth century to posterity as characteristically as the present Library represents the eighteenth century'.[82]

By the closing date, 218 entries had been received from 29 countries. The panel of judges consisted of the Vice-Chancellor, Lord Rosse; Raymond McGrath, Principal Architect of the Office of Public Works; two non-Irish architects, Sir Hugh Casson and Franco Albini; and an expert on library buildings, Keyes Metcalf, the former Director of Harvard University Library, though he fell ill before the judging and was replaced by Ralph Esterquest, the Harvard Medical Librarian. The successful candidate was Paul Koralek, a young British architect and one of the founder partners of the firm of Ahrends, Burton and Koralek, established in 1961. (See Figure 25.) The decision of the jury was not unanimous, Professor Albini abstaining on the grounds that the proposed building did not harmonise with its surroundings. It was certainly anything but a neo-Georgian pastiche, being constructed of reinforced concrete faced with granite. Features of the proposed design that particularly attracted the assessors were Koralek's use of natural light and the arrangement of the building to minimise the distance that readers, staff and books would have to travel.[83] It was assumed that the Library would not need the whole of the storage space to start with, and so part of the basement was initially designated as a temporary teaching area and exhibition gallery.

Once the competition had been successfully concluded, McConnell needed to complete the fundraising. He wrote to Lemass asking for a government grant of £413,880, which represented the revised estimated cost of £640,880 less the £227,000 that had been raised by the appeal. The Department of Education declined to provide the full sum but agreed to match the

---

[81] University of Dublin, Trinity College, *International architectural competition for a new library building*, 1960, TCD EPB 147.c.42, No. 14.

[82] *Ibid.*

[83] MUN/V/6/10, p. 28; 'Dublin library competition', *Architects' Journal*, 133 (1961), 870–83. For detailed information about the existing and proposed operation of the Library, and comments on the competition entries, see University of Dublin, Trinity College, *Official answers to questions, international competition for a new library building*, October 1960 (MUN/LIB/32/Box 40), and *Decisions and report of the Jury of Award, International competition for a new library building*, June 1961, TCD EPB 147.c.42, No. 15.

Figure 25 President de Valera (centre) with Paul Koralek, architect (right), at the ceremony to announce the result of the design competition for the New Library, 8 June 1961. Also in the picture are Dr A. J. McConnell, Provost (far left), and the Earl of Rosse, Vice-Chancellor (*Irish Times*)

amount raised by the College on a pound-for-pound basis up to a combined maximum of £640,900 and, if the total available were not sufficient to meet the eventual cost, the Department would supply the remainder in the form of a loan. The conditions of the grant were that library facilities would be available to members of the public, that a technical library service would be provided for government departments and commercial firms and that Trinity would co-operate with the National Library to avoid unnecessary duplication and expense, all conditions that were acceptable to the Board.[84]

The contract for the new building was issued to the Dublin firm G. and T. Crampton and work began on site after President de Valera had cut the first sod on 20 November 1963.[85] The appeal was still attracting significant donations, including one of £30,000 from Jack Morrison, a London businessman, and $280,000 from the Ford Foundation.[86] The cost, however, rose to about £800,000 and the College had to seek further government funding, which was provided on the same 50:50 basis, up to a total of

[84] NAI, Department of the Taoiseach, S13962 C/61; MUN/V/5/29, 11 October 1961.
[85] MUN/V/6/11, p. 49; MUN/LIB/32/40 (press release 20 November 1963).
[86] *Irish Times*, 26 July 1963; MUN/V/5/30, 29 January 1964.

£736,000.[87] This level of state support was not universally popular. Michael Tierney, the President of University College Dublin, objected to it on the grounds that Trinity claimed to be a suitable university for Catholics as well as Protestants and had denounced as bigotry the hierarchy's ban on Catholic students attending the College.[88]

It was clear that a large new building would require more staff and a new approach to library services and, under pressure from the College, recurrent funding from the government was gradually increased to meet these new commitments. The Library budget, which was £25,000 in 1961, was planned to rise to £57,000 by 1967.[89] Additional posts, such as those of Science Librarian, Information Librarian (to provide a service to outside organisations), a Superintendent for a new temporary reading room, and more 'boys' to fetch books, were created. The annual grant that had been provided to reduce the cataloguing backlog was incorporated into the recurrent budget and the staff employed on that grant were made permanent. O'Sullivan was promoted to be Keeper of Manuscripts. The Board recognised the 'new stature' of the Deputy Librarianship by placing Hurst on the same salary scale as professors who were heads of department, and a new post of Sub-Librarian was created to plan the transition to the new building and then to run it on a day-to-day basis. William Dieneman (see Figure 26) was appointed to that post from 21 September 1962.[90]

An important move away from the practices of the past and in the direction of those prevailing elsewhere was the closure in 1963 of the Accessions Catalogue, which by then comprised 436 volumes of pasted-in slips. It was replaced by a card catalogue. The 'Secondaries Catalogue' was also closed at the same time and replaced for subject access by a classified card-catalogue based on the Dewey Decimal System, which was to be used to classify open-access books in the new building.[91]

By now the Library was also playing a more prominent role in the wider library world. An Chomhairle Leabharlanna (The Library Council) had been established by the Public Libraries Act of 1947 to provide advice and assistance to the public library service, and from the start senior Trinity Library staff were appointed as members of the Council. The College was also a founder member of SCONUL, the Standing Conference of National and University Libraries, which was established in 1950 to represent academic libraries in Britain and Ireland.

[87] NAI, Department of the Taoiseach, S13962 C/63.   [88] *Irish Times*, 29 June 1964.

[89] MUN/V/6/11, p. 115.

[90] MUN/V/5/29, 16 November 1960, 24 and 31 May 1961, 7 March and 1 October 1962; MUN/LIB/15/86–MUN/LIB/15/87; MUN/LIB/32/35, 21 May 1962.

[91] [Trinity College Library] *Notes for readers*, May 1964.

Though approval had been given in 1953 for the building of a new library, it was 1963 before construction started and 1967 by the time it was completed. In the meantime, space had to be found for those legal-deposit books and journals which could not be accommodated in the Colonnades, and for the increasing numbers of readers as the College grew in size. For books, additional storage was provided in 1962 in the basement of a building formerly occupied by J. J. O'Hara, a builders' merchant, in Lincoln Place, at the south-east corner of the College.[92] In 1961, huts were erected against the south side of the Old Library to create a temporary reading room for about a hundred users. These were extended in 1963 and included an open-access collection of books and periodicals, as well as providing accommodation for the Library's cataloguing staff.[93]

Departmental libraries

In November 1950, the Board received proposals, which had been drawn up by Moody in consultation with Parke, for the reconstitution of the Lecky Library. Since its arrival in 1912, that library had been housed in locked cupboards in the Council Room in the Museum Building and had been hardly used. Moody recommended that the collection should be split, with some books transferred to the College Library, and the remainder made available for borrowing by students. The Council Room also contained the Lending Library, which he described as even more disused and useless than the Lecky. Any books of value should, he said, go to departmental libraries, and the rest should be disposed of. Finally, he proposed that the Joint Lending Library, which was managed by three departmental societies (the Commerce and Economics, History and Law Societies) should be merged with the Lecky, that its annual grant should be transferred to the reconstituted Lecky and that the Council Room should be converted into a reading room for students in relevant subjects. In this way the Lecky could be transformed from 'a mausoleum into a living collection of books'.[94] The Board approved Moody's proposals and appointed him as the Trustee of the new Lecky Library, which initially contained about 2,500 volumes and was formally opened by the Provost on 2 May 1951.[95]

---

[92] MUN/V/5/29, 7 February 1962.

[93] MUN/V/5/29, 7 June 1961; MUN/V/5/30, 13 March 1963; MUN/LIB/32/35, 1 May, 27 October 1961, 2 September 1963.

[94] MUN/P/54/14/137.

[95] MUN/LIB/3/3, 16 February 1951; MUN/V/5/27, 7 and 14 March 1951; MUN/V/6/8, pp. 73 and 105; MUN/LIB/15/605.

In 1959, the collections in the various modern-language departments were brought together to create a 'Regent House Library', housed over the Front Gate, and in the Medical School a reading room for pre-medical students and those reading natural sciences was opened.[96] Two years later, it was decided that the planned Biochemistry Building would contain a biomedical library formed by the merger of several of the scientific departmental libraries, and for this the Wellcome Trust provided a grant of £16,000.[97]

Planning for the new College Library building inevitably raised the question of the role of the other libraries that received money from the Board. A committee set up in 1962 identified no less than thirty-six of them, of which seventeen received direct grants from the Board. The remainder were financed by allocations from their departments. Between them they contained about 45,000 volumes, had about 200 seats and a combined annual expenditure of £3,000. The principal reasons given for their existence were the convenience of having books in the department and the inadequacy of the College Library, especially in its reading room provision, its lack of books for undergraduates and its prohibition on borrowing. The committee supported the plans for a biomedical library, which would be administratively part of the College Library, staffed by a qualified medical librarian and with generous opening hours. It recommended that the relationship between the College Library and the remaining libraries in science departments should be clarified, especially as far as the receipt of legal-deposit periodicals was concerned. Once the New Library was open, the justification for the continued existence of the various arts libraries would cease, and they should be incorporated into the College Library system.[98]

These important recommendations were received by Parke without great enthusiasm, as he was concerned that they would lead to an increased pressure being placed on the College Library without the provision of the necessary additional resources. He would only be able to support the plan, he said, when his own staff numbers were large enough 'to meet reasonably' the demands placed upon them.[99] In 1964, the College Library took over administrative responsibility for the Lecky and Regent House libraries as a first stage in the development of an undergraduate lending library.[100] At the same time as this consolidation was taking place, the mathematicians moved in the opposite direction, gaining approval to set up a new Mathematics library. This was approved only as a temporary measure pending

[96] MUN/V/5/28, 18 March, 10 June 1959; MUN/V/6/9, p. 69.
[97] MUN/LIB/32/35, 1 December 1961; MUN/V/5/29, 6 December 1961, 24 January 1962.
[98] MUN/V/6/11, p. 10.   [99] MUN/V/6/11, p. 43.
[100] MUN/V/5/31, 8 July 1964; MUN/V/6/11, p. 111.

the opening of the new College Library, and the Library Committee took the opportunity to reaffirm its view that the 'fragmentation' of the College Library into departmental libraries was 'undesirable in both principle and practice'.[101]

Books and manuscripts

After the end of the Second World War, attention turned to the early Irish manuscripts. The Swiss publisher, Urs Graf Verlag, was given permission to photograph the Book of Kells and, initially, the illustrated pages from the Book of Durrow, with a view to printing facsimiles of both. An edition of 500 copies of the Book of Kells was published in November 1950, at the same size as the original and with 48 pages in colour. Copies were given to the President of Ireland, King George VI, the Roman Catholic and Church of Ireland primates, and various libraries and other institutions.[102]

An inspection, carried out before the photography began, revealed that both manuscripts needed to be rebound and that more than twenty leaves of the Book of Kells had become detached. Having seen the effect of earlier rebindings, Parke was disinclined to commit the College's treasures to a commercial binder, and for a time suspended any binding or repair of manuscripts.[103] He was advised by the British Museum to employ the conservation binder Roger Powell for the Book of Kells. Powell adopted a very different approach from that of his predecessors. By tensioning the leaves he was able to flatten them and, in order to avoid the use of adhesive, which had caused problems with previous bindings, the leaves were sewn onto linen guards. The extra thickness thus created would have produced a very unwieldy book and so it was decided that the manuscript would be divided into four volumes, one for each Gospel, as this would also facilitate the display in the Long Room. The work was carried out in the Library during 1953.[104]

[101] MUN/V/6/12, p. 3; MUN/V/5/32, 24 February 1965.

[102] MUN/V/5/26, 30 January 1946, 25 February, 23 June 1948; MUN/V/5/27, 1 October 1949, 22 November 1950; MUN/V/6/8, p. 27; E. H. Alton and P. Meyer, eds., *Evangeliorum quattuor Codex Cenannensis* (Bern: Urs Graf, 1950–1); G. O. Simms, 'Codex Cenannensis', *Annual Bulletin*, (1950), 16–17.

[103] William O'Sullivan, 'Binding memories of Trinity Library', in *Decantations*, pp. 168–76.

[104] MUN/V/5/27, 22 April 1953; MUN/LIB/3/3, 21 November 1952, 11 April, 19 June, 16 October 1953; MS 2586 (Powell's binding notes); R. O. Dougan, 'The rebinding of the Book of Kells', *Annual Bulletin* (1953), 11–12; R. Powell, 'The Book of Kells, the Book of Durrow: comments on the vellum, the make-up and other aspects', *Scriptorium*, 10 (1956), 3–21; Bernard Meehan,

Satisfaction with Powell's treatment of the Book of Kells, the condition of the binding of the Book of Durrow and Urs Graf Verlag's interest in publishing a facsimile, all combined to provide an incentive to rebind that manuscript, too. It was taken to the British Museum, so that it could be disbound and photographed in full, and so that A. A. Luce and the Celtic scholar Ludwig Bieler could attempt to determine the original order of the pages. Powell then rebound the manuscript in a single volume. Noting the commercial success of Urs Graf's facsimile of the Book of Kells, the Board insisted that not only was the College to receive free copies of the facsimile of Durrow, as it had with that of Kells, but that a royalty on sales should also be paid. The book was published in 1960.[105]

For the next two decades Powell continued to work on other early Irish manuscripts, both for Trinity and the Royal Irish Academy. In 1957, it was the turn of the Book of Armagh and the Book of Dimma; in 1961, the *Liber hymnorum* was left for him to work on in London after the end of the Burlington House exhibition; and in 1963, the Ricemarch Psalter was rebound.[106] Powell's final bindings for Trinity were some of the genealogies and brehon law manuscripts, including the *Seanchas Már*.

The Library's acquisitions continued to be dominated by those received from the Copyright Agency, which, by 1960, was supplying 23,000 new books a year and a similar number of periodical issues, as well as maps and music. The staff of the Agency had increased to six, including the Agent, George Copp, who took over on 1 August 1953, following Osborne's retirement. The annual cost of the Agency was £1,600 to each library.[107]

The purchasing budget rose steadily from the insignificant sum of £1,100 immediately after the war, though Trinity's level of buying was on a very modest scale compared to that of many other university libraries. By 1954, it was spending £3,000 on acquisitions, a figure that rose over the next decade

---

'Bindings: documentary evidence', in *Kells facsimile*, pp. 193–5; Anthony Cains, 'Bindings: technical description', *ibid.*, pp. 197–207; Anthony Cains, 'Roger Powell and his early Irish manuscripts in Dublin', in Nicholas Hadgraft and Katherine Swift, eds., *Conservation and preservation in small libraries* (Cambridge: Parker Library Publications, 1994), pp. 151–6.

[105] MUN/V/5/27, 27 January, 10 February 1954; MUN/LIB/3/3, 19 June 1953, 2 February, 3 December 1954; A. A. Luce, G. O. Simms, P. Meyer and L. Bieler, eds., *Evangeliorum quattuor Codex Durmachensis*, 2 vols. (Olten: Urs Graf, 1960).

[106] MUN/V/5/28, 27 February 1957; MUN/V/5/29, 15 February 1961; MSS 2587–8; Anthony G. Cains, 'Roger Powell's innovation in book conservation: the early Irish manuscripts repaired and bound, 1953–1981', in John L. Sharpe, ed., *Roger Powell: the compleat binder* (Turnhout: Brepols, 1996), pp. 68–87; William O'Sullivan, 'Notes on the Trinity *Liber hymnorum*', *ibid.*, pp. 130–3.

[107] CUA ULIB/7/2/26/2–7/2/26/5.

to £9,000.[108] Additional support came from the Rockefeller Foundation which, from 1948, provided an allocation of $1,300 as part of a scheme to enable British and Irish universities to obtain foreign books and journals.[109] Antiquarian material was bought as the opportunity and funding permitted. Webb and Parke were authorised to spend up to £200 at the sale of the Duke of Leinster's library from Carton House, Maynooth in 1949, and for this they were able to obtain about 350 volumes, mainly seventeenth- and eighteenth-century French books and Dublin printings.[110] In 1957, the College bought Townley Hall near Drogheda, the former home of the Balfour family, and 3 years later the Library acquired books and manuscripts that had been collected at the Hall since the eighteenth century. The 2,500 printed items included works of classical literature, theology and travel, but the strength of the collection was its musical material. There were about a thousand pieces of printed music dating from 1760 to 1820, including operas, songs and chamber music, and manuscripts of the same period, including an early copy of Handel's *Messiah*.[111] The purchase of 400 eighteenth-century plays from J. Barry Brown of Naas in 1964 marked the start of the Library's policy of building up its collection of drama in English.[112]

Donations included the Somerville and Ross collection, bequeathed by Alain, comte de Suzannet, of Lausanne, in 1950, which consisted of about 800 letters, first editions, notebooks and drafts of the books as well as Edith Somerville's drawings for several of her books.[113] The exhibition on W. B. Yeats in the Long Room in 1956 included a number of books and manuscripts that had been borrowed from Yeats' widow, and at the end of the exhibition Mrs Yeats donated the manuscript of *Mosada* (MS 3502) and rare privately printed editions of the poet's work.[114] In 1955, Aileen Crofton of Ashford, County Wicklow, gave a collection of 2,000 seventeenth- and eighteenth-century pamphlets, principally concerned with economics and

[108] MUN/V/5/27, 26 June 1954; MUN/V/6/12, p. 43.

[109] MUN/V/5/26, 28 April 1948; MUN/V/5/27, 19 January 1949; MUN/LIB/12/59.

[110] MUN/V/5/27, 1 June 1949; MUN/LIB/3/3, 18 November 1949; 'The Carton Library', *Annual Bulletin* (1949), 10.

[111] Stanley, note 13 above; Eimear Saunders, 'The music in the Library', in *Old Library*, pp. 286–300. The manuscripts are MSS 3590–3629.

[112] Charles Benson, '"Here's fine work! Here's fine suicide, paracide and simulation"', in *Treasures*, pp. 148–57.

[113] MUN/V/5/27, 24 January 1951; Cresap S. Watson, 'The Somerville and Ross Collection', *Annual Bulletin* (1951), 16–17. The manuscripts are MSS 3279–3331.

[114] R. O. Dougan, *W. B. Yeats: manuscripts and printed books, exhibited in the Library of Trinity College, Dublin* (Dublin: Three Candles, 1956); Nicholas Grene, 'Modern Irish literary manuscripts', in *Treasures*, pp. 230–8; 'Gifts and acquisitions, 1956–7', *Annual Bulletin* (1957), 14.

trade, which had been assembled by her ancestor, the eighteenth-century gentleman-book-collector Christopher Earbery.[115]

The Long Room became the venue for regularly changing exhibitions as well as the permanent display of the Irish manuscripts, and in 1958 the Carnegie United Kingdom Trust donated new display cases.[116] Following a theft of money from the Room, the Library's gold fibula and other pieces of Irish metalwork were transferred to the National Museum.[117] Parke was also concerned about the condition of the 'Brian Boru' harp, and so at the end of the Burlington House exhibition it was moved to the British Museum to be restored and re-strung before being returned to the Library and installed in a new case donated by Arthur Guinness and Company.[118]

* * *

Parke resigned as Librarian with effect from 12 July 1965, though he continued as Vice-Provost, Professor of Ancient History and a Senior Fellow.[119] The Library that he left was in a far better shape than that which he had inherited. The new building was well under way, major progress had been made in clearing up the mass of uncatalogued material scattered around the College and the budget, though still far from adequate, had been increased substantially and was no longer a matter of shame for the College.

---

[115] Now MSS 3575–3587. MUN/V/5/27, 2 July 1955; 'The Crofton pamphlets', *Annual Bulletin* (1956), 15–18.

[116] 'Exhibition cases', *Annual Bulletin* (1958), 16; Shane Mawe, '"Would you look at that!": a chronological list of library exhibitions', in *Old Library*, pp. 389–97.

[117] MUN/V/5/28, 6 May 1959; MUN/V/6/9, p. 71

[118] MUN/V/5/29, 25 January, 6 December 1961; *Irish Times*, 19 February 1962.

[119] MUN/V/5/32, 24 February 1965.

18 | Professional management: 1965–1983

John Hurst

The reforms that had been initiated by Parke continued under his successors. John Hurst was appointed as Librarian from 12 July 1965, but the Board, which had previously shown generosity in placing him on the professorial salary scale as the Deputy Librarian, remarkably saw no need to increase his salary or change his conditions when he became the Librarian. William Dieneman replaced him as the Deputy Librarian in April 1966.[1] For the first time in its history the College not only had a professionally qualified Librarian but also one whose appointment was full-time and not held in conjunction with teaching or other offices. However, the Board found itself unable to relinquish academic control completely. It created for Parke a new honorary office of Curator of the Library, which had no clear terms of reference except to chair the Library Committee. Parke remained as Curator throughout the tenure of Hurst and his successor, Denis Roberts, and relinquished the title only in 1972, shortly before his retirement from the Vice-Provostship and Chair of Ancient History. Hurst's tenure as Librarian was brief and uncomfortable.

As the completion date for the New Library approached, it became ever clearer that the building would be inadequate to meet the demands about to be placed upon it. Whilst he was the Deputy Librarian, Hurst had been closely involved with the planning and was aware of the new building's shortcomings. He sought to reduce their impact, but he received little support from the academic community in the College. The divergence of views between the Librarian and some of the Fellows came to a head at a contentious Board meeting in November 1966 when the Board refused to overturn its earlier decision to use part of the basement of the New Library as an exhibition hall, despite Hurst's pleading that he needed the space to transfer books from their various stores around the College.[2]

---

[1] MUN/V/5/32, 24 February 1965; MUN/V/5/33, 15 June 1966.
[2] MUN/V/5/34, 2 November 1966; MUN/LIB/15/315.

Figure 26 Four Trinity librarians: (left to right) John Hurst, Librarian 1965–7; William Dieneman, Deputy Librarian 1966–70; Denis Roberts, Librarian 1967–70; Peter Fox, Librarian 1984–94 (MS 4717/192)

Provost McConnell realised that there was an urgent need to consider the Library's problems, not just as an emergency measure to deal with the current situation but in the context of a longer-term strategy. He asked for a ten-year plan, but by this time Hurst had already tendered his resignation, following his appointment as the first Librarian of the New University of Ulster at Coleraine. Rather than produce the requested plan, therefore, and aware that he was shortly to leave Trinity, he gave vent to his frustration, criticising previous policy, some of it fundamental to the nature of the Library. He wrote a strongly worded letter to the Provost, asserting that the difficulties faced by the Library sprang largely from two decisions taken in the past: to remain a legal-deposit library 'without apparently taking into account that this would become an extremely expensive responsibility well outside the College's financial resources'; and to plan a new building without having a policy for the Library's future role and services, which was a case of putting 'the cart before the horse'. As a result, the New Library would be unable to cope with the level of activity that was expected of it. It was, he said, 'depressing to talk of library "development" when in fact we still need to reach basic minimum standards', and for that the Library needed £1 million 'to salvage what we already have', when it was having to manage on less than £125,000 a year.[3]

---

[3] MUN/LIB/32/169, Hurst to Provost, 9 November 1966.

In a further letter, and with a eye to the position of his successor, he criticised the lack of status of the Librarian in the College, the role of Parke as Curator, and the fact that the institution was required to function as an undergraduate library, a research library, a legal-deposit library and a public library, with inadequate financial and staffing resources.[4] Though there was little the College could do about it, given its own financial situation, Hurst's assessment of the problems facing the Library was an accurate one. It was no longer subject to the severe financial constraints of the first half of the twentieth century, but Hurst and all his successors have been forced to find ways of meeting a growing level of demand with resources that have ranged over time from the minimally acceptable to the seriously inadequate.

Hurst left Trinity on 31 March 1967 and was succeeded on 1 June by Denis Roberts, Secretary of the National Library of Scotland.[5]

The New Library completed

A month after Roberts' tenure began, honorary degrees were conferred on five 'distinguished librarians': William Beattie (National Library of Scotland), H. R. Creswick (Cambridge), R. J. Hayes (National Library of Ireland), K. W. Humphries (Secretary of SCONUL) and Robert Shackleton (Bodley's Librarian).[6]

The following day, 12 July 1967, the New Library was opened by President de Valera. With its crisp lines of concrete and granite, it was a dramatic addition to the College landscape. Koralek set his building behind the line of the Old Library and the Museum Building, with a podium linking the two, creating not just an imposing entrance to his Library but also 'the only really carefully thought out transition from one square to another in the whole College'.[7] The Library consisted of three elements: a bookstack in the basement; offices and a catalogue and reference room on the ground floor; and reading rooms and open-access bookstacks on the first and second floors. There were seats for 470 readers, more than had originally been specified, but necessary given the growth in student numbers. However, this had an inevitable impact on the amount of book-storage space available, which was calculated to be 829,000 volumes once the temporary teaching area and exhibition gallery in the basement had been handed

[4] *Ibid.*, 15 December 1966.   [5] MUN/V/5/34, 7 December 1966, 6 March 1967.
[6] MUN/V/5/34, 6 March 1967; *DU Calendar*, 1967–8.
[7] E. J. McParland, 'The College buildings', in Holland, pp. 153–84 (p. 180).

over to Library use. The basement stack had an initial capacity of 272,500 volumes, which would eventually increase to 667,000. The upper floors contained over 150,000 volumes directly accessible to readers, which re-introduced an element of convenience that users of the Old Library had not experienced for over a century.[8] The building quality was high. Koralek's use of light and space, and his creation of a series of interior cell-like 'rooms', prioritised 'the reader and the experience of reading over the previously sacrosanct accommodation of books'.[9] (See Figure 27.) The new build-ing became the administrative focus of the Library, with the Librarian's Office and almost all the staff transferring there from the Old Library and the huts. From the outset, however, criticism was levelled at its structural inflexibility.[10] This proved to be a major problem for future librarians try-ing to adapt the building to the digital world and the changing demands of readers.

Some remodelling of the East Pavilion, to provide a link between the Old Library and the New, had been part of the brief for the competition, and the two buildings were now linked by a tunnel. It was intended that modern books, periodicals and government documents would be consulted in the New Library, and readers using older books from the Long Room and Gallery would be accommodated in a new reading room in the Old Library.[11] Mary ('Paul') Pollard, who had been working part-time in Trinity and Marsh's Library since 1957, was appointed as a full-time Assistant Librarian to take charge of a new Department of Older Printed Books (later renamed Early Printed Books).[12]

Following the production of a report by Koralek and the College architect Ian Roberts on the poor condition of the woodwork in the East Pavilion, the Board realised that a more extensive intervention was required than had originally been envisaged. It accepted Koralek's proposed solution, which was to rebuild the interior of the Pavilion in the brutalist style of his New Library.[13] His plan involved the creation of a new shop and an entrance

---

[8]   University of Dublin, Trinity College, *The New Library, opened by Eamon de Valera, President of Ireland, July 12th 1967* (Dublin University Press, 1967); 'Library, Trinity College Dublin', *Architect and Building News*, 232 (1967), 611–18.

[9]   Raymund Ryan, 'The Ussher Library at Trinity College', *Irish Arts Review*, 19/1 (Summer 2002), 82–9 (p. 85).

[10]   See, for example, Alan Colquhoun, 'Library, Trinity College, Dublin', *Architectural Review*, 142 (1967), 264–77.

[11]   Parke, 'Library project', 11 January 1963, MUN/LIB/32/40.

[12]   Charles Benson, 'Introduction', in Charles Benson and Siobhán Fitzpatrick, eds., *That woman! Studies in Irish bibliography: a Festschrift for Mary 'Paul' Pollard* (Dublin: Lilliput Press, 2005), pp. viii–xiii.

[13]   MUN/V/5/33, 1 and 8 June 1966; MUN/LIB/5/34, 21 January 1967.

Figure 27 The interior of the Berkeley Library (Gillian Whelan, Digital Resources and Imaging Services, TCD)

for tourists, a reading room for Older Printed Books and a new concrete staircase to bring visitors up to the Long Room. This required the removal of half the Fagel collection from the room where it had been housed since the early nineteenth century. It was a wholly unsympathetic intrusion into an eighteenth-century building.

During the construction work on the East Pavilion, the Library was faced with a near disaster when wooden shuttering collapsed and about four thousand books in the Colonnades were covered in wet concrete.[14] The cost of the damage was estimated at £10,000, most of which was eventually reimbursed by the contractor. Some of the books could be repaired, but the bulk of the compensation was used to buy replacements or new titles in modern languages, the subject of the majority of books that had been damaged.[15]

The disturbing report on the state of the woodwork in the East Pavilion led to a similar investigation of that in other parts of the Old Library, and it was discovered that major repairs were also needed elsewhere. The Long Room was closed from August 1968 for the work to be carried out and to allow lighting, heating and a fire-detection system to be installed.[16] It reopened for the summer of 1970.

Planning for a new Arts and Social Sciences Building had started by this time, and Denis Roberts realised that the Magnetic Observatory, which was still being used as the Manuscripts Reading Room and store, would have to be moved, as it stood in the way of the proposed building. He saw this as an opportunity to provide more suitable accommodation for the Library's manuscripts and their readers, and recommended that the West Pavilion should be adapted for this purpose. He also recognised the need for a conservation bindery, something that had been proposed by Roger Powell in the 1950s. In this he was supported not only by William O'Sullivan, now Keeper of Manuscripts, but also by Rollin McCarthy, an American engineer who had paid for air-conditioning in the Magnetic Observatory and who was anxious to help with funding the construction not simply of a bindery but of a conservation laboratory.[17] In 1970, the Board approved a remodelling of the West Pavilion that was rather less drastic than that at the east end of the building. An office, reading room and store were provided for the Manuscripts Department, the former Librarian's Office was converted into a meeting room and the attic was left vacant for a conservation laboratory, to be created when funding became available. The new Manuscripts Room opened to readers on 1 June 1971.[18] Responsibility for the College archives,

---

[14] Hurst to Provost, 6 January 1967, MUN/LIB/32/169.

[15] MUN/LIB/15/379; MUN/V/6/15, p. 85; MUN/V/6/16, p. 42.

[16] MUN/V/5/34, 6 March 1967; MUN/V/6/13, p. 56.

[17] MUN/V/6/13, p. 88; MUN/V/5/35, 7 August 1968; William O'Sullivan, 'Binding memories of Trinity Library', in *Decantations*, pp. 168–76.

[18] MUN/V/6/15, p. 63; MUN/V/5/37, 18 February 1970; William O'Sullivan, 'The new Manuscripts Room', *Long Room*, 5 (Spring 1972), 23–5.

or 'muniments', had been transferred to the Manuscripts Department in 1969, and in 1971 Margaret Griffith, who had retired as Deputy Keeper of the Public Records of Ireland, was appointed to organise and catalogue them.[19]

With the majority of readers now using the New Library, the 1937 Reading Room was converted into a Modern Languages Lending Library, housing the lending collection formerly in the Regent House and providing a reading room for students in modern languages. It opened in October 1967, as did the Biomedical Library, which contained research-level books and journals in biology and medicine and was housed in the new Biochemistry Building.[20]

Denis Roberts

The opening of the New Library and the appointment of Denis Roberts as Librarian marked a further stage in the process of rehabilitation which had begun with Parke's reforms. The building acted as a catalyst for what was to be a complete transformation of library services in the College, and from the 1960s onwards the Library increasingly assumed its proper place in Trinity and in the library community in Ireland and further afield. The Librarian's status as a senior College officer was recognised by the invitation to Roberts and his successors to attend Board meetings.[21] Roberts applied his considerable administrative skills to reorganising the staff structure and establishing procedures to meet the needs of the rapidly developing organisation that the Library had now become. By 1970, the number of staff had reached ninety, including thirty-five in professional grades, and as well as expanding their numbers, Roberts also sought to improve their salaries.[22] The transfer of legal-deposit books to the libraries in science departments was stopped, because of concern that the College Library had no control of them once they were there, though the departments continued to receive new issues of those periodical titles that they already held.[23]

Planning for the College's capital needs was influenced throughout the late 1960s and early 1970s by the government's proposals to merge Trinity

---

[19] M. C. Griffith, 'The muniments of Trinity College', *Long Room*, 12/13 (Autumn 1975/Spring 1976), 6–12.

[20] MUN/LIB/15/368; *DU Calendar*, 1968–9.   [21] MUN/V/5/36, 11 June 1969.

[22] MUN/LIB/15/161; MUN/LIB/15/Box II ('Further particulars, vacancy for Librarian', January 1970).

[23] MUN/LIB/15/337c.

and University College Dublin into a single university. Those plans took various forms as ministers came and went, and they were finally laid to rest in the mid 1970s, when it was decided that the two universities would retain their separate existences. One factor that was clear throughout the period was that, whatever form the Dublin universities might eventually take, the demand for places in them would rise, a factor exacerbated for Trinity following Archbishop McQuaid's decision in 1970 to remove the ban on Catholic students from the Dublin archdiocese attending the College. During the later stages of planning the New Library, the number of reader places had been increased from 320 to 470, but even those were inadequate, given that the size of the student body for which it had been planned – 2,700 – had already risen to 3,500, and was projected to rise to 6,000 over the following decade. The reduced storage capacity, of just over 800,000 volumes, represented closer to 20 years' intake than the 60 that had originally been estimated, and since that 20 included the 18 years since the earlier calculation had been made, the building was effectively full as soon as it opened. Indeed, as the Board had refused Hurst's plea to relinquish the exhibition space in the basement, the entire capacity of the building was not available to the Library until the 1970s.

Some potential future relief was offered by the proposed Arts and Social Sciences Building, which was to be built on the south side of the Fellows' Garden, at right angles to the New Library and with an entrance from Nassau Street. As well as lecture theatres and offices for the academic staff, the original plan also included 'departmental specialised libraries'.[24] In July 1969, Roberts produced a lengthy paper on Library development for submission to the Higher Education Authority (HEA) as part of a general statement on the College's capital requirements.[25] He recommended that the proposed Arts Building should not perpetuate the small departmental libraries but should contain an undergraduate library for all arts and social-science students and form an integral part of the College Library. This would allow the New Library to become principally a research library. His plans also included the construction of a new science library as part of the development of science facilities at the east end of the College. The most radical recommendation was to abandon the vain hope of providing proper Library storage within the College, relinquish the makeshift arrangements that had operated hitherto, and construct a purpose-built repository away from the campus for that part of the legal-deposit intake which was in relatively low use. Such a building could be designed to be built in phases as

[24] MUN/V/6/13, p. 127.   [25] MUN/V/6/14, pp. 83–7.

needed, and, if shared with other Dublin libraries, it might prove more likely to attract government funding. Roberts' repository scheme was approved in principle by the Board in July 1968 as a solution not just to the storage of future legal-deposit material but also as a way of clearing the remaining 'dumps' of books in O'Hara's, the basements of the Zoology Building and the Chapel, and the Catacombs under the 1937 Reading Room.[26]

More buildings

In 1970, Roberts returned to Edinburgh as Librarian of the National Library of Scotland and Dieneman left to become Librarian of the University College of Wales, Aberystwyth. Roberts was replaced on 1 October by Peter Brown, Keeper of Catalogues at the Bodleian Library, but the post of Deputy Librarian was left unfilled, pending a decision by the new Librarian.[27] (See Figure 28.)

The Library that Brown inherited still had major funding problems, but its needs were now being taken more seriously by the College and the HEA, and attempts were being made to redress the neglect of the past, though the resources available to achieve this were limited. During the 1970s Brown was gradually able to implement Roberts' plans for developing and rationalising the Library's buildings, but delays in the provision of funding by the HEA meant that, for much of the decade, readers – especially undergraduates – had to manage with a series of ad hoc arrangements.

Paul Koralek was selected as the architect for the Arts and Social Sciences Building and the final plan, approved in 1971, was for it to contain a library with 600 seats and a capacity of 75,000 volumes, which would be linked to the New Library at basement level.[28] It was to be principally a collection of borrowable books for undergraduates, based partly upon two existing libraries, the modern languages collection in the 1937 Reading Room, and the Lecky, which was transferred from the Museum Building to the former teaching area in the New Library in 1971.[29] Both needed to be substantially augmented to create a library of sufficient size and breadth, and the HEA agreed to include the cost of developing this collection as part of its capital provision.[30] To these purchased lending collections would be added appropriate legal-deposit books, which the students would not be

[26] MUN/LIB/15/380.   [27] MUN/V/5/37, 21 January, 1 April, 24 July 1970.
[28] MUN/V/5/37, 8 October 1969; MUN/V/6/16, p. 51.   [29] MUN/V/6/18, p. 29.
[30] MUN/V/6/20, p. 31.

Figure 28 Peter Brown, Librarian 1970–84 (MS 4717/193)

able to borrow. Other demands on the HEA's funding programme, however, meant that completion of the new building was not expected before 1977.

A medical library for clinical staff and students opened in the new College Teaching Unit at St James's Hospital in 1973, but in the early 1970s the long-term plan for the construction of a central science library at the east end of the College remained an even more distant prospect than the Arts

Building.[31] With the College expanding and space at a premium, a collection of huts began to appear in the Fellows' Garden and against the south wall of the Old Library. These huts were used for lectures, to house the computer and to accommodate the undergraduate lending collection for the sciences. That collection remained in the huts when a new science reading room was opened in the Chemistry Building in October 1971.[32] In 1976, the science books were moved from the huts to the basement of the New Library, and 2 years later they were transferred across Pearse Street into the redundant St Mark's Church, which had been bought by the College.

The need to resolve the Library's book-storage problems had again become acute. A site for the proposed repository had been found at the College's sports ground in Santry, but the government wanted the building to be a shared one. Both the National Library and the Dublin public library service expressed an interest, with the public library wishing to have half the space and meet half the cost, but neither of those two institutions – nor indeed the HEA – was in a position to make a financial commitment. Trinity's need was urgent, however, and so in July 1973 it decided to pre-empt the confirmation of funding and proceed.[33] The building was completed in 1974, but within 2 years 400,000 volumes of new acquisitions and books transferred from O'Hara's and elsewhere had almost filled the College's share of the space. As the city council had still not committed itself to funding, it was agreed that Trinity could encroach into the space allocated to the public library and release the equivalent amount in the next phase. Peter Brown calculated that a second phase would be required by 1980, but when that year arrived it had not even been included in the list of projects for the HEA's capital works programme.[34]

The completion of the Arts and Social Sciences Building in 1978 meant that the summer of that year was a busy one, with a series of interrelated bookmoves taking place. The whole of the Arts Building library became known as the Lecky, and the New Library was renamed the Berkeley. In the later stages of planning, the initial concept of the Arts Building library had been revised in order to provide a more coherent structure for the humanities and social sciences collections. The new Lecky Library was no longer, as originally envisaged, a purely undergraduate collection, but

[31] MUN/V/6/17, p. 77.
[32] MUN/V/6/18, p. 29; *DU Calendar*, 1971–2; TCD Library information sheets 1971–3, MUN/LIB/15, Box II.
[33] MUN/V/6/16, p. 59, MUN/V/5/40, 4 July 1973.   [34] Annual Report, 1980–1.

contained books at all levels in literature, fine arts and social sciences, as well as the whole of the undergraduate lending library in humanities and social sciences. The Berkeley housed the remainder of the humanities collection of books and all open-access periodicals in non-scientific subjects. (See Plate 11.)

Following the transfer of modern-language books from the 1937 Reading Room to the new Lecky, that building was used for the mathematics and engineering collections and their readers, as well as for the Music Library. St Mark's housed the remainder of the scientific books and the undergraduate lending library for the sciences. The library buildings now provided a total of about 1,500 seats, which was regarded as acceptable for a College of 5,000 undergraduates. However, the dilapidated state of St Mark's meant that many science students soon began to use the Lecky as a reading room, leading to overcrowding in that building and renewed complaints about the inadequacy of Library facilities.[35] In 1981, the science collection was transferred from St Mark's Church to the ground floor of the Luce Hall, the College's new sports centre. This provided much-improved reading facilities and was seen as a satisfactory interim arrangement pending the construction of a permanent science library.

In his annual report for 1977–8 Brown recognised that science-library provision was still unsatisfactory, but he nonetheless felt able to claim that the recent changes marked 'a significant further step in the development of the College Library from its primitive and unorganised state of only twelve years ago'.[36]

Automation

During the 1960s, experiments took place in a handful of public and academic libraries to establish whether electronic data-processing could be applied to some routine administrative tasks. Trinity was an early participant in that work, and a close relationship developed between the Library and the College's Department of Electrical Engineering. In February 1966, groups of Library staff visited the Department 'to see the computer at work', and investigations into the use of automation in the Library began.[37] The Ford Foundation had contributed towards the cost of the New Library, and

---

[35] MUN/V/5/46, 6 December 1978.   [36] Annual Report, 1977–8.
[37] MUN/LIB/15/310; Neville Harris, 'Pilot projects using variable length library records', *Program*, 8 (1968), 13–16.

the College submitted three proposals to it for possible further support, including a 'Library-Electronics Project'.[38] In 1967, an IBM 360 computer was bought, to be used partly for Library purposes, and a feasibility study was undertaken into whether magnetic tapes of catalogue data produced by the British National Bibliography (BNB) could be used to create catalogue records.[39] Roberts proposed the establishment of a systems section within the Library, and Alan Tucker, a computer programmer from the University of California, Los Angeles, was appointed as the systems analyst.[40]

Trinity quickly became a leading exponent of the use of computers in libraries. In 1968, it was chosen as the primary participant in an experiment funded by the (British) Office for Scientific and Technical Information to determine the feasibility of using catalogue data created in one institution to produce records for another. It was estimated that, since about 80 per cent of the Library's intake of books consisted of legal-deposit material, that proportion of the cataloguing ought to be covered by BNB records, leaving only 20 per cent to be produced locally.[41] The files from the BNB were initially used to create catalogue cards, which were interfiled with those for books that were being catalogued locally, and Trinity soon became the first university library in Britain and Ireland to have an operational cataloguing system based on BNB records. Serious technical problems soon developed, however, and the production of catalogue cards for the legal-deposit intake was abandoned and replaced, first by computer printout and then, in 1972, by computer-output-microfilm. Entries for books without BNB records continued to be added to the existing card catalogue until 1973, when they, too, were computerised.[42]

This meant that, until the retrospective conversion projects started in the 1980s, the reader was faced with no less than four public catalogues: the Printed Catalogue of acquisitions to 1872, the Accessions Catalogue covering 1873 to 1963, a card catalogue for all books received between 1964 and 1969 plus items catalogued up to 1973 for which there were no BNB records, and a microfilm (microfiche after 1978) catalogue for the newer books.

---

[38] MUN/V/5/33, 18 May, 7 July 1966.   [39] MUN/LIB/15/372.

[40] MUN/LIB/15/333 and MUN/LIB/15/336; MUN/V/5/35, 1 May 1968.

[41] E. F. D. Roberts, 'MARC tapes in Trinity College Library', December 1968, MUN/LIB/15, Box II; Alan Tucker, 'Library automation in Trinity College Dublin: a progress report', *Long Room*, 2 (Autumn/Winter 1970), 36–7.

[42] W. Dieneman, 'MARC tapes in Trinity College Library', *Program*, 4 (1970), 70–5; Alan M. Tucker, 'Experiences with MARC-based systems at Trinity College, Dublin', in *The exchange of bibliographic data and the MARC format*, 2nd edn (München-Pullach: Verlag Dokumentation, 1973), pp. 157–71.

Such was Trinity's pre-eminence in library automation at this time that in 1974 Eric Ceadel, the Cambridge University Librarian, invited Tucker to test his programs on that University's computer, and a modified version of the Trinity system was subsequently introduced at Cambridge.[43]

Acquisitions

The budget for acquisitions grew rapidly during the 1960s in order to enable the collection for the New Library to be built up. From £9,000 in 1965 it reached £15,000 in 1967 and £35,000 by 1971.[44] For Peter Brown this was still far from adequate. He estimated that the total value of the legal-deposit books and journals received that year was £85,000, of which about one-third (£30,000-worth) were titles that a normal university library might have been expected to buy. That provided him with a total figure of £65,000 (£35,000 + £30,000) to represent the value of the Library's academic acquisitions, which he claimed was less than half that being spent by libraries in other universities of a similar size. By 1983, the Library's acquisitions expenditure (which included periodicals) had risen to about £250,000, but because of the effects of inflation the number of books bought each year in the previous decade had hardly increased, remaining at an annual figure of between 4,500 and 5,500.[45] On the other hand, the number of books published each year, and therefore acquired by legal deposit, continued to rise. In 1973, 33,700 books and 5,600 periodical titles were received either from the Agency or directly from Irish publishers. A decade later the figures were 44,800 books and 8,500 periodicals.[46]

In the United Kingdom, the Copyright Act of 1956 (which included no reference to legal deposit) came under review in 1973 by a committee (the 'Whitford Committee') established by the Department of Trade. The submissions made in respect of legal deposit were predictable. The libraries, supported by SCONUL and the Library Association, argued for the maintenance of the status quo. The publishers objected that legal deposit was an unjust financial burden and proposed that there should be just one deposit copy, with perhaps a second for lending purposes. The Publishers'

[43] MUN/LIB/32/154; Eric B. Ceadel, *Adaptation of computer programs for catalogues for use in another library*, British Library Research and Development Report, 5352 (Cambridge University Library, 1977).

[44] MUN/V/6/12, p. 43; MUN/V/6/18, p. 29.

[45] Annual Report, 1983–4.   [46] Annual Report, 1972–3 and 1982–3.

Association criticised Trinity's position outside the United Kingdom as an anomaly, but the College pointed out that, apart from its value for Ireland generally, it was the most accessible deposit library for scholars from Northern Ireland and was extensively used by them. The accusation, repeated from the 1940s, that the Library failed to catalogue books which had been deposited, was refuted. Indeed, the College was now able to argue that this was particularly inapplicable when Trinity, thanks to automation, was now more advanced than 'almost every other library in the British Isles' in the full recording of its accessions.[47] In its report, the committee made no formal recommendations on legal deposit, and so there was no change to the legislation.[48]

George Copp retired as the Copyright Agent in 1977 and was succeeded by Tom Smail, recruited from the National Library of Scotland. The increasing amount of material being processed through the Agency meant that its accommodation was again becoming too small, and in 1978 it moved to new premises close to Euston Station.[49] The National Library of Wales, which had been receiving books independently since it became a legal-deposit library in 1911, joined the Agency in 1982 and began to acquire material on the same basis as the other four libraries.[50] Planning for the introduction of automation into the Agency began in 1980 in collaboration with the British Library and, after the abandonment of the first attempt, a new system was successfully introduced during 1985–6.[51]

The importance of making the Library's legal-deposit collection more widely accessible within Ireland was recognised after the National Board for Science and Technology demonstrated that requests from Irish libraries for books and journal articles were being sent to the British Library Lending Division, even though 90 per cent of them could have been met from within the country, principally from Trinity.[52] In 1980, the National Board for Science and Technology provided funding to establish an

---

[47] *Bookseller*, 31 August 1974 (summary of Publishers' Association submission); Trinity College submission, 10 September 1974, MUN/SEC/151.

[48] *Copyright and designs law: report of the committee to consider the law on copyright and designs*, [Cmnd. 6732], 1976–7, VII, 441 (pp. 204–11).

[49] Minutes of the Copyright Conference, 19 July 1978, MUN/LIB/32/98.

[50] Minutes of the Copyright Conference, 22 September 1982, CUA ULIB 7/2/26/13.

[51] Minutes of the Copyright Conference, 16 July 1980, CUA ULIB 7/2/26/11; ibid., 28 July 1983, CUA ULIB 7/2/26/14; Annual Report, 1985–6.

[52] Barré Carroll and Norman Wood, *Scientific and technical information in Ireland: the findings of the National Documentation Use Study a report presented to the Documentation Co-ordinating Committee of the National Science Council*, 2 vols. (Dublin: National Science Council, 1978).

experimental document-delivery network based on Trinity College Library, and this continued as a self-financing service from the following year.

As a former curator of manuscripts, Denis Roberts encouraged the acquisition of modern literary papers, and during his tenure of office several major collections were received.[53] This policy continued after his departure and the Library is now an important repository for the papers of modern Irish writers. The first such collection to arrive was that of John Millington Synge, consisting of his correspondence with other writers, diaries and almost fifty 'commonplace books' containing drafts, notes and scraps of dialogue that he had overheard. They were offered to Trinity in 1968 by the Synge estate at a price of £50,000, a sum that was beyond the College's resources, but Roberts was able to persuade the Board to take the unusual step of selling a pair of eighteenth-century silver soup tureens to meet the cost.[54] The following year, Lily Stephens, the widow of Edward Stephens, Synge's nephew and literary executor, donated over three hundred of Synge's letters (MS 4428), and in 1972 she gave more Synge material, including his camera and typewriter. At her request, these became part of a small permanent display in the Long Room.[55] Samuel Beckett donated several notebooks and drafts containing unfinished pieces in 1969 at the suggestion of R. B. D. French (MSS 4661–4).[56] The Library's Beckett collection was augmented in succeeding years by a considerable number of donations and purchases.[57]

Seumus O'Sullivan was the pen name of James Starkey, the founder of the *Dublin Magazine* and a man who was at the centre of the Dublin literary scene for half the twentieth century. In 1969, his papers and those of his wife, the artist Estella Solomons, were bought for the Library by the sisters Laetitia and Naomi Overend. As well as the archive of the *Dublin Magazine*, the collection consisted of correspondence, about two thousand

[53] Nicholas Grene, 'Modern Irish literary manuscripts', in *Treasures*, pp. 230–8.

[54] MUN/V/5/35, 8 June 1968; MUN/V/5/36, 27 November 1968, 16 April 1969; Ann Saddlemyer, '"Infinite riches in a little room": the manuscripts of John Millington Synge', *Long Room*, 3 (Spring 1971), 23–31; W. O'Sullivan and N. Grene, *The Synge manuscripts in the Library of Trinity College Dublin: a catalogue prepared on the occasion of the Synge centenary exhibition, 1971* (Dublin: Dolmen Press, 1971). The manuscripts are MSS 4328–4428.

[55] MUN/V/5/36, 8 January 1969; MUN/V/6/17, p. 103.   [56] MS 9795/2/11.

[57] Jane Maxwell, 'Waiting for an archivist: the Samuel Beckett Collection', in *Old Library*, pp. 370–6; Matthijs Engelberts, Everett Frost and Jane Maxwell, '*Notes diverse holo*': *catalogues of Beckett's reading notes and other manuscripts at Trinity College Dublin, with supporting essays* (Amsterdam: Rodopi, 2006); Martha Dow Fehsenfeld and Lois More Overbeck, eds., *The letters of Samuel Beckett*, vol. I – (Cambridge University Press, 2009–).

printed books, including publications of Irish private presses and a considerable number of Solomons' paintings, which now form part of the College Collection.[58]

In the same way that the 1960s marked the start of the Library's role as a home for modern literary papers, from the mid 1970s a similar development took place with modern political papers. Among the collections acquired were those of John Dillon, one of Ireland's leading politicians around the turn of the twentieth century; of his father John Blake Dillon, co-founder of the *Nation*; papers of the Irish republican, Erskine Childers; and of the radical nationalist politician, Michael Davitt. Other donations received during the 1970s included the archives of the stained-glass artist and illustrator Harry Clarke and the papers of Thomas Bodkin, Director of the National Gallery of Ireland.[59]

The Department of Older Printed Books acquired several collections of Irish printing, of which the first was a donation of books published by Sáirséal agus Dill, the country's most important Irish-language publishing house, founded in 1945. The gift contained all the publications of the company, with reprints and later editions, and new items continued to be donated until the late 1970s.[60] In 1979, the Library bought a complete collection of Dolmen Press publications, together with related ephemera and account books.[61]

Peter Brown

During the 1970s, the College began to recognise the revenue-generating potential of some of its treasures, chief of which was the Book of Kells. Approaches were received from publishers wishing to produce expensive facsimile editions at a quality that was claimed to be higher than that of the Urs Graf edition of 1950–1, and others wanted to produce books 'at a lesser standard'.[62] Nothing came of the proposals for expensive facsimiles at that stage, but in 1974 a book reproducing over a hundred pages of the

[58] MUN/V/5/36, 11 June 1969; MUN/V/6/14, p. 58; MUN/V/6/15, p. 29; Stuart Pressley, 'The archives of the *Dublin Magazine*, 1923–58', *Long Room*, 7 (Spring 1973), 27–32. The manuscripts are MSS 4461–4657.

[59] See Appendix 2.

[60] M. Pollard, 'The Sáirséal agus Dill collection', *Long Room*, 1 (Spring 1970), 43.

[61] Christine Nudds, 'The Dolmen Press Collection', in *Treasures*, pp. 239–47.

[62] MUN/V/6/15, p. 15.

manuscript in colour was published with a text by the distinguished art historian Françoise Henry. Trinity received substantial royalties from this, which were used first to buy the Dillon papers and then to act as a fund for the future purchase of manuscripts.[63]

In the late 1960s, the possibility of exhibiting the Book of Kells in the USA as a means of promoting the College and the country – and in the hope of a substantial financial return – was considered. The Metropolitan Museum of Art in New York was enthusiastic, but the plan foundered through lack of support from the government, a factor that the Board considered to be essential to the success of the venture.[64] By the mid 1970s the political climate had changed, however. A fundraising campaign for the College was being planned and the Board regarded an American exhibition as an important component of this. The government realised that such an exhibition could create positive publicity for Ireland at a time when most of the news about the country was negative.[65] As a result of government pressure, the exhibition that eventually took place became a joint one with the National Museum of Ireland and the Royal Irish Academy. It was held at venues in New York, San Francisco, Pittsburgh, Boston and Philadelphia between October 1977 and May 1979 and was seen by a total of over 800,000 visitors. It was then placed on view in the National Museum of Ireland in 1980–1 and a modified version toured five locations on the European mainland between 1982 and 1984.

The benefit of having had the Book of Kells bound in four volumes was apparent, as two could form part of the travelling exhibition, whilst the other two remained on display in the Long Room. The provision of a Library Shop as part of the remodelling of the late 1960s had proved to be very successful, and by 1971 its accumulated profit had reached a level sufficient to fund the construction of the Conservation Laboratory that had been proposed by Denis Roberts. Anthony Cains, who had been working as part of the British team restoring the books damaged by the 1966 floods in Florence, was appointed as the Technical Director to plan and equip the laboratory, which opened in 1974. Under Cains' direction it became one of the leading library conservation units in the world.[66] Rollin McCarthy, who

[63] Françoise Henry, *The Book of Kells: reproductions from the manuscript in Trinity College, Dublin* (London: Thames and Hudson, 1974); MUN/V/6/20, p. 2.

[64] MUN/V/6/14, p. 71; MUN/V/5/36, 25 June, 24 September 1969.

[65] MUN/V/5/43, 19 January 1976.

[66] MUN/V/6/17, pp. 24, 65; W. E. Vaughan, 'The foundation of the Conservation Laboratory', in *Old Library*, pp. 423–36; Edward Simpson, 'Anthony Cains, Director of Conservation at Trinity College Dublin', *Paper Conservation News*, 74 (June 1995), 1–4.

had advised on the planning of the Laboratory, provided $100,000 towards its running costs.[67]

Visitor numbers continued to rise and by 1980, when a donations box was placed in the Long Room (with a suggested contribution of 50 pence), the Library was attracting over 100,000 tourists a year. This marked the start of a more commercial approach, and the suggested donation became an admission charge of 50 pence for the summer of 1983, raising about £45,000. By that time the Library Shop was also making an annual profit of a similar amount, which was used to support the work of the departments in the Old Library (Manuscripts, Early Printed Books and the Conservation Laboratory).[68] The income from the admission charge was added to this, in order to fund a programme of conservation of the books in the Long Room, managed by the Conservation Laboratory.[69]

As the Library grew in size and complexity, its staff structure needed to be reorganised to create appropriate lines of communication and decision-making. In 1974, Brown reduced the twelve people reporting to him to a more manageable five: the heads of Printed Books (later Reader Services), Technical Services, Manuscripts, Older Printed Books and the Conservation Laboratory.[70] Instead of appointing a Deputy Librarian to replace Diene-man, he converted the post into that of Library Secretary and appointed Brian McCarthy in 1971. This was a short-lived arrangement, and on McCarthy's resignation the post reverted to that of Deputy Librarian when Sean Phillips was appointed in October 1975.[71] Phillips left in 1978 to become Librarian of University College Dublin and was replaced the following year by Peter Fox.[72]

The 1970s were marked by growing student unrest, deteriorating industrial relations and an increasingly unstable situation in Northern Ireland. The Library was affected by all of these. On several occasions it was occupied by students, sometimes as part of a campaign to improve Library facilities or increase opening hours, sometimes as a convenient focus of disruption in support of campaigns on other issues. Though tiresome for those Library staff who had to be involved, the occupations were usually peaceful and well organised. Industrial relations were also contentious, with an increasingly assertive group of trades unions determined to ensure that any changes made to their working conditions were compensated at a level that they deemed appropriate. This was particularly difficult for Brown, who

[67]   McCarthy to Treasurer, 6 October 1986, MUN/LIB/32/203.
[68]   Annual Report, 1982–3.   [69] Annual Report, 1978–9.   [70] MUN/V/6/20, p. 23.
[71]   MUN/V/5/38, 11 November 1970, 17 February 1971; MUN/V/5/42, 30 April 1975.
[72]   MUN/V/5/46, 27 September 1978, 16 May 1979.

was trying to modernise the Library processes and structures and introduce what the unions referred to as 'new technology'. On more than one occasion demarcation disputes or issues of assimilation of grades led to lengthy delays in implementing change.[73] Industrial relations reached their nadir with a two-week strike in the College in 1983; some Library staff were involved, but services were largely maintained.

The security of the Long Room and the Book of Kells became a matter of concern, especially after the theft of the 'Brian Boru' harp in 1969. On that occasion a window in the Old Library was broken and the harp stolen as part of a plan to secure a ransom from the College for its return. It was recovered by the police within a few weeks, with only minor damage.[74] A proposal to secure the windows of the Colonnades with grilles was rejected by the Board, but it was agreed that laminated glass could be installed.[75] However, it took another attempted theft, that of the shrine of Dimma in February 1974, before any action was taken.[76] By that time Brown was also concerned at the risk posed by the increased violence in Northern Ireland and the potential damage from fire-bombs in the Old Library. Only a month after his paper on security had been considered by the Board, parts of the College suffered damage from bombs in Nassau Street, but the Library was spared.[77]

The period between Brown's appointment and about 1975 was one when the seeds of improvement that had been planted by Parke and Roberts began to bear fruit: the number of books being bought each year had risen to about 5,500, the number of Library staff rose from 99 to 134, the book repository had resolved some of the chronic storage problems, an advanced computer system was in place, books were being catalogued within a reasonable time of their arrival, there were now records for all current periodicals and adequate accommodation for readers would soon be provided in the Arts Building library. The main areas still to be addressed were the poor science-library facilities and the remaining 'dumps' of books and other materials, such as maps. In his annual report for 1974–5 Brown recorded the improvements, but noted that the Library was still operating

---

[73] For example, a dispute with the Workers' Union of Ireland over Library Attendant and Library Assistant grades dragged on from 1972 to 1978, MUN/SEC/67.

[74] *Irish Times*, 26 March, 18 April 1969; Veronica Morrow, 'The harp that once . . .', *Newsletter, Friends of the Library, Trinity College Dublin*, Number 43 (Autumn 2004).

[75] MUN/V/5/39, 21 June 1972.   [76] MUN/V/5/41, 20 February, 17 April 1974.

[77] Brown to Board, 'Old Library security', 10 April 1974, MUN/SEC/151; MUN/V/5/41, 29 May 1974.

at what he described as 'a low level compared with similar libraries in other countries'.[78]

After a promising start to the decade, the second half was beset by increasing problems. A high level of inflation eroded the Library's purchasing power, the book repository was filling rapidly, with no sign of the next phase being funded, and increasing student numbers were putting more pressure on services and accommodation. Brown's annual reports showed growing signs of desperation: 'very serious problems' in the coming year were predicted; staff numbers were 'inadequate to carry out all the Library operations efficiently'; there were 'unavoidable...inadequacies in the Library's operations and services'; 'the financial position of the Library [was] deteriorating very seriously and alarmingly'.[79] The statements accurately reflected Brown's frustration with the Library's situation, but constant repetition of these apocalyptic predictions inevitably convinced some in the College that the Librarian was crying 'wolf'. Some of his demands were indeed unrealistic. In 1979, for example, he announced that he needed nineteen new posts and an increase in the book budget from £50,000 to £130,000.[80]

Nonetheless, it was clear to those who used the Library that its problems were serious and that there was a realistic prospect that the gains of recent years would be lost. In 1980, the Provost, Leland Lyons, set up a working party to investigate and make recommendations for a long-term policy. The report, published in May 1981, was sympathetic, noting the transformation of the service since the opening of the Berkeley Library and remarking that the Library's success had aroused expectations 'which, given its limited resources and the expanding calls upon those resources, it is simply not capable of fulfilling'.[81] Judged by normal university library standards, it said, the College Library was expensive, but it was not a normal university library. The two British universities closest in size to Trinity were Reading and Southampton, both of which had libraries about a quarter the size of Trinity's and accessions of one-third, but library budgets that were 75 per cent and 90 per cent that of Trinity. The library at University College Dublin received roughly the same proportion of the college budget as did Trinity's, but the Trinity Library was four times the size and its accessions three times greater. In a thinly veiled criticism of Brown's scattergun approach, the

---

[78] Annual Report, 1974–5.   [79] Annual Report, 1975–6 to 1978–9.
[80] 'Development of the College Library', 22 May 1979, MUN/LIB/32/98.
[81] 'Library Working Party report', May 1981, MUN/LIB/32/178.

report noted that the case for more resources needed to be 'persuasively argued' and made 'in the context of a well-defined and coherent Library plan'. The report concluded: 'we are accustomed to regard it [the Library] as our greatest treasure. It is time we regarded it as our heaviest responsibility'.[82] Despite those fine words, the report had little practical effect and, as the College's financial situation worsened during the early 1980s, frozen posts and reduced opening-hours became the order of the day.

* * *

On 7 January 1984, Brown suffered a fatal heart attack. Peter Fox (see Figure 26) was appointed as Acting Librarian whilst the process of advertising and interviewing for a successor took place; he was appointed as Librarian in July.

---

[82] *Ibid.*

19 | Epilogue: 1984–2003

The death of Peter Brown and the start of the present writer's incumbency of the Librarianship might seem an appropriate point to end this narrative. The final years of the twentieth century, however, saw such dramatic changes in universities and their libraries that to conclude in 1983 seems premature. This final section must inevitably be less analytical than previous chapters, but it seeks to chronicle as objectively as possible the main development of the Library up to the formal opening of the Ussher Library in 2003.[1]

During these two decades the Library was served by three Librarians: Peter Fox from 1984 until 1994, when he was appointed Librarian of the University of Cambridge; Bill Simpson, who had been the Librarian of the University of London and was at Trinity from 1994 until 2002, when he moved to Manchester as University Librarian and Director of the John Rylands Library; and Robin Adams, who had been the College's Deputy Librarian since 1991 and was appointed Librarian in 2002.

The information revolution

The late twentieth century was the period of the 'information revolution', a process that continues today and is changing libraries more profoundly than any development since the introduction of printing with moveable type more than a century before Trinity College was founded. During the 1970s and 1980s the use of computers, referred to at the time as 'library automation', was largely confined to the machine-processing of routine manual tasks. By the mid 1980s most of Trinity College Library's management systems had been automated: legal-deposit accessions, book-ordering, cataloguing and lending. The programs had been written at various times by the College's Computer Laboratory and some of them had been in use

---

[1] Unless otherwise indicated, the information in this chapter is based on the Library's annual reports for 1983/4–1992/3 (MUN/LIB/32/178), 1993/4–1999/2000 (MUN/LIB/32/177) and 2000/1–2002/3 (held in the Librarian's Office).

for almost 20 years. Because of their piecemeal development, each system operated independently, and records could not easily be transferred from one to another. Many libraries had by now begun to adopt 'integrated library-management systems', in which a record, once created, could be used for a range of purposes, including book-selection, ordering, cataloguing and lending, and could be shared across the world. Trinity's in-house system was not capable of that form of development, and so, in 1986, it was decided to move to a commercial library-management system, Dynix, which was in use in many North American libraries and a number in the United Kingdom. However, Trinity's peculiar requirements, resulting mainly from its legal-deposit status, caused the supplier major problems, and it eventually took more than 2 years until Dynix was operating satisfactorily. This was a source of frustration for both Library staff and users, but the online catalogue and integrated lending system were welcomed when they finally became operational in 1989.

The increased availability of machine-readable catalogue records from sources such as the British Library and the Library of Congress provided the opportunity to reduce the number of catalogues in the Library. In 1983, the user was faced with four public catalogues, covering acquisitions received at different periods. In that year, the Library embarked upon a pilot project to examine the feasibility of converting the records in the card catalogue into a form in which they could be added to the computer-produced microfiche catalogue. The pilot was successful and a project, christened Stella, ran until 1994, when the conversion of the cards was completed.[2] This was followed by work on other catalogues and, by the end of the century, online records were available for most of the books in the Library, including many listed in the Printed and Accessions Catalogues. At the same time, the Professor of Computer Science, John Byrne, applied optical character recognition and automatic correction software to the Printed Catalogue, to produce a database which could be searched online and which then presented the viewer with an image of the relevant page in the original Printed Catalogue. That version was offered as an alternative to the Printed Catalogue itself.[3]

By the end of the twentieth century, the use of computers in libraries was as ubiquitous as it was in all other aspects of life. They were no longer

---

[2] John Fitzgerald, Gail Hogan, Colette Ní Mhoitleigh and Trevor Peare, 'Retrospective conversion at Trinity College Dublin', *Vine*, 69 (1987), 13–24.

[3] John G. Byrne, 'The Trinity College Dublin 1872 online catalogue', in *Document analysis systems VI*, Lecture notes in computer science, 3163 (Berlin: Springer, 2004), pp. 17–27; John G. Byrne, 'The 1872 printed catalogue online', in *Old Library*, pp. 217–29.

confined to running the technical services invisible to readers but, following the invention of the World Wide Web, they had become for many the preferred means of access to information. Forms of scholarly communication, which had hitherto been provided in print, were now available electronically, not just within the library building but from anywhere in the world. The process started with the development of electronic journals, first in the sciences but soon embracing all areas of scholarship, and was followed by the proliferation of full-text databases and digitised versions of print publications. By 2003, Trinity College Library provided access to 30,000 electronic journals, compared to 25,000 journals in traditional print form, and to over a quarter of a million electronic and digitised books.

More books, more readers, more buildings

Paradoxically, as electronic resources grew in importance, the number of printed books and journals published around the world also increased each year. The Library's acquisition of such material continued to be dominated by its legal-deposit intake, which accounted for about 85 per cent of the physical items received. The result was an unprecedented growth in the number of books acquired each year. In 1950, the annual intake had been about 10,000 volumes; by 1984 it had risen to 50,000 and in 2003 it was over 100,000. This was a tenfold increase within 50 years and meant that, in little more than a decade, over a million books would be added to the collection. Shortly after the turn of the century the number of printed volumes in the Library passed the 5 million mark.

At the same time as the collections were growing at an increasing rate, the College was also undergoing a major process of expansion. The student body grew from 7,200 in 1984 to over 15,000 in 2003. In addition, the Library served 800 academic staff and had 12,000 registered external readers. This inevitably had an impact on demand for working space, and the 20 years after 1984 saw the most ambitious building programme in the history of the Library. (See Plate 1.)

In 1986, the second phase of the book repository at Santry was completed and 300,000 items were moved into it. With the exception of the maps, all books and other material belonging to the Library were now housed in acceptable conditions and, for the most part, were available to users. Phase three of the Santry repository was opened in 1990; it accommodated about 500,000 volumes transferred from the Colonnades as part of the reconstruction of that area. Phase four was completed in 2001. The book repository provided good-quality storage at a much lower cost than would have been possible within the College, but the accommodation of an ever greater proportion of the Library's stock away from the campus meant that the material housed there was no longer simply the little-used items, as had been originally envisaged, but books in moderate demand. As a result, readers were frequently subjected to delays in obtaining books that they needed.

The provision of adequate science-library facilities, which had been an aspiration since the 1970s, was finally achieved with the opening of the Hamilton Library in 1992. This brought together the science and engineering collections that had hitherto been housed in the 1937 Reading Room and the Luce Hall. The Hamilton was the first part of the Library to offer regular access to electronic information, which at that time was provided mainly in the form of CD-ROMs and Library-staff-mediated searching of the emerging online resources. The removal of science books from the 1937 Reading Room released that building to be used, first, as an undergraduate library for students in economics and social sciences, and later as a study centre for postgraduate students.

The John Stearne Medical Library at St James's Hospital opened in 1993 to serve staff and students in health sciences; it replaced the portacabins that had served as the College's Medical Library on that site for many years. The School of Occupational Therapy, at Rochestown Avenue in the south of the city, was integrated into the Faculty of Health Sciences in 1987 and the College Library assumed responsibility for the Faculty's library.

The most important new building was the James Ussher Library, completed in 2002 and formally opened by the President of Ireland, Mary McAleese, on 11 April 2003. It was designed by a partnership of two Irish architectural firms, McCullough Mulvin and Keane Murphy Duff, and was funded through the Irish government's Programme for Research in Third-Level Institutions, with donations from Lewis and Loretta Glucksman and the Atlantic Philanthropies.[4] The Ussher is located between the Berkeley Library and Nassau Street and links the Berkeley and Lecky to create a library complex (the 'BLU') serving the arts, humanities and social sciences, with a combined total of 2,100 reader places, 800,000 books on open

[4] University of Dublin, Trinity College, *The James Ussher Library: incorporating the Glucksman Map Library and Conservation Department, opened by the President of Ireland, Mary McAleese, 11 April 2003* (Dublin: Trinity College, 2003); Valerie Mulvin, 'Ideas for a library', *Long Room*, 46 (2001), 35–8; Raymund Ryan, 'The Ussher Library at Trinity College', *Irish Arts Review*, 19/1 (Summer 2002), 82–9.

access and a further 400,000 in closed stacks. The interior of the Ussher is dominated by an atrium that spans the full eight storeys, of which six are above ground. The reading areas on the upper floors overlook the College Park, and glass-fronted balconies open on to the atrium on each floor. (See Plate 12.)

The Old Library was not spared during this period of building development. The books that were housed in the Colonnades dated mainly from the nineteenth and early twentieth centuries and were in relatively little demand, but the inflexible nature of the shelving meant that major reconstruction would have been required to make it suitable for more modern material. Most of the books were, therefore, moved to the book repository at Santry and, as part of the College's quatercentenary celebrations of 1992, the area was converted into a stack for special collections, an enlarged shop and an exhibition gallery. A new entrance for visitors was created in the centre of the building and the Book of Kells and the other early Irish manuscripts on display were moved into a new 'Treasury' in the East Pavilion. This offered greatly improved display facilities and better security than had been possible in the Long Room, a fact that provided some reassurance when it became known that a major Dublin criminal had been showing interest in stealing the Book of Kells.[5] A complete full-colour facsimile of that manuscript, which had originally been proposed in 1979 by the Swiss publisher Faksimile Verlag, was published at the end of 1989, and the first copy was presented to the President of Ireland, Patrick Hillery, in the Long Room.[6]

The appointment of a Map Librarian in 1986 marked the beginning of the process of sorting the vast collection of maps, the most substantial part of the Library's collection that was still suffering from the neglect of the past. The Old Gymnasium was converted into a Map Library, and about 350,000 maps were moved from their temporary store in St Mark's Church, cleaned and sorted. The Map Library opened to readers in October 1988 and the remaining 150,000 maps, mostly stored in poor conditions in the basement of the Chapel, were gradually moved into new premises. The Andrew W. Mellon Foundation donated $30,000 towards the cost of conserving the nineteenth-century Ordnance Survey maps of Ireland, and a donation from the Glucksman family funded the construction of purpose-built premises in the Ussher Library, into which the Map Library moved in 2002,

---

5   *Irish Times,* 20 August 1994; Paul Williams, *The General: godfather of crime* (Dublin: O'Brien Press, 1995), p. 212.
6   *Kells facsimile; Irish Times,* 28 November 1989.

leaving some of the lesser-used maps in a store away from the main College campus.[7]

The Conservation Laboratory also moved into space in the Ussher Library, funded by the Glucksman gift. Over the 30 years of its existence the Laboratory's role had broadened from the binding of manuscripts to encompass the full range of preservation issues relating to collections of library materials, both on paper and vellum and, increasingly, in electronic form, and it had developed a close relationship with the National Preservation Office, established in 1984 at the British Library. The condition of the books in the Long Room had become a source of concern. In 1985, a programme of cleaning and refurbishing was started, with funding from the admission charge paid by visitors, and the books in the Old Library that had been published between 1830 and 1940 were examined to establish the incidence of brittle paper.[8]

Legal deposit in an electronic age

As electronic publishing grew in importance at the end of the century, it became apparent to the legal-deposit libraries that a gap was developing between what was being published and what they were able to claim, since the legislation, in both Ireland and the United Kingdom, covered only printed material. Publications such as reports from academic, scientific or commercial organisations, newsletters and other relatively ephemeral items, which would have been collected by the deposit libraries in the past, were now appearing on websites without any printed equivalent, and many then simply disappeared without being preserved for the use of future scholars.

In 1993, the British Library sought legislation to bring non-print publications within the legal-deposit provisions. Two working parties, on both of which Trinity was represented, first developed the case and then, in collaboration with representatives of the publishers, examined how the legislation might be extended.[9] Through the work of these groups a level of trust and

---

[7]   M. Cains and P. Ferguson, 'Map conservation project at Trinity College Library Dublin', *Cartographic Journal*, 27 (1990), 3–6.

[8]   Anthony Cains and Paul Sheehan, 'Preservation and conservation in the Library of Trinity College, Dublin', *International Library Review*, 18 (1986), 173–8; Anthony Cains and Katherine Swift, *Preserving our printed heritage: the Long Room Project at Trinity College Dublin* (Dublin: Trinity College Library, 1988); Paul Sheehan, 'A condition survey of books in Trinity College Library Dublin', *Libri*, 40 (1990), 306–17.

[9]   British Library, *Proposal for the legal deposit of non-print publications: to the Department of National Heritage, from the British Library* (London: British Library, 1996); Anthony Kenny,

goodwill developed between libraries and publishers, which had not been the case with previous attempts at legal-deposit legislation, and although it took until 2002 for a Bill to be proposed, its passage through the Westminster Parliament was a relatively smooth one, with a consensus on what was required. The Legal Deposit Libraries Act 2003 (2003 c. 28) reaffirmed the provisions of the 1911 Act as far as printed publications were concerned and empowered the Secretary of State to make regulations for extending its coverage to non-print material. This was an important principle, as it meant that the Act would cover not just existing online and offline publications but was sufficiently flexible to include new formats yet to be invented, without the need to return to Parliament. Trinity's rights were confirmed in this British Act on condition that any new regulations relating to electronic publications in either British or Irish legislation would have to confer equivalent levels of protection for British publishers.[10] The protection that the publishers sought was the assurance that readers' access to deposited material would resemble as closely as possible that granted to printed publications. In the same way that a deposited book can be read by only one person at a time in a deposit library, access to an electronic publication was to be limited to a single user within the library building. This meant that networking of the deposited publications across the universities at Trinity, Oxford and Cambridge, as is the norm for material acquired by purchase, was not permitted.

In the matter of electronic deposit, the Irish government had in fact moved ahead of its British counterpart, with the passing of the Copyright and Related Rights Act 2000, which extended the coverage of legal deposit to include such material. Both Acts, however, were written simply as enabling legislation, and their implementation had to await the results of detailed discussions between publishers, librarians and civil servants.

Collecting of a more traditional nature continued at Trinity, as it did in most research libraries.[11] The Cuala Press, which had been founded in 1902 as the Dun Emer Press, published the works of living Irish writers

---

Report of the working party on legal deposit to the Department for Culture, Media and Sport (London: British Library, 1998).

[10] Clive Field, 'Securing digital legal deposit in the UK: the Legal Deposit Libraries Act 2003', *Alexandria*, 16 (2004), 87–111; John Byford, 'Publishers' and legal deposit libraries' cooperation in the United Kingdom since 1610: effective or not?', *IFLA Journal*, 28 (2002), 292–7; Adrienne Muir, 'Legal deposit of digital publications' (unpublished Ph.D. thesis, Loughborough University, 2005).

[11] For details, see Appendix 2; Charles Benson, 'Department of Early Printed Books: a review of accessions', *Long Room*, 46 (2001), 9–11; Bernard Meehan, 'Manuscript accessions in Trinity College Library Dublin, 1982–2003, part I', *Long Room*, 48 (2003), 38–55; Charles Benson,

and made an important contribution to the development of modern Irish culture. It ceased operating in 1986, and its archive was presented to the Library. Printing equipment was also given to augment that of the Trinity Closet Press, a hand press founded in 1973 in the basement of the Printing House and run by the Department of Early Printed Books as a teaching tool.[12] The collecting of modern Irish literary archives remained a priority, and a new departure was to arrange for the acquisition of the papers of living writers, such as John Banville and John B. Keane. Among the early manuscripts bought, the most important was the 'Red Book' of the Earls of Kildare, compiled in the early sixteenth century and consisting of transcripts of 200 documents relating to lands of the Fitzgerald family in various parts of Ireland (MS 9825).

Less happily, when Dr Steevens' Hospital closed in 1988, the building was left empty and the library, which had been donated to the hospital by Edward Worth and was still housed in its original eighteenth-century room, was at risk of theft or damage. With the agreement of the trustees, the books were moved to Trinity, both for safe-keeping and so that they could be made available to scholars. However, when the hospital premises were eventually bought by the Eastern Health Board as its corporate headquarters, the Board sought the return of the collection. This was opposed by the trustees and the College, but the High Court ruled in favour of the Health Board and the collection was moved back to the former hospital building.[13] Through an agreement with the Health Board, the College Library now oversees the running of the Worth Library at Dr Steevens'.

The national role and its cost

A feature of the late twentieth century was the growth in co-operation between libraries, as the rapid increase in both the quantity and the cost of scholarly publishing, combined with constraints on budgets, meant that individual institutions were less able to remain self-sufficient. As the largest library in Ireland, Trinity played a leading role in this co-operation through its membership of bodies such as the cross-border Committee for

---

'"Must do better": enhancing the collections of early printed books and special collections', in *Old Library*, pp. 437–44.

[12] *Cuala Press archive 1902–1986: a general descriptive listing* (Dublin: Trinity College Library, 1998); Vincent Kinane, 'Some aspects of the Cuala Press', *The Private Library*, ser. 4, 2 (1989), 118–29; Karen E. Brown, 'The Cuala Press Archive, 1902–86', in *Old Library*, pp. 272–85.

[13] J. C. Brady, 'Charities: a rare case of cy-près', *Dublin University Law Journal*, 16 (1994), 153–60.

Library Co-operation in Ireland (COLICO), the Consortium of National and University Libraries (CONUL) and the Library Council/An Chomhairle Leabharlanna. In 1997, Trinity and the other universities in the Dublin area (University College, Dublin City University and St Patrick's College Maynooth) established the ALCID (Academic Libraries Co-operating in Dublin) scheme by which academic staff and postgraduate students at any of the participating institutions could obtain access to the libraries of any of the others without formality. The scheme was subsequently extended to include the other Irish universities. The Document Delivery Service, established in 1980 to supply copies of documents from Trinity to other libraries, was incorporated into a national online request service, IRIS, in 1994, providing access to the holdings of six participating libraries, including Trinity.[14]

The cost of the Library's national and legal-deposit role, as distinct from the normal support for undergraduate and research activities appropriate to any university library, was explicitly recognised by the Higher Education Authority in 1984 with an earmarked grant of £72,000. This was well below the figure that the College estimated to be the actual cost and, though it was gradually increased, it remained at less than half the amount allocated to Oxford and Cambridge for the same purpose by the University Grants Committee (later Higher Education Funding Council for England). Furthermore, in the 1990s, the HEA's application of a new unit-costing model created major difficulties, as it appeared to show that the Library was much more expensive than it should have been, were a formula based purely on the number of staff and students in the College to be applied, as it was in the other universities. The Librarian, Bill Simpson, pointed out that there were several reasons why the running costs of Trinity's Library were bound to be higher than those of other Irish university libraries: it was several times larger than any of those libraries; it was collecting material on behalf of the nation; and it was making it available to a large clientele outside the College and, indeed, outside the higher-education sector. The cost of providing this service was not being fully met by the state, and the HEA's unit-costing mechanism meant that the College was in effect 'subsidising a national resource whilst being penalised' by the HEA for the cost it incurred in doing so.[15]

The importance of the Library as a tourist destination, and the contribution of the revenue from those tourists both towards the Library's costs

[14] J. D. Trevor Peare, 'IRIS: a Z39.50 national information system', *New Review of Information Networking*, 1 (1995), 17–32.
[15] Annual Report, 1995–6.

and to the College as a whole, continued to grow. The 50p admission charge for the Long Room was raised to £1 in 1985, with little effect on visitor numbers, and over the next two decades it was gradually increased. In 2003, the charge was €7.50, providing, with the profits from the Library Shop, a contribution to the College's finances of €600,000, raised from half a million visitors a year.

✳✳✳

Trinity College Library began as a collection of books and manuscripts to support the education of Protestant clergy. It is now an internationally important resource for scholarship, not just in the College but through the whole of Ireland and beyond. Until the nineteenth century its role, like that of most university libraries, was principally a custodial one and its use was restricted almost exclusively to senior members of the College, who were able to 'glory much in their library' but inclined to use it relatively little.[16]

The recommendations of the Royal Commissions on the universities of Ireland, Scotland and England in the middle of the nineteenth century led to reform of the curriculum and to a greater demand for library facilities that better met the needs of teaching staff and, increasingly, students. Trinity Library's ability to meet those needs varied with the financial state of the College, but the intake of legal-deposit books underpinned the collections, at least as far as British and Irish books were concerned. This reliance on books and journals received under the terms of the Copyright Acts, and the demands that it placed on the Library's staffing and other resources in an institution that was rarely well-resourced, meant that there were relatively few periods when the collections were being developed in a balanced way. The closest the Library came to this was when periods of affluence in the College coincided with the tenure of energetic Librarians keen to undertake extensive purchasing. For the most part, however, it is not the purchases that have made the Library great but the donations that it has received, either of important collections – Ussher, Gilbert, Fagel – or of individual treasures such as the Book of Kells.

For more than a century, the legal-deposit intake has represented between 70 per cent and 80 per cent of the total number of volumes acquired, compared to figures closer to 50 per cent at the other two university legal-deposit libraries, Oxford and Cambridge. Those two institutions not only enjoy a substantial budget for purchasing to augment the legal-deposit collections but the existence of college and faculty libraries largely relieves

---

[16] Sir William Brereton, *Travels in Holland, the United Provinces, England, Scotland and Ireland, 1634–1635*, ed. by Edward Hawkins (Manchester: Chetham Society, 1844), p. 143.

the central university library of the requirement to meet undergraduate demand, and allows it to concentrate on the needs of researchers. Trinity Library, on the other hand, as the only significant library in the University, has to process the legal-deposit intake, support the research of the academic staff and make both printed and electronic books available for large numbers of undergraduates, as well as providing a service to external readers – all of this on a budget less than half that of its sister academic legal-deposit libraries.[17]

It is possible that, during the coming years, the importance of the legal-deposit intake will diminish. Restrictions on the networking of electronic material acquired through legal deposit mean that, if electronic publication becomes predominant, as seems likely, the value of receiving such material on deposit will inevitably come under scrutiny. The problem will be exacerbated by the increasing variety in the nature of electronic 'publications', some of which incorporate an element of interactivity between the product and its users that renders irrelevant the concept of a publication fixed in time. The legislation will need to keep up with technological developments and the libraries will need to be able to handle the range of products offered to them. The question, however, is: will they want to?

And what of the role of the academic library in general? This narrative ends at a time when questions are being raised about its future and that of the book itself. It has been argued that all the information worth having – and much that is not – will be available online. It is claimed by some that libraries will become museums of manuscripts and old books, which themselves will be less and less used as projects to digitise them become more comprehensive. However, the 'death of the book' has been predicted since at least the early 1990s, and yet more physical books are being published today than ever before. The printed book is proving more resilient than many believed and the library is enjoying a renaissance as a place to study, a 'vibrant hub', where users meet to share ideas and work collaboratively, and where new users, their interest ignited by digital access, want to acquire a closer relationship with the writers of the past through handling the original artefacts.

There is no reason to believe that the developments of the next half-century in information provision will be any less dramatic than those of the last 50 years. But what direction they will take us in, and what effect they will have on libraries and their users, is anybody's guess. The role of

---

[17] University of Dublin Trinity College, 'Consolidated accounts'; *Cambridge University Reporter, passim*; *Oxford University Gazette, passim*.

the library and the librarian has traditionally been to select, organise and preserve information, to make it available to users and to help those users navigate their way through the mass of material to the resources they need. That role will continue to be an essential one, regardless of whether the information is in the form of a manuscript or a printed book, whether it is born digital or appears in a format yet to be invented.

Appendix 1 | Librarians, Assistant Librarians and Deputy Librarians[1]

Library Keeper

1601	Ambrose Ussher
1605	John Egerton
1608	Edward Warren
1610	Randall Holland
1614	William Smith
1616	Charles Clinton
1617	Joshua Hoyle
1618	John Garrald (Fitzgerald)
1630	Thaddeus Lysaght
1631	Charles Cullen
1633	Arthur Ware
1634	Charles Cullen [*again*]
1636	Thomas Seele
1637	James Bishop [Bushop]
1641	Richard Welsh [Walsh]

Between about 1644 and 1661, there were several unfilled posts in the College, including that of Library Keeper.

1661	John Jones
1664	George Walker
1669	James Kyan
1670	George Mercer
1672	Giles Pooley
1675	Richard Acton
1676	Edward Walkington
1677	John Barton
1680	Thomas Smyth
1682	Thomas Patrickson
1683	Richard Reader
1684	Edward Smith
1685	John Hall
1687	Jeremiah Allen

In 1689, most of the Fellows fled to England.

1692	William Carr
1693	Claudius Gilbert

---

[1] For biographical details of the Librarians, see Peter Fox, 'The Librarians of Trinity College', in *Essays*, pp. 11–24.

Library Keeper

1696	Thomas Coningsby
1697	William Grattan
1699	John Dennis
1700	Matthew French
1701	Thomas Squire
1703	Robert Howard
1705	John Walmsley
1706	Robert Howard [*again*]
1707	Richard Helsham
1709	George Berkeley
1710	Charles Grattan
1711	Thomas Bindon
1712	John Kearney
1713	John Hamilton
1714	Robert Clayton
1715	John Kearney [*again*]

Librarian[2]

1716	William Thompson
1717	James Stopford
1718	Thomas Skelton
1719	William Lewis
1720	Joseph Caddy
	Charles Stuart
1722	James King
1723	Lambert Hughes
1724	Robert Berkeley
1726	Richard Dobbs
1727	John Pellisier
1728	Henry Hamilton
1729	Edward Hudson
1730	Edward Molloy

Assistant or senior Assistant Librarian

1731	Edward Hudson [*again*]	
1740	William Clement	
1742		John Lyon
1743	John Forster	James Knight
	John Lawson	
1744	Brabazon Disney	Henry Mercier
1747	John Lawson [*again*]	John Boswell
1748		Henry Mercier [*again*]
1750	John Whittingham	Theaker Wilder

[2] From the early eighteenth century, the word 'Librarian' was used with increasing frequency, rather than 'Library Keeper', and from 1716 it became the term employed in the Board registers.

	Librarian	Assistant or senior Assistant Librarian
1751	James Knight	Thomas Leland
1752	John Whittingham [*again*]	Theaker Wilder [*again*]
1753	John Lawson [*again*]	Joseph Grace
1757		John Stokes
1759	John Stokes	William Martin
		Richard Murray
1760	Joseph Grace	
1761	Thomas Leland	
	William Martin	
	William Andrews	
1762	Theaker Wilder	
1764		Thomas Wilson
1765	Thomas Wilson	William Dobbin
1766	William Andrews [*again*]	Michael Kearney
1767		William Dobbin [*again*]
1768	Thomas Leland [*again*]	John Waller
		Henry Dabzac
1769	Richard Murray	John Forsayeth
1771	Thomas Leland [*again*]	
1774	Thomas Wilson [*again*]	
1776	Thomas Leland [*again*]	
1777		Joseph Stock
1778		John Kearney
1781	Henry Ussher	Gerald Fitzgerald
	John Forsayeth	
1782	Gerald Fitzgerald	John Waller [*again*]
	Thomas Wilson [*again*]	
1783		William Day
1784		John Barrett
1785	Henry Dabzac	
1790	George Hall	
1791	Arthur Browne	Robert Burrowes
	John Barrett	
1795		William Magee
		Richard Graves
1798		Whitley Stokes
1799		William Magee [*again*]
1800		George Miller
1804		Joseph Stopford
1806	Richard Graves	Cornelius Ussher
1807		Richard Nash
1808	Joseph Stopford	Cornelius Ussher [*again*]
1809	Thomas Prior	William Davenport
	John Barrett [*again*]	
1812		Bartholomew Lloyd

	Librarian	Assistant or senior Assistant Librarian
1813	Thomas Prior [*again*]	Samuel Kyle
1814	John Barrett [*again*]	
1815		James Wilson
1820		Franc Sadleir
1821	Franc Sadleir	Charles Elrington
1828		Thomas Gannon
1837	Charles William Wall	James Henthorn Todd
1850		Benjamin Dickson
1852	James Henthorn Todd	
1855		Thomas Fisher
1867		William Brownrigg Hunt
1869	John Adam Malet	Benjamin Dickson [*again*]
1877		Thomas French
1879	John Kells Ingram	
1887	Thomas Kingsmill Abbott	
1889		Thomas Keenan
1896		Alfred de Burgh
1914	Josiah Gilbart Smyly	
1929		Joseph Hanna
1949	Herbert William Parke	

		Deputy Librarian
1952		Robert Ormes Dougan
1958		Francis John Embleton Hurst
1965	Francis John Embleton Hurst	
1966		William Dieneman
1967	Edward Frederick Denis Roberts	
1970	Peter Brown	
1971		Robert Brian McCarthy (*Library Secretary*)
1975		Sean Phillips
1979		Peter Kendrew Fox
1984	Peter Kendrew Fox	
1985		Elizabeth Duffin
1991		David Robert Hutchinson (Robin) Adams
1994	William George Simpson	
2002	David Robert Hutchinson (Robin) Adams	Jessie Kurtz

Appendix 2 | Growth of the collection

Until the nineteenth century, major increases in the growth of the Library were the result of large donations, principally those of Ussher in 1661, Palliser in 1727, Gilbert in 1743 and Fagel in 1802. It took until 1847 for the number of printed books to reach 100,000. The next 100,000 were added in 37 years (by 1884), and by 1947 the figure of half a million had been reached (see Table 2). The enormous growth in publishing after the Second World War and the consequent increase in the number of books received by legal deposit meant that, by the late twentieth century, as many books were being added in a single year as in the whole of the first 250 years of the Library's existence.

Table 1 Number of printed volumes, 1600 to 1820

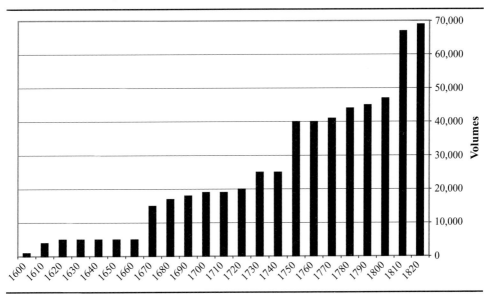

Table 2 Number of printed volumes 1780 to 2000

Major donations and purchases

Figures in square brackets after entries refer to page numbers in the main text where the acquisitions are described in greater detail. Numerically large acquisitions are indicated in bold type.

pre-1601	Christopher Ussher: manuscripts [*donation*] [p. 7]
pre-1601	Richard Latewar: books and manuscripts [*donation*] [p. 7]
1601–13	**Purchases, mainly by Challoner and Ussher** [pp. 9–11]
1629	Ambrose Ussher: papers [*donation*] [p. 20]
1630–52	Miles Symner: manuscripts [*donation*] [p. 33]
*c.*1661	Henry Jones: Book of Kells and Book of Durrow [*donation*] [pp. 23–4]
1661	**Irish House of Commons: Ussher's library of 10,000 volumes** [*donation*] [p. 29]
1670	Sir Jerome Alexander: library of 600 books and manuscripts [*donation*] [pp. 34–5]
1671	Countess of Bath: books to the value of £200 [*donation*] [pp. 36–7]
1680s	Michael Boyle, Jeremiah Hall, Thomas Otway: £100 to buy books [*donation*] [p. 48]
1684	Samuel Ladyman: theological books [*donation*][1]

[1] John Davis White, 'Extracts from the original wills formerly preserved in the Consistorial Office, Cashel, but now removed to the Court of Probate, Waterford', *Proceedings and Papers of the Kilkenny and South-East of Ireland Archaeological Society*, n.s., 2 (1858–9), 317–22.

1691	Charles Willoughby: £200 to buy books [*donation*] [p. 45]
1698?	Thomas Herbert, Earl of Pembroke: £500 for the Library [*donation*] [p. 49]
1718	St George Ashe: mathematical books [*donation*] [p. 45]
1726	Robert Gibbon: £100: 16th- and 17th-century classical texts [*donation*] [p. 61]
1727	**William Palliser: library of 4,000 volumes** [*donation*] [p. 61]
1735	John Hall: £100 to buy books [*donation*] [pp. 88–9]
1741–5	John Stearne: books, pamphlets and manuscripts [*donation*] [pp. 74–8]
1742	Edward Worth: books from the collection of his uncle, John Worth [*donation*] [p. 74]
1743	**Claudius Gilbert: library of 13,000 volumes**, £500 for busts [*donation*] [pp. 78–83]
1757	Henry Maule: £10 to buy books on Ireland[2] [*donation*]
1766	John Fergus sale: Irish manuscripts [*purchase*] [p. 96]
1766	Francis Stoughton Sullivan sale: Irish manuscripts [*purchase*] [p. 97]
1766–7	Irish manuscripts from Muiris Ó Gormáin [*purchase*] [p. 97]
1772?	Theophilus Butler: 17th- and 18th-century printed books [*donation*] [p. 106]
1772–	English Houses of Parliament: *Journals* [*donation*] [p. 106]
1774	Thomas Hollis: £100 to buy books for the Library [*donation*] [p. 105]
1776	Irish manuscripts from John O'Brien [*purchase*] [p. 97]
1778	Edward Smyth: printed books [*donation*] [p. 107]
1781–1800	Irish House of Lords: *Journals* [*donation*] [p. 106]
1782	William Burton Conyngham: 'Brian Boru' harp [*donation*] [p. 108]
1784	Charles Vallancey: painting of Battle of Kinsale [*donation*] [p. 104]
1786	Sir John Sebright: Irish manuscripts [*donation*] [p. 100]
1786	William Digges La Touche: oriental manuscripts [*donation*] [p. 107]
1791	Books from the collection of Henry Ussher [*purchase*] [p. 112]
1792	Books and manuscripts from Charles Vallancey [*purchase*] [p. 104]
1794	Edmund Burke: manuscript of the *Bustan* by the Persian poet Sa'di (MS 1563) [*donation*][3]
1795	Lord Mornington sale: printed books [*purchase*] [p. 113]
1797	Antonio Vieyra: printed books [*donation*] [p. 113]
1800	John Wilson Croker: 'Mary Queen of Scots' Sallust' [*donation*] [p. 113]
1800	William Murray: Richard Murray's mathematical and philosophical books (used to create Lending Library) [*donation*] [p. 148]
1800	Scientific papers of Matthew Young [*purchase*] [p. 102]
1800	Richard Murray sale: printed books [*purchase*] [p. 113]
1800	Archbishop Newcome sale: printed books [*purchase*] [p. 113]
1800	Icelandic manuscripts from James Johnstone [*purchase*] [p. 113]
1802	**Erasmus Smith Trust: Fagel collection (20,000 volumes)** [*donation*] [pp. 115–28]
1802	Irish House of Commons: *Journals* [*donation*] [p. 107]

---

[2] *DU Calendar*, 1858, p. 248.   [3] *DU Calendar*, 1858, p. 248; MUN/V/5/5, 20 December 1794.

1802	Charles Vallancey: Sanskrit manuscripts [*donation*] [p. 140]
1805	Henry George Quin: printed books [*donation*] [p. 141]
1805	Claudius Buchanan: printed books on oriental subjects [*donation*] [p. 140]
1805	Arthur Browne sale: Shakespeare first folio [*purchase*] [p. 139]
1806	East India Company: oriental manuscripts [*donation*] [p. 140]
1806	Sir Richard Musgrave: 1798 manuscripts [*donation*] [p. 140]
1806	John Beresford sale: printed books [*purchase*] [p. 139]
1808	Oriental manuscripts from Sir William Ouseley [*purchase*] [p. 140]
1812	Thomas Wogan Browne sale: printed books [*purchase*] [p. 139]
1820	Monck Mason sale: printed books [*purchase*] [p. 139]
1836	Book of Dimma from Sir William Betham [*purchase*] [p. 162]
1837	Franc Sadleir: 'Dublin Apocalypse' [*donation*] [p. 162]
1838?	Lord Kingsborough: Greek papyri [*donation*] [p. 163]
1840	Robert McGhee: books and documents on the 'Roman Catholic controversy' [*donation*] [p. 165]
1840	William King letters and papers [*purchase*][4]
1841	1,200 German Reformation pamphlets [*purchase*] [p. 161]
1842	Joseph D'Arcy Sirr: Dopping manuscripts [*donation*] [p. 162]
1842	1798 manuscripts from Joseph D'Arcy Sirr [*purchase*] [p. 162]
1842	Lord Kingsborough sale: letters from Queen Elizabeth I to Sir Henry Sidney, 1565–70 (MS 745) [*purchase*][5]
1851–2	William King letters [purchase and donation][6]
1853	Frederick Conway sale: incunabula [*purchase*] [p. 205]
1854	Lord Beresford: Book of Armagh [*donation*] [pp. 205–7]
1854	Charles Wall: Roman Inquisition documents [*donation*] [pp. 207–8]
1855	James Ussher memorandum book (MS 455) [*purchase*][7]
1855	Rocque printed maps [*purchase*] [p. 205]
1856	Robert Jager: scientific papers of Matthew Young [*donation*] [p. 103]
1857	Charles, comte de Meuron: manuscripts of the Reformation in Switzerland [*donation*] [p. 208]
1858	John Chapman: manuscript of Berkeley's Introduction to his *Principles of human knowledge* (MS 453) [*donation*][8]
1865	Richard Robert Madden sale: 1798 manuscripts [*purchase*] [p. 205]
1866	Joseph Singer sale: Irish pamphlets [*purchase*] [p. 205]
1870	Edward Hincks sale: manuscripts [*purchase*][p. 228]
1879	Sir Thomas Larcom pamphlets [*donation*] [p. 229]
1879	Correspondence of Joseph Cooper Walker [*purchase*] [p. 229]
1880s	Papyri from Charles Graves and Flinders Petrie [*donation*] [p. 251]

---

[4] MUN/V/5/7, 5 March 1840.
[5] MUN/V/57/11, December quarter 1842; Tomás Ó Laidhin, ed., *Sidney state papers 1565–70* (Dublin: Irish Manuscripts Commission, 1962).
[6] MUN/LIB/11/24/11; MUN/LIB/11/24/12; MUN/V/57/12, March quarter 1852; MUN/LIB/17/13.
[7] MUN/LIB/11/32/9.   [8] MUN/V/5/11/1, 28 April 1858.

1881	Aiken Irvine: 1,500 theological books and pamphlets [*donation*] [p. 229]
1885	William Neilson Hancock: books and pamphlets [*donation*][9]
1887	Royal Geological Society of Ireland: library of books and journals [*donation*] [p. 251]
1889	British Museum duplicates (1,000 volumes) [*donation*][10]
1890	Robert Graves: Rowan Hamilton books and papers [*donation*] [p. 251]
1892	War Office 18th- and 19th-century maps of Ireland [*donation*] [p. 243]
1892	Henry Sheares Perry bequest: 800 volumes [*donation*][11]
1892	William Reeves sale: Irish manuscripts [*purchase*] [p. 249]
1895	Sir Thomas Phillipps sale: 15th-century manuscripts [*purchase*] [p. 249]
1896	Deposit of James Goodman's collection of Irish traditional music [p. 252]
1898	Joseph Carson bequest: 335 volumes [*donation*][12]
1898	Sir Thomas Phillipps sale: 17th-century manuscripts [*purchase*] [p. 249]
1900	British Museum duplicates (500 volumes) [*donation*][13]
1904	George Salmon bequest: theological and mathematical books and pamphlets [*donation*][14]
1908	Hewitt Poole Jellett, Serjeant-at-Law: 74 volumes of legal books [*donation*][15]
1910	Ebenezer Prout library [*purchase*] [p. 252]
1912	**Lecky Library (6,000 volumes)** [*donation*] [pp. 250–1]
1918–	Samuel Tickell: early-printed books [*donation*] [p. 279]
1919	Rupert Magill: recruiting posters [*donation*] [p. 279]
1919	Owen Tweedy: Sinn Féin newspapers [*donation*][16]
1919	Lyons collection of William King letters [*purchase*] [p. 278]
1919	W. G. Strickland: 16th- to 18th-century papers [*purchase*][17]
1921	Bonaparte-Wyse collection of Provençal literature [*purchase*] [pp. 278–9]
1923	Katherine Maxwell: Wolfe Tone papers [*donation*] [p. 279]
1923	Lady Kathleen Bushe: 114 volumes of pamphlets relating to Ireland [*donation*][18]
1924	General James Berkeley: books from George Berkeley's library [*donation*][19]
1932–41	Albert Bender: private-press books [*donation*] [pp. 279–80]
1934	John Tait: Rowan Hamilton papers [*donation*]
1945	Richard Prior-Wandesforde: notebooks and diaries of Thomas Prior (MSS 3360–84) [*donation*][20]

[9] MUN/V/5/15, 11 December 1885.   [10] Harris, p. 353; MUN/LIB/17/42.
[11] MUN/LIB/2/5, 25 June 1892.   [12] MUN/V/5/16, 21 May 1898.
[13] Harris, pp. 413–14; MUN/LIB/17/42.   [14] MUN/LIB/2/7, 13 February 1904.
[15] MUN/V/6/5, 8 May 1908.   [16] MUN/LIB/17/69.
[17] MUN/LIB/17/68.   [18] MUN/LIB/17/73.   [19] MUN/V/5/23, 30 April 1924.
[20] MUN/P/54/35/112–4; R. B. McDowell, 'The journal of a disappointed man', *Annual Bulletin* (1954), 7–9.

1949	Duke of Leinster's library, Carton House: 17th- and 18th-century printed books [*purchase*] [p. 317]
1950	Somerville and Ross collection: manuscripts and drawings (bequest of Alain, comte de Suzannet) [*donation*] [p. 317]
1953	Clogher Diocesan Library: 18th- and 19th-century books [*purchase*][21]
1953	Killeen Castle, Dunsany: 18th- and 19th-century books [*purchase*][22]
1954	George A. Birmingham (James Hannay): manuscripts and correspondence (donated by his daughter) (MSS 3430–3459) [*donation*][23]
1954	Markree Castle: 17th-century pamphlets [*purchase*][24]
1954	***Parke's recalculation of the number of volumes in the Library*** [p. 291]
1955	Aileen Crofton: 17th- and 18th-century pamphlets [*donation*] [p. 317]
1956	Mrs W. B. Yeats: Yeats manuscript and editions [*donation*] [p. 317]
1956	Captain J. K. Ingram: £10,000 to purchase books or papers in memory of John Kells Ingram [*donation*][25]
1959	James Sullivan Starkey: 250 vols. of 18th and 19th-century hymnals and psalters [*donation*]
1960	Aileen Crofton: estate papers of the Earbery and Crofton families (MSS 3573–3587) [*donation*] [p. 318]
1960	Townley Hall: printed books and printed music [*purchase*] [p. 317]
1964	J. Barry Brown: 18th-century plays [*purchase*] [p. 317]
1964	Katherine Dickason: Wolfe Tone papers [*donation*] [p. 279]
1966	John Purser Shortt: approx. 900 liturgies, hymnals and psalters [*donation*]
1967	Music manuscripts of Ina Boyle (MSS 4047–4173) [*donation*][26]
1968	John Millington Synge correspondence and papers [*purchase*] [p. 334]
1969	Samuel Beckett: notebooks and drafts [*donation*] [p. 334]
1969	Lily Stephens: 300 letters of J. M. Synge [*donation*] [p. 334]
1969	Papers of Seumus O'Sullivan and Estella Solomons, the archive of the *Dublin Magazine* and paintings by Solomons [*donation*] [pp. 334–5]
1969	Publications of Sáirséal agus Dill [*donation*] [p. 335]
1972	Lily Stephens: J. M. Synge material, including his camera and typewriter [*donation*] [p. 334]
1973	Archives of the Harry Clarke studio (MSS 5970–6167) [*donation*][27]
1974	Papers of Thomas Bodkin (MSS 6910–7079) [*donation*][28]
1975	Papers of John Dillon, and his father John Blake Dillon (MSS 6455–6909) [*purchase*][29]
1976	John Dillon: further Dillon papers [*donation*]
1976	Papers of Thomas MacGreevy (and 1978) (MSS 7985–8190) [*donation*][30]

[21] 'Acquisitions 1953–54', *Annual Bulletin* (1954), 14.   [22] *Ibid.*

[23] R. B. D. French, '"George A. Birmingham"', *Annual Bulletin* (1955), 11–16.

[24] 'Acquisitions 1953–54', *Annual Bulletin* (1954), 14.

[25] MUN/V/5/28, 10 October 1956, 20 February 1957.

[26] Elizabeth Maconchy, *Ina Boyle: an appreciation, with a select list of her music* (Dublin: Trinity College Library, 1974); MUN/V/5/38, 24 February 1971.

[27] Fiona Griffin, 'The Harry Clarke studios', in *Old Library*, pp. 347–56; 'Accessions: manuscripts acquired during the years 1973 and 1974', *Long Room*, 11 (Spring/Summer 1975), 35–7.

[28] 'Accessions', note 27 above.   [29] Stuart Ó Seanóir, 'The Dillon papers', in *Treasures*, 215–21.

[30] Thomas MacGreevy Archive, www.macgreevy.org/index.jsp.

1977	Papers of Erskine Childers and his son, Erskine Hamilton Childers (MSS 7781–7931 and 9935–10046) [*donation*][31]
1977	Rowan Hamilton papers [*purchase*]
1979	18th-century playbills, ballads and printed half-sheets from Terence Vigors [*purchase*][32]
1979	Dolmen Press publications and records from Michael Freyer [*purchase*] [p. 335]
1982	Cahir Davitt: correspondence and diaries of Michael Davitt (MSS 9320–9681) [*donation*][33]
1984	Red Book of Kildare [*purchase*] [p. 348]
1985	Denis Johnston: diaries, correspondence and other papers [*donation*] (MS 10066)[34]
1986	Cuala Press archive [*donation*] [pp. 347–8]
1987–90	John Banville: literary papers (MS 10252) [*purchase*]
1988	Hubert Butler: correspondence, literary and family papers (MS 10304) [*purchase*][35]
1990	Thomas MacGreevy: letters from Samuel Beckett (MS 10402) [*bequest*][36]
1990	James Stephens: papers and printed books (MS 10408) [*donation*][37]
1990	John B. Keane: literary papers and correspondence (MS 10403) [*purchase*][38]
1993	Oliver St John Gogarty: literary papers and correspondence (MS 10609) [*donation*][39]
1995	*Abidil Gaoidheilge agus Caiticiosma* (Dublin, 1571) [*purchase*][40]
1996	Máirtín Ó Cadhain: literary papers and correspondence (MS 10878) [*donation*][41]
1996	1,200 French plays, mainly 17th-century [*purchase*][42]
1996	10,000 pamphlets relating to the French Revolution [*purchase*]
1997	Samuel Beckett estate: notebooks and manuscripts (MSS 10962–71) [*donation*][43]
1997	Samuel Beckett: letters to his BBC producer Barbara Bray (MS 10948) [*purchase*][44]

[31] John Bowman, '"*Entre nous*": some notes by Erskine Childers on the making of the Anglo-Irish Treaty, 1921', in *Treasures*, pp. 222–9.

[32] Annual Report, 1979–80; M. Pollard, 'The Burgage Collection', *Long Room*, Nos. 20/21 (Spring/Autumn 1980), 38–9.

[33] Carla King, 'The Davitt Papers', in *Old Library*, pp. 246–8; Felicity O'Mahony, 'Michael Davitt's travels abroad, 1884–1905', in *Treasures*, pp. 205–14.

[34] Nicholas Grene, 'Modern Irish literary manuscripts', in *Treasures*, pp. 230–8.

[35] Bernard Meehan, 'Manuscript accessions in Trinity College Library Dublin, 1982–2003, part I', *Long Room*, 48 (2003), 38–55.

[36] *Ibid.*   [37] Felicity O'Mahony, 'James Stephens: a life in letters', in *Old Library*, pp. 310–24.

[38] Meehan, note 35 above.   [39] *Ibid.*

[40] 'Bibliophile's diary', *Long Room*, 40 (1995), 7–15.   [41] Meehan, note 35 above.

[42] Charles Benson, '"Probationary starts and unprovok'd rants": the drama collection at Trinity College Dublin', *Antiquarian Book Monthly Review*, 14 (1987), 216–18.

[43] Meehan, note 35 above.   [44] *Ibid.*

1997	Nicholas Robinson collection of 1,000 political cartoons, 1789 to 1830 [*donation*][45]
1999	Jennifer Johnston: literary papers and correspondence (MS 11063) [*donation*][46]
2002	1,400 stained-glass designs from the Harry Clarke studio (MS 11182) [*donation*][47]

---

[45] Nicholas K. Robinson, 'Some Irish stereotypes in the "Golden Age" of caricature', in *Old Library*, pp. 155–63.
[46] Meehan, note 35 above.   [47] *Ibid.*

Appendix 3 | The Library oath and declaration

Library oath

Ego, . . . , sancte coram Deo promitto, et juro, me quoties in Bibliothecam hujus Collegii venire contigerit, libros caeteramque supellectilem sic tractaturum, ut superesse quam diutissime possint. Juro etiam, quod neque ipse librum aliquem asportabo, sponte corrumpam, interscribam, aut alio quovis modo abutar, nec ab aliis haec fieri (quantum in me est) permittam. Eorum vero nomina, qui in hisce deliquerint, intra triduum postquam de iis cognovero, Praeposito vel Bibliothecario deferam. Quae omnia et singula, et omnia Bibliothecae statuta, quantum ad me attinet, me fideliter observaturum promitto et spondeo. Ita me Deus adjuvet tactis Sancrosanctis Christi Evangeliis.[1]

I, . . . , do solemnly promise before God, and swear, that as often as I shall enter the Library of this College I will handle the books and other furniture so as they may last as long as possible. I also swear that I will not carry away, willingly spoil, write in, or in any other way abuse, any book myself, or (as far as in me lies) suffer such things to be done by others. Moreover I shall report to the Provost or Librarian the names of any who are guilty of such offences within three days of learning about them. All and each of which things, and all the statutes of the Library, as far as they concern me, I promise and pledge faithfully to observe. So help me God, touching the Holy Gospels of Christ.

Library declaration

Ego, . . . , solemniter promitto, me quoties in Bibliothecam hujus Collegii venire contigerit, libros caeteramque Bibliothecae supellectilem sic tractaturum, ut superesse quam diutissime possint. Promitto etiam quod neque

---

[1] *Literae patentes, sive 'Statutum de Bibliotheca bene ordinanda'*, 8 George II, reprinted in *Chartae et statuta Collegii Sacrosanctae et Individuae Trinitatis Reginae Elizabethae juxta Dublin* (Dublin: Gill, 1844), pp. 327–37.

ipse librum aliquem asportabo, sponte corrumpam, interscribam, aut alio quovis modo abutar, nec ab aliis haec fieri (quantum in me est) permittam. [Eorum vero nomina, qui in hisce deliquerint, intra triduum postquam de iis cognovero, Praeposito vel Bibliothecario deferam.] Quae omnia et singula, et omnia Bibliothecae statuta (quantum ad me attinet), me fideliter observaturum promitto, et spondeo.[2]

I, . . . , do solemnly promise that whenever I enter the Library of this College, I will handle the books and other furniture of the Library in such a manner that they may last as long as possible. I further promise that neither will I myself take away any book nor designedly damage or write in or badly treat in any way whatever any book, nor so far as in me lies will I permit such things to be done by others. [Moreover, I will communicate to the Provost or Librarian the names of those who commit such offences within three days after I shall know of them.] All and each of which things and all the statutes of the Library, in as far as they concern me, I promise and vow faithfully to observe.[3]

---

[2] Letters patent, 18 Victoria (31 January 1855), *Chartae et statuta Collegii Sacrosanctae et Individuae Trinitatis Reginae Elizabethae juxta Dublin*, 3 vols. (Dublin: University Press, 1898), vol. II, pp. 59–110.

[3] The words in square brackets were removed in 1938. See page 281.

1 Aerial view of Trinity College Dublin, showing location of libraries and buildings (*Peter Barrow, European Photo Services*).

Library buildings currently in use
1   Old Library (1732)
2   Reading Room (1937)
3   Berkeley Library (1967)
4   Lecky Library (1978)
5   Hamilton Library (1992)
6   Ussher Library (2002)

Buildings used at various times as Libraries, or to store books
7   Biochemistry Building (and approximate site of Campus House and OTC huts)
8   Board Room
9   Chapel

10   Chemistry Building
11   Luce Hall
12   Magnetic Observatory (site of)
13   Museum Building
14   J. J. O. Hara (site of)
15   Old Gymnasium (site of)
16   Provost's stables
17   St Mark's church
18   Zoology Building

Other buildings mentioned in the text
19   Front Gate
20   Public Theatre (Examination Hall)
21   Rubrics

2 Colonel Thomas Burgh, architect of the Old Library (*Hubie de Burgh*).

3 *Prospect of the Library of Trinity College Dublin*, by Joseph Tudor, *c.*1753 (*College Art Collections, TCD*).

4 Watercolour of the Long Room, by James Malton, c.1793 (*College Art Collections, TCD*).

5 John Stearne, Bishop of Clogher (*College Art Collections, TCD*).

6 One of the hinged cases installed in the gallery in the 1840s (*Brian McGovern, Audio Visual and Media Services, TCD*).

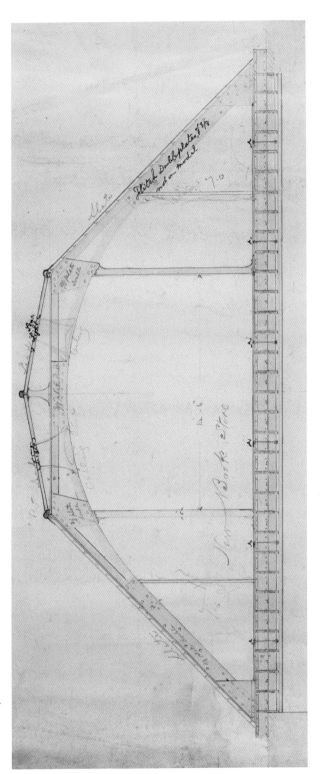

7 Proposal from Turner & Gibson, Hammersmith Iron Works, in 1858, accompanying Robert Mallet's plan to create book-storage space in the roof void above the Long Room by inserting iron girders above the existing ceiling to support a new floor. The plan included the replacement of the slates at the apex of the roof with new roof-lights (*Irish Architectural Archive*, 79/17.58/1).

8 McCurdy and Mitchell's proposed reading room, between the west end of the Old Library (on the left) and the Public Theatre, 1874 (*MUN/MC/92a*).

9 Thomas Newenham Deane's proposed link between the east end of the Old Library (on the right) and the Museum Building, 1878 (*MUN/MC/98*).

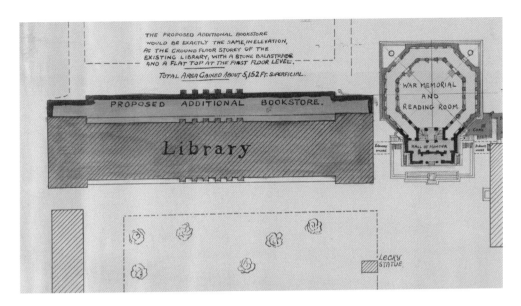

10 Sir Thomas Manly Deane's proposed bookstore along the south side of the Old Library and his plan for the Hall of Honour and Reading Room (*MUN/MC/47*).

11 The Berkeley Library (left) and the Arts and Social Sciences Building, with the sloping windows of the Lecky Library (*Gillian Whelan, Digital Resources and Imaging Services, TCD*).

12 The interior of the Ussher Library (*Gillian Whelan, Digital Resources and Imaging Services, TCD*).

Sources and select bibliography

Throughout this book references to MUN and MS numbers without any further indication of location are invariably to documents in Trinity College Library. In all other cases the holding library or archive is indicated.

Trinity College Dublin muniments

The main archival sources for the history of the Library are the College muniments held in the Manuscripts and Archives Research Library, a department of Trinity College Library.[1] The relevant muniments are the following:

MUN/LIB/1	Library catalogues, book lists, etc.
MUN/LIB/2	Library minute books (1785–1958)
MUN/LIB/3	Library Committee minute books (1845–84, 1943–60)
MUN/LIB/4	Diaries and notebooks of Library staff
MUN/LIB/5	Binders' and booksellers' accounts
MUN/LIB/6	Records of book use
MUN/LIB/7	Records of manuscript use
MUN/LIB/8	Records of the Lending Library
MUN/LIB/9	Miscellaneous items
MUN/LIB/10	Accounts and book lists to 1799
MUN/LIB/11	Accounts and book lists (nineteenth century)
MUN/LIB/12	Miscellaneous papers and correspondence (nineteenth century)
MUN/LIB/13	Correspondence (nineteenth century)
MUN/LIB/14	Miscellaneous papers and correspondence (nineteenth century)
MUN/LIB/15	Invoices and receipts (twentieth century)
MUN/LIB/16	Correspondence (twentieth century)
MUN/LIB/17	Library (annual) reports
MUN/LIB/18	Counting sheets recording number of volumes (1855–1950)
MUN/LIB/19	Long Room counting books
MUN/LIB/20	Register of publications received
MUN/LIB/21	Lists of periodicals received
MUN/LIB/22	Papers and correspondence relating to legal deposit

[1] For more detail, see Jane Maxwell, 'A guide to manuscript sources in TCD for the history of the Library', in *Essays*, pp. 91–103.

MUN/LIB/23	Material connected with the admission of readers
MUN/LIB/24	Printing and binding accounts
MUN/LIB/25	Bank statements, etc.
MUN/LIB/26	Friends of the Library
MUN/LIB/27	Exhibitions
MUN/LIB/28	Library Shop
MUN/LIB/29	Long Room visitors
MUN/LIB/30	Faksimile Verlag, Book of Kells facsimile
MUN/LIB/31	Staff societies and conferences
MUN/LIB/32	Miscellaneous files (twentieth century)
MUN/MC	Maps and plans of the College
MUN/P/1	Miscellaneous documents (17th to 19th centuries)
MUN/P/2	Documents relating to the College buildings
MUN/P/4	Bursars' vouchers
MUN/P/7	Bursars' accounts (seventeenth century)
MUN/V/5	Board registers (minute books)
MUN/V/6	Companion volumes of papers to Board registers
MUN/V/57–8	Bursars' accounts (from 1697)

Archives of the Copyright Agency

Cambridge University Archives, Archives of Cambridge University Library, CUA ULIB/7/2

Biographical information about members of Trinity College:

A catalogue of graduates who have proceeded to degrees in the University of Dublin from the earliest recorded Commencements (Dublin: Hodges, Smith and Foster, 1869–)

Bartlett, J. R., ed., *Trinity College Dublin record volume 1991*, compiled by D. A. Webb (Dublin: Trinity College Press, 1992)

Burtchaell, G. D. and Sadleir, T. U., eds., *Alumni Dublinenses: a register of the students, graduates, professors and provosts of Trinity College in the University of Dublin (1593–1860)*, new edn (Dublin: Thom, 1935)

General works about the College

Bailey, Kenneth C., *A history of Trinity College, Dublin, 1892–1945* (Dublin University Press, 1947)

The Book of Trinity College Dublin: 1591–1891 (Belfast: Ward, 1892)

Dixon, W. Macneile, *Trinity College Dublin* (London: Robinson, 1902)

Holland, C. H., ed., *Trinity College Dublin and the idea of a university* (Dublin: Trinity College Dublin Press, 1991)

Luce, J. V., *Trinity College Dublin: the first 400 years* (Dublin: Trinity College Dublin Press, 1992)

McDowell, R. B. and Webb, D. A., *Trinity College Dublin, 1592–1952: an academic history* (Cambridge University Press, 1982)

Mahaffy, John Pentland, *An epoch in Irish history: Trinity College Dublin, its foundation and early fortunes, 1591–1660* (London: Fisher Unwin, 1903)

Maxwell, Constantia, *A history of Trinity College, Dublin, 1591–1892* (Dublin University Press, 1946)

Murphy, Harold Lawson, *A history of Trinity College, Dublin from its foundation to 1702* (Dublin: Hodges, Figgis, 1951)

Stubbs, John William, *The history of the University of Dublin, from its foundation to the end of the eighteenth century* (Dublin: Hodges, Figgis, 1889)

Taylor, W. B. S., *History of the University of Dublin* (London: Cadell & Cumming, 1845)

Urwick, William, *The early history of Trinity College Dublin, 1591–1660* (London: Fisher Unwin, 1892)

Works about the Library

Annual Bulletin of the Friends of the Library of Trinity College Dublin, 1946–58

Boran, Elizabethanne, 'Libraries and learning: the early history of Trinity College Dublin from 1592 to 1641' (unpublished Ph.D. thesis, University of Dublin, 1995)

Buschkühl, Matthias, 'Die Bibliothek des Trinity College in Dublin' (unpublished thesis, Bibliothekar-Lehrinstitut des Landes Nordrhein-Westfalen, Köln, 1980)

Fox, Peter, ed., *Treasures of the Library: Trinity College Dublin* (Dublin: Royal Irish Academy, 1986)

Kinane, Vincent and Walsh, Anne, eds., *Essays on the history of Trinity College Library Dublin* (Dublin: Four Courts Press, 2000)

Long Room, 1– (1970–)

Vaughan, W. E., ed., *The Old Library, Trinity College Dublin: 1712–2012* (Dublin: Four Courts Press, 2013)

Published catalogues of Library collections

The Trinity College Manuscripts and Archives Research Library contains handlists and catalogues of specific collections, some of which have been transferred to the online catalogue of the manuscripts and archives collection, MARLOC. For unpublished catalogues of both manuscripts and printed books see the 'General index' to this book under 'catalogues'.

Abbott, T. K., *Catalogue of fifteenth-century books in the Library of Trinity College, Dublin, and in Marsh's Library, Dublin, with a few from other collections* (Dublin: Hodges, Figgis, 1905)

Catalogue of the manuscripts in the Library of Trinity College, Dublin; to which is added a list of the Fagel collection of maps in the same library (Dublin: Hodges, Figgis, 1900)

and Gwynn, E. J., *Catalogue of the Irish manuscripts in the Library of Trinity College, Dublin* (Dublin: Hodges, Figgis, 1921)

Bcheiry, Iskandar, *Catalogue of Syriac manuscripts in Trinity College Dublin* (Kaslik: Parole de l'Orient, 2005)

Bernard, Edward, *Catalogi librorum manuscriptorum Angliae et Hiberniae*, 2 vols. (Oxford: Sheldonian, 1697)

Catalogus librorum in Bibliotheca Collegii Sanctae et Individuae Trinitatis Reginae Elizabethae juxta Dublin (Dublin: Hyde [1721?])

Catalogus librorum impressorum qui in Bibliotheca Collegii Sacrosanctae et Individuae Trinitatis Reginae Elizabethae juxta Dublin adservantur [The Printed Catalogue], 9 vols. (Dublin University Press, 1864–87)

Colker, Marvin L., *Trinity College Library Dublin: descriptive catalogue of the mediaeval and renaissance Latin manuscripts* (Aldershot: Scolar, 1991), and supplement 1 (Dublin: Four Courts Press, 2008)

Engelberts, Matthijs, Frost, Everett and Maxwell, Jane, *'Notes diverse holo': catalogues of Beckett's reading notes and other manuscripts at Trinity College Dublin with supporting essays* (Amsterdam: Rodopi, 2006)

Esposito, Mario, 'Inventaire des anciens manuscrits français des bibliothèques de Dublin', *Revue des bibliothèques*, 24 (1914), 185–98; 30 (1920), 127–47; 31 (1921), 374–80

Garau Aunós, M., 'Manuscritos españoles de la biblioteca del Trinity College de Dublin', *Il Biblioteconomia* (1965), 52–8 [with appendix: José Miguel Santamaría, 'Apéndice al catálogo de manuscritos españoles en la biblioteca del Trinity College de Dublin (Fagel Collection)', *Revista alicantina de estudios ingleses*, 1 (1988), 171–80]

Hincks, Edward, *Catalogue of the Egyptian manuscripts in the Library of Trinity College Dublin* (Dublin: Milliken, 1843)

McGing Brian C., ed., *Greek papyri from Dublin (P. Dub.)* (Bonn: Habelt, 1995)

Mahaffy, J. P. and Smyly, J. G., *The Flinders Petrie papyri*, 3 vols. (Dublin: Royal Irish Academy, 1891–1905)

Malet, J. A., *A catalogue of Roman silver coins in the Library of Trinity College Dublin* (Dublin: Graisberry, 1839)

O'Sullivan, W. and Grene, N., *The Synge manuscripts in the Library of Trinity College Dublin: a catalogue prepared on the occasion of the Synge centenary exhibition, 1971* (Dublin: Dolmen Press, 1971)

Skulerud, Olai, *Catalogue of Norse manuscripts in Edinburgh, Dublin and Manchester* (Kristiania: Moestues Boktrykkeri, 1918)

Smyly, J. G., *Greek papyri from Gorub* (Dublin: Royal Irish Academy, 1921)

'Notes on Greek manuscripts in the Library of Trinity College', *Hermathena*, 23 (1933), 163–95

'Old Latin deeds in the Library of Trinity College', *Hermathena,* 66, 69, 70, 71, 72, 74 (1945–9)

Todd, James Henthorn, *The books of the Vaudois: the Waldensian manuscripts preserved in the Library of Trinity College, Dublin* (London: Macmillan, 1865)

Busts in the Long Room

Crookshank, Anne and Webb, David, *Paintings and sculptures in Trinity College Dublin* (Dublin: Trinity College Dublin Press, 1990)

Strickland, W. G., *A descriptive catalogue of the pictures, busts and statues in Trinity College Dublin* (Dublin University Press, 1916)

Index of Trinity College Dublin manuscripts

General index